DRAMATICA®

DRAMATICA®

A New Theory of Story

Melanie Anne Phillips
& Chris Huntley

Tenth Anniversary Edition

Write Brothers Press

TENTH ANNIVERSARY EDITION: November 2004

The Dramatica Theory was developed by Melanie Anne Phillips and Chris Huntley and was not researched nor based on any other theories of story design or analysis.

Write Brothers Press is an imprint of Write Brothers Incorporated.

WWW.DRAMATICA.COM • WWW.WRITE-BROS.COM

10   9   8   7   6   5   4   3   2   1

ISBN 0-918973-04-X

Acknowledgments

The authors would like to thank all those who have been influential in guiding our paths and inspirational in shining a light for us to follow. Though each of us can point to scores of such friends, relatives, associates and distant pioneers, Chris would particularly like to thank Stephen Greenfield for bugging him (for ten years!) about writing down the stuff in this book. Melanie would like to thank her mother, whose brilliance laid the foundations for many of the insights that eventually led to the Dramatica theory.

The concise and extensive support materials contained in this book would not have been possible without the help and input of many dedicated and insightful contributors. We would like to give a special thank you to members of the industry who attended our early seminars. We thank our compatriots in the academic community who reviewed and inspected our work for accuracy. In addition, special thanks goes to Mark Haslett, who started as an intern with the Dramatica Project and developed into an expert of the theory, and contributed many side notes and corrections to this book. Finally, our deepest appreciation goes to Sandy Stone, Mary Parrillo, Katy Monahan-Huntley, and J.D. Cochran. And cheers to friends and relatives who suffered our long-winded requests for opinions of these materials perhaps more than we suffered in creating them. Our deep gratitude goes to a gathering of great minds in support of a new idea.

FOREWORD

(ONWARD)

I know. You don't read forewords. You always skip them.
I understand.

Just don't skip this one.

> *Looking at story in a new way is like*
> *falling into a fast river of cold water*
> *with all your clothing on: it's a big shock.*

Dramatica is a theory, a paradigm, a model, a philosophy of
story. It's got a different perspective on many of the ideas you may
have already learned in books and classes on writing, or from the raw
experience of writing.

> *At first, you struggle,*
> *intensely aware of your situation.*
> *Will you get whisked away?*
> *Smash head first into a rock?*

It takes some time to get used to Dramatica's unique perspective,
novel terminology, and dramatic concepts that predict relationships
between character, theme, plot and genre.

> *Kick off your shoes,*
> *shed some of your excess clothing.*
> *You can always get dressed later on.*
> *Right now, you need to get accustomed*
> *to your new environment.*

What is story? What are the underlying principles? The beginning
of this book introduces concepts about story that will amaze many,
surprise others and confuse the rest (this is normal!).

Shooting the rapids,
quite unsure if you're going to make it,
you dodge a few nasty-looking bounders.
Whew!

Throughlines. Throughlines. Perspectives. Overall Story and Subjective characters. Dynamic pairs. Contagonists. Thematic Issues

Where did all this stuff come from?

A low branch, conveniently hanging over the water.
You reach for it as you get whisked
over the thundering waterfall,
sailing through thin air into...

Storyforming. Story Encoding. Story Weaving. Story Reception. As you move through these Four Stages of Communication, things begin to look more familiar.

...a nice, calm, shallow pool of water.
You're alive!
Heck, the water's not cold -- it's refreshing.
You might even want to stay in for a while...

You begin to see how Dramatica can be used to accurately describe story problems, fix faulty structure, and improve storytelling. Wow!

...As you paddle toward the shore,
you notice a group of familiar faces
applauding you: friends,
fellow writers, your agent.

The journey to learn more about the mysterious art and craft of creating stories is always worth the effort. As you approach the end of the book, much of what you've read will come together. After the final page turns, I hope Dramatica will occupy a unique place in your heart and mind when considering this thing we call "story."

Your best friend extends a hand
to hoist you out of the water.
You're buck ass naked, but who cares?
You just had an adventure.

Stephen Greenfield
President, Write Brothers, Inc.
Chief Software Architect, Dramatica

Contents

Preface

Ten years ago, the first version of this book hit the market. It holds up pretty well for its age. Sure, we've tweaked the language a bit here and there. We've even broadened and deepened our understanding of the Dramatica theory of story. But happily, our initial concepts remain true and sound.

We've spent a lot of time discussing story theory and teaching it to others. One big problem we've found in talking about "story," is that there are as many definitions of story elements as there are writers. Ask any three writers to define "theme" and you may end up with three or more different answers. Dramatica strives to solve this problem by providing terminology with specific definitions. And there is a LOT of terminology in Dramatica. With that volume of terminology has come a tremendous benefit. Writers can now talk to other writers about abstract concepts…and understand each other better than ever before.

Before you explore Dramatica's take on story, let's find out what *you* think stories are about. Ask yourself the following questions. If you want, take moment or two to write your answers down on a sheet of paper. Be as specific as you can. You may find it interesting (and surprising) to read your answers again after reading this book.

- Why do you think stories exist?

- Why do you like to tell stories?

- Why do you like to listen to stories?

- What is your definition of a story?

- What is a character?

- What is a theme?

- What is a plot?

- What is a genre?

- What isn't a story?

One of the most noticeable changes since the first edition of this book are the changes in some of the Dramatica terminology. If you are new to Dramatica, you won't notice these changes. If you're a long time Dramatica supporter, here's a list of the changed words:

New Term	Original Term
Overall Story	Objective Story
Impact Character	Obstacle Character
Main vs. Impact	Subjective Story*
Throughline	Domain
Situation	Universe
Activity	Physics
Fixed Attitude	Mind
Manipulation	Psychology
How Things Are Changing	Progress
Gathering Information	Learning
Developing A Plan	Conceptualizing
Conceiving An Idea	Conceiving
Playing A Role	Being
Changing One's Nature	Becoming
Memories	Memory
Impulsive Responses	Preconscious
Contemplation	Conscious
Innermost Desires	Subconscious
Symptom [*element*]	Focus [*element*]
Response [*element*]	Direction [*element*]
Issue	Range
Benchmark	Stipulation
Main Character Growth	Main Character Direction
Main Character Problem-Solving Technique	Main Character Mental Sex*
Logical / Linear	Male* [*Mental Sex*]
Intuitive / Holistic	Female* [*Mental Sex*]
Story Driver	Story Work
Story Point	Appreciation

* The original term is used in this version of the theory book in lieu of the new term.

Enough said. Now, kick back and enjoy the read.

Chris Huntley
Glendale, California

Dramatica and the Creative Writer

A Place to Start

Mastering the craft of writing requires a skill in communication and a flair for style. Through communication, an audience receives meaning. Through style, an author achieves impact. The Dramatica theory of story explores both aspects of the writing process providing structural guidelines for clarifying communication and artistic techniques for improving style.

Therefore, this book is divided into two principal sections: *The Elements of Structure* and *The Art of Storytelling*. Separating these two aspects of the writing craft allows us to see more deeply into each. This arrangement also splits the experience of writing into two parts, when in practice, they are usually blended in a simultaneous effort.

Many other books have been written which explore the blended creative process. In contrast, this is a book of theory, designed more to educate than to inspire. Still, the motivation to write is one of inspiration. So, before we rush headlong into a detailed, accurate, and revolutionary explanation of story, let us put everything in context by describing the relationship of Dramatica with the Creative Writer.

Communication

The process of communication requires at least two parties: the originator and the recipient. For communication to take place, the originator must be aware of the information or feelings he wishes to relay. The recipient must be able to receive and decipher that meaning.

Similarly, storytelling requires an author and an audience. And, to tell a story, one must have a story to tell. Only when an author is aware of the message he wishes to pass on can he decide how to couch that message for accurate reception.

An audience is more than a passive participant in the storytelling process. When we write the phrase, "It was a dark and stormy night," we communicate a message, although a vague one. Besides the words, another force is at work creating meaning in the reader's mind. The readers themselves may have conjured up memories of fragrant fresh rain on dry straw. They may recall the trembling fear of blinding explosions of lightning, or a feeling of contentment that recalls a soft fur rug in front of a raging fire. But all we wrote was, "It was a dark and stormy night." We mentioned nothing in that phrase of straw or lightning or fireside memories. In fact, once the mood is set, the less said, the more the audience can imagine. Did the audience imagine what we, the authors, had in mind? Not likely. Did we communicate? Some. We communicated the idea of a dark and stormy night. The audience, however, did much creating on its own. Did we tell a story? Definitely not!

Grand Argument Stories

The question arises: Is telling a story better than telling a non-story? No. Stories are not "better" than any other form of communication—just different. To see this difference we need to define "story" so we can tell what a story is and what it is not. Here lies a political problem. No matter how one defines "story," there will be an author someplace who finds his favorite work left out. He feels his work diminished by the classification. Rather than risk the ire of countless creative authors, we have limited our definition to a special form of story: The Grand Argument Story.

As its name suggests, a Grand Argument Story presents an argument. To be Grand, the argument must be a complete one. It must cover all the ways the human mind might consider a problem and showing that only one approach is suitable to solving it. Obviously, this limits out many creative, artistic, important works—but not out of being stories, just out of being Grand Argument Stories. So, is a Grand Argument Story better than any other kind? No. It is just a specific kind.

What's In A Grand Argument Story?

A Grand Argument Story is a conceptually *complete* story with both an emotional and logical comprehensiveness. There are many qualities that identify whether a story is a Grand Argument or not. These exist in the story's Structure, Dynamics, Character, Theme, Plot, and Genre.

Structure: The underlying relationships between the parts of a story describe its structure. A Grand Argument Story has a specific structure that we explore thoroughly in the first half of this book entitled *The Elements of Structure*.

Dynamics: The moving, growing, or changing parts of a story describe its dynamics. A Grand Argument Story has eight essential dynamics that we explore in the second half of this book entitled *The Art of Storytelling*.

Character: Grand Argument Stories deal with two types of Characters: Objective Characters and Subjective Characters. These Characters provide the audience with the experience of moving through the story in both a passionate and an intellectual sense.

Theme: Theme, in a Grand Argument Story, is tied to every structural and dynamic element. Theme provides the various biases and perspectives necessary to carry the story's subject matter or meaning.

Plot: Plot in a Grand Argument Story is the sequence in which a story's thematic structure unfolds. Plot details the order in which dramatic elements must occur within that story.

Genre: Genre in a Grand Argument Story classifies the audience's experience of a story in the broadest sense. Genre considers the elements of structure, dynamics, character, plot, and theme to define significant differences between various complete Grand Argument Stories.

These parts of a Grand Argument Story combine in complex relationships to create its Storyform. A Storyform is like a blueprint that describes how these parts fit in a particular story, regardless of how they are symbolized for the audience. It is such a Storyform that allows such different stories as WEST SIDE STORY and ROMEO AND JULIET, to share the same meaning while bearing little likeness to each other. The same is true for CYRANO DE BERGERAC and ROXANNE. These two pairs of stories share almost the same Storyform.

The Free-form Author

While some authors write specifically to make an argument to an audience, many others write because they want to follow their personal muse. Sometimes writing is a catharsis, or an exploration of self. Sometimes writing is a sharing of experiences, fragmented images, or just of a point of view. Sometimes writing is marking a path for an audience to follow, or perhaps just presenting emotional material the audience can form into its own vision. Interactive communications challenge the power of a linear story itself, and justifiably so. There are many ways to communicate, and each has just as much value as the next *depending on how one wishes to affect one's audience.*

The Scope of Dramatica

With all these forms of communication, isn't Dramatica severely limited in addressing only the Grand Argument Story? No. The Grand Argument model described by Dramatica works to present all the ways a mind can look at an issue. As a result, all other forms of communication will be using the same pieces, just in different combinations, sequences, or portions. In our example, we suggested the less we said the more the audience could use its imagination. A Grand Argument Story says it all. It makes every point, even if hidden obscurely in the heart of an entertainment. Other forms of communication use "slices" of the model, chunks, or levels. Even if an author is unaware of this, human minds share common essential concepts. This means the author communicates using concepts and patterns found in the Dramatica model.

Symbolizing Concepts

It has been argued that perhaps the symbols people use are what create concepts, and therefore no common understanding between cultures, races, or times is possible. Dramatica works because indeed there ARE common concepts: *Morality*, for example. Morality, a common idea? Yes. Not everyone shares the same definition of morality, but all cultures and individuals understand some idea that means "morality" to them. In other words, "morality" may have many different meanings—depending on culture or experience—but they all qualify as different meanings of "morality." Thus there can be universally shared essential concepts even though they drift apart through various interpretations. It is through this common reference of essential concepts that communication is possible.

Communicating Concepts Through Symbols

How can we communicate essential concepts? Not in their pure, intuitive form direct from mind to mind. (Not yet, anyway!) To communicate an idea, an author must symbolize it, either in words, actions, juxtapositions, interactions, or some form or another. By symbolizing the idea, however, it becomes culturally specific and therefore inaccessible to much of the rest of the world.

Even within a specific culture, the different experiences of each member of an audience will lead to slightly different interpretations of the complex patterns represented by intricate symbols. On the other hand, it is accepting common symbols of communication that defines a culture. For example, we see a child fall and cry. We do not need to know what language he speaks or what culture he comes from to understand what has happened. However, interpreting the reaction to the fall may be culturally specific. We may experience emotions of sadness at the event. However, the author's culture may hold a child who succumbs to tears in low esteem. In this case, the differing cultural reactions inhibit communication of the author's intent.

Author's Intent

Simply having a feeling or a belief does not an author make. One becomes an author the moment one shows an intent to communicate. Usually some intriguing setting, dialog, or bit of action springs to mind and with it the wish to share it. Almost immediately, most authors leap ahead in their thinking to consider how the idea might best be presented to the audience. In other words, even before a complete story has come to mind most authors are already trying to figure out how to tell the parts they already have.

As a result, many authors come to writing carrying baggage. They have favorite scenes, characters, or action, but no real idea how they are all going to fit together. A common problem is that all of these wonderful inspirations often don't belong in the same story. Each idea is fine by itself, but there is no greater meaning when added together—the whole is no greater than its parts. To be a story, each part must also work as a piece of the whole.

Some writers run into problems by trying to work out the entire dramatic structure of a story in advance. They finish with a formulaic and uninspired work. Conversely, other writers seek to rely on their muse and work their way through the process of expressing their ideas. They find they have created nothing more than a mess. If a way could be found to bring life to tired structures and to knit individual ideas into a larger pattern, both kinds of authors might benefit. This is why we developed Dramatica.

When to Use Dramatica

For some authors, applying Dramatica at the beginning of a creative project might be inhibiting. Many writers prefer to explore their subject, moving in whatever direction their muse leads them until they eventually settle on an intent. In this case, the storytelling comes before the structure. After completing the first draft, such an author can look back at what he has created with the new understanding he has arrived at by the end. Often, much of the work will no longer fit the story as the author now sees it. By telling Dramatica what he *now* intends, Dramatica will be able to suggest which parts of the existing draft are suitable. It will also show which parts are not suitable, and what is missing. In this way, the creative process is both free and fulfilling, with Dramatica serving as analyst and collaborator.

Following the Muse

Some authors write with no intent at all. They apply themselves to recording their journey through a topic or subject or simply wander, musing. The resulting work is almost always open to all kinds of interpretation, yet may elicit strong emotions and conclusions in almost everyone who sees the work. Even when an author meanders, he does so with the same mental tools everyone shares. So although no intended message might be sent, the subconscious patterns of the author's mental processes are recorded in the work. For those authors who prefer a more freeform approach, a Grand Argument Story is nearly useless. It is not that the Dramatica model cannot describe the nature of their communication. Rather, a freeform author simply has no need of it.

Dramatica as a Tool

None of the creative techniques an author might use are better or worse than others. They are simply different approaches to the creative process. The key is to find the ones that work for you. Sometimes what works is not to create a full argument, but to break the rules, shatter expectations, and play with the minds of your audience members. Even here Dramatica can help. Because it defines a complete argument, Dramatica aids in predicting the effect that breaking an argument will have on the message going to the audience. It can describe how the communication has been altered. When all is said and written, Dramatica provides authors with a tool for understanding the process of communication, whenever they want it.

How This Book Is Arranged

Part of what makes a story great is its underlying dramatic structure and part is the manner in which that structure relates to an audience, often called "storytelling". Therefore, we have divided this book into two principal sections: *The Elements of Structure* and *The Art of Storytelling.*

In The Elements of Structure we explore the essential items that occur in all complete stories as they appear in *Character*, *Theme*, *Plot*, and *Genre*. In the Art of Storytelling we examine the Four Stages of Communication that occur between an author and an audience: *Storyforming*, *Storyencoding*, *Storyweaving*, and *Story Reception*.

When you have finished, you will have gained a whole new understanding of what stories are, and a whole new set of tools for creating them.

Want to see how Dramatica's basic concepts improve a story? Take a look at a constructive criticism of the motion picture JURASSIC PARK in the Epilogue section.

You will note that we draw most of the examples in this book from motion pictures. This stems from the authors' personal backgrounds in the motion picture industry. Dramatica, however, is a theory of story—*not* a theory of screenplay. All the dramatic concepts presented here are equally applicable to any medium of story expression. This includes novels, stage plays, teleplays, radio plays, and even short stories, poems and ballads.

Note about Pronoun Usage: It's best to see some characters by their dramatic functions. To help keep this perspective, we use the impersonal pronoun "it" when referring to such characters. It's best to explore other characters in terms of their growth. To help draw the reader into a closer relationship with such a character, we use the personal pronoun, "he."

Earlier editions of this book used "she" as the personal pronoun. Because of this uncommon usage, it jarred readers out of a relationship with personal characters rather than drawing them in. This defeated our purpose. As a result, this edition employs masculine pronouns.

SECTION I

The Elements of Structure

Foundations

Central Concepts

In Dramatica, there are some central concepts that prove immediately useful. Presenting these up front reveals the practical side of the theory and provides a firm foundation for more explorations to come.

These central concepts are:

1. The Story Mind

2. The Four Throughlines

3. The Overall Story Throughline

4. The Main Character Throughline

5. The Impact Character Throughline

6. The Subjective Story Throughline

7. The Grand Argument Story

The Story Mind

One of the unique concepts that sets Dramatica apart from all other theories is the assertion that every complete story is a model of the mind's problem solving process. This *Story Mind* does not work like a computer, performing one operation after another until reaching the solution. Rather, it works more holistically, like our own minds, bringing many conflicting considerations to bear on the issue. It is the author's argument about the relative value of these considerations in solving a particular problem that gives a story its meaning.

To make his case, an author must examine all significant approaches to resolving the story's specific problem. Leave out parts of the argument and the story will have holes. Make the argument unevenly and the story will have inconsistencies.

Characters, Plot, Theme, and Genre are the different *families* of considerations in the Story Mind made tangible. This allows audience members to see them at work and gain insight into their own methods of solving problems. Characters represent the motivations of the Story Mind (which often work at cross-purposes and come into conflict). Plot documents the problem-solving methods employed by the Story Mind. Theme examines the relative worth of the Story Mind's value standards. Genre shows the Story Mind's overall attitude, which casts a bias or background on all other considerations. When a story is fully developed, the model of the Story Mind is complete.

The Four Throughlines

It is not enough, however, to develop a complete Story Mind. That only creates the argument the audience will consider. Equally important is how the audience is positioned relative to that argument.

Does an author want the audience to examine a problem dispassionately or to experience what it is like to have that problem? Is it more important to explore a possible solution or to weigh the benefits and drawbacks of alternative solutions? In fact, you must develop all of these points of view for a story to be complete.

An author's argument must go beyond telling audience members what to look at. It must also show them how to see it. It is the relationship between object and observer that creates perspective.

In stories, ***perspective provides context, and context creates meaning***.

There are four different perspectives that must be explored as a story unfolds to present all sides of the issue at the heart of a story:

- Third person perspective ("They")

- First person perspective ("I")

- Second person perspective ("You")

- First person plural perspective ("We")

Each perspective offers a unique context in which problems can be identified and resolved. Together, these four perspectives represent all the ways in which we experience the real world

When we connect these perspectives in stories, they create four story "lines" that reach from the beginning of the story to its end. We call these story threads, Throughlines. Each throughline has a different name. They are the Overall Story Throughline, the Main Character Throughline, the Impact Character Throughline, and the Subjective Story Throughline.

The Overall Story Throughline

The first perspective we'll look at is the Overall Story Throughline, so called because it is the broadest, most dispassionate, objective look at the Story Mind. This is the third person, "They" perspective.

Imagine the argument of a story as a battle between two armies. The Overall Story view is like that of a general on a hill overlooking the battle. The general focuses on unfolding strategies and, from this perspective, sees soldiers not by name but by their role on the field: foot soldier, grenadier, cavalry officer, scout. Though the general may care for the soldiers, he must concentrate on the events as they unfold. Because it highlights events, the **Overall Story Throughline** is often thought of as plot, but as we shall see later, plot is so much more.

Other names for this throughline include the Objective Story Throughline, the "head" line, the "Big Picture," and others.

The Main Character Throughline

For a story to be complete, the audience needs another view of the battle as well—that of the soldier in the trenches. Instead of looking *at* the Story Mind from the *outside*, the **Main Character Throughline** is a view *from* the *inside.* What if that Story Mind were our own? That is what the audience experiences when it becomes a soldier on the field. Audience members identify with the Main Character of the story. This is the personal, first person, "I" perspective.

Through the Main Character we experience the battle as if we were directly taking part in it. From this perspective we are much more concerned with what is happening immediately around us than we are with the larger strategies that are too big to see. This most personally involved argument of the story is the **Main Character Throughline**.

Other names often associated with the Main Character are the Primary Character, the Principle Character, the Hero, the Protagonist, and others.

As we shall explore shortly, the Main Character does not have to be the soldier leading the charge in the battle as a whole. Our Main Character might be *any* of the soldiers on the field: the cook, the medic, the bugler, or even the recruit cowering in the bushes.

The Impact Character Throughline

To see the third perspective, keep yourself in the shoes of the Main Character for a moment. You are right in the middle of the story's battle. Smoke from dramatic explosions obscures the field. You are not sure which way leads to safety. Still, before there was so much turmoil, the way was clear and you are confident in your sense of direction.

Then, from the smoke a shadowy figure appears, solidly blocking your way. The shadowy figure is your **Impact Character**. You can't see well enough to tell if he is friend or foe. He might be a compatriot trying to keep you from stepping into a minefield. Or, he might be the enemy luring you into a trap. What to do! Do you keep on your path and run over this person or try the other path instead? This is the dilemma that faces a Main Character.

To explore the issue at the heart of a story completely, an Impact Character must present an alternative approach to the Main Character. The **Impact Character Throughline** describes the promoter of this alternative path and the manner in which he impacts Main Character. This is the impersonal, second person, "You" perspective.

Other names for this character include the Obstacle Character, Influence Character, Mirror Character, and possibly others. Don't be distracted by the name. Though the label implies a single character, the Impact Character can be represented by one character or a group of characters. The consistency of perspective is the important quality of the throughline.

The Subjective Story Throughline

As soon as the Main Character faces his Impact Character, a skirmish results at a personal level amid the battle as a whole. The two characters close in on each other in a theatrical game of "chicken," each hoping the other will give in.

The Main Character shouts at his Impact to get out of the way. The Impact Character stands fast, insisting the Main Character change course and even pointing toward the fork in the road. As they approach one another, the exchange becomes more heated until the two are engaged in heart-to-heart combat.

While the Overall Story battle rages all around, the Main and Impact Characters fight their private engagement. The **Subjective Story Throughline** describes the course this *passionate* battle takes. This is the first person, familiar, plural, "We" perspective.

Other names for this throughline include the MC/IC Throughline, the Relationship Throughline, the "heart" line, the "B" story line, and others. Though the Main Character and Impact Character take part as characters in this throughline, the subject of this throughline is *their relationship*, not them as individuals.

The Four Throughlines Of A Story You Know

Here are some examples of how to see the four throughlines of some well-known stories. Completed stories tend to blend these throughlines together in the interest of smooth narrative style. From a structural point of view, however, it is important to see how they can be separated.

STAR WARS

Overall Story Throughline: The Overall view of STAR WARS sees a civil war in the galaxy between the Rebels and the evil Empire. The Empire has built a Death Star that will destroy the Rebels if it isn't destroyed first. To even hope for a successful attack, the Rebels need the plans to the Death Star that are in the possession of a farm boy and an old Jedi master. These two face many other characters while delivering the plans, ultimately leading to a climactic space-battle on the surface of the Death Star.

Main Character Throughline: The Main Character of STAR WARS is Luke Skywalker. This throughline follows his personal growth over the course of this story. Luke is a farm boy who dreams of being a star pilot, but he can't allow himself to leave his foster parents to follow his dreams. He learns that he is the son of a great Jedi Knight. When his foster parents are killed, he begins studying the religion of the Jedi: The Force. Surviving many dangerous situations, Luke learns to trust himself more and more. Eventually he makes a leap of faith to trust his feelings over his computer technology while flying into battle as the Rebel's last hope of destroying the Death Star. It turns out well, and the experience changes Luke for the better.

Impact Character Throughline: The Impact Character of STAR WARS is Obi Wan Kenobi and this throughline describes his impact (especially on Luke Skywalker) over the course of the story. Obi Wan is a wizened old Jedi who sees everything as being under the mystic control of the Force. He amazes people with his resiliency and ability, all of which he credits to the Force and one's willingness to open oneself to the Force.

Subjective Story Throughline: The Subjective Story throughline of STAR WARS describes the relationship between Luke and Obi Wan. Obi Wan needs Luke to help him and he knows Luke has incredible potential as a Jedi. Luke, however, needs guidance because his desires are so strong and his abilities so new. Obi Wan sets about the manipulations that will help Luke see the true nature of the Force and learn to trust himself.

TO KILL A MOCKINGBIRD

Overall Story Throughline: The Overall view of *TO KILL A MOCKINGBIRD* sees the town of Maycomb with its horns locked in various attitudes over the rape trial of Tom Robinson. Due process has taken over, however many people think this case should never see trial. As the trial comes to fruition, the people of the town argue back and forth about how the defense lawyer ought to behave. They also discuss the role people should take in response to this alleged atrocity.

Main Character Throughline: The Main Character of *TO KILL A MOCKINGBIRD* is Scout and her throughline describes her personal experiences in this story. Scout is a young tomboy who wants her life to remain as simple as it's always been. Going to school, however, and seeing the town's reaction to her father's work introduces her to a new world of emotional complexity. She learns there is much more to people than you can see.

Impact Character Throughline: Boo Radley presents the Impact Character point of view in *TO KILL A MOCKINGBIRD*. Boo is the reclusive and much talked about boy living next door to Scout. The mystique surrounding this boy, fueled by the town's ignorance and fear, make everyone wonder what he is like and if he's as crazy as they say.

Subjective Story Throughline: The Subjective Story view of *TO KILL A MOCKINGBIRD* sees the relationship between Scout and Boo Radley. This throughline explores what it's like for these two characters to live next door to each other and never get to know each other. It seems any friendship they might have is doomed from the start because Boo will always be locked away in his father's house. The real problem, however, turns out to be one of Scout's prejudice against Boo's mysterious life. Boo has been constantly active in Scout's life, protecting her from his position in the background. When Scout finally realizes this she becomes a changed person who no longer judges people without first trying to stand in their shoes.

Summary - The Grand Argument Story

We have described a story as a battle. The perspective that takes in the full scope of the battle is the *Overall Story Throughline*.

Within the fray is one special soldier through whom we experience the battle firsthand. How he fares is the *Main Character Throughline*

The Main Character confronts another soldier, blocking the path. Is he friend or foe? Either way, he is an obstacle, and exploring his impact on the Main Character is the *Impact Character Throughline*

The Main and Impact Characters engage in a skirmish. Main says, "Get out of my way!" and Impact says, "Change course!" In the end, the steadfast resolution of one will force the other to change. The growth of this exchange forms the *Subjective Story Throughline*.

Taken together, the four throughlines comprise the author's argument to the audience. They answer the questions: What does it feel like to have this problem? What's the other side of the issue? Which perspective is the most suitable for dealing with that problem? What do things look like in the "big picture?"

Only through developing these four simultaneous throughlines can the Story Mind truly reflect our own minds. We pit reason against emotion and immediate advantage against experience in the hope of resolving a problem in the most favorable manner.

Why The Four Throughlines Are Important

In real life, each of us only sees three perspectives clearly within a single context.

In our own lives, we know what it's like to stand in our shoes sharing the "I" (Main Character) perspective. We know what it is like to have someone in our face with a contrary position and directly experience the "You" (Impact Character) perspective. We know what it is like to have a relationship with others and directly experience the "We" (Subjective Story) perspective. But we can never stand outside and see ourselves objectively. We cannot directly experience the "They" (Overall Story) perspective when it comes to our own lives. We can only guestimate what it might be based on what we experience, and don't experience, in the other three perspectives.

In other people's lives, we can look at them objectively and see how they fit in. We can directly experience the "They" (Overall Story) perspective. We can have a relationship with other people and directly experience the "We" (Subjective Story) perspective. We can hold positions contrary to other people and directly experience the "You" (Impact Character) perspective. But we can never stand in other people's shoes. We can never directly experience what it is like to *be* another person and share the "I" (Main Character) perspective with them.

Grand argument stories are special. Grand argument stories give us more than we get in real life. Grand argument stories give us all four perspectives within a single context. They provide us experiences we cannot have in real life.

This quality of grand argument stories helps explain why audiences can watch some stories over and over, long after the storytelling has gone stale. They give meaning to the ambiguous. They provide possible answers to unanswerable questions. They simply allow us the opportunity to experience more than we can in our day-to-day lives.

Moving On

Now that you've added Story Mind, Overall Story Throughline, Main Character Throughline, Impact Character Throughline, and Subjective Story Throughline to your writer's vocabulary, you have all the background you need to explore a whole new world of understanding: The Dramatica Theory of Story.

The Elements Of Structure

CHARACTER

Introduction to Characters

Hero Is a Four-Letter Word

It is easy to think of the principal character in a story as "the hero." Many beginning writers base their stories on the adventures or experiences of a hero. As writers become more mature in their craft, they may come to think of their central character as a "protagonist," or perhaps a "main character." And yet, through all of this, we still don't have any consistent, agreed on definitions of these terms. Before we continue then, it seems prudent to show what Dramatica means by each of these concepts.

A Main Character is the player through whom the audience experiences the story firsthand.

A Protagonist is the prime mover of the plot in the Overall Story throughline.

A Hero is a combination of both Main Character and Protagonist.

In other words, a hero is a blended character who does two jobs: He moves the plot forward and serves as a surrogate for the audience. When we consider all the characters other than a Protagonist who might serve as the audience's position in a story, suddenly a hero becomes severely limited. It is not wrong, just limited.

We see the value of separating the Main Character and Protagonist into two different characters in the motion picture and book, TO KILL A MOCKINGBIRD. Here, the character, Atticus (played by Gregory Peck in the film version), is clearly the Protagonist, yet the author tells the story through the experiences of Scout, Atticus' young daughter.

Later, we will explore many other ways to employ the Main Character in much less typical terms than as a hero. For now, the key point is that Dramatica identifies two different kinds of characters: Those who represent an audience point of view, and those who fulfill a dramatic function in the Overall Story throughline.

Objective and Subjective Characters

The reason there are two kinds of characters goes back to the Story Mind. We have two principal views of that mind: The Objective view from the outside looking in, and the Subjective view from the inside looking out. In terms of the Story Mind, the objective view is like looking at another person, watching his thought processes at work (the "They" perspective). For an audience experiencing a story, the objective view is like watching a football game from the stands. All the characters are most easily identified by their roles on the field. The objective view is tied to the Overall Story throughline.

The Subjective view is as if the Story Mind were our own. From this perspective, only two characters are visible: Main and Impact. The Main and Impact Characters represent the inner conflict of the Story Mind. In fact, we might say a story is of *two* minds. In real life, we often play our own devil's advocate, entertaining an alternative view as a means of arriving at the best decision. Similarly, the Main and Impact Characters make the Story Mind's alternative views tangible. To the audience of a story, the Main Character experience is as if the audience was one of the players on the field. The Impact Character is the player who blocks the way.

To summarize then, characters come in two varieties: Objective and Subjective. Objective Characters represent dramatic functions; Subjective Characters represent points of view. When we attach the Protagonist role to the Main Character point of view, commonly we think of the resulting character as a *hero*.

Looking Forward

In the next chapter we will begin an exploration of Objective Characters found in the Overall Story throughline. Here we meet the Protagonist, Antagonist, and several other archetypes. Next we dissect each archetype to see what essential dramatic elements it contains. Finally, we examine how those same elements can be combined in different, non-archetypal patterns to create more realistic and versatile *complex* characters.

Then we turn our attention to the Subjective Characters: Main and Impact. We examine how the audience point of view is shifted through the Main Character's growth. We also explore the forces that drive these two characters and forge the beliefs they possess.

Objective Characters

Objective Characters are found in the Overall Story throughline and are sometimes called Overall Story Characters. We call them "objective" characters because we look *at* them analytically and identify them by their functions in the Overall Story throughline. As authors, we use the Objective Characters to explore the appropriate and inappropriate ways to resolve the Overall Story problem. We make Objective Characters interesting to our audiences with clever storytelling.

A convenient way to describe Objective Characters is to divide them into two groups: Archetypal Characters and Complex Characters. Archetypes are commonly used objective characters, simple in function and easily recognizable by most audiences. Complex characters use the same character functions as Archetypes, but distribute the functions in more varied patterns. Both Archetypal Characters and Complex Characters are useful in developing your Overall Story throughline.

Archetypes often appear in children's stories and stories in which characters in the Overall Story have limited development. They are simplistic, often too simplistic for most novels, plays, and screenplays. But, their simplicity gives us a useful place to start exploring Objective Characters.

Archetypal Characters

Introduction to Archetypes

Archetypal Characters (Archetypes) are eight, simple Objective Characters that can be found in the Overall Story throughline. The eight Archetypal Characters are Protagonist, Antagonist, Reason, Emotion, Sidekick, Skeptic, Guardian, and Contagonist. Several of these are familiar to most authors. Some are a bit more obscure. One is unique to Dramatica. We will introduce all eight, show how they interact, then explore each in greater detail.

Archetypes exist as a form of storytelling shorthand. Because they are instantly recognizable, an author may choose to use archetypal characters for various reasons. An author may use them because of limited storytelling time or space, or to highlight other aspects of story such as Plot or Theme. Authors use Archetypes to play on audience familiarity, and for other reasons we'll explain. The main advantage of Archetypes is their basic simplicity. This can sometimes work as a disadvantage if you do not develop the characters fully enough to make them seem real.

Protagonist

Players and Characters?

We described how authors often assign the roles of both Protagonist AND Main Character to the same *player* in the story. We mentioned this in our earlier discussion of what sets the Subjective Characters apart from the Objective Characters.

We find the idea of a "player" throughout Dramatica. It differs from what we mean by "character." Dramatica defines a character as a set of dramatic functions that must be portrayed to make the complete argument of a story. Several functions may be grouped and assigned to a person, place, or thing that will represent them in the story. The group of functions defines the nature of the character. The personage representing the functions is a *player*.

In other words, a player is like a vessel into which we place a character (and therefore a set of character functions). If we place more than one Overall Story Character into a single player, the player will have multiple personalities. For example, the dual characters contained in the player DR. JEKYLL & MR. HYDE, or the many personalities of SYBIL.

Describing the Protagonist

No doubt the most well known of all the Archetypal Characters is the Protagonist. As with all the Archetypal Characters, there is a specific "shopping list" or "recipe" of dramatic functions that describes the Protagonist. The archetypal Protagonist is the chief proponent and principal driver of the effort to achieve the story's goal.

At first, this description seems far too simple for even the most archetypal of Protagonists. This is because we see the Main Character most often combined with the Protagonist. We seldom see a Protagonist player representing the archetypal functions alone.

Still, pursuing the goal is the essential function of the Protagonist, and beginning here we can build a network of relationships that describe the remaining archetypes. As a side note, the entire exploration of the Main Character throughline is an independent job of the Main Character. For the Archetypal Protagonist, therefore, we consider only its role in the Overall Story Throughline as just another player on the field (although a crucial one).

So, for our current needs, consider the Archetypal Protagonist as the chief proponent and principal driver of the effort to achieve the story's goal.

Antagonist

What is an Antagonist?

The Archetypal *Antagonist* is diametrically opposed to the Protagonist's successful attainment of the goal. Often this results in a Protagonist who has a purpose and an Antagonist comes along and tries to stop it. Sometimes, however, it is the other way around. The Antagonist may have a goal of its own that causes negative repercussions. The Protagonist then has the goal of stopping the Antagonist. Dramatica defines the Protagonist's goal as the story's goal, regardless of which kind it is. This sets up a consistent way to analyze how all Archetypal Characters relate to the goal of any story,

Antagonist and the Impact Character

Just as the Protagonist is often "doubled up" with the function of the Main Character, the Antagonist is sometimes (though less often) combined with the Impact Character. We explore the Impact Character fully in the Subjective Characters section of this book. For now, a simple description of the Impact Character will serve our purposes.

Just as the Antagonist opposes the Protagonist in the Overall Story, the Impact Character stands in the way of the Main Character in the Subjective Story. Note we did not say the Impact Character *opposes* the Main Character, but rather *stands in the way*. The Impact Character's purpose in the story is to represent an alternative belief system or worldview to the Main Character. This forces the Main Character to avoid the easy way out and to face his personal problem.

When combining the Impact Character and the Antagonist in the same player, keep in mind the difference between their respective functions. This allows you to express the dramatic purposes of each fully.

Reason & Emotion

Why Reason and Emotion Characters?

Having briefly described the Protagonist and Antagonist, we can already see how they represent basic functions of the Story Mind. The Protagonist represents the drive to try to solve a problem; the Antagonist represents the drive to prevent or avoid success. These two characters teeter back and forth over the course of the story as each in turn gains the advantage.

Even in the most Archetypal terms, this conflict is not enough to describe an argument fully. It fails to address many other basic concerns that occur naturally in the minds of audience members. Therefore, we must incorporate these other concerns into the Story Mind as well. That is why there are six other Archetypal Characters. Just as Protagonist and Antagonist form a pair, the other six Archetypal Characters form three other pairs. *Reason* and *Emotion* make up the first of these pairs.

Reason and Emotion Described

The Reason Archetypal Character is calm, collected, and cool, perhaps even cold. It makes decisions and takes action wholly based on logic. (Remember, we say *wholly* because we are describing an *Archetypal* Character. As we shall see later, *Complex* Characters are much more diverse and dimensional.)

The Reason character is the organized, logical type.

The Emotion character is uncontrolled and driven by feelings.

As in real life, Reason is not inherently *better* than Emotion, nor does Emotion have the edge on Reason. They just have different areas of strength and weakness that may make one more suitable than the other in a given context.

Functionally, the Emotion Character has its heart on its sleeve. It is quick to anger, but also quick to empathize. Because it is frenetic and disorganized, however, most of its energy is uncontrolled. It wastes energy by lashing out in so many directions that it ends up running in circles and getting nowhere. In contrast, the Reason Character seems to lack "humanity" and seemingly has no ability to think from the heart. As a result, the Reason Character often fails to find support for its well-laid plans. It wastes its effort because it has unknowingly violated the personal concerns of others.

In terms of the Story Mind, Reason and Emotion describe the conflict between our purely practical conclusions and considerations of our human side. Throughout a story, the Reason and Emotion Archetypal Characters will conflict over the proper course of action and decision, illustrating the Story Mind's deliberation between intellect and heart.

Sidekick & Skeptic

The next pair of Archetypal Characters are the *Sidekick* and the *Skeptic*, who represent the conflict between confidence and doubt in the Story Mind.

The Sidekick is the faithful supporter. Usually, a Sidekick attaches itself to the Protagonist. Sometimes, however, it may be a supporter of the Antagonist. This gives a good clue to the way Dramatica sees Overall Story Characters: The purpose of the

Sidekick is to show faithful support. That does not decide *who* or *what* it supports, but just that it must loyally support someone or something. Other dynamics of a story control whom the Sidekick supports to make the story's argument.

The Skeptic balances the Sidekick.

The Skeptic is the disbelieving "opposer." Where the Sidekick has faith, the Skeptic disbelieves; where the Sidekick supports, the Skeptic opposes. The line from a song, "Whatever it is, I'm against it," fittingly describes the nature of the Skeptic. In the Story Mind, it is the function of the Skeptic to note the indicators that foreshadow failure. In contrast, the Sidekick notes the indicators that point to success.

The interactions between Sidekick and Skeptic describe the Story Mind's consideration of the likelihood of success.

Guardian & Contagonist

What are the Guardian and Contagonist?

Finally we come to the remaining pair of Archetypal Characters. The first of these archetypes is a common yet often loosely defined set of functions; the second archetype is unique to Dramatica. The first of these characters is the *Guardian*. The Guardian functions as a teacher/helper who represents the Conscience of the Story Mind. This is a protective character that removes obstacles and brightens the path ahead. In this way, the Guardian helps the Protagonist stay on the proper path to achieve success. Balancing the Guardian is a character representing Temptation in the Story Mind. This character works to place obstacles in the path of the Protagonist, and to lure it away from success. Because this character works to hinder the progress of the Protagonist, we coined the name "*Contagonist*."

Contagonist: "Whose side are you on?"

Because the Contagonist and Antagonist both have a negative affect on the Protagonist, they can easily be confused with each other. They are, however, two completely different characters because they have two completely different functions in the Story Mind. Where the Antagonist works to stop the Protagonist, the Contagonist acts to deflect the Protagonist. The Antagonist works to prevent the Protagonist from making further progress, the Contagonist works to delay or divert the Protagonist for a time.

As with the Sidekick, the Contagonist allies itself with either the Antagonist or the Protagonist. Often, Contagonists are cast as the Antagonist's lackey or second-in-command. However, Contagonists sometimes attached themselves to the Protagonist, where they function as a thorn in the side and bad influence. As a pair, Guardian and Contagonist function in the Story Mind as Conscience and Temptation. They provide both a light to clarify the proper path and the enticement to step off it.

Archetypes—a Balanced Part of the Complete Argument

As a group, the Archetypal Characters represent all the essential functions of a complete Story Mind. They are grouped in simple patterns. However, because the Archetypes can be allied in different ways, a degree of versatility can be added to their relationships.

Complex Characters

What is a Complex Character?

Complex Characters are created from the same set of dramatic functions as Archetypes. The principal difference is that Archetypal Characters group functions that are most similar and compatible, and Complex Characters don't. Although Archetypal Characters may conflict with one another, an Archetypal Character is never in conflict with its own drives and attitudes. This is why the Archetypal Characters often seem less developed than Complex Characters and perhaps less *human*.

To create characters that more closely represent our own inconsistencies, we must redistribute their functions so they are less internally compatible. We refer to any arrangement of character functions other than an Archetypal grouping to be Complex. A character containing such a grouping is a *Complex Character*.

Complex Characters provide us opportunities to explore the Overall Story throughline and Objective characters to greater depth.

Archetypes and Complex Characters Together

A single story may have both Archetypal and Complex Characters. Deciding how to group the functions is open to an author's storytelling desires. The problem is, until one is aware of exactly what these functions are and how they interact, it is difficult to know how to combine them. These essential functions are at such a basic level that they form the elementary building blocks of Overall Story Characters. Therefore, we refer to these functions as character *Elements*. Listing the character Elements gives little feel for the characters created from them. Similarly, listing the Periodic Chart of Elements in chemistry gives no feel for the natures of the compounds engineered by combining them.

As a result, the best way to present the character Elements with meaning is to start with the Archetypal Characters. By definition, Dramatica Archetypal Characters collectively contain all the Elements. We then break the Archetypal Characters down, step-by-step, level-by-level, until we expose their elemental ingredients. In this manner, understanding is carried down to the Elements, which may then be combined in non-archetypal ways to create Complex Characters.

Drivers and Passengers

Dynamic Pairs

We have now created four distinct pairs of Archetypal Characters. Each pair presents the birthing ground of a particular conflict. Two Characters bonded in such a relationship form a *Dynamic Pair*. Here are the Eight Archetypal Characters organized by dynamic pairs.

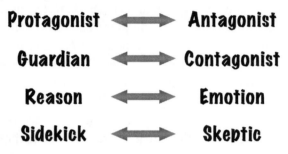

Protagonist	⟷	Antagonist
Guardian	⟷	Contagonist
Reason	⟷	Emotion
Sidekick	⟷	Skeptic

Functions of Dynamic Pairs

We easily see how these Archetypal pairs represent a broad analogy to a human mind dealing with a problem. The Protagonist represents the wish to work at resolving the problem. Its dynamic pair, the Antagonist represents the wish to leave the problem alone. As with the Archetypal Characters, we face an internal battle between making decisions based on Reason or on Emotion. Like the functions of the Sidekick and Skeptic, the Story Mind will contain a struggle between Faith and Disbelief. And finally, in an Archetypal sense, the Mind will be torn between the Contagonist's temptation for immediate indulgence and the Guardian's counsel to consider the consequences.

Forcing the Story Forward

There is another useful grouping of the Archetypal Characters which helps uncover their essential Elements. Four of the characters seem to be the prime movers of the story, and it is their interactions that determine the thrust of the effort to address the story's problem. The other four are "backseat drivers"—perhaps interested in the outcome, but rather than forcing the plot, they *influence* those who do force the plot. Remember, these descriptions are only applicable in a general way but serve to make comparisons between similar traits of characters. In Dramatica, we group four similar, interrelated items into a simple table called a *quad*. So, we can create a quad of Driver Characters and a quad of Passenger Characters.

Drivers

The Driver Quad

Quad One: The Driver Characters

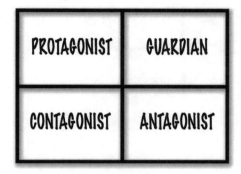

In simple stories, the Protagonist, Antagonist, Guardian, and Contagonist are all major drivers of the story. Whatever the object of their efforts, the Protagonist tries to achieve it. The Antagonist tries to prevent its achievement. The Guardian acts to aid the achievement, and the Contagonist acts to hinder (although Guardian and Contagonist may not be directly concerned with the goal itself or even each other). Regardless of their personal levels of awareness, each of these Characters seen *objectively* acts with a unique drive that represents a basic Motivation of the Story Mind.

For example, if the Protagonist wants to build a shopping center, the Antagonist will not want it built. The Contagonist might get an injunction delaying construction so it can profit from a stock deal, even though it may like to see the center built eventually. The Guardian might find a legal loophole to overturn the injunction, perhaps just as a by-product of another matter it is representing in court.

Remember, these Overall Story Characters are not judged by how THEY see the story, but how WE see them *affecting* the story.

Passengers

The Passenger Quad

Quad Two: The Passenger Characters

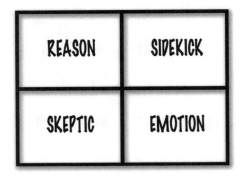

   Unlike the first quad, these four Characters are not the prime movers of the story, but rather ride the coattails of the Driver Characters. If not for the Drivers, the Passengers would not even be involved with the problem. Each represents an approach or attitude in the story. Sidekick is forever faithful while Skeptic is forever doubting. Reason acts based on logic and Emotion responds from feelings. Of course, each of these Characters also has its own motivations, but seen objectively as part of the Story Mind they represent different approaches and attitudes toward solving the problem.

   Before we subdivide the Archetypal Characters into their basic Elements, let's get a better feel for them by examining the Drivers and Passengers in several well-known stories.

Drivers and Passengers in STAR WARS

Archetypes in STAR WARS (1977)

Most people would agree that Luke Skywalker is the Protagonist in STAR WARS and Dramatica sees it the same way. The Empire itself, embodied in the Gran Mof Tarkin and his troops, is the force *diametrically* opposed to the story's goal of destroying the Death Star. It is the Antagonist. Obi Wan Kenobi is the Guardian, protecting Luke and company and providing "moral" guidance. Darth Vader is the Contagonist, representing the temptation of the "Dark side of the Force" and hindering progress at every turn.

Han Solo functions as the Skeptic, arguing his disbelief in the Force as well as his opposition to just about every course of action anyone tries to take. R2D2 and C3PO jointly fill the role of Sidekick, forever faithful to whomever they attend. Princess Leia is Reason, coldly calculating (although the storytelling tempers this), calm-headed and the real planner of the group. Chewbacca, in contrast, responds often with little or no thought and acts solely based on his feelings. This clearly defines him as Emotion.

(Please note that R2D2 and C3PO have a well-developed *subplot* between them that is forefront as the movie opens. This gives them much more personality and versatility. It also spells out differences between them that would not occur if they both simply shared the sidekick function. Subplots are dealt with later in the Storyweaving section of this book.)

Drivers and Passengers in STAR WARS

Having described our eight characters in STAR WARS, let us organize them into Drivers and Passengers.

Driver Characters

PROTAGONIST LUKE	GUARDIAN OBI WAN
CONTAGONIST DARTH VADER	ANTAGONIST EMPIRE

Passenger Characters

REASON LEIA	SIDEKICK R2D2 & C3PO
SKEPTIC HAN SOLO	EMOTION CHEWBACCA

Drivers and Passengers in
THE WIZARD OF OZ

Archetypes in THE WIZARD OF OZ

We can label Dorothy as the Protagonist in THE WIZARD OF OZ with some confidence. The Scarecrow seems to be Reason since he is the planner of the group ("I'll show you how to get apples!"), but he is not calm or collected. In fact, he is the opposite. Similarly, the Tin Man looks like Emotion as he cries in the poppy field. Yet he is anything but frenetic when he rusts himself from the tears. Clearly, our original Archetypes don't seem as true-to-form as they did in STAR WARS.

Let's file that away for later and press on. The Cowardly Lion fills the role of Skeptic and Toto performs as the Sidekick. Glinda is an unabashed Guardian and the Wicked Witch of the West balances her as the Contagonist. But just a moment, doesn't the Wicked Witch act more like an Antagonist? Indeed she does, yet she seems to also fill the same role compared to Glinda as Darth Vader fills compared to Obi Wan. Assuming for a moment the Wicked Witch IS the Contagonist, then who is the Antagonist?

There is only one major character yet unaccounted for --the Wizard himself.

The Wizard as Antagonist? Somehow it doesn't sound right. At this point it becomes clear the characters in Oz are not all exactly Archetypal. Something is going on with the Scarecrow and Tin Man and the Witch and the Wizard that doesn't fit. Exploring these failings of the Archetypal Character model as applied to Oz will eventually offer some insight into the essential character Elements.

However, let's pencil in the Witch as Antagonist and the Wizard as the Contagonist so we have a place to start. Here are the Eight Simple Characters of THE WIZARD OF OZ in Quad format, ignoring any inconsistencies for the moment.

Drivers and Passengers in
THE WIZARD OF OZ

Driver Characters

PROTAGONIST DOROTHY	GUARDIAN GLINDA
CONTAGONIST WIZARD	ANTAGONIST WITCH

Passenger Characters

REASON SCARECROW	SIDEKICK TOTO
SKEPTIC LION	EMOTION TIN MAN

Drivers and Passengers in JAWS

Archetypes in JAWS

Chief Brody fills the Protagonist's shoes in JAWS, and few would doubt the Shark is the Antagonist. Hooper, with all his gizmos, takes the Reasonable stand, while Quint, who simply hates sharks, functions as Emotion. The Mayor is a strong Contagonist and Brody's wife is a weak Sidekick although it almost seems as if Hooper fills that role sometimes as well. Once again, we need more versatility than the Archetypal Characters provide.

We still need a Guardian—someone to protect Brody as well as stress the proper moral course. Simply put, JAWS has no character that performs BOTH functions. Rather, Hooper plays the **moral** half of the Guardian's role. Hooper reminds Brody of his duty and urges him into taking action against the shark problem. The **protective** role is filled in turn by the land itself, Hooper's boat, and lastly Quint's boat.

Non-Archetypal Roles in JAWS

There is no reason a character must be a *person*. A boat can be a player as well as a person, as long as it can show its function to the audience. Again, in Dramatica, the point of a story is to illustrate all aspects of the Story Mind dealing with a problem. As long as each aspect is accounted for, the specific carrier of that Element is *structurally* irrelevant and may only have storytelling ramifications.

So far we have not determined the Skeptic in JAWS. Who refuses to believe evidence of the shark problem or the need for taking action against it? Clearly the Mayor embodies that characteristic well, and yet was previously identified as the Contagonist. Obviously some "doubling up" is going on here. If we look at who is across from whom in quad form, we can see some of the basic dramatic Character conflicts in JAWS.

Drivers and Passengers in JAWS

Driver Characters

PROTAGONIST BRODY	GUARDIAN HOOPER
CONTAGONIST MAYOR	ANTAGONIST SHARK

Passenger Characters

REASON HOOPER	SIDEKICK WIFE
SKEPTIC MAYOR	EMOTION QUINT

From this breakdown, we see a good example in both the Mayor and Hooper of single players who portray two distinct Archetypal characters. The Mayor functions as Contagonist and Skeptic. Hooper portrays both Guardian and Reason. Some of these broad labels fit better than others which is why there are some Complex Character arrangements in JAWS, that do not fall into the strict Archetypal mold.

Action and Decision Elements
of Drivers and Passengers

Recap of Archetypal Characters

Now that we have become familiar with Archetypal characters and some of their limitations, let us recap our list of the eight Archetypal Characters as a prelude to resolving the inconsistencies we saw in THE WIZARD OF OZ and JAWS:

- **PROTAGONIST**: The traditional Protagonist is the driver of the story: the one who forces the action. We root for it and hope for its success.

- **ANTAGONIST**: The Antagonist is the character directly opposed to the Protagonist. It represents the problem that must be solved or overcome for the Protagonist to succeed.

- **REASON**: The Reason character deliberates and takes action based on logic, never letting feelings get in the way of a rational course.

- **EMOTION**: The Emotion character responds with its feelings without thinking, whether it is angry or kind, without regard for practicality.

- **SKEPTIC**: The Skeptic doubts everything—courses of action, sincerity, truth—whatever.

- **SIDEKICK**: The Sidekick is unfailing in its loyalty and support. The Sidekick often aligns with the Protagonist though it may also attach itself to the Antagonist.

- **GUARDIAN**: The Guardian is a teacher or helper who aids the Protagonist in its quest and offers a moral standard.

- **CONTAGONIST**: The Contagonist hinders and deludes the Protagonist, tempting it to take the wrong course or approach.

Splitting Archetypes Into
Action and Decision Characteristics

Reexamining the list, we can learn something new that will help us in analyzing THE WIZARD OF OZ and JAWS: each of the Eight Archetypal Characters contains one action characteristic and one decision characteristic.

PROTAGONIST

Action Characteristic:
Pursues the goal. The traditional Protagonist is the driver of the story: the one who forces the action.

Decision Characteristic:
Urges the other characters to consider the need to achieve the goal.

ANTAGONIST

Action Characteristic:
The Antagonist physically tries to prevent or avoid the successful achievement of the goal by the Protagonist.

Decision Characteristic:
The Antagonist urges the other characters to reconsider the attempt to achieve the goal.

GUARDIAN

Action Characteristic:
The Guardian is a helper who aids the efforts to achieve the story goal.

Decision Characteristic:
 The Guardian represents conscience in the mind, based on the Author's view of morality.

CONTAGONIST

Action Characteristic:
The Contagonist hinders the efforts to achieve the story goal.

Decision Characteristic:
The Contagonist represents temptation to take the wrong course or approach.

REASON

Action Characteristic:
The Reason character is calm or controlled in its actions.

Decision Characteristic:
 The Reason makes decisions based on logic, never letting emotion get in the way of a rational course.

EMOTION

Action Characteristic:
The Emotion character is frenzied or uncontrolled in its actions.

Decision Characteristic:
The Emotion character responds with its feelings without regard for practicality.

SIDEKICK

Action Characteristic:
The Sidekick supports, playing a cheering section.

Decision Characteristic:
The Sidekick is almost gullible in the extent of its faith—in the goal, in the Protagonist, in success, and so on.

SKEPTIC

Action Characteristic:
The Skeptic opposes—everything.

Decision Characteristic:
The Skeptic disbelieves everything, doubting courses of action, sincerity, truth—whatever.

Split Archetypes in Quads

Having split them in two, we can see that each of the Archetypal Characters has an attitude or Decision characteristic and an approach or Action characteristic. When we arrange both characteristics under each of the eight Archetypes in our Driver and Passenger Quad format, we get a graphic feel for the Archetypal Overall Story Characters and the Elements they represent.

Driver Quad

PROTAGONIST Pursue Consideration	GUARDIAN Help Conscience
CONTAGONIST Hinder Temptation	ANTAGONIST Prevent Reconsideration

Passenger Quad

REASON Control Logic	SIDEKICK Support Faith
SKEPTIC Oppose Disbelief	EMOTION Uncontrolled Feeling

In Dramatica, we refer to these 16 characteristics as the *Motivation* Elements because they describe what drives the Archetypal Characters.

The 16 Motivation Elements in STAR WARS

Elements of STAR WARS Characters

Let's see how well these sixteen Motivation Elements line up with the characters we have examined so far. As Protagonist, Luke does indeed seem to be the **pursuing** character. He is also the one who urges all to **consider** the need to achieve the goal ("We've got to help the Princess!"). The Empire wants to **prevent** Luke from succeeding, and urges him and all others to **reconsider** the propriety of their actions—*reconsider or you will die.*

Obi Wan provides a sense of **conscience**, while **helping** Luke when he gets into trouble. Darth, on the other hand, clearly represents the **tempting** "Dark side of the Force." Darth also **hinders** Luke's progress, the Rebel's progress, and even hinders progress by the Empire itself!

R2D2 and C3PO are ever **faithful** and **supportive**. Han is the never-ending **disbeliever** and **opposer**. Chewbacca acts on his **feelings** and behaves in an **uncontrolled** way. Leia is **controlled** and driven by **logic**.

Charted out, the assignment of characteristics to the various characters has a good feel to it.

Character Quads with Elements

Driver Quad

PROTAGONIST LUKE Pursue Consider	GUARDIAN OBI WAN Help Conscience
CONTAGONIST DARTH VADER Hinder Temptation	ANTAGONIST EMPIRE Prevent Reconsider

Passenger Quad

REASON LEIA Control Logic	SIDEKICK R2D2 & C3PO Support Faith
SKEPTIC HAN SOLO Oppose Disbelief	EMOTION CHEWBACCA Uncontrolled Feeling

The 16 Motivation Elements in
THE WIZARD OF OZ

Archetypal Elements of "OZ" Characters

Returning to OZ, Dorothy is both **pursue** and **consideration**. Toto is **faith** and **support**. The Cowardly Lion is clearly **disbelief** and **oppose**, and Glinda is **conscience** and **help**. But here is where breaking the Eight Archetypal Characters into 16 characteristics solves our previous problems.

Tin Man and Scarecrow Swap Meet

When we look at the Scarecrow he represents **logic** ("If I only had a brain"), but his approach, rather than being in **control**, is **uncontrolled**. Similarly, although the Tin Man is undoubtedly **feeling** ("If I only had a heart"), his behavior is just as surely described by **control** (he freezes stiff when he cries).

Archetypal Arrangement

	Reason	Emotion
Decision Element	Logic	Feeling
Action Element	Control	Uncontrolled

WIZARD OF OZ

	Scarecrow	Tin Man
Decision Element	Logic	Feeling
Action Element	Uncontrolled	Control

Clearly, the Scarecrow and the Tin Man have swapped characteristics: logic goes with uncontrolled and feeling goes with control. In a sense, both of these Characters now contain two Elements that are in conflict. The Action Element does not reflect the Decision Element. This creates two interesting Characters who have an added degree of depth to them: an internal friction, inconsistency, and conflict. This is the kind of arrangement that begins to make characters more complex.

Witch and Wizard Ways

But what about the Witch and the Wizard? What is it that makes them diverge from the Archetypal molds? Could it be a similar "swapping" of Elements? As it turns out, it is a *similar* swapping, but not the same. To be the Archetypal Contagonist, the Wizard would have to be **temptation** and **hinder**. To be the Antagonist, the Witch would have to be **reconsideration** and **prevent**. But rather than swapping an Action Element for another Action Element, the Witch ends up with **both** Action Elements and the Wizard with **both** Decision ones!

Archetypal Arrangement

	Antagonist	*Contagonist*
Decision Elements	Reconsideration	Temptation
Action Elements	Prevent (avoid)	Hinder

WIZARD OF OZ

Wizard Decision Elements	Reconsideration	Temptation
Witch Action Elements	Prevent (avoid)	Hinder

The Witch tries to prevent Dorothy from leaving Oz by putting her into a magic induced sleep, and later by trying to kill her. She also works to hinder Dorothy's efforts by attacking her friends and getting her ejected from the safety of the Emerald City.

The Wizard acts as temptation with the promise of easy answers for Dorothy and her friends (a diploma for Scarecrow, an award for the Cowardly Lion, a balloon trip for Dorothy, and so on). As "The Great and Powerful Oz," his threatening reputation, nature, and tasks make Dorothy's group think twice before continuing. Even the Wizard's disguise as the Emerald City gatekeeper is designed to convince Dorothy to "go away."

"OZ" Elements in Quads

When we put this information into our Quad formation, the Elements do not line up in a simple way.

Driver Quad

PROTAGONIST	GUARDIAN
DOROTHY Pursue Consider	GLINDA Help Conscience
WIZARD Reconsider Temptation	WITCH Prevent Hinder

Passenger Quad

	SIDEKICK
SCARECROW Uncontrolled Logic	TOTO Support Faith
SKEPTIC LION Oppose Disbelief	TIN MAN Control Feeling

Everyone still has two characteristics. However, the arrangements are not Archetypal for *all* the Characters in THE WIZARD OF OZ. As a result, the Archetypal role names have been removed where they do not apply.

The 16 Motivation Elements in JAWS

Elements of JAWS Characters

Brody, as Protagonist, is nicely **pursue**, and with his bell ringing and whistle-blowing Brody is **consideration** as well. Hooper does provide the sense of **conscience** and **helps** Brody. The Mayor **hinders** our Protagonist and dishes out plenty of **temptation** to give up the quest. The shark forces **reconsideration** of the propriety of the goal and goes out of its way to **prevent** Brody from achieving his goal of adjusting its feeding habits. Brody's wife is his **faithful supporter**. Hooper adds to his functions by filling the role of **logic** as well, yet he is **uncontrolled** in his approach, as made obvious by the variety of devices he employs to no clear success. Quint is clearly acting from his **feelings**, but his approach is simple and in **control**. The Mayor, in addition, supplies us with **disbelief** and **oppose**.

Driver Quad

PROTAGONIST **BRODY** Pursue Consider	GUARDIAN **HOOPER** Help Conscience
CONTAGONIST **MAYOR** Hinder Temptation	ANTAGONIST **SHARK** Prevent Reconsider

Passenger Quad

QUINT Control Feeling	SIDEKICK **WIFE** Support Faith
SKEPTIC **MAYOR** Oppose Disbelief	**HOOPER** Uncontrolled Logic

Grouping the 16 Motivation Elements

A Better Way to Group Elements

A better way to organize these characteristics is to separate the Action Elements from the Decision Elements. The Eight Archetypal Character Types describe a specific pairing of Action characteristic to Decision characteristic. When we separate the sets, we cannot keep the Archetypal Character names as their contents are split. Nevertheless, it is much more useful to arrange the Elements by their similar natures rather than by the simple arrangement contained in the Archetypal Characters.

With 16 characteristics, we can create four quads of four characteristics each. This grows from starting with a Driver Character Quad and a Passenger Character Quad. We split each quad in two (Action Quad and Decision Quad), giving us four Quads. The resulting quads are the Action Driver Quad, the Decision Driver Quad, the Action Passenger Quad and the Decision Passenger Quad.

Motivation Element Quad

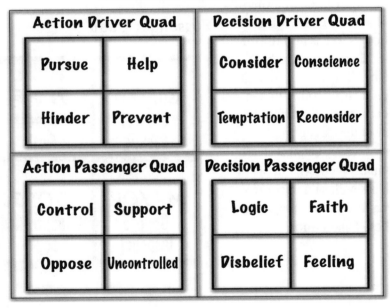

Action Driver Quad		Decision Driver Quad	
Pursue	Help	Consider	Conscience
Hinder	Prevent	Temptation	Reconsider
Action Passenger Quad		**Decision Passenger Quad**	
Control	Support	Logic	Faith
Oppose	Uncontrolled	Disbelief	Feeling

Using the Quads to Gain Meaning

In Dramatica, we call a group of four Quads a *Set*. Note how the set above provides added meaning. For example, when dealing with a problem of Action in terms of Drivers, one would have the choice to Pursue, Prevent, Help, or Hinder. When a Character represents the Drive to Pursue, it applies itself to achieving the goal. Although it may also want the goal to be achieved, a Help Character focuses its efforts on being useful to the Pursuit of the goal rather than starting its own effort. This explains the functions of and relationship between the Protagonist's Drive (Pursue) and the Guardian's Drive (Help).

Similarly, when a Protagonist' Drive is Pursue, an Antagonist's Drive is Prevent. And, of course, the Contagonist Hinders the Protagonist's Pursuit. In fact, when we consider all four Quads, we gain a precise understanding of why the Eight Archetypal Characters are created as they are and exactly how they relate.

Complex Arrangements of Character Elements

So far we have only explored sixteen different character Elements. One way to create complex characters is by assigning these sixteen Elements to characters in non-archetypal patterns. However, as great as the number of potential characters that can be created is, this limited set of sixteen Elements is *still* not enough to describe all the rich complexities of the Overall Story Characters we see in sophisticated stories. This is because these sixteen Elements only represent character *Motivations*. In fact, we call them the Sixteen Motivation Elements.

Characters Do Not Live By Motivations Alone

Like real people, characters are driven by Motivations, but they also aspire to different *Purposes*, employ different *Methodologies* in the effort to achieve those purposes, and use different standards of *Evaluation* to determine the effectiveness of their efforts. The adage that one should create three-dimensional characters falls short by one dimension. Fully realized characters are four-dimensional consisting of an Action and Decision Element in each dimension.

In the following sections we will explore two kinds of character complexity. First we will look at ways to rearrange the Motivation Elements, and second, we will outline how to bring the other three character dimensions into play.

STAR WARS Characters in Four Motivation Quads

Once again, to enhance our "feel" for these relationships, let's add the names of the Characters in STAR WARS to the quads.

STAR WARS

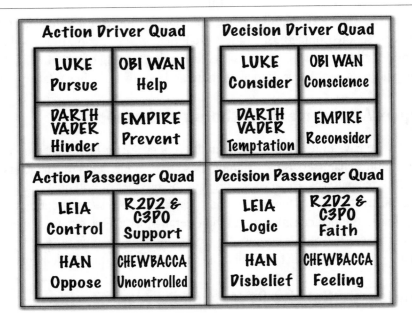

Action Driver Quad		Decision Driver Quad	
LUKE Pursue	OBI WAN Help	LUKE Consider	OBI WAN Conscience
DARTH VADER Hinder	EMPIRE Prevent	DARTH VADER Temptation	EMPIRE Reconsider
Action Passenger Quad		**Decision Passenger Quad**	
LEIA Control	R2D2 & C3PO Support	LEIA Logic	R2D2 & C3PO Faith
HAN Oppose	CHEWBACCA Uncontrolled	HAN Disbelief	CHEWBACCA Feeling

As before, the amazingly pure Archetypal Characters of STAR WARS translate into a symmetrical pattern. Each Character has an Action Quad characteristic and a Decision Quad characteristic. Each pair of Characters is in direct opposition, both internally and externally. Further, Driver Archetypes are represented only in the Driver Quads and Passenger Archetypes are found only within the Passenger Quads.

"OZ" Characters in Four Motivation Quads

THE WIZARD OF OZ

Action Driver Quad		Decision Driver Quad	
DOROTHY Pursue	**GLINDA** Help	**DOROTHY** Consider	**GLINDA** Conscience
WICKED WITCH Hinder	**WICKED WITCH** Prevent	**WIZARD** Temptation	**WIZARD** Reconsider
Action Passenger Quad		**Decision Passenger Quad**	
TIN MAN Control	**TOTO** Support	**SCARECROW** Logic	**TOTO** Faith
LION Oppose	**SCARECROW** Uncontrolled	**LION** Disbelief	**TIN MAN** Feeling

In looking at these patterns, the Passenger Characters in THE WIZARD OF OZ seem much like the Passenger Characters in STAR WARS, with one notable exception. The difference is the "flipping" of Logic and Feeling in relation to Control and Uncontrolled. The Reason and Emotion Characters simply traded places on one Dynamic Pair of Elements in a single Quad. It makes sense that a stereotypical Reason Character would be logical AND controlled. It follows that a stereotypical Emotion Character would be feeling AND uncontrolled. But if you simply flip the Action Characteristics in relation to the Decision Characteristics, far more versatile Characters emerge. You create characters whose approach no longer *complements* their attitude, but *conflicts* with it. In a sense, these Characters are made more interesting by creating an inequity *within* them even as they continue to represent methods of problem solving within the Story Mind.

Looking at the Wizard and the Wicked Witch we see swapping characteristics creates much less stereotypical characters. Rather than a tempter, the Wicked Witch becomes an action-oriented pest. She not only works to prevent Dorothy from achieving her goal but also hinders her every step on the way as well. The Wizard becomes a purely decision-oriented tempter. He represents taking the seemingly easy way out. Through his fearsome reputation, displays, and requests, he also urges Dorothy and her friends to reconsider their decisions. This lack of action characteristics may help explain why the Wizard is so physically absent during most of the story, although his influence is felt throughout. Obviously, the nature of the combinations of characteristics has a great impact on which decisions and actions the audience expects and accepts from an Objective Character.

JAWS Characters in Four Motivation Quads

JAWS

Action Driver Quad	
BRODY Pursue	HOOPER Help
MAYOR Hinder	SHARK Prevent

Decision Driver Quad	
BRODY Consider	HOOPER Conscience
MAYOR Temptation	SHARK Reconsider

Action Passenger Quad	
QUINT Control	WIFE Support
MAYOR Oppose	HOOPER Uncontrolled

Decision Passenger Quad	
HOOPER Logic	WIFE Faith
MAYOR Disbelief	QUINT Feeling

Clearly, the Driver Character characteristics in JAWS are as simple as those in STAR WARS. In fact, they are identical in terms of which characteristics are combined into a single Character. However, when we look at the Passenger Character characteristics, we see a new phenomenon: some of those Elements are present in the Driver Characters, two of whom are doing multiple duty.

The Mayor represents Temptation and Hinder as a Driver Character but also represents the Passenger characteristics of Disbelief and Oppose. Hooper, a Driver in Conscience and Help, also represents Logic and Uncontrolled, putting him in conflict with Quint. Clearly these "multi-characteristic" Characters are much more complex in their make-up and therefore in their interactions than Archetypes. Therefore we refer to them as Complex Characters.

Complex Motivation Characteristics

Rules for Building Characters?

The question now becomes, "Is there a definitive set of rules that govern how characteristics may combine without violating the analogy of the Story Mind?" Let's find out.

A Character Cannot Serve Two Masters

The first thing we notice when examining the Motivation Characters is there is never an instance where a Character contains both characteristics in a Dynamic Pair. This makes common sense: "One cannot serve two masters." Essentially, how can you be AGAINST something at the same time you are FOR it? So, our first rule of combining characteristics is: **Characters should never represent more than one characteristic in a Dynamic Pair.**

Can't Serve Two Masters at the Same Time....

Sounds good, but what if you want to create a Character who represents one view and then the other. For example, if you had a one-woman show, you would need to combine ALL 16 Motivation characteristics into one person. This is doable because of the difference between a character and a player. A player is a person, place, or thing that embodies one or more characters. In stage terms, a player is often an actor who "plays" one or more characters in the work. In a one-woman show, even if it is a single story argument, there might be a multitude of characters but only one player. The key to keeping them separate is to have the player change from one character to another, never simultaneously portraying more than one, such as by donning different apparel or adopting a different voice.

Because of this extra information we add a second rule of thumb to our first: Players should never represent more than one character at a time.

The Meaning of Overall Story Character Elements

In truth, there are many valid reasons for combining opposing characteristics in one body. An example is DOCTOR JEKYLL AND MISTER HYDE. As Jekyll and Hyde, this player has a split personality representing, in effect, two *Characters* in the same body.

Dramatica sees a player as a shopper filling a grocery sack full of characteristics. You can select whatever you want, as long as you don't put in both Elements of a Dynamic Pair. You can also carry as many bags as you can handle.

But wouldn't a fixed grouping of characteristics prevent a Character from growing? For the answer, look back at what these characteristics are. They are the problem-solving processes within the Story Mind *seen Objectively*. They are Overall Story Characters. Objectively, characters remain the same; it is *Subjectively* that they grow as points of view change. In a sense, the Overall Story nature of characters describes their inherent disposition, in which no changes can be made. The Subjective nature of characters describes their learned behavior, which is what can change over the course of a story.

What does all this mean in a practical sense to us as Authors? First, Dramatica tells us there are only 16 Motivations to spread among our players. If we use the same characteristic twice, it clutters our story. If we neglect to employ one, there will be a hole in our story's argument. Finally, we have much flexibility to create unique and memorable characters while fulfilling all the requirements an audience will look for in a Story Mind.

Complex Characters in GONE WITH THE WIND

Simply "Gone With The Wind"

As an exercise, let's take a look at how the Motivation characteristics are represented and combined in some familiar well-written stories. Why don't we tackle something simple like *GONE WITH THE WIND*?

"Simple?" you say. In terms of thematics, *GONE WITH THE WIND* is an extremely rich and complex story. But in terms of the characters, *GWTW* is no more complex than any of the other stories we have analyzed so far. Let's see how.

Scarlett and Rhett

A list of the most notable Characters might include: Scarlett O'Hara, Rhett Butler, Ashley Wilkes, Melanie Wilkes, Scarlett's sister Suellen, Frank Kennedy,

Scarlett's father Gerald O'Hara, and Prissy. Taking them one at a time, we can see the stuff they are made of.

Intuitively, we sense that Scarlett and Rhett are the two most important characters. Looking at the 16 characteristics, Scarlett is clearly Pursue. She pursues Rhett, she pursues Ashley, she pursues the tax money, and she pursues a fortune. She is motivated to get people to consider things they normally would not. Based on this analysis we will call Scarlett PURSUE and CONSIDERATION.

Rhett, on the other hand, spends most of his time avoiding. He avoids getting involved in the war, and by his contraband dealings he avoids financial hardship. He avoids Scarlett's advances, avoids the firing squad, avoids paying her the tax money, and on and on. Nonetheless, it is Rhett that continually urges Scarlett (and everyone else) to reconsider their actions. So Rhett comes down as AVOID and RECONSIDERATION.

Comparing Scarlett to Rhett, each contains one action characteristic and one decision characteristic. Solely in terms of Motivations, Scarlett and Rhett are Archetypal Protagonist and Antagonist.

Melanie and Ashley

There is little to disguise Ashley's affect as TEMPTATION on Scarlett. Just because he never *actively* tempts her does not reduce his temptation value. And this is a good point to file for later: **A character does not have to employ a characteristic actively or even consciously represent it.**

Looking for Ashley's physical characteristic, we find him to be HINDER. Since his physicality is the source of Scarlett's temptation, Hinder was downplayed to make him more attractive. This explains why they underplayed his Hinder characteristic. Nevertheless, Ashley repeatedly threatens Scarlett's situation. Temptation and Hinder make Ashley a Contagonist.

Melanie, in complement to Ashley, is CONSCIENCE and HELP. She continually tutors Scarlett in the "correct" morality, simultaneously cleaning up the real world messes that Scarlett leaves in her wake. Melanie is forever smoothing ruffled feathers and it is she who handles hiding the Yankee renegade soldier that Scarlett shoots. Conscience and Help make Melanie the Guardian.

Look at the Character pairings designed into this story. Scarlett (Pursue and Consideration) is paired with Rhett (Avoid and Reconsideration). Ashley (Temptation and Hinder) is paired with Melanie (Conscience and Help). Obviously, Margaret Mitchell had an amazingly intuitive sense of where the dramatic potentials lay. (But then, we knew that already, didn't we?) Let's see if this pattern continues.

Frank Kennedy, Suellen O'Hara, Gerald O'Hara, and Prissy

Scarlett's screaming sister Suellen plays nicely as FEELING and UNCONTROLLED, making her the Emotion Character. Her choice of husband, Frank Kennedy (who is snatched by Scarlett) is again, an opposite. Kennedy, by his steadfast business development and religion of practicality defines LOGIC. And by his steadfast business development and resistance to diverging from his plans shows that he represents CONTROL (restraint). Kennedy fits nicely as the Reason Character, again, in a complementary posture to his intended bride.

Finally, we reach a most telling pair. First, we notice Scarlett's father Gerald O'Hara has FAITH. He believes that a war will never happen, and then believes the South will win. Even when they have already lost he won't give up his faith. He goes into a fantasy world rather than admit his faith is in error. On the flip side, he constantly OPPOSES Scarlett's wishes. In the opening scene, Scarlett wants love but her father is pushing real estate. After the fall, he keeps jumping in with inane comments about the way Scarlett is handling the house. Consistently (although gently) he opposes her.

Prissy, on the other hand, has no faith at all. She is absolutely convinced that no matter what the situation, the worst will happen. She is a DISBELIEVER pure and true. And yet, she SUPPORTS Scarlett in every self-serving endeavor Scarlett starts. As with other characters we have examined, Mr. O'Hara and Prissy have swapped characteristics, this time between the Skeptic and Sidekick. They are a complementary pair. This is a wonderful twist from a thematic standpoint, pairing and swapping characteristics between a rich white landholder and a poor black slave.

Complex Characters in REAR WINDOW

Principal Characters in REAR WINDOW

If there is anything that can be seen as "typical" about a Hitchcock film it would be his forefront use of thematics. REAR WINDOW is no exception. As with GONE WITH THE WIND, enjoying the story comes largely from what happens between the lines. But unlike *GWTW*, the characters in REAR WINDOW are complex.

At first glance, it may seem there are many characters. There's the Composer, trying to sell his first hit song. There's Miss Lonely Heart, who can't get a date. We see Miss Torso who exercises in front of her open window. Upstairs is the Couple With the Dog, downstairs, the Sunbather. And, of course, Thorwald the murderer.

More prominent, of course, is Jeffries and the characters we see in his apartment: His girlfriend Lisa; Doyle, the detective; and his Nurse. (Note that Thorwald also shows up in Jeffries' apartment near the end of the story and is the only neighbor to do so.)

The Top Five

The purpose of characters is to show how aspects of the Story Mind deal with a problem. This shows us why the neighbors are not Overall Story Characters. Apart from Thorwald, they all have their own little stories, but only interact with one another peripherally, if at all. Their private stories heighten the thematic atmosphere of the overall story but neither advance nor clarify the plot.

If we remove the neighbors who do not interact, we pare our list down to five characters: Jeffries, Lisa, Doyle, Nurse, and Thorwald. If REAR WINDOW is well written, we would expect all sixteen motivation Elements to be divided among these five. Let's see if they are.

Elements of the Top Five

Who represents FAITH? Unquestionably Jeffries. He keeps his belief that a murder has been committed in the face of objections by each of the other characters. Lisa can't talk him out of it and neither can his Nurse. Thorwald denies it by his actions and Doyle is not convinced until after the proof is irrefutable. In fact, Doyle personifies DISBELIEF, even while HELPING Jeffries gain information to which he would not have access. Lisa comes around to accepting the possibility and so does Nurse. Thorwald already *knows* the truth, but Doyle is *never* convinced until he sees the proof with his own eyes.

In addition, Doyle relies on LOGIC to support his disbelief. He will not accept Jeffries' claims without logical arguments. Then is Jeffries FEELING? No. Jeffries does not ignore Logic in his considerations; he merely can't supply it. Jeffries urges the others to CONSIDER what he knows and what he suspects. Lisa, on the other hand, continually acts on impulse without regard for logic, illustrating nicely the characteristic of FEELING.

If Jeffries is CONSIDERATION, we would expect his nemesis, Thorwald, to cause RECONSIDERATION, and he does. Thorwald's seemingly guilt-free actions are a constant force that urges Jeffries (and the others) to RECONSIDER. All we ever see of him is that he acts *methodically* to carry out his plan, whatever that might be. It is his methodical approach that makes Thorwald the CONTROL Character as well. He wastes no time or energy on anything but the task, whereas Jeffries dabbles at whatever fills his view, even when it interferes with his goal of getting the goods on Thorwald. Jeffries plainly illustrates the Element of being UNCONTROLLED.

Even though Lisa SUPPORTS Jeffries in his quest, she manages to HINDER his efforts through distraction and redirection of their conversations. She clearly TEMPTS him to give up PURSUING this crazy scheme. In contrast, Jeffries' Nurse OPPOSES his efforts, even while providing a moralistic philosophy or CONSCIENCE to his every comment. And, of course, Thorwald would prefer to AVOID the whole matter.

Characteristic Lists

If we take a slightly different form, we can arrange the five Characters as column headings and list their characteristics beneath them.

REAR WINDOW

JEFFRIES	LISA	DOYLE	NURSE	THORWALD
Faith	Temptation	Disbelief	Conscience	
Consideration	Feeling	Logic		Reconsideration
Uncontrolled	Support		Oppose	Controlled
Pursue	Hinder	Help		Avoid

REAR WINDOW Characters
in the Motivation Set

Assigning the Character names of REAR WINDOW to the Motivation Characteristic Quads we get:

Action Driver Quad		Decision Driver Quad	
JEFFRIES Pursue	DOYLE Help	JEFFRIES Consider	NURSE Conscience
LISA Hinder	THORWALD Prevent	LISA Temptation	THORWALD Reconsider
Action Passenger Quad		**Decision Passenger Quad**	
THORWALD Control	LISA Support	DOYLE Logic	JEFFRIES Faith
NURSE Oppose	JEFFRIES Uncontrolled	DOYLE Disbelief	LISA Feeling

Using the grid above we can predict the principal conflicts of REAR WINDOW simply by noting which characters are in Dynamic (diagonal) positions and the issues (Elements) over which each pair will diverge.

In summary, the set of sixteen Motivation Elements offers a valuable tool for understanding some of the essential building blocks of Overall Story Characters. They also show how their distribution creates both Archetypal and Complex characters.

Other Character Dimensions

What's the Purpose?

When authors describe their characters, they are often asked to state a character's motivations. A common reply might be, "The character Jane wants to be president." Often that is accepted as a valid motivation. In fact, becoming president is Jane's *Purpose,* <u>not</u> her motivation. Her motivation may be that she felt no control over her life as a child. Or she might be motivated by a love of the natural world, hoping to start a national conservation plan. She might be motivated by a desire for an equal rights amendment.

Just knowing what her purpose is does not tell us anything about what Jane is driven *by* but only what she is driven *toward*. Any of the stated motivations would be enough to explain Jane's purpose of becoming president. Conversely, if Jane's motivation were the first example—a lack of control over her life as a child—several different purposes might satisfy that motivation. She might become a schoolteacher, a drill sergeant, or a religious leader. Clearly, motivations do not specifically dictate purposes, nor are purposes indicative of any particular motivations.

Step into the Fourth Dimension....

In Dramatica, we refer to Motivation as a Character Dimension. Often it is said that characters must be three-dimensional to seem like real people. Dramatica sees *four* dimensions as necessary to flesh out a character. Motivations and Purposes are the first and last dimensions, but that is not enough. Motivation gives a character the force to move, Purpose gives a character a direction in which to move. But how is he going to get to where he wants to go? For this, he needs a Methodology, which is the third dimension of character. Methodologies describe the kinds of approaches a character might use in its efforts to achieve its purposes.

This might seem like enough dimensions. After all, we have a beginning (motivation), a middle (methodology), and an end (purpose). Still, there is one remaining dimension lacking: Evaluations. Evaluations are the standards by which characters measure their progress.

All right, Buddy... Where's the conflict?!

As an example of the concept of Evaluation, imagine two business partners who share motivations, methodologies and purposes. They might agree on what drives them (a motivation to be independent), what they want to achieve (a purpose of creating a thriving business), and how to achieve that (word-of-mouth advertising as a methodology).

However, they might argue about why sales are up but satisfaction is low because their evaluations suggest different reasons. If one evaluates success based on gross sales, he might argue that their word-of-mouth methodology brings in more business because their prices are good. If the other evaluates based on customer satisfaction, he might argue that repeat business is non-existent because of poor customer satisfaction. As a result, the two partners argue all the time, even though they agree in all three dimensions of Motivation, Methodology, and Purpose.

Difficulties can arise between characters in any one of the four dimensions, even though they might agree in one or more of the other dimensions. In short, characters are never fully developed unless they are represented in all four dimensions, and they may come into conflict over any combination of Motivations, Methodologies, Means of Evaluation, or Purposes.

The Sixty-Four-Element Question

Each of the character dimensions contains sixteen Elements, as we have already seen with Motivations. Each character dimension is referred to as a *Set* of Elements. All four Sets come together to create a *Chess Set* (because of its eight by eight grid) as illustrated below:

Purpose Set				Evaluation Set			
Knowledge	Ability	Actuality	Aware	Proven	Theory	Effect	Trust
Desire	Thought	Self-Aware	Perception	Hunch	Unproven	Test	Cause
Order	Equity	Inertia	Projection	Accurate	Expectation	Result	Ending
Inequity	Chaos	Speculation	Change	Determin-ation	Non-accurate	Unending	Process
Consider	Logic	Pursuit	Control	Certainty	Probability	Proaction	Inaction
Feeling	Reconsider	Un-controlled	Avoid / Prevent	Possibility	Potentiality	Protection	Reaction
Faith	Conscience	Support	Help	Deduction	Reduction	Acceptance	Evaluation
Temptation	Disbelief	Hinder	Oppose	Production	Induction	Re-evaluation	Non-acceptance
Motivation Set				Methodology Set			

A good way to get a feel for the content of and relationships between character dimensions is through the Archetypal Characters. When we superimpose the Archetypal Characters onto the character Elements, an "archetypal pattern" appears. Let's begin with the Motivation Set:

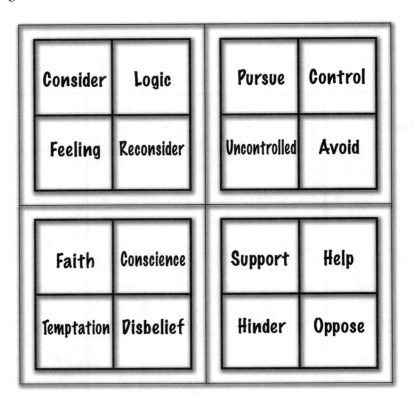

Mapping the Archetypal Pattern

The archetypal pattern formed in the Motivation Set clearly illustrates the consistency and balance of the character Elements. In each quad of four Elements, the items that are diagonal from one another hold the greatest potential for conflict because they are exact opposites.

For example, Pursuit is the opposite of Avoid. As a result, when we place the Protagonist on the Motivation of Pursuit, we would expect the Antagonist to represent Avoid. As we have illustrated in the previous section, that is exactly the case. Similarly, when we place the Reason Archetype on Logic, it comes as no surprise to find Emotion positioned on Feeling, since it is diagonal from Logic. In fact, every pair of Archetypes that are in a diagonal relationship will produce the greatest dynamics between them. This is why we call two Elements in diagonal opposition a Dynamic Pair.

PROTAGONIST Consider	REASON Logic		PROTAGONIST Pursue	REASON Control
EMOTION Feeling	ANTAGONIST Reconsider		EMOTION Uncontrolled	ANTAGONIST Avoid
SIDEKICK Faith	GUARDIAN Conscience		SIDEKICK Support	GUARDIAN Help
NURSE Temptation	CONTAGONIST Disbelief		DOYLE Hinder	CONTAGONIST Oppose

Archetypal Methodologies

Shifting our attention to the Methodology Set, a useful pattern becomes obvious. Because the Methodology Elements are also arranged in Dynamic Pairs, we can simply copy the Archetypal pattern from the Motivation Set and the Archetypal Characters will cover the Methods they represent in stories as well.

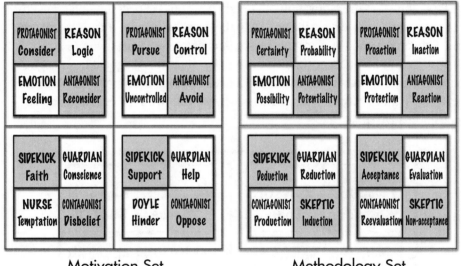

Motivation Set   Methodology Set

For example, a Protagonist Motivated by Pursuit employs a Methodology of Proaction, and a Skeptic Motivated to Oppose employs a Methodology of Non-Acceptance.

This Archetypal Pattern continues through all four character dimensions. A Protagonist is motivated by Pursuit, employs a Methodology of Proaction, Evaluates its progress by the Effect it has, and strives toward achieving Actuality as its Purpose. Each of the Archetypal Characters follows the same pattern for both its External and Internal characteristics, resulting in an alignment of character Elements in four dimensions.

Complex Dimensional Patterns

Most stories emphasize one dimension over the others. Character Motivations are often most prominent. Still, many stories compare the methods used by characters, question their purposes, or carry a message that a means of evaluation is actually the cause of the problem. Some characters become famous for characteristics other than Motivations, such as a notable detective who employs a methodology of Deduction.

Being aware of all four character dimensions adds versatility in creating complex characters as well. Characters might be Archetypal in one dimension, but fall into complex patterns in another. Also, a character may have three Motivations that drive it, yet strive toward a single Purpose that it hopes will satisfy all three. Some characters may not be represented at all in one or more dimensions, making them both more complex and less well rounded at the same time. To make the argument of any story fully, however, all sixty-four Elements must be represented in one character or another. In addition, a key point to remember is: Unless a character represents *at least one* Element, it is not fulfilling a dramatic function and is there for storytelling only.

What's In a Pair?

Finally, we can use our Chess Set of Elements to learn something more about our character's relationships. In each quad of Elements, we find not only Dynamic (diagonal) Pairs, but horizontal and vertical pairs as well. Horizontal Elements are called Companion Pairs, and vertical Elements are Dependent Pairs. Each pair describes a different relationship between the Elements, and therefore between the characters that represent them.

Besides the three types of pairs, we can look at each Element as a separate part and compare it to the overall nature of the quad itself. This Component approach describes the difference between any given Element and the family of Elements in which it resides (quad). Therefore, the degree of individuality the characters represent within the "group" can be explored.

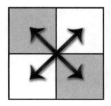 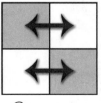 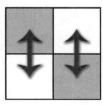 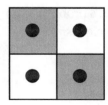

Dynamic Pairs   Companion Pairs   Dependent Pairs   Components

Dynamic Pairs describe Elements with the greatest opposition to each other. Whenever two opposing forces come together they will create either a positive or negative relationship. They can form a *synthesis* and create something greater than the sum of the parts or they can simply tear away at each other until nothing remains (*destructive*). Within a quad, one of the Dynamic Pairs is a positive relationship, the other a negative one. Which is which depends on other story dynamics.

Companion Pairs contain the Elements that are most compatible. However, just being compatible does not preclude a negative relationship. In a positive Companion Pair, characters will continue along their own paths, side by side. What one does not need they will offer to the other (*positive impact*). In a negative Companion Pair, one character may use up what the other needs. They are not against each other as in a negative Dynamic Pair, but still manage to interfere with each other's efforts (*negative impact*).

Dependent Pairs are most complementary. In a positive sense, each character provides strengths to compensate for the other's weaknesses (*cooperation*). Together they make a powerful team. In its negative incarnation, the Dependent Pair Relationship has each character *needing* the other to survive (*codependency*).

Components describe the nature of the Elements in relationship to the overall quad. On the one hand, the individual characters in a quad can be a group that works together (*interdependency*). The group is seen to be greater than the individual characters that comprise it, at the risk of overwhelming the individuality of its members. This is contrasted by identifying the disparate nature of each character in the quad (*independency*). Seen this way, the characters are noted for their distinguishing characteristics at the risk of losing sight of shared interests.

Dynamic Relationships are the most familiar to writers, simply because they create the most obvious forms of conflict. Companion and Dependent Pairs are used all the time without fanfare, as there has previously been no terminology to describe them. Components are useful to writers because they allow characters in groups to be evaluated in and out of context.

By building characters with thought and foresight, an author can use the position of Elements in the Chess Set to forge relationships that are Dynamic in one dimension while being Companion and Dependent in others. Characters created with Dramatica can represent both the *structural* Elements of the Story Mind's problem solving techniques and the *dynamic* interchange between those techniques.

Summary

Altogether we have outlined four dimensions of characteristics, each fostering an aspect of the eight Archetypes. We can subdivide each of the Archetypes into internal and external Elements resulting in sixteen Elements in each dimension—a total of sixty-four characteristics from all four dimensions with which to build characters. Stepping out of the archetypal patterns and relationships can create complex characters.

Subjective Characters

In *The Elements of Structure: Foundations* we described four throughlines in a story—the Overall Story Throughline, Main Character Throughline, Impact Character Throughline, and Subjective Story Throughline. The Overall Story Throughline describes the relative value of the approaches of the Overall Story Characters. The Main Character Throughline describes the point of view and growth of the Main Character. The Impact Character Throughline describes the alternative point of view and growing impact of the Impact Character. The Subjective Story Throughline describes the growing relationship between the Main and Impact Characters.

A good way to think of these four throughlines is as four different points of view through which the audience relates to the Story Mind—the same four points of view we use in all of our relationships. The Main Character represents the "I" point of view. The Impact Character represents the "you" perspective. The Subjective Story Throughline covers the "we" perspective, and the Overall Story Throughline explores the "they" perspective. Taken together, the four points of view range from the most personal to the most impersonal, and provide all the angles we use to examine the nature of our problems and the relative value of alternative solutions.

We have previously looked at the Elements of Character from a purely objective perspective. When we stand in the shoes of a character, however, we get an entirely different perspective. Rather than seeing how the events of a story relate to one another, we become more concerned with how events affect us personally. Providing this experience is the purpose of the Main Character.

The Main Character: One of a Kind

There is only one Main Character in a story. Why is this? Because each complete story is a model of the Story Mind that reflects our own minds, and in our minds we can only be one person at a time. At any given moment, we have a position in our own thoughts. Our state of mind on a particular problem reflects the biases of the position on which we stand. If a story is to involve an audience fully, it must reflect this point of view.

What Is the Story Mind?

Dramatica is built on the idea that the structure and dynamics of a story are not random, but represent an analogy to a single human mind dealing with a problem. We call this idea the Story Mind. A Story Mind is not a character, the author, or even the audience, but the story itself. It's as if the audience's experience of a complete story were like looking inside someone's head. Every act and scene, the thematic progression and message, the climax, plus all the characters and all they do represent the parts and functions (or *thoughts* if you will) of the Story Mind.

A complete story successfully argues all possible sides of its message, thus it will address all the possible human perspectives on that specific issue. That is how the structure and dynamics of a single story create a single Story Mind. This is also why characters are common elements in all stories, along with theme, plot, acts and scenes. Each of these represent the way in which essential human psychology is recreated in stories so we can view our own thought processes more objectively from the outside looking in.

Now before we go on, we'll note that there can be many Main Characters in a completed work, but there will be only one Main Character in a completed story. This is because a *work* is the finished product an author puts before an audience. It may contain a single story, several stories, or several partial and complete stories all woven together or at least nestled in the same fabric of storytelling. This means that a book or a movie, a stage play or teleplay, may have no Main Character at all, or it may have many. But for any single story in that work, there will be only one Main Character. [NOTE: It is permissible to have several players act as one Main Character. For this to work, each of the players must represent the same worldview, the same view of the story's inequity.]

A Grand Argument Story does not allow the audience to stand in the shoes of every character, every Element, and see what the story looks like from there. Such a work would simply be too big to handle. Rather, the purpose of a Grand Argument Story is to discover if the Main Character is looking at the problem from the right place, or if he should change his bias and adopt another point of view instead.

An Alternative Point of View

There is also one other special character that represents the argument for an alternative point of view. The character who spends the entire story making the case for change is called the Impact Character, for he acts as an obstacle to the direction the Main Character would go if left on his own.

As with each of us, the last thing we question when examining a problem is our part in it. We look for all kinds of solutions both external and internal before we finally (if ever) get around to wondering if maybe we have to change ourselves and learn to see the problem differently. We *can* learn to like what we currently hate, but it takes convincing for us to make that leap.

When a Main Character makes the traditional *leap of faith* just before the climax, he has explored all possible means of resolving a problem short of changing who he is. The Impact Character has spent the entire story trying to sell the Main Character on the idea that change is good, and in fact, pointing out exactly how the Main Character ought to change. The clock is ticking, options are running out. If the Main Character doesn't choose one way or the other, then failure is certain. But which way to go? There's no clear-cut answer from the Main Character's perspective.

A History of Success

The Main Character came into the story with a tried-and-true method for dealing with the problem featured in the story. That method has always worked for the Main Character before: it has a long history. Suddenly, a situation arises where that standard approach *doesn't* work, perhaps for the first time ever. This marks the beginning of the story's argument. As the story develops, the Main Character tries everything to find a way to make it work anyway. He holds out in the hope the problem will eventually go away, or work itself out, or is resolved by the tried-and-true method.

Along the way, the Impact Character comes into the picture. He tells the Main Character there is a better way, a more effective approach that not only solves the same problems the Main Character's tried-and-true method did, but solves this new one as well. It sounds a lot like pie in the sky, and the Main Character sees it that way. Why give up the old standby just because of a little flak?

As the story develops, the Impact Character makes his case. Slowly, an alternative paradigm builds up that becomes rather convincing. By the climax, the long-term success of the old view is perfectly balanced by the larger, but untried, new view. There is no clear winner, and that is why it is a leap of faith for the Main Character to choose one over the other.

Please note that the Impact Character need not even know he is having an effect on the Main Character. He may know, but he may easily not even be aware. Main Characters are defined by the point of view, Impact Characters by the impact on that point of view.

A Leap or a Creep?

As a final thought in this brief introduction to Subjective Characters, the "leap of faith" story is not the only kind that occurs. Equally reflective of our own mind's processes is the *slow change* or *non-leap of faith* story. The Main Character gradually shifts his perspective until, by the end of the story, he has already adopted the alternative paradigm with little or no fanfare (for example, Hamlet in Shakespeare's HAMLET).

Usually, in such stories, a particular dramatic scenario occurs near the beginning of the story and repeats (in some similar manner) near the end. The Main Character reacted one way in the first scenario and the audience gets a chance to see if he responds the same way again or not. In the Slow Change story, the Main Character may never even realize he has changed. We, the audience, are able to evaluate the worth of the journey the Main Character has been through by seeing whether the Main Character has been changed and whether that is for better or worse.

In our current Western culture, the leap of faith story is favored, especially in Hollywood-style motion pictures. In other media and cultures, however, the Slow Change story predominates. In theory, each reflects the way our minds shift belief systems: Sometimes in a binary sense as a single decisive alternation, and other times in an analog sense as a progressive realignment.

Main Character Resolve:

Does the Main Character eventually Change or Remain Steadfast?

In empathizing with the Main Character of a story, we nearly become this person. There are certain dynamics we expect to be able to find out about a Main Character as part of experiencing conflicts from his point of view. One of these is called Main Character Resolve.

Main Character Resolve answers the question "Does the Main Character ultimately Change or Remain Steadfast?" At the beginning of the story the Main Character is driven by a particular motivation. When the story ends, he will either still be driven by the same motivation (Steadfast) or have a new motivation (Change).

Main Character Resolve describes the relationship between the Main Character and the Impact Character. The impact of the Impact Character is what forces the Main Character to even consider changing. If the Main Character eventually does change, it is the result of the Impact Character's affect on the Main Character's perspective. If, on the other hand, the Main Character remains steadfast, then his impact on the Impact Character will force the Impact Character to change.

Some Examples:
STAR WARS:
    Main Character: Luke Skywalker (Change)
    Impact Character: Obi Wan Kenobi (Steadfast)

THE STORY OF JOB:
    Main Character: Job (Steadfast)
    Impact Character: The Devil (Change)

TO KILL A MOCKINGBIRD:
    Main Character: Scout (Change)
    Impact Character: Boo Radley (Steadfast)

THE FUGITIVE:
    Main Character: Dr. Richard Kimble (Steadfast)
    Impact Character: Agent Gerard (Change)

Subjective Characters
and the Overall Story

One of the most common mistakes made by authors of every experience level is to create a problem for their Main Character that has nothing to do with the story at large. This usually occurs because an author works out a story and then realizes that he has not made it personal enough. Because the whole work is already completed, it is nearly impossible to tie the Main Character's personal problem into the larger story without a major rewrite. To improve the work, the author *tacks on* a personal issue for the Main Character.

Of course, this leads to a finished piece in which removing either the story's issues or the Main Character's issues still leaves a sound tale behind. In other words, to an audience it feels like one of the issues is out of place and shouldn't be in the work.

Now, if one of the two different problems were removed, it wouldn't leave a complete story, yet the remaining part would still feel like a complete *tale*. Dramatica distinguishes between a "tale" and a "story". If a story is an argument, a tale is a statement. A story explores an issue from all sides to discover what is better or worse overall, a tale explores an issue down a single path and shows how it turns out. Most fairy tales are just that, tales.

There is nothing wrong with a tale. You can write a tale about a group of people facing a problem without having a Main Character. Or, you could write a personal tale about a Main Character without needing to explore a larger story. If you simply put an Overall Story-tale and a Main Character tale into the same work, one will often seem incidental to the real thrust of the work. But, if the Main Character tale and the Overall Story-tale both hinge on the same issue, then suddenly they are tied together intimately. What happens in one influences what happens in the other.

This, by definition, forms a Grand Argument Story, and opens the door to all kinds of dramatic power and variety not present in a tale. For example, although the story at large may end in success, the Main Character might be left miserable. Conversely, even though the big picture ended in failure, the Main Character might find personal satisfaction and solace. We'll discuss these choices at great length in *The Art Of Storytelling* section. For now, let us use this as a foundation to examine the relationship between the Subjective Characters and the Overall Story.

The Crucial Element

One point at which the Overall Story and the Main Character hinge is called the *Crucial Element*. In fact, the Crucial Element is one of the sixty-four Overall Story Character Elements we have already explored. When we look at the Objective Character Elements as the soldiers on the field (from our earlier example), there is one special Element from which the audience experiences an internal perspective on the story. This is the Main Character position in the Overall Story, and the Element at that point is the Crucial Element. As a result, whichever Overall Story Character represents the Crucial Element should be placed in the same player as the Main Character. In that way, what happens during the Main Character's growth will have an impact on his Overall Story function. Similarly, pressures on his Overall Story function caused by the story's situations will influence his decision to change or remain steadfast.

We can see that a Protagonist will only be a Main Character if the Crucial Element is one of the Elements that make up a Protagonist. In other words, a Protagonist has eight different Elements, two from each dimension of character. If one of them is the Crucial Element, then the player containing the Protagonist must also contain the Main Character. This means we can create eight different kinds of *heroes*. An action hero might have a Crucial Element of Pursue, while a thinking hero might have a Crucial Element of Consider. Clearly, the opportunities to create Main Characters who are NOT Protagonists are also extensive. Main Character are often complex Objective Characters.

The Impact Character has a special place in the Overall Story (Objective) Character Elements as well. We have already discussed Dynamic Pairs. As it turns out, the point at which an Impact Character will have the greatest dramatic leverage to try to change the Main Character is the other Element in the Dynamic Pair with the Crucial Element. In simpler terms, the Main and Impact Characters are opposites on this important issue. Often one will contain the story's problem, the other the story's solution.

If the Main Character (and Crucial Element) stands on Pursue, the Impact Character will occupy Avoid. If the Main Character is Logic, the Impact Character is Feeling. In this manner, we explore the essential differences between the two opposite points of view in an objective sense, looking from the outside in, and in a subjective sense, from the inside looking out. All four throughlines come into play (Overall Story, Main Character, Impact Character, and Subjective Story). By the end of the story, the audience will feel the central issue of concern to the Story Mind has been examined fully from all relevant angles.

To summarize, a complete story requires that both the Overall Story and Subjective views are provided to an audience, and that they are hinged together around the same central issue. We do this by assigning the Main and Impact Characters to the Overall Story Characters who contain either the story's problem or solution Elements. The Element held by the Main Character becomes the Crucial Element, as both the Objective and Subjective Stories revolve around it.

The Crucial Element: Where Subjective meets Objective

The Crucial Element is an item that is at the heart of a story from both the Overall Story and Subjective points of view. How this happens depends on the Main Character. The Crucial Element is the one of the connections between the Main Character and the Overall story and makes the Main Character special enough to be "Main." This issue at the heart of the Main Character is thematically the same issue that is at the heart of the Overall Story.

For Example:

TO KILL A MOCKINGBIRD Crucial Element is INEQUITY

Inequity is the problem that is causing all the conflict around the town of Maycomb. The trial of Tom Robinson brings all the towns' people into squabbles about inequity in the treatment of different races, inequity among the social classes of people, their levels of income, and their educations.

Scout, as the Main Character, is driven by her personal problem of inequity. This is symbolized most clearly in her fear of Boo Radley. Kept at the margins of the Overall Story dealings with the problem of inequity, Scout however comes to see her prejudice against Boo Radley as being every bit as wrong.

Don't Sweat Over The Crucial Element

Despite the name, proper assignment of the Crucial Element isn't critical. Your story is stronger if you assign the Crucial element to the player that is also the Main Character, but it is only one of many connections between the throughlines.

Deep Theory

The following section delves deeply into the inner workings of a Main Character and how that character grows over the course of a story. The material covered will address the following questions: How does a Main Character come to have a particular problem? How does that problem relate to the Overall Story as well? If the Main Character has a problem, why doesn't he just solve it? How can an Impact Character bring a Main Character to the point of change?

This discussion can get theoretical at times, and we present it more for those interested in details, rather than as essential reading. If you have an interest in theory, read on! If not, you may wish to skip to the next chapter on Theme, or jump ahead to *The Art Of Storytelling* for a more practical approach.

Problem Solving and Justification

What are Justifications?

At the moment we act in response to a problem, each of us sees our approach as justifiable. If we later regret our actions or are called to task, we have reasons we should not be blamed or at least not held accountable. We call these reasons "Justifications." To us, these justifications legitimize our actions. To others who find our actions unwarranted, our reasons seem more like excuses, and our actions unjustified.

Sometimes, we may be unsure if our actions are justified because there is a conflict between what our reason and our feelings are telling us. When we see no clear-cut response, we go with the side of ourselves that makes the stronger case.

Excuses, Excuses!

To convince ourselves (and others) that our actions are justified, we make excuses like, "This is going to hurt me more than it's going to hurt you," "It's for your own good," "I had to teach him a lesson," "She had it coming," "I had no other choice," "I couldn't help myself," "There was nothing I could do," "It was the right thing to do," and "The end justifies the means." Each of these statements implies that even though feeling says this is wrong, reason makes a stronger case that it is right (or the reverse).

Whenever the "proper" response is unclear, the legitimacy of our actions is open to interpretation. If there were a way to stand outside it all and take an objective view, we could see which actions were justifiable and which were not.

Unfortunately, we are not granted this objective view in real life. So, we create stories to try to estimate the objective truth.

The Author Giveth; the Audience Taketh Away

An author builds an argument that the Main Character's actions are either justified or not. He then "proves" the point by ending the story with an outcome of success or failure and a judgment of good or bad. In this way, the author hopes to convince an audience that actions taken in a particular context are appropriate or inappropriate. The audience members hope to become convinced that when the proper course of action is unclear, they can rely on a more "objective" truth to guide them.

In real life, only time reveals if our actions achieve what we want and if that will bring us more happiness than hurt. In stories, it is the author who decides what is justified and what is not. Within of the story, the author's view IS objective truth.

The author's ability to decide the truth of actions "objectively" changes the meaning of justification from how we have been using it. In life, when actions are seen as justified, it means that everyone agrees with the reasons behind the actions. In stories, reasons don't count. Even if all the characters agree with the reasons, the author might show that all the characters were wrong. Reasons just explain *why* characters act as they do. Consensus on the reasons does not determine correctness.

What is Problem Solving?

All characters are driven by their justifications, but only some of the actions they take will end up solving a problem. From the author's "objective" view, approaches that lead to solutions are "problem solving." Approaches that do not are simply justifications.

The process of "problem solving" describes the paths an author promotes as being the most suitable approaches to the story's problem. The process of justification describes all paths that are not as suitable.

In a binary sense, the best path of all will be represented by either the Main or Impact character. The remaining character of the two will represent the worst path. Of Main and Impact, one will be problem solving, the other justifying. All the remaining characters represent alternative approaches between the two extremes.

From an author's perspective, it is just as important to know how things got started as it is to know how everything turns out. How is it that people can become so misguided? How is it that characters can become so justified?

Problems Start Innocently Enough....

It is the nature of people and characters as well, to try to find a source of joy and a resolution to that which hurts them. This hurt might be physical suffering or mental torment. The resolution may be to rearrange one's environment or to accept the environment as it is. Regardless of the source of the inequity or the means employed to resolve it, all thinking creatures try to maximize their pleasure and minimize their pain. That is the primal force that drives us in our lives, and the dramatic force that drives a story.

If our environments would instantly respond to our desires, and if our feelings would immediately adjust to new attitudes, all inequities between our environments and us would equalize at once. Unfortunately, this is not the case. Rather, to solve external problems we must apply effort to rearrange the material that surrounds us, and to solve internal problems we must adopt a series of paradigm shifts to arrive at a perspective that minimizes our anguish.

Getting to the Heart of the Problem

Because it takes time to resolve inequities, we define problem solving as a process we engage in over time. Step by step we chip away at pieces of a problem until we arrive at a solution. We meet prerequisites that give us the resources to fulfill the requirements that must be completed to clear the way to our goal. Or, we change the nature of the forces at work that determine the processes that preserve the inequity, so it dissolves when its foundation erodes.

Problem solving requires identifying the source of the inequity and the nature of the effort that will end it. Each of these requirements depends on an accurate assessment of the mechanism that produces the inequity, and there lies the opportunity for error.

Characters, Problems, and Justification

Stories are about one character who is problem solving and a second character who believes they are problem solving but are in error. One will be the Main Character and the other the Impact Character. In terms of the Story Mind, these two characters represent our own inability to know in advance if the method we have chosen to apply to a problem will lead to success or failure. When our approach leads to failure Dramatica does not refer to the process as problem solving, but calls that process *Justification*.

Why We Justify

No one justifies because they are stupid or mean. They simply adopt the best approach they can imagine, based on their life experience. Neither justification nor problem solving are intrinsically good or bad. In fact, they are the same process, the main difference being how things eventually turn out. With the value of hindsight we can judge if the decisions made and actions taken were correct, but we cannot judge this as the effort is happening since none of us can see the future. So, no character or person can be certain whether their approach to an inequity will resolve it, not effect it, aggravate it, or create another inequity somewhere else that might be even more disturbing. All any of us can do—all any of us EVER do is to make the decisions and take the actions our experience dictates as the best choices toward resolving our inequities.

Poor, Misguided Souls....

From this perspective, no character is bad, merely misguided. However, that is not the only perspective. If we step into the story and see a misguided character hurting others and us, from OUR life experience we decide that character must be stopped. Perhaps we argue with them, try to educate them, fight with or kill them. Maybe we write them off, severing our emotional ties and letting them spiral down into self-destruction because it is the only way to avoid them dragging us down.

Or, we might argue with them and find ourselves convinced of their point of view. We might try to educate them but learn something instead, fight with them and lose or be killed. We might be written off BY them or hold on to them and be dragged down as well, or drag them down with us.

The point is, both Main and Impact characters will feel they are right, believe in what they do, try to convince or thwart their counterpart and eventually prove to be correct or misguided.

Uniqueness Means Never Having to Say, "I Agree"

As we are driven by life experiences and since the experiences of each of us are unique, it is no wonder we come into conflict and confrontation over most everything we can think of. Stories are about the incompatibility of two life experiences and the best ways to resolve an inequity.

If a character stands by his life experience, then his approach served him well in other scenarios. Similarly, his counterpart has had different life experiences that served him equally well. For the current inequity in question, each life experience creates an approach incompatible with the other. In one context, each set of experiences was problem solving. In the current context, one will be seen to be problem solving, the other justification.

Tell Me A Message, Mommy....

This is the purpose and function of story: To show when something that has previously served you well one hundred percent of the time may not continue to hold true, or conversely, that it will always hold true. Either message is equally valid and depends on the author's personal bias on the issue which arbitrarily controls the slant of the message. Obviously, the outcome is not arbitrary to the author, but it is arbitrary to the story.

Several factors determine the audience's position in relationship to the correct and incorrect approaches to the problem. For example, whether the Main Character is change or steadfast, the outcome is success or failure, and the judgment is good or bad. These choices, and others, therefore control the impact of the story message on the audience.

Step By Step, Slowly We Argued....

So far we have only identified the difference between problem solving and justification in terms of the results they create. From this point of view, no character can tell for sure if he is on the right or the wrong track until he sees the results. This is fine for the characters, but an author will want to fashion a story so judgment is passed on each action and decision as it is taken. This is what forms the theme of the story and builds the emotional side of the story's argument event by event until (hopefully) the audience is buried under overwhelming evidence to support the author's message and positions.

Note the difference between the result-oriented *rational* argument and the more holistic *passionate* argument. In a story, the author hopes to convince the audience of his point of view both in terms of its reasonable nature and that it simply feels good as well. In this manner, the audience members adopt the author's bias on the issue and are moved to alter their behavior in their everyday life. In a broader sense, engaging in the story has added to the life experience of the audience and will affect their future choices for problem solving.

To carry an emotional appeal to an audience, a story must not only show the results of a method of problem solving, but must document the appropriateness of each step as well. To do this an author requires an understanding of the *process* of problem solving and its justification counterpart. Let us examine both.

A Simple Example of Problem Solving

Imagine a waitress coming through the one-way door from the kitchen into the restaurant. Her nose begins to itch. She cannot scratch her nose because her hands are full of plates. She looks for a place to lay down the plates, but all the counter space is cluttered. She tries to call to a waiter, but he cannot hear her across the noisy room. She hollers to a busboy who gets the waiter who takes her plates so she can scratch her nose. Problem solved! Or was it justification?

What if she could have solved the problem just by shrugging her shoulder and rubbing her nose? Then there were two possible solutions, but one was much more direct. Rationally, either one would serve as well in that particular context, yet one was much more efficient and therefore more emotionally satisfying because it required less unpleasant work than the other method.

There's a Problem In Your Solution!

If the waitress could not use her hand to scratch her nose, then using her shoulder was another potential solution to the same problem. However, trying to find a place to put down the plates is a generation removed from solving the original problem. Instead of trying to find another way to scratch her nose, she was using her problem solving efforts to try to solve a problem with the first solution. In other words, there was an obstacle to using her hand to scratch her nose, and rather than evaluating other means of scratching she was looking for a place to get rid of her plates. When there was a problem with that, she compounded the inefficiency by trying to solve the plate problem with the solution devised to solve the problem with the first solution to the problem: she tried to flag down the waiter. In fact, when she got her nose scratched, she had to take a roundabout path that took up all kinds of time and was several generations removed from the original problem. She made one big circle to get to where she could have gone directly.

But, what if there was a limit: her itching nose was about to make her sneeze and drop everything. Then, going on that long circular path might mean she would sneeze and fail, whereas the only suitable path would be to use her shoulder to scratch before she sneezes. But what if her stiff uniform prevents her shoulder from reaching her nose? AND what if the extra time it took to try the shoulder delayed trying the roundabout method just long enough to make her sneeze before the waiter arrived? If she had only taken the great circle route first, she would have had just enough time to solve the problem.

Paying the Price For a Solution

Clearly, problem solving turns into justification and vice versa, depending on the context. So how is it that achieving results in the rational sense is not the only deciding factor? Simply because sometimes the costs paid in suffering in a long, indirect path to a goal far outweigh the benefits of achieving the goal itself. When we try to overcome obstacles that stand between a goal and us (prerequisites and requirements) we pay a price in effort, resources, physical and emotional hardship. We suffer unpleasant conditions now in the hope of a reward later. This is fine as long as the rewards justify the expenses. But if they do not, and yet we continue to persevere, we cannot possibly recoup enough to make up for our losses, much as a gambler goes into the hole after losing his intended stake.

My Kingdom for a Solution!

Why is it that we (as characters) throw good money after bad? This occurs because we are no longer evaluating what we originally hoped to achieve but are trying to solve the problems that have occurred with the solutions we have employed. With our waitress, she wasn't thinking about her nose when she was calling to the waiter or yelling to the busboy. She was thinking about the problem of getting their attention. Because she lost sight of her original objective, she could no longer tally up the accruing costs and compare them to the benefits of resolving the inequity. Rather, she compared each cost individually to the goal: putting down the plates, calling to the waiter, yelling at the busboy. And in each case, the *individual* costs were less than the benefits of resolving the *individual* sub-goals. However, if taken as a whole, the costs may far outweigh the benefits of resolving the original problem. And since the prerequisites and requirements have no meaning except as a means to resolving that original problem, any benefits she felt by achieving those sub-goals should have had no bearing on deciding if the effort was worth the benefits. But, as she had lost sight of the original problem, that measurement could not be made. In fact, it would never occur to her, until it was too late to recoup the costs even if the problem came to be resolved.

Does this mean the only danger lies in the roundabout path? Not at all. If it were to turn out there were NO direct paths that could work, ONLY an indirect one could resolve the problem at all. And if the existence of the problem is not just a onetime event but continues to cause friction that rubs one physically or mentally raw, then the inequity itself grows the longer the problem remains. This justifies ANY indirect method to resolving the issue as long as the rate at which the costs accrue is less than the rate at which the inequity worsens.

Accelerating Inequities!

But let's complicate this even more... Suppose the inequity doesn't worsen at first, but only gets worse after a while. Then what may have been the most correct response for problem solving at one stage in the game becomes inappropriate later. In such a complex web of changing conditions and shifting context, how is an individual to know what choices are best? We can't. That is the point. We can never know which path is best because we cannot predict the future. We can only choose what our life experience has shown to be most often effective in similar situations and hope for the best. It does not matter how often we reevaluate. The situation can change in unpredictable ways at any time. This can put all of our plans and efforts into new contexts that change our evaluation of them from positive to negative or the vice versa.

Stories serve as collective truisms, much like the way insurance works. Through them we strive to contain the collective knowledge of human experience. Although we cannot predict what will happen to any specific individual (even ourselves), we can tell what is *most likely* the best approach to inequity, based on the mean average of all individual experience.

Strategy vs. Analysis

Although we have covered a lot of ground, we have only covered one of two kinds of problem solving/justification: the effort to resolve an inequity. In contrast, the second approach to problem solving/justification refers to efforts made to understand inequities so we might come to terms with them. In a sense, our first exploration has dealt with strategies of problem solving whereas this other area of exploration deals with defining the problem itself.

Defining the Problem

We cannot move to resolve a problem until we recognize the problem. Even if we feel the inequity, until we can pinpoint it or understand what creates it, we can neither arrive at an appropriate response nor act to nip it at its source.

If we had to evaluate each inequity that we face with an absolutely open mind, we could not learn from experience. Even if we had seen the same thing one hundred times before, we would not look to our memories to see what had turned out to be the source or what appropriate measures had been employed. We would be forced to consider every little friction that rubbed us the wrong way as if we have never seen it before. This is another form of inefficiency, as "those who do not remember the past are condemned to repeat it."

In such a scenario, we would not learn from our mistakes, much less our successes. But is that inefficiency? What if we meet an exception to the rules we have come to live by? If we rely completely on our life experience, when we face a new context in life, our whole paradigm may be inappropriate.

You Idiom!

We know the truisms, "Where there's smoke, there's fire," "Guilt by association," "One bad apple spoils the bunch," "The only good (fill in the blank) is a dead (fill in the blank)." In each of these cases we assume a different causal relationship that is generally examined in our culture. Each of these phrases asserts that when you see one thing, another thing will be there also, or will follow. Why do we make these assumptions? Because, in context, they are often true. But as soon as we apply them *out of context* they are just as likely false.

Associations in Space and Time

When we see something occur enough times without exception, our mind accepts it as an absolute. After all, we have never seen it fail! This is like saying that every time you put a piece of paper on hot metal it will burst into flame. Fine, but not in a vacuum! You need oxygen as well to create the reaction you expect.

In fact, every time we believe THIS leads to THAT or whenever we see THIS, THAT will also be present, we make assumptions without regard to context. And that is where characters get into trouble. A character makes associations in their backstory. Because of the context in which they gather their experiences, these associations always hold true. But then the situation (context) changes, or they move into new areas in their lives. Suddenly some of these assumptions are untrue!

Hold on to Your Givens!

Why doesn't a character (or person) simply give up the old view for the new? There are two reasons one will hold on to an outmoded, inappropriate understanding of the relationships between things. We'll outline them one at a time.

First, there is the notion of how many times a character has seen things go one way, compared with the number of times they've gone another. If a character builds up years of experience with something being true and then faces one time it is not true, they will treat that single false time as an exception to the rule. It would take as many false responses as there had been true ones to counter the balance.

Context is a Sneaky Thing

Of course one is more sensitive to the most recent patterns so an equal number of false items (or alternative truths) are not required when one is aware he has entered a new situation. However, situations often change slowly and even in ways we are not aware. So context is in a constant state of flux. If something has always proven true in *all contexts up to this point* then one is not aware of entering a whole new context. Rather, as we move in and out of contexts, a truism that was ALWAYS true may now be true sometimes and not true at other times. It may have an increasing or decreasing frequency of proving true or may *tend* toward being false for a while, only to *tend* toward being true again later. This style of dynamic context requires that something be seen as false as often as it has been seen as true. This produces a neutral point where one perspective is held evenly with the other.

Building Paradigms

The second reason characters hold onto outmoded views is that they have built other views on the outmoded ones. In fact, this is how we learn. We see something as an unerring truth, stop considering it every time we see it and accept it as a given. Then, we assemble our givens, look for patterns and accept the relationships *between givens* as being givens in their own right. Layer on layer we weave an intricate web of interconnections, some based on the order in which things are expected to occur, some based on items or activities we associate as always occurring together.

Strength in Paradigms

When we encounter something at the top level of the most recently determined givens, it can be a small feat to rethink our conclusions. If one of our base assumptions is wrong, however, there may be no way to reconcile the instance with our understanding without completely dismantling the foundations of our whole belief system. Not an easy task! It is much easier to discount the variance as an exception. Even more important, because we have not added the unusual incident to our knowledge base, but simply let it bounce off, the next instance of the same "new" truth will meet with the same strength of resistance as the first. We can hold onto our old paradigm unless so many *different* new truths hit us all at once that it becomes easier to create a new paradigm than to try to dismiss them all.

The Justified Main Character

This is the nature of the Main Character's struggle in a story. He has either built up an understanding of how to try to solve problems that no longer fits, or he has built up an understanding of what causes problems that is no longer correct. The backstory builds on one of these scenarios. A context is set up that creates one form of problem solving about a specific problem. The story begins when the context changes and the problem solving technique is no longer appropriate. The question then becomes whether the Main Character should Change to conform to the new situation or remain Steadfast until things get back to "normal."

Dancing Toward Neutral Ground

The story unfolds as the Main and Impact Characters argue over direct vs. indirect, repetition vs. framework, strategy vs. analysis, and problem solving vs. justification. As the story progresses, it is the Impact Character's function to force the Main Character through all four of these conflicts. Each conflict represents a different "level" of justification (problem solving). Finally, they both stand at the neutral point where one means of problem solving/evaluation is as good as the next. This is the moment of the Leap of Faith, where life experience has been counterbalanced by what has been recently learned. This is the moment the Main Character must step into the void without personal experiences to guide him, and choose to continue with the path he has always taken or adopt a new one.

The story then resolves in Success/Good, Success/Bad, Failure/Good, or Failure/Bad. These four resolutions are the "Author's Proof," in which he states his personal bias about the most appropriate and inappropriate choices were.

Sequence and the Passionate Argument

From this perspective, we can see how the sequence in which dramatic events occur has tremendous impact on the meaning drawn from that structure. The "feel" of the passionate argument will be determined by the order in which the Main Character passes through the levels of justification to face the real source of the story's inequity.

This sequence not only affects character, but plot and theme as well, and is therefore a complex series of cycles within cycles that is unpredictable during viewing a work, but falls into understanding at the conclusion or *denouement*. Because it is so complex, this is the part of Dramatica best left to computer calculation or to the intuition of the author himself.

The Elements Of
Structure

THEME

What Exactly *Is* Theme?

It seems every author is aware of theme, but try to find one who can define it! Most will tell you theme has something to do with the mood or feel of a story. But how does that differ from *genre*? Others will say that theme is the message of the story. Some will put forth that theme is the *premise* of a story that illustrates the results of certain kinds of behavior.

Taking each of these a bit farther, a story's mood or feel might be "anger." A message might be "nuclear power plants are bad." A premise could be "greed leads to self-destruction." Clearly each of these might show up in the same story, and each has a thematic feel to it. But just as certainly, none of them feels complete on their own. This is because each is just a different angle on what theme really is.

In fact, theme is perspective. Perspective is relationship. Theme describes the *relationship* between what is being looked at and from where it is being seen. This is why theme has traditionally been so hard to describe. It is not an independent thing like plot or character, but is a relationship *between* plot and character.

As a familiar example, think of the adage about three blind men trying to describe an elephant. Each is like a character in a story, and their investigation of the beast is like the plot. One, feeling the tail comments, "It is long and thin like a snake." Another, feeling the ear replies, "No, it is wide and flat like a jungle leaf." The final investigator feels the leg and retorts, "You are both wrong! It is round and stout like a tree." How each of those men *felt* about the elephant, how they *understood* it, depended on his point of view, and that it was an elephant each examined. It is also true, that had another animal been the object of study, the perspectives would have changed as well.

Where we are looking from are the four points of view represented by the four throughlines (Overall Story, Main Character, Impact Character, and Subjective Story). In stories, *what* we are looking at is the problem the Story Mind is considering. So, to understand perspective (and therefore theme) we must be able to describe the nature of the story's problem accurately, and then see how its appearance changes when seen from each different point of view.

Describing The Story's Problem

When we seek to classify something, we try to narrow its definition, such as when we ask if something is animal, vegetable, or mineral. When classifying problems that might be of concern to the Story Mind, the first thing we might want to know is if the problem is an external issue (such as an intolerable situation) or an internal one (such as a bad attitude). External problems occur in the environment, a Situation (Universe). Internal problems occur in the mind, a Fixed Attitude (Mind).

Further, some problems don't have to do with states of things (an external situation or an internal attitude) but are processes that have gone awry. An external process falls in the category of Activity (Physics), which simply means physical activity of some kind. An internal process that results in a problem has to do with Manipulation (Psychology), which simply means a manner of thinking. Note that a manner of thinking (Psychology) is different from a fixed attitude (Mind). Manipulation (Psychology) describes problems like spending too much time with details, whereas Mind problems would be more like a prejudice.

Having identified four categories by which we might classify the nature of the Story Mind's problem, we can arrange them in a quad pattern, much as we did earlier with the Character Elements.

Since these four categories classify the problem, Dramatica refers to them as CLASSES.

More Resolution

So far, we have been able to show that a problem might be an external or internal state or process, represented by the four Classes. Already we can get a more refined view of the problem we will describe in our story. We need only consider which of these four Classes best describes the problem about which we want to write.

For example, if we have an idea for a story about people trapped underwater in a sunken ship, that would be an external problem, best described as a state of things. An external state is the definition of a Situation problem, so this story idea takes place in the Situation Class.

If we wish to write about a harrowing trek through the jungle to a lost city, we are describing an Activity problem: An external activity from which difficulties arise.

A story exploring a father who will not let his daughter marry below her station in life is a Fixed Attitude problem, for it stems from a fixed attitude, bias, or preconception.

And finally, an author who wishes to comment thematically on a group of friends manipulating one another would select Manipulation as his Class of problem. The thematic issue is changing one's manner of thinking. Again, this differs from changing one's Fixed Attitude (about something).

ALL FOUR Classes play a role in every complete Grand Argument Story. As we shall explore a bit later, each Class will describe the problem as it appears from a different throughline.

Throughlines

Earlier we illustrated how one could see four throughlines of STAR WARS. Below are illustrations of STAR WARS' four throughlines seen in terms of *Throughlines*.

STAR WARS

Overall Story Throughline: Activity—STAR WARS is about a war between the Empire and the Rebellion. There is not any set location where this needs to take place; rather it is an exploration of the feints, attacks, and battles that occur between the two forces.

Main Character Throughline: Situation—Luke Skywalker is a whiny farm-boy from a small desert planet. He has unrealized talent because his father was a Jedi, but everyone sees him as a kid from the edge of the galaxy.

Impact Character Throughline: Fixed Attitude—Obi Wan Kenobi lives in the world of the Force. His attitude about the Force's power and impact, the existence of the Light and Dark sides of the Force, and the importance of the Force is unshakable.

Subjective Story Throughline: Manipulation—Obi Wan clearly manipulates Luke through psychological means. He tries to pressure Luke to help him get to Alderaan, which Luke resists. Obi Wan does not reveal the fate of Luke's aunt and uncle to Luke even though Obi Wan is clearly not surprised when he hears the news. Obi Wan purposely keeps Luke in the dark about his resources while bartering with Han Solo, hushing him up when Luke can barely contain himself. Obi Wan keeps Luke under his thumb by doling out information about the Force, the Empire, the Past, and everything else. It is Obi Wan who whispers into Luke's head at several critical moments, "Run, Luke, run!" and "Trust your feelings, Luke."

At this point, we have achieved a clearer understanding of our story's theme by classifying the story's problem. In our own lives, however, this would be insufficient information to identify the problem clearly enough to begin solving it. The same is true of the Story Mind. We need to dig deeper and be more precise if eventually we are to pinpoint the source of the story's problem so it can be addressed at the root.

To increase our precision, we can subdivide each of the Classes into different TYPES of problems within each Class, much as the classification "animal" and "vegetable" subdivide into various species.

Situation Types		Activity Types	
Past	How Things Are Going (Progress)	Under-standing	Doing
Future	Present	Obtaining	Gathering Information (Learning)
Developing A Plan	Playing A Role	Memory	Impulsive Responses (Preconscious)
Changing One's Nature	Conceiving An Idea	Innermost Desires (Subconscious)	Contempla-tions (Conscious)
Manipulation Types		Fixed Attitude Types	

Types

As you can see, the TYPE level of resolution on our story's problem is much more refined. Already the names of the Types carry much more of a thematic feel than those of the broad-stroke Classes. Some of the Types seem more familiar than others. This is because our culture has its own built-in biases and favorites and tends to focus on certain kinds of problems more than others.

If we compare the Types in one Class to those in the others, we can see how the chart does not cater to our culture's biases. Rather, it presents a neutral set of subcategories so any problem an author might wish to address is treated with equal weight.

One of the first things we can begin to feel about the Types is that their position within each quad has an influence on the nature of the Type, which is reflected in its name. For example, in the upper left hand corner of the Situation Class we find the Type, "Past." By comparison, in the upper left hand corner of the Fixed Attitude Class we find the Type, "Memory." The balance of the chart can be easily illustrated in the phrase, "Past is to Situation as Memory is to Fixed Attitude." In fact, all the categories and subcategories we have explored (and the two remaining levels) share this relationship.

We have found that it helps to get a feel for a story's problem by running this kind of comparison over in our minds as we examine the chart. Patterns of relationships begin to emerge, and the process of choosing the Class and Type of problem at the heart of our story's theme becomes almost a game.

Concerns:

Choosing the Type most prominent in a particular throughline sets up the Concerns which is most important from that point of view. To show how this might work, let's look at the Concerns of STAR WARS.

STAR WARS

Overall Story Concern: Doing (Engaging in an activity)—The Empire is building the Death Star and searching for the Rebels. The Rebels are trying to keep their location secret by moving it around. The smuggler is trying to transport passengers to Alderaan. The passengers are trying to get the plans of the Death Star to the Rebels who will decipher the plans and launch an attack on the Empire.

Main Character Concern: How Things Are Going (Progress)—Luke Skywalker constantly is concerned with how things are going—"At this rate I'll never get off this rock!" He is impatient and never satisfied with how things are progressing. Once he gets off Tatooine, he is concerned with how long it will take for him to become a Jedi Knight—the progress of his training. When

Darth Vader slices Obi Wan, Luke's loss is compounded because he has lost a friend and a tutor. When they get to the Rebel base, he is concerned about how preparations are going and eventually with his own progress as a pilot in the Rebel attack on the Death Star.

Impact Character Concern: Impulsive Responses (Preconscious)—To be "one with the Force," a person must let go of himself and let the Force act through him. This allows the Force to guide one's unthinking responses and reflexes and to become an unbeatable power for good or evil. This is Obi Wan's greatest concern and his efforts here impact everyone around him, especially Luke.

Subjective Story Concern: Playing A Role (Being)—Obi Wan wants Luke to be the faithful student. Luke just wants to be a Hero without understanding what good it does to be quiet and controlled like Obi Wan. Luke's farm-boy lifestyle is not in sync with his true nature as Obi Wan sees him. Obi Wan knows that Luke is the son of a Jedi and therefore he tries to manipulate Luke out of being what he's not.

Limitations of space prevent us from describing every Type through example. At the back of this book, however, you will find an appendix with a complete definition of each, as well as reproductions of the complete chart of categories.

Even with this degree of refinement, our story's problem has still not been identified with the precision required to focus our theme. It is time to move into the next level of the problem chart.

When we subdivide the Types, we can set up four different VARIATIONS of each. This creates the extended chart below:

Situation Variations   ### Activity Variations

Fate	Prediction		Fact	Security		Instinct	Senses		Wisdom	Skill
Interdiction	Destiny		Threat	Fantasy		Interpreta-tion	Condition-ing		Experience	Enlighten-ment

Openness	Delay		Work	Attract		Approach	Self Interest		Pre-requisites	Strategy
Choice	Destiny		Repel	Attempt		Morality	Attitude		Analysis	Pre-conditions

State of Being	Situation		Knowledge	Ability		Truth	Evidence		Value	Confidence
Circum-stances	Sense of Self		Desire	Thought		Suspicion	Falsehood		Worry	Worth

Rationali-zation	Commit-ment		Permission	Need		Closure	Hope		Investiga-tion	Appraisal
Responsi-bility	Obligation		Expediency	Deficiency		Dream	Denial		Re-appraisal	Doubt

Manipulation Variations   ### Fixed Attitude Variations

Now we can finally begin to see some familiar thematic topics: Morality, fate, commitment, and hope, for example. We can also see some unfamiliar terms about theme that we may not have considered before. As before, Western culture (as do all cultures) favors certain areas of exploration and almost ignores others. For an author who wishes to explore new ground, these unfamiliar terms provide a wealth of choices. For the author who writes for the mainstream, all the old standbys are there, but with much more detail than before.

You will not find terms on this chart like "love" or "greed." Although these concepts figure prominently in many discussions of theme, they are more descriptive of subject matter, rather than the perspectives one might take *about* that subject matter. For example, suppose we decide to write a story about love. All right, what kind of love? Brotherly love? Romantic love? Paternal, lustful, spiritual, or unrequited love? Clearly, love is in the eye of the beholder. In other words, love is shaded by the nature of the object that is loved.

In our chart of Variations, we find terms such as "Attraction", "Obligation", "Desire", or "Instinct", each of which can be used to describe a different kind of love. For example, love in the context of Attraction could be physical love or puppy love. Love in the context of Obligation could be parental love or familial love. Love in the context of Desire could be passionate love or obsessive love. Love in the context of Instinct could be animal love or love at first site, and so on. Use the Variations to say something specific *about* Love.

Similarly, you won't find "Greed" on this chart, but you will find "Self-Interest" (near the lower left corner of the Activity Variations). "Self-Interest" is not as emotionally charged as "Greed." It more clearly defines the issues at the center of a rich man's miserliness, a poor man's embezzlement, and a loving parent who must leave her child to die in a fire to save herself. And other Variations such as "Fantasy", "Need", "Rationalization", or "Denial" each reflect a different form of "Greed".

It is not our purpose to force new, sterile and unfamiliar terminology on the writers of the world. It is our purpose to clarify. So, we urge you to pencil in your favorite terms to the chart we have provided. Stick "Love" on "Attraction," place "Greed" on "Self-Interest," if that is how you see them. In this manner, you create a chart that already reflects your personal biases, and most likely incorporates those of your culture as well. The original bias-free chart, however, is always available to serve as a neutral framework for refining your story's problem.

As a means of zeroing in on the Variation that best describes the thematic nature of your story's problem, it helps to look at the Variations as pairs. Just as with characters, the Variations that are most directly opposed in nature occur as diagonals in the chart. A familiar dynamic pair of Variations is Morality and Self-Interest. The potential conflict between the two emerges when we put a "vs." between the two terms: Morality vs. Self-Interest. That makes them feel a lot more like the familiar *thematic conflict*.

Later we shall return to describe how each dynamic pair in the chart can form the basis for a thematic premise in your story. We will also show how this dynamic conflict does not have to be a good vs. bad situation, but can create a "lesser of two evils" or "better of two goods" situation as well.

Issues

Identifying the Variation of a throughline sets up the Issue of thematic concepts explored from that point of view. To show how this might work, let's look at the Issues of STAR WARS.

STAR WARS

Overall Story Issue: Skill (Practiced ability)—Everyone in this galaxy compares themselves to one another in terms of their skills; piloting a spacecraft, fighting their way out of tight situations, and standing up for themselves. The princess immediately evaluates her rescuers (Han, Chewbacca, and Luke) in terms of their obvious lack of skill. The entire war between the Rebellion and the Empire is a match between skills and experience. The Empire has experience in quashing upstart groups, but its skills at doing so are rusty. The Rebellion, which has far less experience, consists of great numbers of raw talent like Luke. Skill is an advantageous quality in this story.

Main Character Issue: Fantasy (Belief in something unreal)—Fantasy is an important part of Luke Skywalker's life. He has no idea what wars are like, but he wants to hear all he can about them because his fantasy is to be a hero in one. He plays with toy space ships, he is intrigued by messages from damsels in distress, and he cares more about these fantasies than about the humdrum life of farming on a desert planet. These fantasies help set him apart from the unimaginative people around him (for example his uncle), yet they also make him seem inexperienced and naive (he is almost killed in Mos Isley cantina). Fantasy is advantageous for Luke.

Impact Character Issue: Worth (A rating of usefulness or desirability)—Obi Wan's impact forces considerations of what should be thought to have true worth (as opposed to objective value). Obi Wan makes it clear that he believes the Force is what everyone should see as having the greatest worth in the galaxy. He backs up his opinion by using it to get himself and others out of tight jams. He also appears at first to be a nutty old hermit, but is revealed to be a person of great worth in the eyes of Princess Leia, an important leader in the Rebellion. Because Obi Wan shows that things are seldom what they seem, his impact often causes people to reevaluate what they find of worth and what they don't. These reevaluations of worth lead to a greater understanding—especially for Luke Skywalker. Obi Wan shows Worth to be advantageous.

Subjective Story Issue: Ability (The inherent capacity to do or be)—The most focused aspect of Luke's and Obi Wan's relationship has to do with developing the abilities of a Jedi Knight. When Luke is either improving his own abilities or admiring Obi Wan's, everyone sees this relationship as a positive one for both people involved. Obi Wan's influence helps Luke see abilities which he didn't ever allow himself to see, such as the ability to leave home and join the Rebellion. Clarifying these abilities, however, would not be positive to their relationship if these two didn't also share similar desires. Fortunately for them, every time Obi Wan uncovers a new ability, such as being able to use a light saber without looking, it makes Luke want more. These kinds of demonstrable abilities make others, such as Han Solo, see there is something good happening between this teacher and student--even if it does involve ancient religion. Ability in this relationship is advantageous.

We still have one final level of the thematic chart of a story's problem to encounter. In fact, we have already seen it. It is the same chess set of sixty-four Character Elements we created earlier:

Knowledge	Ability		Actuality	Aware		Proven	Theory		Effect	Trust
Desire	Thought		Self-Aware	Perception		Hunch	Unproven		Test	Cause

Order	Equity		Inertia	Projection		Accurate	Expectation		Result	Ending
Inequity	Chaos		Speculation	Change		Determin-ation	Non-accurate		Unending	Process

Consider	Logic		Pursuit	Control		Certainty	Probability		Proaction	Inaction
Feeling	Reconsider		Un-controlled	Avoid / Prevent		Possibility	Potentiality		Protection	Reaction

Faith	Conscience		Support	Help		Deduction	Reduction		Acceptance	Evaluation
Temptation	Disbelief		Hinder	Oppose		Production	Induction		Re-evaluation	Non-acceptance

Each Variation can be subdivided again into four Elements. And, it turns out that when we get to the heart of the thematic issues in a story, no matter what kind of problem we began with it all comes down to the same thing: Character. Not surprising at all, really. Characters represent the different ways the Story Mind can go about solving the story's problem. The Main Character sits on the Crucial Element, and must either stick with it, if it is the solution, or abandon it if it turns out to be the problem itself.

Problems

Identifying the Element at the heart of each throughline puts a specific name on the Problem that drives that throughline in the story.

STAR WARS

Overall Story Problem: Test (A trial to find out something's validity)—Rather than trusting in the design and efficiency of the Death Star, the Empire decides it must have a test run on Alderaan. This clues Princess Leia, Obi Wan, and subsequently the Rebellion, to the terrifying nature of what they are facing. This also allows the Rebellion forces to prepare for the worst, which is the Empire's undoing. The Rebellion, on the other hand, does not fully trust their information about the Empire's secret weapon and tests its accuracy by waiting until they have the plans in their hands. Had they trusted their early reports they could have moved the base and remained out of the Empire's reach.

Main Character Problem: Test (A trial to find out something's validity)—Luke is constantly driven to test his skills—as a wannabe Jedi, as a daring doer, as a sharpshooter, and eventually as a pilot. By constantly testing himself, he gets into situations that he would have avoided if he had confidence (or trust) in himself. For example, he knew better than to go alone into the Sand people's territory; the scuffle he created at the bar could easily have been avoided; the messy breakout of the Princess was partially motivated by his testing his limits.

Impact Character Problem: Unproven (A rating of knowledge that has not been tested)—Because of his devout faith in the Force, Obi Wan is driven by the idea that everything remains unproven—even if common sense might dictate otherwise. He finds exceptions to every generality that people mention around him. The impact of his character is to make others draw their most cherished beliefs into question, because the true nature of "the Force" is so unimaginable, yet so powerful.

Subjective Story Problem: Non-Accurate (Not within tolerances)—Obi Wan's secrecy and misleading comments to Luke keeps their relationship off balance. Obi Wan tries to lure Luke away with him to Alderaan. He feigns indifference when Luke wimps out. Obi Wan warns Luke to be careful at the cantina without giving Luke a real idea of the dangers within. Obi Wan's vagueness about the necessary "pains" associated with Luke's Jedi training (like getting zapped by the trainer robot) jostles their relationship.

We need to take a breather here! Much new material has been covered and it takes some time to assimilate. We suggest you put the book down for a while, ponder what we've just explored, have a snack, watch a program on TV, and then return once the dust has settled. If we could, we'd provide some soothing mood music right about now. Since that is a bit difficult, we'll do the next best thing—pull it all together in a simplified image.

Because each level "falls" under the one above it, we can create a "3-D" representation of the thematic chart that illustrates its nested nature:

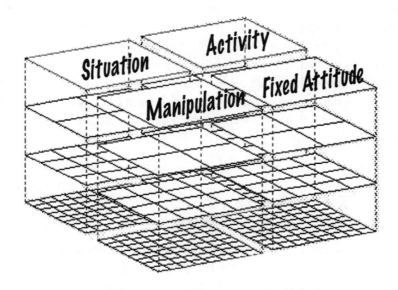

The Dramatica Structural Model

This projection gives a good feel for how Classes, Types, Variations, and Elements relate to one another. We start at the top by loosely classifying our story's problem, and then subdivide each Class into Types. Each Type is refined into Variations and then defined in terms of its basic Elements. Remember, our purpose here is only to identify the components of theme. Later in *The Art Of Storytelling* we will illustrate how to build and develop your story's theme.

Matching Points Of View To The Chart

To reiterate: Theme is perspective. Perspective is created by the relationship between two things: what is being looked at and where it is being seen from. In stories, what is being looked at is the nature of the problem and its ramifications.

To define the story's problem we start with its Class, then find out what Type of problem it is within that Class. Next we see what Variation of that Type the problem is. We finally work down to the Elemental nature of the problem, which is reflected in Character.

Now we need to see what each of those aspects of the problem looks like from each of the four points of view an audience will expect in a complete story. Let's begin with the Class level.

Overall Story Throughline

All four of the Classes of problem (Situation, Fixed Attitude, Activity, and Manipulation) show up in every complete grand argument story. As it turns out, one represents the way the Overall Story view sees the problem. Another represents the Main Character's view of it. Another represents the Impact Character's view. The remaining Class tells us how the problem looks from the Subjective Story view.

Each perspective is assigned to only one of the four Classes. No repititions or omissions are allowed. Four perspectives combined with the four Classes gives you the four throughlines. For example:

Overall Story + Fixed Attitiude	=	OS Throughline
Main Character + Activity	=	MC Throughline
Impact Character + Manipulation	=	IC Throughline
Subjective Story + Situation	=	SS Throughline

The first key to creating thematic perspectives in a story is to assign each of the four throughlines to the four Classes in the structure. Once we do this, the most broad stroke foundations of the author's biases on the story's issues have been laid.

As an example, objectively, the problem in a particular story might be a situation. This means the Overall Story point of view and the Situation Class match or link in such a story. When we *assign* a point of view to a Class, we say that Class is the point of view's *Throughline*. In other words, everything we see in our story from the Overall Story view is in the Situation Class, so the Situation Class is the Overall Story Throughline.

Assigning a point of view to a Class creates the perspective, and therefore changes the way dramatic items in that Class appear.

For example, if the Overall Story Throughline is Situation, the story at large is about a situation that affects all the characters in the story to some degree. Such a story might be about people in a post-nuclear holocaust world, prisoners of war in a concentration camp, or two rival gang families stranded together on a deserted island. In each case, the external situation is the cause of the story's problems, when we see them objectively. Also in each case, the same situation affects all the characters in the story. This is the definition of the problem seen from the "they" point of view, like that of the general on the hill watching the battle. The audience wants to see what the problem looks like from this point of view. It gives them the feel that they explore the issues of the story fully.

In contrast, by assigning the Main Character point of view to the Situation Class, the Situation Class becomes the Main Character Throughline. In a different story with this arrangement, only the Main Character is in the situation. The other characters would be involved in one of the remaining Classes. In such a story where the Main Character Throughline is in a Situation, the situation might be the Main Character as second in command on a battleship. Or, perhaps he has a physical deformity like THE ELEPHANT MAN, or a particular race or sex. In other words, we describe the Main Character by his personal situation, which is an external condition causing difficulties only for that character. This is different from an Overall Story situation that affects *all* the characters in a story (including the Main Character).

Before we move to the Type, Variation, and Element levels, let's take a brief look at each of the sixteen Class/throughline combinations that might be created.

Situation as Overall Story Throughline

When Situation is the Overall Story Throughline, the story's troubles grow from a problematic Situation. All the Overall Story Characters in the story have the common source of their troubles emanating from an external situation. Just because the situation is external and objective does not mean it must be without feeling. It simply means the audience does not experience the situation personally.

Activity as Overall Story Throughline

An Overall Story Throughline of Activity means an activity gone wrong causes the story's troubles. This might be an activity engaged in by people or existing in nature. Either way, the "perpetuation" of this activity is what causes all the difficulties faced by the Overall Story Characters. There is often the tendency to think of an activity in the large scale, making it macroscopic—larger than life. But dry rot works as well as a marauding horde in creating problems big enough to drive a story. The only constraint is the activity must be an external one that is causing the difficulties for all.

Situation vs. Activities

It is easy to think of kinds of activities that border on being situations. For example, we might want to tell a story about a disease. If the story's problem stems from having the disease, it is a situation. If fighting the disease causes the story's problem, it is an activity. Because all four Classes will show up in a complete story, it is likely that both having and fighting the disease will show up as things unfold. The thematic question here is: which one do we see objectively, or phrased another way, which one do we see as the cause of the problems for all the characters throughout the story—having it or fighting it?

Fixed Attitude as Overall Story Throughline

Fixed Attitude is an internal state, describing problems that come from fixed attitudes. When we choose Fixed Attitude as the Overall Story Throughline, the problems that affect all the characters will stem from internal attitudes, biases, and fixations. For example, an Overall Story Throughline of Fixed Attitude might be about how prejudice affects a town or how a humiliating memory affects a kingdom. In contrast, Situation and Activity Overall Stories deal with external states and processes. A selection of Fixed Attitude as the Overall Story Throughline specifically means the source of the difficulties between all the Overall Story Characters is best seen as a problematic state of mind or conflict between problematic states of mind.

Manipulation as Overall Story Throughline

Manipulation is an internal process, describing problems that come from the ways in which people think. When we choose Manipulation as the Overall Story Throughline, the problems that affect all the characters will stem from manipulations and conflicting processes of thought. As opposed to the fixed attitudes described in the Fixed Attitude Class, Manipulation is about problems that arise from manners of thinking. For example, an Overall Story Throughline of Manipulation might be about the problems caused by a regiment overly trained to follow orders. Another example is a dysfunctional family that tries to manipulate one another into nervous breakdowns.

Main Character Throughline

Because an audience identifies most strongly with the Main Character, choosing a Main Character Throughline is like asking your potential audience, "Where's your mind at?" This Throughline describes the realm in which the Main Character operates. Each Class, therefore, provides a different mindset for the Main Character.

Situation as Main Character Throughline

Situation is a Class of problematic situations. A Situation Main Character finds himself in a troublesome situation. The situation in question can be a social status issue, such as being a certain race or gender or being queen or king. It could be a predicament such as being a rock star, or it could be a physical condition such as having an extremely large nose or exceptional beauty. Each of these illustrations shows a Main Character defined by the situation in which he is found.

Fixed Attutyde as Main Character Throughline

A Fixed Attitude Main Character is defined as holding onto a fixed attitude. Such a character might be suffering from a prejudice, haunted by a suppressed memory, or unable to shake a crush on the kid down the street. In each case, it is a fixed state of mind that causes the Main Character's difficulties.

Activity as Main Character Throughline

An Activity Main Character is a person of action. For example, he might be doing something just to do it, or he might be trying to get or achieve something. Other activities of an Activity Main Character might be learning or seeking to understand something. At first learning and understanding might seem too internal to be Physics, but consider these activities *applied* externally. Learning is gathering information about something and understanding is seeking the meaning of something. This is different from *coming up with original thought* which *would* be internal.

Manipulation as Main Character Throughline

A Main Character Throughline of Manipulation suggests an individual best described by how he thinks. This could be a flighty person, someone who jumps to conclusions, or even a calculating, manipulative person. In each of these scenarios, the opinions the Main Character holds are not what set him apart, but rather the kinds of mental processes he goes through. Though there may be many Overall Story Characters who represent manners of thinking, only the Main Character will provide the audience with the experience of thinking that way.

The Main Character has Class

Clearly, the nature and concerns of a Main Character change radically from Class to Class. If your main interest is to explore your Main Character in a story, then choosing the Main Character Class before any others is the way to approach developing a story. Keep in mind, though, that once you assign a Class to one of the four Throughlines in a story, you cannot assign it to any of the others. So whatever you might pick for your Main Character's Class will not be available for the Overall Story, Subjective Story or Impact Character throughlines.

Impact Character Throughline

It is important to be clear about the difference between the Main Character and the Impact Character. The audience looks through the Main Character's eyes, and through them looks *at* the Impact Character. Through the Main Character, we feel what it is like to be in a particular predicament. With the Impact Character we see an external view of what someone else looks like in the same predicament. Since we cannot climb into and become this character, we can only judge him by how he affects the characters and events around him.

As an example, imagine a handicapped Main Character. During the duration of the story, the audience members also feel handicapped. They suffer the problems the Main Character's handicap creates as if it is a problem in their own lives. By contrast, if the Impact Character has a handicap, the audience would examine the problem from the outside, learning more about the difficulties logistically, not experientially. The focus would be on how this handicap impacts others. "Impact" is the key word to keep in mind when examining the story's problem in the Impact Character Throughline.

Situation as Impact Character Throughline

An Impact Character with a Throughline of Situation will impact others because of his social status, race, gender, physical qualities, position or station. Whatever the situation might be, it provides the alternative paradigm to the Main Character's view of things.

Activity as Impact Character Throughline

An Activity Impact Character is a person who acts in the areas of Learning, Understanding, Doing, or Obtaining (the four Activity Types). The Impact Character makes a case against the Main Character's point of view. At the end of such a story, the audience will not have experienced what it feels like to engage in these activities, but will know a lot about what *impact* these activities have.

Fixed Attitude as Impact Character Throughline

The Fixed Attitude Impact Character displays a fixation or attitude dealing chiefly with memories, desires, immediate responses or considerations. It is this attitude that causes the Main Character to reconsider or justify his position.

Manipulation as Impact Character Throughline

A Manipulation Impact Character influences others through direct manipulation or may just have an impact because of the way in which he thinks. In either case, the focus of this Throughline is an external view of how thought processes affect those whom interact with them.

Subjective Story Throughline

The Subjective Story Throughline is the story's Passionate Argument. This is where the author creates meaning for the audience's emotional appraisal of a story's message. The primary focus is on the *relationship* between the Main and Impact Characters. Since the Main and Impact Characters are, by definition, at odds with each other, the Subjective Story Throughline forms the background against which the battle between them is fought. As a result, choosing a Class as the Subjective Story Throughline affects how a story *feels* to an audience.

Situation as Subjective Story Throughline

A Subjective Story Throughline of Situation has the Main and Impact Characters in conflict over a situation that exists between them. This includes a marriage contract, a business partnership, or a chain of military command. It also includes being a caregiver to an invalid, any kind of employment situation, and all other relationships "stuck" in the real world. To illustrate a Subjective Story Throughline of Situation properly, you need to create a situation principally limited to a relationship between the Main and Impact Characters. It should involve the past, present, progress, or future.

Activity as Subjective Story Throughline

If Activity is the Subjective Story Throughline, the Main and Impact Characters grapple over an activity. This could be an activity that is leading toward a purpose or just something engaged in for its own rewards. It might even be a harmful activity engaged in as a means of punishing oneself to relieve guilt. Both Main and Impact may be striving to outdo each other at this activity. Or, one may be for the activity and the other against it. Anyway, the activity lies at the heart of the difficulties between them and forms the subject of the story's passionate argument of Activity is the Subjective Story Throughline.

Fixed Attitude as Subjective Story Throughline

When you select Fixed Attitude as the Subjective Story Throughline, fixed attitudes or mindsets form the battleground of the Main and Impact Characters. How many fixed attitudes can we see as a personal point of conflict between two people? A prejudice, political view, religion, an attitude toward a child or parent, or a feeling of worthlessness does the trick. A scenario that portrays the troubles between the Main and Impact Characters revolving around a fixed state of mind, successfully represents Fix Attitude as the Subjective Story Throughline.

Manipulation as Subjective Story Throughline

Manipulation as the Subjective Story Throughline has the Main and Impact Characters diverging over a manner of thinking. They do not conflict over *what* they think, but *how* they think. Phrases like, "You always get this way when we argue," and "No, I don't - it's *you* that keeps changing subjects," suggest a psychological conflict between the Main and Impact Characters. When *how* someone works something out becomes the issue between the Main and Impact Characters, the Subjective Story Throughline most likely is Manipulation.

Throughlines and Beyond

As we have seen, each of these sixteen perspectives has a slightly different flavor because of the particular point of view linked with a specific Class. This alone is a more quantitative way to look at Theme than has previously been available, yet we still have three more levels of the thematic structure to explore! Each level has its own kind of perspectives. For convenience, we call the thematic perspectives created at any level *story points (appreciations)*, which simply means that is how we understand a problem at that level from that point of view.

Because of practical constraints on the size of this book, we won't be able to go into as much detail for story points at the Type, Variation, and Element levels as we might like. What we *can* do is provide a general description of the story points found in each throughline. Once one gets a feel for how a throughline changes the meaning of a structural item in general, one can apply that understanding to any item in the structure and arrive at an accurate dramatic appreciation.

To recap, the Main Character Throughline represents the audience point of view in a story. The Impact Character Throughline is the opposing point of view the audience is asked to consider. The Subjective Story Throughline contains the passionate argument tied to the relationship between those two points of view. The Overall Story Throughline encompasses the practical argument about the relative value of all possible approaches to solving the story's central problem *including those of the Main and Impact Characters*.

So, a Main Character *Throughline* explores what it looks like and feels like to have a particular kind of problem (often seen as drive). The Impact Character Throughline explores what kind of impact someone with that kind of problem (or drive) has on the people and events around him. The Subjective Story Throughline explores how the problem affects the relationship between Main and Impact Characters. The Overall Story Throughline explores which is the better position to be in for the benefit of everyone.

Keeping these points of view in mind, let's see what other story points are created at the Type, Variation, and Element levels.

CONCERNS

Just as combining a throughline and a Class creates a Throughline in which the problem appears from that point of view, combining a throughline and a Type creates an area of Concern. So, there will be an Overall Story Concern, a Main Character Concern, an Impact Character Concern and a Subjective Story Concern in every complete story. As its name implies, a Concern reflects the area in which the problem will be of greatest concern for each throughline.

Overall Story Concern

The Overall Story Concern is the area in which all the characters share a common concern. This might be a single item they are all concerned about, or it might be that each of them has a personal concern of this nature. For example, if the Overall Story Concern were the Type "Obtaining," then all the characters would be concerned with Obtaining (or losing) something. In such a story, everyone might be trying to Obtain the same thing, such as a buried treasure. In another story with an Overall Story Concern of Obtaining everyone might be trying to Obtain something different. The Protagonist might want to Obtain the treasure, but the Reason Character might want to Obtain a diploma. The Overall Story characters share the nature of the Concern, though not necessarily the specific expression of it.

Later, in the Plot and Encoding sections, we will touch on how one can pull these different items of Obtaining together into the same story. In the example above, the Protagonist could be a treasure hunter wanting to Obtain the treasure. The Reason Character who wants to Obtain a diploma in archeology joins the Protagonist's team because he seeks the quest for the treasure as the basis for his doctoral thesis. Tying items together in this manner is not a structural aspect of story, but one of storytelling, and is therefore beyond the scope of this section on *The Elements of Structure*.

Keep in mind that a Concern of Obtaining might also mean a Concern of *getting rid of* something. Whether one wants to Obtain or wants to stop Obtaining does not change the nature of the *area* of Concern. So, for this appreciation and all the following, remember to consider it as either meaning *not enough of something* or *too much of something*.

Main Character Concern

As one would expect, the Main Character Concern is of interest only to the Main Character. This appreciation describes the area that most worries or interests the Main Character. It suggests the way the Main Character sees the problem without being as specific as the problem.

If Obtaining were the Main Character Concern, the Main Character alone would be trying to get or get rid of (hold on to or refuse to hold on to, gain or lose) something. None of the other characters would share this Concern because the other throughlines are all in other Classes with different Types. This divergence is what gives a story some breadth and a sense of completeness for an audience. Rather than focusing on just one issue, every point of view on the story's problem falls into a different Throughline with its own unique Concern.

Similarly, a Main Character with a Concern of Memory would be trying to remember, to forget, to fix a memory, or to prevent one from forming.

Impact Character Concern

Because we explore the Impact Character Throughline in terms of its impact, the Concern explores the area in which the Impact Character has its greatest effect. A way of phrasing this is to say the Impact Character's impact chiefly Concerns this area. So, an Impact Character Concern of Obtaining here would describe an Impact Character who changes what is or can be Obtained (or refused) because of his impact on the people and events around him.

Subjective Story Concern

The Subjective Story Concern describes the area of greatest conflict or divergence between the Main and Impact Characters. They might see eye-to-eye everywhere else, but when it comes to the Subjective Story Concern, they always come to blows. The Concern of the Subjective Story Throughline grows out of the Main and Impact Concerns.

If the Subjective Story Concern were Obtaining, the Main and Impact would argue over whether they should have something. It might be something only one of them has or can have. Who should have it? It might be something they must either have together or not. Obtaining is not only gaining. It can also refer to something lost or missing.

Wrapping Up Our Concerns

As we have seen, matching a Type with a throughline creates a Concern. Each Concern provides a deeper appreciation of a different side of the story's problem for the audience.

Variations On A Theme

Moving down to the Variation level, we find story points that further refine the story's problem as seen from each throughline. We call each of these an *Issue*. The *Issue* describes the subject matter explored in context of the Concerns in a given Throughline. In a sense, think of the Issue as the thematic topic for each throughline.

Overall Story Issue

This story point describes the kind of value judgments that apply to all the characters and events in a story. For example, an Issue of Morality will have a dynamic counterpoint of Self-Interest. This means the thematic conflict in the Overall Story Throughline would be Morality vs. Self-Interest. Because Morality is the Issue, it would be in the forefront and appear as the topic or subject matter of the Overall Story Throughline's Theme.

Because Morality is the *Overall Story* Issue, it will appear almost everywhere. In a hypothetical story, we might see a man taking candy from a baby, a headline proclaiming that a company's profits are up, while behind the newsstand we see the company dumping toxic waste in the background. Illustrations of the Overall Story Issue can focus on the characters or can act as a flavoring for the story as a whole. We shall explore this in greater detail in the Encoding section.

NOTE: The Overall Story Issue is the closest touch point with the traditional use of the term, "theme."

Main Character Issue

The Main Character Issue (and its counterpoint) represents the thematic conflict of personal interest to the Main Character. You see it in the kinds of things this character notices that no one else does. Because it is a personal value judgment, the author can use this appreciation to whisper his point of view, rather than shouting it overtly, as might happen with the Overall Story Issue. Because it is so personal, the Main Character Issue helps bring humanity to the Main Character. It is through the issues explored through the Issue the audience can identify not only with the Main Character's head but his heart as well.

Impact Character Issue

The Impact Character Issue provides a way of evaluating the appropriateness of the Impact Character's impact. The Impact Character Issue and Counterpoint act as a balance or scale to measure the results of the Impact Character's point of view. This is where an author can tip the balance to favor one point of view over another. Later we shall explore how to tip that balance back and forth over the course of the story, making a more realistic and less heavy-handed statement of the author's bias.

Subjective Story Issue

The Subjective Story Concern describes the area of shared concern for the Main and Impact Characters. The Subjective Story Issue and Counterpoint describe why they conflict over it. The Main Character will believe the Subjective Story Issue (or counterpoint) is the value standard to use when looking at the Subjective Story Concern. As a result, The Main Character will see the Concern in a particular light. In contrast, the Impact Character will believe the other Variation (Issue or counterpoint) is the proper way to evaluate the Concern. Since this standard of measure results in different conclusions about the Concern, the Main and Impact Characters come into conflict. They use these two points as they argue over two issues: What to do about the Concern, and which is the best way to look at it?

It's Elemental!

Finally, we have arrived at the most basic and precise level of understanding about a story's problem: The Element level. It is here we find the source of difficulties experienced in each throughline. The Overall Story Problem is something that will affect all the characters and all that they do.

In contrast, the Main Character's Problem will be the source of his drive. Eventually, it may turn out to be (or reflect) the Overall Story Problem, or have the potential to solve the Overall Story Problem, if only the Main Character can bring himself to apply it.

The Impact Character Problem is the source of his drive as well, but rather than experience it, the audience examines it from the outside. "What is driving *him* or *her*?"

Lastly, let's examine the Subjective Story Problem. Unlike the Problems in each of the other throughlines, this one is not about an item, but a relationship—the relationship between Main and Impact Characters. What is at the heart of their disagreements? What is the most essential subject from which all their conflict grows? The Subjective Story Problem describes the most refined view of what drives (or pulls) the Main and Impact Characters apart.

At this point we have defined all the principal thematic perspectives in a story. We have determined that any Problem might be understood in terms of its Class, Type, Variation, and Element. We have further described the story's central Problem itself can never be seen directly, but is approximated by exploring how it appears from four different points of view. Each view provides its own understanding of the nature of the Problem's Class, Type, Variation, and Element. Each of these is called a *story point*. When all the story points are considered together in the mind of the audience, the author's bias on the issues at the heart of a story is established.

Deep Theme

What we have done so far is describe the Elements of Theme. Now we have to put them in motion as well.

The Thematic Argument

What moves Theme forward is the Thematic Argument. Why an argument? Because unless the audience shares the author's bias on the story's issues, it will not accept a blanket statement the author's proposed way of dealing with a particular problem is the best. The audience does want to be convinced—it wants to learn something useful in real life while being entertained at the same time. But, unless an author can successfully make an emotional argument supporting his bias through his Theme, he will not be able to change the heart of his audience.

Premise and the Thematic Argument

One of the most familiar attempts to describe the nature of the thematic argument relies on an idea called the *premise*. A premise usually takes this form: *Some activity or character trait leads to a particular result or conclusion*. An example of this would be *Greed leads to Self-Destruction*. A premise can be useful in describing what a thematic argument is about in a nutshell, but provides little information about how that argument will advance.

For the example above, there are many ways in which greed might lead to self-destruction. In addition, each of the four throughlines has its own view of the thematic nature of the problem, so each one needs its own thematic argument. The traditional premise looks at a story's Theme from one point of view only. If greed leads to self-destruction, is this a problem for everyone, just for the Main Character, just the Impact Character, or does it perhaps describe the nature and outcome of the relationship between Main and Impact? We simply don't have enough information to decide that. As a result, the traditional premise is fine for summing up a story, but does little to help an author create a thematic argument.

Dramatica's view of a thematic argument begins with the thematic conflict. Each of the throughlines has its own thematic conflict that we have already described to some degree during our discussion of Issue.

The Issue itself forms one side of the thematic conflict and the Counterpoint forms the other. As suggested earlier, you won't find Greed in Dramatica's thematic structure, but you will find Self-Interest. The Counterpoint for Self Interest is the Variation dynamically opposed to it in the chart, which is Morality. Thus, the premise of a thematic argument dealing with Greed might begin with the conflict, Self-Interest vs. Morality.

The advantage of the thematic conflict is that it spells out *both* sides of the thematic argument. Both Issue and counterpoint must be played against each other over the course of the story if the author is to make a case that one is better than the other.

The component of a traditional premise that describes growth is in the phrase "leads to." Sometimes this may also be "prevents," "creates," "hinders" or any other word that shows the relationship of the topic (such as Greed) to the conclusion (such as self-destruction). Again, this describes what an audience comes to understand at the end of a story, but does not give a clue about how to develop that understanding while creating a story.

Because it begins with a conflict rather than a topic, Dramatica's version of a thematic argument supports an author creating as many scenes or events as he may choose in which the Issue is weighed against the Counterpoint. Each time the Issue or Counterpoint is illustrated does not have to be shown in terms of all good vs. all bad. The illustration can be shades of gray. Using our example from above, in a series of scenes Self-Interest might be moderately positive, largely negative, slightly negative, then largely positive. At the end of the story the audience can sum up or average out all the instances in which they have seen it.

Similarly, the counterpoint of Morality in its own scenes might be largely positive, moderately positive, largely negative and largely negative again. At the end of the story the audience will sum up the counterpoint and decide whether Morality by itself is positive or negative.

The audience does not consciously work out these averages. Rather, it is simply affected by the constant layering of value judgments created by the author's bias. In fact, audience members are constantly balancing the Issue against the counterpoint in their hearts until the story is over and they feel more toward one or the other.

The advantage of this approach is that an author does not have to be heavy-handed by saying only negative things about one side of the thematic conflict and only positive things about the other. An audience will be much more open to a balanced emotional argument where decisions are seldom black and white.

Finally, as reflected in traditional premise, an audience will want to see the results of adhering to one value standard over another. In our example of Greed, it led to Self-destruction. This is a generic conclusion. It could mean either a failure in one's goals or a personal loss of the heart.

Dramatica sees goals and yearnings as two different things: One born of reason and one born of emotion. How completely we achieve our goals controls our degree of satisfaction. How well we accommodate our yearnings controls our degree of fulfillment. So, one thing we need to know at the end of thematic argument is whether our goals ended in success or failure, and whether things feel good or bad.

The degree of success or failure, good or bad, is determined in storytelling. The thematic story points of Success, Failure, Good, and Bad simply suggest on which side of the fence the conclusion settled. As a result, there are two different parts to the conclusion of a Dramatica thematic argument—the Outcome (Success or Failure) and the Judgment (Good or Bad).

From these considerations we can see that four broad conclusions to a thematic argument are possible:

1. The Success/Good conclusion   =   Happy Ending

2. The Failure/Bad conclusion   =   Tragedy

3. The Success/Bad conclusion   =   Personal Tragedy

4. The Failure/Good conclusion   =   Personal Triumph

A Failure/Good story, for example, does not mean the Failure is Good but that despite a lack of satisfaction, the feel of the story is fulfilling. Such is the case in the motion picture RAIN MAN in which Charlie (Tom Cruise) fails to get the inheritance, yet overcomes his hatred of his father. This is a Personal Triumph.

Similarly, Success/Bad stories are like REMAINS OF THE DAY in which Mr. Stevens (Anthony Hopkins) successfully preserves the household through wars and owners, yet in the end finds himself empty and alone. This is a Personal Tragedy.

Another Success/Bad story is "ROMEO AND JULIET" by William Shakespeare. It is Success because the families cease their feud after the death of their favored children. It is Bad because Romeo (the Main Character) dies unhappily.

Sewing Together The Themes

In this section we have learned the traditional premise is too blunt a tool to do more than describe the gist of a finished work. In contrast, Dramatica explores the idea of a thematic argument through thematic conflict, development of the relative value of different standards, and ends with an assessment of both the level of satisfaction and fulfillment. Such an approach is much more in line with the organic flow of a story's emotional impact as felt through Theme, and is much more accessible as a creative guideline.

The Storyform: How Does All This Stuff Hold Together?

In our present exploration of Theme we are looking at Thematic Story Points one by one. From this point of view Story Points can appear rather independent, with each carrying its own meaning which needs clarification and development.

This point of view is deceptive, however. The meaning, which Story Points hold, is partly in their individuality and partly in their relationships to each other. The nature of any single Story Point has an impact on how to see every other Story Point in that story. Altogether, the collective impact of a specific arrangement of Story Points describes the underlying structure of a single complete story.

The connections these Story Points have with one another is complex. Beyond the obvious links between such items as Throughlines/Concerns/ and Issues, the web of dramatic relationships between the Story Points of a single story can only be kept fully consistent using a computer.

The purpose of this section, *The Elements of Structure*, is just to catalog the pieces of story structure. The second half of this book, titled *The Art of Storytelling*, will explore exactly how creating a story controls what relationships will exist between a story's Story Points.

Additional Story Points

Throughline, Concern, Issue, and Problem are not the only story points in Dramatica. In fact, there are six other story points for each of the four throughlines, plus others that affect the whole story. Whether an author consciously considers them while writing, these story points will clearly appear in every complete story.

Additional Element Level Story Points:

At the Element level where we already found each throughline's Problem, each of the four throughlines also has three more story points. Since each throughline has a Problem, it is not surprising that each also has a Solution. We find the Solution directly opposite the Problem in the thematic structure. For example, the Solution for too much or too little *logic* is more or less *feeling*.

If a Problem were a disease, its Solution would be a cure. A disease will also have symptoms, and treatments for those symptoms. This is reflected in the same quad as the Problem and Solution in each throughline, where one of the remaining Elements will be the Symptom or and the other the Response (treatment). The reason we call them Symptom and Response is that characters, like real people, find their attention drawn to the difficulties caused by a problem more than to the problem itself. Whether the Symptom and Direction we are considering falls in the Overall Story, Main Character, Impact Character, or Subjective Story Throughline, they represent the symptoms of the Problem that draw attention (Symptom) and what the characters try to do about it (Response).

In the Overall Story Throughline, the Symptom is where all the characters concentrate, as that is where their troubles are most clear. The Response is how they respond to try to reduce those troubles. If the story were a body with a disease (Problem), sometimes a cure must be found and one must ignore the symptoms, not worry about a treatment, and concentrate on a cure. Other times, one cannot find the cure, but if one simply treats the symptoms, the body will recover enough to heal itself.

In the Main Character Throughline, the decision whether to change is intimately tied to whether the Main Character is driven by the Symptom toward a Response effort, or whether he seeks the cure. The Main Character cannot tell which is the correct approach. A final decision at a leap of faith (or the more gradual shift from one approach to the other) will finally settle whether the conclusion of the thematic argument ends in Success or Failure and Good or Bad.

In the Impact Character Throughline, the Symptom is where this character hopes to have the greatest impact, and Response is how he wants things to change because of that impact.

Symptom in the Subjective Story Throughline is the topic over which Main and Impact Characters argue because it gets their attention. The audience sees the real Problem between them, but the Main Character and Impact Character only see the Symptom. Subjective Story Response describes the direction in which the argument leans.

In practice, the Symptom is seen by the characters as the source of the problem before they grow enough to recognize it only as a symptom. If you walked up to a Main Character and asked him, "What's causing your troubles?" he would say something like, "All my problems come from _____," where the Main Character Symptom fills in the blank. The same is true of the other throughlines and their characters.

Likewise, the Response is seen by the characters as the best way to respond to the Symptom to fix things. It is an apparent "solution" for what they see is the problem.

Additional Variation Level Story Points

At the Variation level each of the four throughlines has two more story points. They function roughly the same way in each throughline, but are most similar between the Main and Impact Character Throughlines and between Overall Story and Subjective Story Throughlines.

Both Main and Impact have a *Unique Ability* and a *Critical Flaw*. In the Main Character, the Unique Ability represents some trait or quality that has the potential to allow that character to resolve the story's Problem. The Critical Flaw, however, undermines that Unique Ability. If the Main Character is ever to solve his troubles, he must overcome his Critical Flaw to employ his Unique Ability fully.

Because we see the Impact Character in terms of his impact, his Unique Ability describes the quality that enables him to have a special impact on the Main Character's point of view. The Impact Character's Critical Flaw is a quality that undermines that impact.

In the Overall Story and Subjective Story Throughlines, these same two items take form as the *Catalyst* and *Inhibitor*. Catalyst and Inhibitor act as the accelerator and brake pedal on the forward progress of each throughline. In the Overall Story Throughline, bringing in the Catalyst moves the plot forward more quickly; applying the Inhibitor slows things down. This is a structural aid in pacing a story.

In the Subjective Story Throughline, Catalyst and Inhibitor control the rate at which the relationship between Main and Impact Characters develops. More Catalyst brings a confrontation to a head; more Inhibitor delays it. Because Catalyst, Inhibitor, Issue, and counterpoint are all Variations, the proper choice of these items insures the story's pacing to come from inside the structure, rather than imposed arbitrarily by the author.

Additional Type Level Story Points

At the Type level, each of the four throughlines has one more appreciation, a *Benchmark*. It gets its name because it is a measure of the growth of each throughline. The Benchmark provides a category in which the progress of each throughline can be charted. For example, an Overall Story Benchmark of Obtaining might be characters gathering cash receipts in their efforts to afford tuition. In the Main Character Throughline, a Benchmark of Obtaining might be the unused concert tickets on a shy man's bed stand from all the times he bought them but then was too afraid to ask someone out to the show.

What about the Class level?

The Class level has no added story points, since it only has four items: The four Throughlines.

Is That About It?

Please keep in mind that this section of the Dramatica Theory Book deals with *The Elements Of Structure*. It describes what the pieces are, not how to put them together. That comes later in *The Art Of Storytelling*.

The Elements Of

Structure

PLOT

Plot vs. Storyweaving

A common mistake made when considering plot is to assume that plot refers to the sequence of events in a finished story. A more accurate view considers the difference between the progression of events in a story's structure, and the order in which these are revealed to an audience.

As an example of the difference between the two, we can look to the novel THE BRIDGE OF SAN LUIS REY by Thornton Wilder. The book opens with five travelers falling to their deaths as the bridge they are crossing collapses. The rest of the book documents how each of the travelers came to be on that bridge at that time. Clearly, the progression of events for the characters was different from the order of revelation granted to the audience.

In contrast, the novel SLAUGHTERHOUSE FIVE by Kurt Vonnegut Jr. follows the adventures of a Main Character who lives his life out of chronological order. In this case, the mixed-up progression of events is *part* of the plot's structure, not simply part of the storytelling.

The key difference between these two aspects of plot is that there is an internal logic to the plot's structure from the character's point of view, and there is an order in which that logic is revealed to the audience.

Looking toward motion pictures for examples, films such as PULP FICTION, MEMENTO, or REMAINS OF THE DAY present their plots in a different order than the order in which events *actually* occurred. In each of these stories, there is an internal logic to the sequence of events as they occurred in the structure. Then, that sequence is mixed up and presented to the audience in the new order. This new arrangement has a different affect on how an audience responds to each story, yet does not alter the internal logic at all. In other words, if we re-edited PULP FICTION, MEMENTO, or REMAINS OF THE DAY to reveal the plot in chronological order, the message of the story's structure would remain the same, but the viewing experience for the audience would change.

A prime example of this kind of impact shift is in the film and video versions of the movie, ONCE UPON A TIME IN AMERICA. The story explores the changing relationships of a group of friends from their days as poor children during the Depression to their eventual stations in life as old men in today's society. In its original theatrical release, episodes from several different periods in their long history together were jumbled up, so the audience would see them as old men, then young boys, old men again, and then teenagers. A large part of the enjoyment in watching this film was to try to sort out how one thing would eventually lead to another, and to discover why some expected things didn't happen after all. In a sense, viewing the movie was like assembling a jigsaw puzzle.

In the video release, however, they presented the story in chronological order. All the same pieces were there, but the story lost much of its charm, appearing absurdly simple and predictable in this new form.

The point is the plot of a story describes the internal logic or sequence of events. These events lead the characters from their situations and attitudes at the beginning of the problem to their situations and attitudes when the effort to solve the problem is finally over. Once that has been established, an author may choose to rearrange the order in which those events are revealed to the audience. This rearrangement may be integral to the feel of the finished work, but has no effect on the internal logic. As a result, such a technique falls into the area of storytelling. In Dramatica, we call storytelling techniques of this nature *Storyweaving*. Storyweaving is explored fully in the portion of this book dealing with *The Art of Storytelling*. Here, we will only examine the nature of the plot itself.

A Thematic Side To Plot

Plot has two sides: One side deals with the sequence of what happens next. The other side is thematic in nature and controls what the plot is about. Terms that describe the sequence of plot include *Acts*, *Chapters*, and *Scenes*. Terms that describe the thematics of plot include *Goal*, *Requirements*, and *Consequences*. We'll examine the thematic side of plot first.

Plot Story Points

As with the thematic perspectives we have already explored, plot thematics are also story points. What sets these apart is that they do not fall in any single throughline. In fact, they are scattered among all four throughlines. This is because these plot story points represent the collective impact of all four throughlines combined. So, when we speak of Goal, we are not talking about one throughline's goal. Rather, we are referring to the Story Goal, which draws from and impacts all four throughlines.

The story-wide effects of plot story points are clear. The Main Character, Impact Character, and Overall Story Characters are *all* caught up in the ripples caused by the quest for the Story Goal. The nature of the goal and the effort to achieve it even impacts the Subjective Story Throughline.

There are eight Plot Story Points that stand at the center of all four throughlines. They are the story *Goal*, *Requirements*, *Consequences*, *Forewarnings*, *Dividends*, *Costs*, *Prerequisites*, and *Preconditions*. All of these story points are at the Type level of the Thematic Structure.

In stories that reflect Western culture—particularly in American culture—the Story Goal is traditionally in the Overall Story Throughline. This results in a story in which the Goal concerns all the Overall Story Characters. The Goal, however, might just as well be in the Main Character Throughline, or either of the other two throughlines. In such a story, the overall Goal could be whatever the Main Character was hoping for or working toward, regardless of what was of concern to the Overall Story Characters.

In fact, it is the Concerns in each throughline that might also double up as the Story Goal. This ties all four throughlines' Concerns together into the issues central to the story as a whole. The relationship among the eight plot story points remains the same no matter which throughline serves as their anchor point. Therefore, we shall describe the nature of the eight Plot Story Points as they appear when the Story Goal is also the Overall Story Throughline Concern. For other perspectives, one merely needs to shift into a different point of view, such as that of the Main

Character. The story points themselves would remain the same; only what they are applied to would change.

Story Goal

The Story Goal will share the same Type as the Overall Story Concern. What then is the difference between a Goal and a Concern? A Concern simply describes the category of the kinds of things the Overall Story Characters worry most about. The Story Goal describes a specific item that is a shared concern. For example, if the Overall Story Concern is Obtaining, then all the characters worry about Obtaining something important to each of them. One might wish to Obtain a diploma, another to Obtain a lost treasure. A Story Goal of Obtaining in the same story might be everyone's wish to Obtain a pirate map. The map would bring recognition leading to a diploma for one character and a lost treasure to another. In such a story, the audience waits to see if the Goal is Obtained or not *because of the character concerns that such an outcome will affect*.

Story Requirements

To achieve a particular Type of Story Goal, a necessary Type of Requirements must be met. Requirements can come in two varieties. One is a series of steps that must occur in a particular order. The other is more like a shopping list that must be filled, no matter the order in which it is completed. Step Requirements can be accomplishments such as winning a series of preliminary bouts to qualify for a shot at the title. List Requirements can be gathered items that must be, such as clues or ingredients. Regardless of the Step or List nature of the Requirements for a particular story, they must all fall into the category described by the Requirement's Type.

Story Consequences

What happens if the characters fail to achieve the Goal? They suffer the Consequences. In some stories, the characters may already be suffering Consequences as the story opens. The Goal then becomes that one thing which will bring an end to the suffering. In this case, the characters's troubles are the Consequences of *not yet having achieved the Goal*. Just as in real life, sometimes Goals are a reward, other times Goals bring relief. It all depends on whether the situation starts out good, but needs improvement, or whether it starts out bad and needs correction.

Story Forewarnings

Just as progress in meeting Requirements signals how close the Goal is to being reached, the progress of Forewarnings points out how close the Consequences are to being imposed. Forewarnings can be as simple as cracks forming in a dam or as subtle as an increasing number of missed appointments. Characters are not only running toward the Goal, but trying to outrun the Consequences as well. Tension increases when one is both the pursuer and the pursued. For stories in which the Consequences are already in place, Forewarnings show how close things are to making the Consequence permanent. We find an example of this kind of Forewarning in Walt Disney's production of BEAUTY AND THE BEAST. Here, petals falling off a rose forebode the point at which the prince must remain a beast forever.

Driver And Passenger Plot Story Points

Just as there are Driver and Passenger characters, there are Driver and Passenger Plot Story Points as well. Goal, Requirements, Consequences, and Forewarnings are the Drivers and set the course of a story's plot. The next four story points, Dividends, Costs, Prerequisites, and Preconditions, are the Passengers which *modulate* the course of the plot set by the Drivers.

Story Dividends

During the effort to achieve the goal, certain benefits are enjoyed or accrued along the way. These serve to add motivation for the characters to continue. No one likes to keep his nose to the grindstone for an extended duration in the hope of eventually receiving a reward. Similarly, if one is already suffering a Consequence, simply accepting that torment while working toward relief quickly becomes unbearable. Characters need to enjoy small rewards along the way—little perks that make the journey bearable and the effort tolerable.

Story Costs

Just as positive benefits accrue during the effort to achieve the goal, so do negative costs have to be paid. Every time a character endures some displeasure while trying to achieve the goal, this added price is a Cost. Costs and Dividends modulate the intensity of the Overall Story Character's drive toward the Goal. These characters cannot know if they will eventually succeed or not. As a result, putting in effort is something of a gamble. Just as with a slot machine in a casino, every spin that simply takes one's money is a Cost. Every small payout is a Dividend. By properly balancing the two, they can preserve their motivation to continue in hopes of a jackpot. Each Dividend is *proof* that rewards can be had, and even if the Costs outweigh the Dividends, the Goal would cover those costs and leave much more profit besides. Of course, as with gambling, characters may slowly accrue so many costs that even achieving the goal would not cover the physical or emotional debt.

Story Prerequisites

Any effort requires supplies, often called *essentials*. The effort to achieve the Goal also requires these essential Prerequisites. You can't make progress without meeting the Prerequisites. Only by gathering the needed materials can you try to meet a story's Requirements. Prerequisites might be a certain kind of transportation, a specific amount of money, a grade point average, or the approval of a bureaucrat. As long as the item in question is essential to mounting the effort to achieve the

Goal, it is a Prerequisite. Prerequisites themselves do not bring the Goal any closer, which is why they are not Requirements. All they do is define the raw materials or foundations that must be in place before the quest for the Goal can advance.

Story Preconditions

In contrast to Prerequisites, Preconditions are like *riders* tacked on to the ends of bills voted on in Congress. With such a bill, the Goal might be to help an endangered species. One of the Requirements would be to pass a bill that gives the species legal status as endangered. One of the Prerequisites would be to get enough votes to pass the bill. One of the Preconditions for getting a block of votes would be to add a rider on the bill that provides subsidies to the tobacco industry. Clearly the rider has nothing to do with the original bill, and might even be philosophically at odds with its intent. But, to get the job done, concessions must be made.

Similarly, Preconditions in a story are non-essential constraints or costs placed on the characters in exchange for the help of someone who controls essential Prerequisites. This might be the only Bedouin who can supply camels so an expedition can cross a desert, who insists they take his uncontrollable daughter with them.

In the movie, THE KARATE KID, the Protagonist is a young boy who wants to be a Karate Champion. To achieve this goal, he must meet the Requirements of winning preliminary bouts. To win these bouts, the Prerequisites are that he receives extra training from a master. The master, who controls this Prerequisite, adds a precondition. He insists the young boy learn new moves by doing chores around the master's house that incorporate those moves, "Wax on... Wax off." Clearly, there are other ways to learn Karate than doing chores, but this Precondition comes from the master's desire for the boy learn humility with his skill.

In Summary

These eight Plot Story Points are the touch points between plot and Theme. Without them, the plot would simply be a series of events that held no particular meaning. With them, the plot supports the thematic argument, and through it touches the other Thematic Story Points such as the Main Character Problem. In this manner, Theme stands as a bridge connecting character to plot so what characters do thematically impacts the progression of events, and events that occur thematically impact the way characters think.

Plot Progression

There are Overall Story Throughline story points, Main Character story points, Impact Character story points and Subjective Story Throughline story points. There are even story points that are the synthesis of all four points of view such as Goal, Requirements, and Consequences. These central story points seem the most plot-like because they affect the Concerns of all four throughlines.

As varied as all of these story points are, there is one quality they share: They stay the same from the beginning to the end of a story. For example, if a story's Goal is Obtaining, that never changes during the story. If the Main Character's Problem is Logic, then Logic is always that character's Problem from "Once on a time" to "They all lived happily ever after." True, the Main Character may solve his Problem, but he will never magically stop being driven by one kind of Problem and start being driven by another. We call Story Points of this stable nature "Static Story Points."

Static Story Points are thematic in nature because they form a bias or commentary on the story as a whole. Even the eight Plot Story Points have a Theme-like feel to them, for they describe what the plot is about. But there is more to plot that this. In fact, there is a different *kind* of appreciation that moves from one issue to another as a story develops. These are called Progressive Plot Points. Through them the story explores the series of events in the Overall Story Throughline. They reveal the growth of the Main Character and the changing nature of the Impact Character's impact. They also show the developing relationship of the Main and Impact Characters in the Subjective Story Throughline.

We can see that each of the four throughlines has, in a sense, a plot of its own, yet they all affect one another in some consistent manner. What is it that makes them separate, yet binds them? A good way to get a feel for this kind of relationship is to think of a story as a football game covered by four different referees. The "real" plot of the game is the series of events that take place on the field. Not one of the four referees can see all the events, for each can only see what is visible from his position. A referee on the opposite side of the field might see interactions that were masked or hidden from the first position, whereas the first referee might report activities not visible from the other side.

Based on what he believes to be happening from his position, each of the referees calls penalties or allows play to continue. Often, the other referees will simply accept that judgment and play will continue. Occasionally though, two or more referees will disagree about what happened simply because the events looked different from each of their perspectives. In this case, the umpire steps in to moderate the referees and settle what the call should be, even if he did not see the play himself.

In stories, each throughline is like one of these referees. Each provides an angle on the events of the story as they unfold. When something appears unfavorable from one of those points of view, the characters in that Throughline cry foul and invoke a penalty to alter the course of action. Each of the throughlines is affected by the series of events that occur, and conversely, each throughline can have an impact on the course of future events. This is how all four throughlines have plots of their own yet affect one another. And, just as the umpire must sometimes step in to settle disagreements, so the author steps in to side with one throughline or another and allow a penalty or revoke it.

In the end, we never see the true plot of the story directly. We see it synthesized as the result of all four throughline plots considered. As Taoist philosophy would explain it, "The Tao that can be spoken is not the eternal Tao." As Dramatica would have it, "The plot that can be seen is not the actual plot."

How then shall we know what must happen in a story's plot? This we can learn by examining the workings of the Progressive Story Points that occur in each throughline. In this manner, we can *plot* the events as seen from each point of view. The synthesis of these into a single understanding of the story's central plot is what occurs in the minds of our audience members as the plots unfolds.

Progressive Story Points

So just what *are* Progressive Story Points? Chances are, you are already familiar with them. They are Acts, Sequences, Scenes, and Events. The Progressive Story Points are not unlike the way we measure time in Days, Hours, Minutes, and Seconds. We can see that a Minute does not stand independently, but *nests* within an Hour, which in turn nests within a Day. Similarly, Scenes are story points that happen within an Act. Events nest in Scenes that nest in Sequences that nest in Acts.

No event stands alone, but bears something of the flavor or identity of the larger units in which it exists and the smaller units it contains. If this begins to sound like the thematic story points we have already explored, it is no accident. Throughline, Concern, Issue, and Problem narrow the issue of the story when we see the story as a state. Act, Sequence, Scene, and Event narrow the issue of the story when we see the story as a process. The Static Story Points tell us what a story is about. The Progressive Story Points tell us how a story unfolds. Taken together, the Static and Progressive Story Points transport a story's meaning.

Acts

Each Class in the Thematic Structure has four Types in the level just below the Class. In the Activity (Physics) Class, for example, the four Types are Learning,

Understanding, Doing, and Obtaining. Because the Activity Class will be assigned as the Throughline of one of the four throughlines, one of these Types will be that throughline's Concern. For this example, let us assume that Activity is the Overall Story Throughline, and the Concern is Obtaining.

Because a Concern is a Static Appreciation, it is felt throughout the story. Therefore, the Overall Story Characters will remain concerned with Obtaining from the beginning to the end of the story. Even so, these characters do not simply sit around concerned with possessing something; rather, they go through a series of endeavors in the attempt to Obtain it (or get rid of it). As it turns out, each of the four Types in a Throughline represents a stage in this attempt.

In our example, the story might begin with the characters Learning something that eventually brings them to an Understanding. Eventually they Understand enough to start Doing something, and when they have Done enough, they just might Obtain whatever it is they are after. The four stages of this endeavor, then, would be Learning, Understanding, Doing, and Obtaining, in that order.

Another story might start with the characters Doing something. Once they have Done enough, they Obtain something. As they come to examine what they have Obtained, an Understanding grows until, after years of accepting what was, they finally begin to Learn again.

The Types in a Throughline can be explored in any order. Each different order, however, will create a different meaning. As an analogy to this, imagine two events: A slap in the face and a scream. A slap followed by a scream might seem as if someone were crying out because of hit. A scream followed by a slap, however, might seem as if someone was hysterical and hit to bring him to his senses. The order in which events occur changes their Progressive meaning, even though their Static meaning might remain the same. This same dynamic holds true for Acts as well, so the order in which we explore the Types changes the Progressive meaning of that throughline's view of the plot at large.

Each Type in a throughline will be the subject matter of one of four Acts in that throughline. The order in which the Types are explored controls the Progressive meaning of that throughline's evolution.

Another View: 3 Act Progressions

Some two thousand years ago, Aristotle proposed that every plot should have a beginning, a middle, and an end. Since then, this notion has evolved into a widely held view there should be three Acts in a complete story. Act one sets up the dramatic potentials. Act two plays these potentials against one another. Act three describes how it all turned out.

At first, a three-act progression might seem in conflict with Dramatica's four act view. As we shall see, however, the two naturally go together.

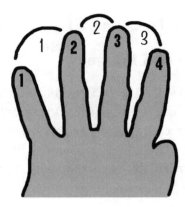

The illustration above shows how a plot that covers four different Acts will automatically produce three different transitions as the subject matter shifts from one concern to the next. In a sense, we might think of a throughline's plot as a road.

At the beginning of the road is the point of departure, City A. At the end of the road is the destination, City D. Along the way are two other cities, B and C. The first leg of the journey begins at City A and ends at City B. The second leg begins at B and ends at C. The final journey begins at City C and ends at the destination, City D.

At each city is a *Signpost* that gives its name. The four signposts in a throughline's plot are the names of the Types. The order in which they will occur in the plot controls where they fall along the road. Between the four signposts are three *Journeys*, each of which described as traveling from one signpost to the next.

Returning to an earlier example, Signposts A, B, C, and D might be Learning, Understanding, Doing, and Obtaining. The Three journeys in this plot would then be Learning—>Understanding, Understanding—>Doing, and Doing—>Obtaining. With four signposts and three journeys, each throughline's plot has *seven* different Progressive Story Points required for that perspective to be complete.

When Aristotle saw a beginning, middle and end, he was seeing Signpost A, all three journeys lumped together, and Signpost D. When successive generations of writers evolved a three-act structure, it became difficult to figure out, "What happens in Act 2?" All three journeys and two of the signposts blended into "the middle". By adopting a Four-Act *structure* that coincides with three *dynamic* acts, the true nature of a throughline's plot is far easier to understand and construct.

Dramatica Act Structures

Dramatica Signposts And Journeys

If we examine the second level of the Dramatica structural model, we see that each throughline has a quad of four items. Dramatica has labels for the quad components of both the three-act structure and the four-act structure.

- The components of the four-act structure are called Signposts.

- The components of the three-act structure are called Journeys.

- There are four Signposts in a four-act structure.

- There are three Journeys in a three-act structure.

MERGING DRAMATICA SIGNPOSTS AND JOURNEYS

Even though signposts and journeys can be seen and understood independently from one another, there are several ways to use them together, each with its own advantages and disadvantages. Writers have a tendency to naturally gravitate toward one of the following methodologies:

Signpost Biased Four-act Structure

In this form, the structure emphasizes the signposts and de-emphasizes the journeys. The signposts take up the bulk of the timeline, breaking the timeline into four not-necessarily-but-usually equally explored acts. The three journeys take the form of transitions between the four signposts, like the joints connecting the bones of an appendage. Even if you do not explicitly explore the journeys, they will be implied by the inherent differences between the explorations of the signposts. This form caters to linearity over holism, emphasizing a writer's use of logistics over a writer's feel for the overall meaning of the story.

Journey Biased Three-act Structure

In this form, the structure emphasizes the journeys and de-emphasizes the signposts. The journeys take up the bulk of the timeline, breaking the timeline into three not-necessarily-but-usually equally explored acts. The four signposts take the form of markers that identify the vague boundaries of the three journeys, like signposts identifying state lines in a cross-country drive. Even if you do not explicitly identify the signposts, they will be implied by the natural changes in "direction" that the journeys make. This form caters to holism over linearity, emphasizing a writer's use of intuition over an attempt to predict the order of events.

Blended Signpost/journey Seven-act Structure

In this form, the structure gives even weight to the signposts and journeys. The timeline is broken into seven not-necessarily-but-usually equally explored acts. This string-of-pearls approach provides a catchall format that blends the two different approaches together. This form offers the best and worst of the three and four-act structures. On the one hand, it ensures that all aspects of the story are explored. On the other hand, it potentially obscures the meaning in the story by providing two, equally balanced contexts. Fortunately, most writers have a natural bias toward the three-act structure or the four-act structure and that bias is usually made evident by an unthinking emphasis of signposts or journeys.

NOTE: The Dramatica software presents the Blended Signpost/Journey structure as a "one-size-fits-all" format, but mitigates it by calling it a four-act structure and emphasizing the signposts.

ACT TRANSITIONS

The transitions between acts as they appear in a quad can be seen as either "straight" or "diagonal."

"Straight" transitions   *"Diagonal" tansitions*

BUMP AND SLIDE

When we look at the straight and diagonal transitions in terms of the dynamic pairs in a quad, we begin to get a "feel" for how smooth or jarring the transition might be.

As was mentioned earlier, the components of a dynamic pair are designed as two ends of a spectrum. The nature of the spectrum is quad content specific. The components of the *co-dynamic pair* represent a related but different spectrum. Because of this difference, transitioning from a component in one dynamic pair to a component of the co-dynamic pair is more noticeable than transitioning between two components within a dynamic pair.

Straight transitions, which move from a component of one dynamic pair to a component of the co-dynamic pair, are relatively noticeable. We describe this transition as a "bump."

Diagonal transitions, which move from one component of a dynamic pair to the other, are relatively smooth. We describe this transition as a "slide."

ACT PATTERNS

When we look at the 1-2-3-4 patterns in terms of their spatial arrangements in a quad, they fall into three distinct patterns: Z's, Hairpins, and U-Turns.

Z-PATTERNS: BUMP-SLIDE-BUMP

A Z pattern is created when the transition between act 1 and 2 is a BUMP, the transition between act 2 and 3 is a SLIDE, and the transition between act 3 and 4 is a BUMP. Here are some examples of the Z pattern in various orientations:

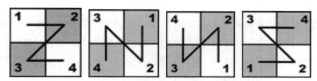

Example Z-Pattern Act Transitions:
BUMP—SLIDE—BUMP

The four-act, Z-pattern structure most closely matches the screenplay/story structure put forward by Syd Field. In his earlier descriptions, he identified a three act structure consisting of an Act 1, a long Act 2 (the slide), and the final Act 3. In a later, modified description of the screenplay act structure, he split the long Act 2 into two parts, thereby more accurately describing the four-act Z-pattern Dramatica structure. This is a popular act progression for modern, American-style, motion picture screenplays.

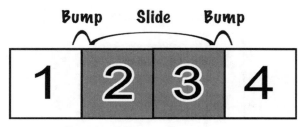

Four-Act Z-Pattern Structure

HAIRPIN PATTERNS: SLIDE-BUMP-SLIDE

A Hairpin pattern is created when the transition between act 1 and 2 is a SLIDE, the transition between act 2 and 3 is a BUMP, and the transition between act 3 and 4 is a SLIDE. Here are some examples of the Hairpin pattern in various orientations:

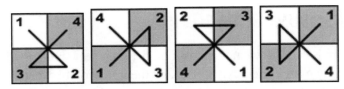

Example Hairpin Pattern Act Transitions: SLIDE—BUMP—SLIDE

The four-act, hairpin pattern structure most closely matches the typical rise and fall story pattern. The first half of the story moves along somewhat smoothly, then there is a noticeable change in the story flow (what we refer to as a "hiccup") and the story goes on in a completely different direction.

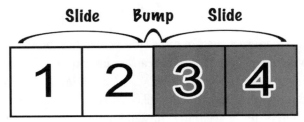

Four-Act Hairpin Pattern Structure

U-TURN PATTERNS: BUMP-BUMP-BUMP

A U-Turn pattern is created when the transition between act 1 and 2 is a BUMP, the transition between act 2 and 3 is a BUMP, and the transition between act 3 and act 4 is a BUMP. Here are some examples of the U-Turn pattern in various orientations:

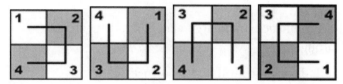

Example U-Turn Pattern Act Transitions: BUMP—BUMP—BUMP

The four-act, U-turn pattern structure most closely matches stories that have an episodic feel to them, such as road stories. Each act transition is pronounced which makes the separation of each act noticeable, emphasizing the segmented nature of the story.

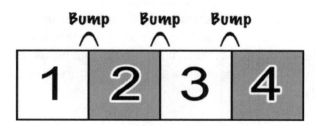

Four-Act U-Turn Pattern Structure

ACT PATTERNS AND THE DRAMATICA THROUGHLINES

Up until now we've referred to the act structures and patterns as if they described an entire story. On the whole, that's the way a story may seem. The reality is far more complex.

- In a Dramatica Grand Argument Story, there are four throughlines.

- Each throughline will have its own act pattern.

- Sometimes these patterns will align and create a predominant pattern.

- Other times the patterns will be wildly different, creating a relatively complex set of act patterns.

The four throughlines in Dramatica are the Overall Story (OS) Throughline, the Main Character (MC) Throughline, the Impact Character (IC) Throughline, and the Subjective Story (SS) Throughline. In the quad structure, the MC and IC throughlines are a dynamic pair, and the OS and SS throughlines are a dynamic pair.

The complexity of patterns is best illustrated through the use of real story examples. The following examples are a sample of the story analyses shipped with the Dramatica Pro software:

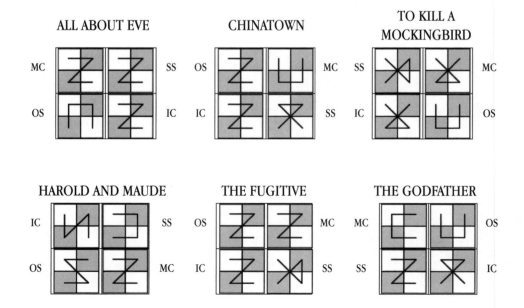

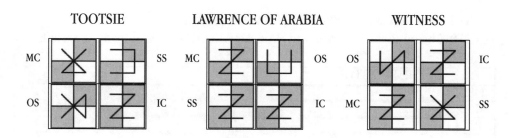

IDENTIFYING SOME FAMILIAR PATTERNS

Some familiar act patterns become apparent when looking at the color-coded, visually blended story timelines. Here is the color coding of the quad we'll use as the color key for the following examples:

TRADITIONAL "SYD FIELD" SCREENPLAY THREE-ACT STRUCTURE—VARIATION I

One of the film's held up as classic proper three-act structure is WITNESS. When we **look** at it's act break structure timeline the reason becomes obvious:

	WITNESS	
OS		Z
MC		Z
IC		Z
SS		H

Three of the four throughlines are the bump-slide-bump type—act 1, long act 2, act three. Not only that, but the relative nature of the three act 1's and act 3's are identical, emphasizing the first and last act turns even further. The relationship in the SS throughline gives a nice accent (and nod) to the midpoint of the story by being a slide-bump-slider.

THE FUGITIVE and HAROLD AND MAUDE also fall into this mold, THE FUGITIVE being slightly simpler and HAROLD AND MAUDE slightly more varied:

	THE FUGITIVE	
OS		Z
MC		Z
IC		Z
SS		H

	HAROLD AND MAUDE	
OS		Z
MC		Z
IC		Z
SS		U

THREE-ACT STRUCTURE-VARIATION II

A popular variation on the traditional three-act structure can be seen in LAWRENCE OF ARABIA and ALL ABOUT EVE.

	LAWRENCE OF ARABIA	
OS		U
MC		Z
IC		Z
SS		Z

	ALL ABOUT EVE	
OS		U
MC		Z
IC		Z
SS		Z

In both these examples, the Overall Story throughlines appear to be more segmented, seemingly more episodic than the traditional three-act structure. Their other throughlines, however, show a remarkable compliance with the bump-slide-bump form. Though more examples will need to be gathered to make anything more definitive, it's possible that this Variation II form is nearly as popular a screenplay form as the Variation I.

OTHER NOTABLE ACT PATTERNS

There are two other "styles" that should be noted at this time. The first one might be tentatively called the "**Complex Act Pattern**." This pattern is complex because of the highly varied combinations of act transition patterns and strong content juxtapositions involved. The two examples from our limited sampling that seem to fit this classification best are CHINATOWN and THE GODFATHER.

	CHINATOWN	
OS		Z
MC		U
IC		Z
SS		H

	THE GODFATHER	
OS		U
MC		U
IC		H
SS		Z

The second notable act pattern is tentatively called the "**Dramatic Arc Pattern**" or "**Rise-and-Fall Act Pattern**" because of its emphasis on the mid-point transition. TO KILL A MOCKINGBIRD is a striking illustration of this act form:

	TO KILL A MOCKINGBIRD	
OS		U
MC		H
IC		H
SS		H

This visualization of TO KILL A MOCKINGBIRD is a particularly accurate view of the film/book. The overall story is segmented, somewhat episodic, while the other throughlines change direction rather rapidly at the story's mid-point. *(The film even has a time transition to identify the story's mid-point.)*

Sequences

Just as Theme has story points that are more character oriented, Progressive Story Points also touch on all four aspects of *The Elements of Structure*. Some story points are more aligned to plot, others that pertain most strongly to genre, and some are closest to the heart of Theme itself.

Acts are the most plot-like of the Progressive Story Points, and therefore fall in the Type level of the structure. Sequences, on the other hand, occur at the Variation level and therefore, like the Issue, are the most Theme-like of the Progressive Story Points.

What Is A Sequence?

Sequences deal with a quad of Variations much as Acts deal with a quad of Types. The quad of interest is the one containing the Issue, as that is the item at the heart of a throughline's Theme. Returning to our example story about an Overall Story Throughline in the Activity Class with a Concern of Obtaining, we shall say the Issue is Morality, as illustrated in the quad below.

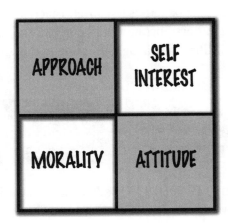

If Morality is the Issue, then Self-Interest is the counterpoint. Theme draws from the balance between items. When examining the quad of Variations containing the Issue, we can see the Issue and counterpoint make up only one pair out of those created in that quad. We have also seen this kind of balance explored in the chapter on Character where we talked about three different kinds of pairs: Dynamic, Companion, and Dependent.

Just as with character quads, we can make two diagonal pairs, two horizontal pairs, and two vertical pairs from the Variations in the Issue quad. For the Morality quad, these six pairs are Morality/Self-Interest, Morality/Attitude, Morality/Approach,

Self-Interest/Attitude, Self-Interest/Approach, and Attitude/Approach. Each of these pairs adds commentary on the relative value of Morality to Self-Interest. Only after we explore all six pairs will the thematic argument be fully made. It could go in a manner as follows:

> ### Morality/Self-Interest
>
> *On face value, which is the better of the two?*
>
> ### Morality/Attitude
>
> *When Morality is the issue, how do we rate the Attitude of those espousing it?*
>
> ### Morality/Approach
>
> *When Morality is the issue, how do we rate the Approach of those espousing it?*
>
> ### Self-Interest/Attitude
>
> *When Self-Interest is the issue, how do we rate the Attitude of those espousing it?*
>
> ### Self-interest/Approach
>
> *When Self-Interest is the issue, how do we rate the Approach of those espousing it?*
>
> ### Attitude/Approach
>
> *Overall, which should carry more weight about this issue?*

By answering each of these questions in a different thematic sequence, the *absolute* value of Morality compared with Self-Interest is argued through the six different *relative* values.

How Sequences Relate To Acts

Three-Act Progressions

With six thematic Sequences and three dynamic Acts, it is not surprising that we find two Sequences each Act. In fact, this is part of what makes an *Act Break* feel like an Act Break. It is the simultaneous closure of a Plot Progression and a Theme Progression. The order in which the six thematic sequences occur does not affect the message of a story, but it does determine the thematic experience for the audience as the story unfolds. The only constraints on order would be that since the Issue is the heart of the thematic argument, one of the three pairs containing the Issue should appear in each of the three dynamic Acts. Any one of the other three pairs can be the other Sequence.

Four-Act Progressions

The three dynamic Acts or Journeys in a throughline's plot represent the experience of traversing the road through the story's issues. The four structural Acts are more like a map of the terrain. Therefore, we associate Types directly with a structural kind of thematic Sequence.

Beneath each Type is a quad of four Variations. Structurally, we examine or judge the Act representing each Type by the four Variations beneath it. In our current example, the Act dealing with Obtaining would be examined in terms of Morality, Self-Interest, Attitude, and Approach. The difference between this and the thematic sequences we have just explored is that we judge Obtaining by each Variation in the quad separately, rather than comparing each Variation with the other Variations in the quad. It is an upward looking evaluation, rather than a sideways looking evaluation.

In this manner, we make a thematic *statement* about the subject matter of concern in each of the four structural Acts. The six Sequences form an *argument* about the appropriateness of different value standards.

Scenes

When we get down to scene resolution, there are so many cross-purposes at work that we need to limit our appreciation of what is going on to see anything in the clutter. First, however, let's touch on some of the forces that obscure the real function of scenes, then strip them away to reveal the dynamic mechanism beneath.

Resolution and Sequence

Earlier we spoke of plot in terms of Types. We also speak of plot here in terms of four resolutions: Acts, Sequences, Scenes, and Events. Both of these perspectives are valid story points *depending on what you need to accomplish*. Because all units in Dramatica relate holographically, no single point of view can completely describe the model. That is why we select the most appropriate view to fit the purpose. Even though looking at plot in terms of Types is useful, it is true that "plot-like" twists and turns are going on at the scene resolution as well. However, these dynamics are not truly *part* of the scene, but merely *in* the scene. An Act, Sequence, Scene, or Event is a temporal container—a box made of time that holds dynamics within its bounds. Much like filters or gratings with different-sized holes, the resolutions "sift" the dynamics trapping large movements at the highest levels and allowing smaller nuances to fall all the way down to the Elements.

What's in a Scene?

At the scene resolution, the effects of Types and Variations are like the tidal pull of some distant moon. But scenes are not the resolution at which to control those forces. Scenes are containers that hold Elements—anything larger cannot get crammed in without breaking. So the richness we feel in scenes is not solely because of what the scene itself contains, but also to the overall impact of what is happening at several larger scales.

What then does a scene contain? Scenes describe the *change* in dynamics between Elements as the story progresses over time. And since Elements are the building blocks of characters, scenes describe the changing relationships between characters.

Characters and Scenes

Characters are made up of Motivations, Methodologies, Means of Evaluation, and Purposes. These terms also describe the four major sets of Elements from which we build the characters. Discovering the driving force of a character in a given scene is valuable, such as whether their argument is over someone's motivations or just the method they are employing.

6 Goes Into 24 Like Theme Goes Into Scenes

We have spoken of the three and four act story points of story. We illustrated how both divisions are valid to specific tasks. When dealing with scenes, we find that no scenes ever hang between two acts, half in one and half in the other, regardless of a three or four act appreciation. This is because there are exactly 24 scenes created at the Element level: Six an act in a four-act appreciation, eight an act in a three-act appreciation. In both cases, the scenes divide evenly into the acts, contributing to the "feel" of each act break being a major turning point in the progress of the story.

Sequences, on the other hand, exist as a six-part partition of the story. Therefore, they divide evenly into a three-act appreciation but not into a four. Since the four-act view is objective, sequences—as they define Thematic movements—are an experiential phenomenon in the subjective appreciation and lose much of their power objectively.

Events

One of the fascinating aspects of the Dramatica model is that it is recursive. It represents one full cycle of considering a problem. In fact, a story's dramatics work in such a way that when you reach the end of the story, you return to reconsider the beginning. Mirroring this looping effect, the smallest dynamic units in the model merge right back into the largest structural units. Time doubles back to meet Space forcing you to decide which one contains the solution.

Events and Throughlines

In Plot, Events are the most defined resolution, yet best described by the most broad stroke structural units: Classes. To recap, there are four Classes: Situation, Fixed Attitude, Activity, and Manipulation. Each is represented as an Event. An Event is an occurrence—something that changes (or remains the same) enough to be noticed by an audience. The dynamics of that incident create dramatic meaning at its most delicate level.

There are four Events within the boundaries of each scene. This means that besides character relationships, each scene must also describe a Situation, an Activity, a Manner of Thinking and a State of Mind. All four Classes should be represented to complete a scene. Immediately, one thinks of action "scenes" that just show something blowing up or deliberation "scenes" where nothing moves. How can these be scenes if they don't contain all four Classes? They can't. In fact, they are Events.

Events Masquerading as Scenes

Twenty-four scenes are *required* for a complete Grand Argument Story. However, if one breaks down those scenes a bit farther, note that 96 Events occur in a complete story as well.

Changing locations during a scene obscures this temporal division of twenty-four scenes. For example, imagine an Activity Event (action) taking place in the jungle. Follow that with a Manipulation Event (deliberation) back home in England. The change in location makes one feel that two different scenes have occurred. Yet, if you design the story well, the Fixed Attitude and Situation Throughlines will also be represented just before, during, or just after changing locations.

Changing locations is part of storyweaving. You have flexibility to bring emphasis to certain aspects of the argument or exploration, and to reduce others. Three Events may occur in one location, followed by the fourth in another. Together, they have filled only one Scene.

The Elements Of

Structure

GENRE

Building Genres

Previously, we have seen that the characteristics, which build the Overall Story Characters, reside at the Element level of the Thematic Structure. Theme itself emanates most strongly from the Variation level. Plot is formed in the Types. It should not be a surprise to find that Genre is most influenced at the Class level. In fact, matching a point of view to a Class creates a story's Throughlines, and it is these Throughlines that have the greatest *structural* impact on Genre.

As one moves up the Dramatica structure, looking from Character to Theme to Plot, the structural components (the Elements, Variations, and Types) take on a *decreasing* significance to the finished work compared with the storytelling aspects involved. Overall Story Characters are easy to define solely in terms of their Elemental dramatic functions. Theme is a bit less tied to the structure as it explores the comparison between dramatic Variations whose balance must be established by the author through storytelling. Plot can be looked at rather precisely in terms of Acts, but is less so when it comes to thematic Sequences. At the Scene resolution of Plot a large part of what goes on is storytelling. At Event resolution, deciding exactly what events ought to occur is almost exclusively storytelling, with the events falling into four broad structural categories.

Following this progression, Genre, which centers on the Class level just above where we find Plot, is the least structural of story qualities. Genre is also the most influenced by storytelling.

In a casual sampling of traditional Genres, we immediately notice that Genre sometimes refers to the setting of a story, as in *Westerns* or *Science Fiction.* Other times, it describes the relationships between characters such as *Love Stories* and *Buddy Pictures*. Genre might refer to the feeling an audience gets from a story as in

Comedy and *Horror Stories*. Even styles of storytelling can have their own Genres like *Musicals* or *Character Studies*.

With all these different duties performed by the word Genre, how can we hope to define it? Video rental stores try to do it. All the old standards are there dividing the movies on their shelves: *Action*, *Drama*, *Children's*. This is fine for picking out what you want to watch some evening, but not much help to authors trying to create stories of their own.

> *Producer: "Write me a war story!"*
> *Writer: "O.K. What do you want, something like* M.A.S.H. *or*
>   PLATOON *or* THE GREAT ESCAPE*?"*

Traditional Genre categories are only useful for grouping finished works. The overall feel of a story is created from a blending of many different components that have an impact on the audience. These range from the underlying dramatic structure (storyform) through the subject matter (encoding) and style (weaving) to audience expectations (reception).

The traditional concept of Genre is most useful to writers by keeping them mindful of the "flavor" of their story, no matter if they are working on character, plot, or theme. Genre would be a lot more useful if it was clearly definable. This is where Dramatica can help.

Dramatica intends to help writers build the deep structure that underlies their stories. This framework functions as the dramatic skeleton on which we build the specifics of a story. Story encoding then places muscle on the skeleton, Story weaving clothes the creation, and Reception affects how the audience might react to such a thing.

When considering Genre from an author's point of view—rather than the traditional audience point of view—the most critical facet will be structural. That is where we lay the foundation on which we build the storytelling. The first step of seeing Genre this way is to look at the four Classes. These four Classes suggest the nature of the subject matter covered in a story's Genre. To recap, the four Classes are:

- **Situation**—an external state; commonly seen as a situation.

- **Activity**—an external process; commonly seen as an activity.

- **Fixed Attitude**—an internal state, commonly seen as a fixed attitude or bias.

- **Manipulation**—an internal process; commonly seen as a manner of thinking or manipulation.

Modes of Expression

Next, we want to consider a new idea: Four *modes of expression* through which we present the story's structure to an audience. The four modes of expression are:

- **Information**—educational tone which focuses the audience on knowledge.

- **Drama**—serious tone which focuses the audience on thought.

- **Comedy**—humorous tone which focuses the audience on ability.

- **Entertainment**—diverting tone which focuses the audience on desire.

The Dramatica Classes describe what the audience sees. The modes describe the light in which they see them. When we match the two categories, we begin to control the feel our story produces within the audience.

This is analogous to the manner in which we create Throughlines by attaching a point of view to a Class. Throughlines are part of the Story Mind itself and represent how a mind shifts its perspective to consider all sides of an issue. Genres, while also creating perspectives, do so outside the Story Mind and represent the four different ways an audience can look *at* the Story Mind as a finished work they are receiving.

The following "Grid of Dramatica Genres," shows the four Dramatica Classes along one axis, and the four modes of expression along the other.

Grid of Dramatica Genres

	Situation	Activity	Fixed Attitude	Manipulation
Information *(Education)*	Where/What it is	How it works	What it means	Why it's important
Drama *(Serious)*	Exploration Drama	Action Drama	Bias Drama	Growth Drama
Comedy *(Humor)*	Situation Comedy	Physical Comedy	Comedy of Manners	Comedy of Errors
Entertainment *(Diversion)*	Entertainment through Atmosphere	Entertainment through Thrills	Entertaining Concept	Entertainment through Twists

- **Where/What it is**—(Information/Situation)—an examination of events and situations with an emphasis on the past, present, progress, and future "state of things" (for example Documentary, Historical and Period Pieces).

- **How it works**—(Information/Activity)—an examination of how specific processes work with an emphasis on instruction (for example Educational, Informational, Instructional).

- **What it means**—(Information/Fixed Attitude)—an examination of opinions and points of view with an emphasis on the context in which they are made (for example Inspirational, Motivational).

- **Why it's important**—(Information/Manipulation)—an examination of value systems with an emphasis on providing context relevant to the audience's personal life (for example Persuasion, Propaganda).

- **Exploration Drama**—(Drama/Situation)—a serious exploration of how the "state of things" is unbalanced (for example Courtroom, Crime, and Classroom dramas).

- **Action Drama**—(Drama/Activity)—a serious take on how problems are created by continuing activities (for example Espionage and War dramas).

- **Bias Drama**—(Drama/Fixed Attitude)—a serious take on what types of conflicts arise from incompatible attitudes (for example Obsession and Prejudice dramas).

- **Growth Drama**—(Drama/Manipulation)—a serious take on the attempts to overcome difficulties resulting from manipulations or evolving identities (for example Coming of Age and Dysfunctional Family dramas).

- **Situation Comedy**—(Comedy/Situation)—humor drawn from the difficulties created by placing characters in some predicament (for example TV Sitcoms).

- **Physical Comedy**—(Comedy/Activity)—pratfalls, slapstick, and other forms of humor drawn from physical activities gone awry (for example The Three Stooges and much of Charlie Chaplin's work)

- **Comedy of Manners**—(Comedy/Fixed Attitude)—humor derived from divergent attitudes, biases, or fixations - often noted as drawing room comedies (for example Jack Benny or Oscar Wilde's THE IMPORTANCE OF BEING ERNEST).

- **Comedy of Errors**—(Comedy/Manipulation)—humor derived from misinterpretation or, in psychological terms, attribution error (for example Abbott and Costello's WHO'S ON FIRST and several Shakespeare comedies including TWELFTH NIGHT).

- **Entertainment through Atmosphere**—(Entertainment/Situation)— entertainment derived from new, unique, or interesting settings or backgrounds (for example Disaster, Fantasy, Horror, Musical, and Science Fiction)

- **Entertainment through Thrills**—(Entertainment/Activity)—entertainment derived from new, unique, or interesting activities/experiences — much like thrill rides at an amusement park (for example Action Adventure, Suspense)

- **Entertaining Concept**—(Entertainment/Fixed Attitude)—entertainment derived from new, unique, or interesting ideas (for example High Concept piece)

- **Entertainment through Twists**—(Entertainment/Manipulation)—entertainment derived from new, unique, or interesting forms of audience manipulation (for example Mysteries, Thrillers)

This grid illustrates how the mode of expression can change the impact a Class will have on an audience. If the Activity Class is expressed in terms of Information it would seem like a "How to" story. If we choose Comedy as the mode of expression, however, the Activity Class looks more like a story involving physical humor or "slapstick."

The beauty of the grid is that it provides authors with a "shopping list" of the kinds of impact they may wish to have on their audience. Take time to examine the table fully. Look at the brief explanation of each mode/Class combination. Unlike most of the previous information in this book, this table lends itself to an intuitive feel that ties in much more closely with the *Art of Storytelling* than with the *Elements of Structure*.

Taken together, Classes and modes of expression determine the feel of the subject matter in a story. Still, there is one aspect of Genre remaining: Positioning the audience in relationship to the subject matter. To do this, we can make use of the four Dramatica *Throughlines*. As a brief recap, they are:

- Main Character Throughline—the first person point of view (I) matched with a Class, this Throughline provides the audience with a "down in the trenches," personal view of the story.

- Impact Character Throughline—the second person point of view (you) matched with a Class, this Throughline provides the audience with a "what's impacting me," impersonal view of the story.

- Subjective Story Throughline—the first person plural point of view (we) matched with a Class, this Throughline provides the audience with a "what's it like to be in this type of a relationship," passionate view of the story.

- Overall Story Throughline—the third person point of view (they) matched with a Class, this Throughline provides the audience with a "big picture," dispassionate view of the story.

By positioning the audience's four points of view on the Class/modes of expression grid, we can accurately predict the feel our story will have.

EXAMPLE #1:

	Situation	Activity	Fixed Attitude	Manipulation
Comedy (Humor)	Situation Comedy	Physical Comedy	Comedy of Manners	Comedy of Errors
(Throughlines)	Overall Story	Main Character	Subjective Story	Impact Character

Suppose we wanted to write a Comedy with the Overall Story Throughline of Situation and the Main Character Throughline of Activity. We could assign all the Throughlines to the grid in the Comedy mode of expression like above.

If we were good storytellers, all four throughlines would have a consistently humorous (comedic) feel to them. The Overall Story would be a situation comedy;

the Main Character would be a physically goofy or funny person (e.g. Stanley Ipkiss in THE MASK). The Impact Character might be someone constantly mistaken for someone else or mistaking the Main Character for someone else. The Subjective Story relationship between the Main and Impact Characters would be conflicting over silly or exaggerated differences of opinion.

Though a story like this covers all the storyforming bases, its single mode of expression lacks the emotional depth that comes from variety. This monotone form of storytelling is fine (and often preferable) for some forms of storytelling. Many audiences, however, prefer to have greater variety of expression in their stories. As it stands, this example story lacks any educational intent (Information), any sense of seriousness (Drama), and any pure diversions (Entertainment).

How does one diversify? Assign each Throughline to a different mode of expression.

A story of such a completely mixed arrangement has no single, overriding feel to it. What it gives up in consistency, however, it gains in variety.

The Overall Story (Situation/Entertainment) set in some unique or viscerally intriguing setting (perhaps a Western, the distant future, or the dark side of the moon) in which something is amiss. In this setting we find our Main Character (Activity/Comedy), perhaps clumsy (for example Inspector Clouseau from THE PINK PANTHER), or excessively active like ACE VENTURA. Providing a contrast to the humorous nature of the Main Character is the serious impact of Impact Character's manipulations (Manipulation/Drama). Finally, we add the Subjective Story relationship (Fixed Attitude/Information) as it describes how the Main and Impact Characters' fixed attitudes conflict over "what it all means."

This is the heart of Dramatica's approach to Genre. At its most basic level it is a choice between four modes of expression. At its most exciting and elegant, it concerns the sophisticated relationship and dynamics created when we bring together the four modes of expression, the four structural Classes, and the four Throughlines. The Class/modes of expressions grid allows authors to select Throughlines using their feelings and intuition. By carefully setting these Dramatica relationships in a story, you can create a powerful Genre experience for your audience with exactly the impact you intended.

Finally, there is a greater depth to Dramatica theory that offers more information about what is really going on in Genre. It may be more than you need to consider for your style of writing and the kinds of stories you create. If you'd like to explore this final aspect of *The Elements of Structure*, read on.

The Class/modes of expression table we have been using makes it appear as if a throughline must remain in one mode for the full duration of a story. In fact, this is only the Static Story Points of Genre. In practice, the Genre of a story develops as the story unfolds. It may "appear" to be simply a Drama as it begins. When it is over it will have defined exactly what kind of Drama it is.

Beginning as one among a broadly identifiable group of stories and ending where no other story has gone before, each story develops its own *unique* Genre. The manner by which this happens relates to the *Progressive Story Points* of Genre, which we will now explore.

First, once you assign a throughline to a Class, creating a Throughline, that particular combination remains for the entire story. Therefore, when we examine how the Mode/Class table is laid out, we can see that each Throughline will fall in a vertical column and stay there. We see the Progressive nature of Genre when each Throughline *slides* up and down its particular column so during the story it may touch on all four modes of expression. Each Throughline always in its same Class gives them consistency; the ability to shift modes of expression gives them versatility.

Just as with Progressive Plot story points there *are* limits to how a Throughline can move from one mode to another. Like the Acts in Plot, Throughlines must move through modes of expression in a particular order. The rule of thumb is that a Throughline cannot *skip over* a mode (according to the order used in the table) but must go through each mode of expression in between to get to the desired one.

This limit is real. Neither the human mind nor the Story Mind can shift mental gears from first gear to third gear without going through second gear. Modes of expression are largely emotional concerns. The human mind must be allowed to experience the transition from one emotional state to the next if it is to feel natural.

A good example of the awkwardness that results from ignoring this rule of thumb exists in the motion picture, HUDSON HAWKE, starring Bruce Willis. The filmmakers made a brave effort to break convention and have a serious heist thriller jumbled up with comedy and even song and dance numbers in the middle of a robbery! This might have worked, had the audience gone through the intermediate modes. Alas, such was not the case and therefore the story simply came out jumbled and impossible to get a grip on emotionally.

Please note that sometimes an author wants to shock an audience. This can be carried out in several ways, including breaking structure or skipping the transitional modes of expression. We explore these kinds of techniques fully in the Storyweaving section of *The Art of Storytelling*. For now, we'll limit our discussion to what a consistent progression of Genre would be.

If you have closely examined the table, you may have wondered if the mode at the top (Information) could ever connect to the mode at the bottom (Entertainment) without having to go through both Drama and Comedy first. The answer to this question is, "Yes."

If you were to clip the Class/modes of expression table out of this book (not recommended!) you could bend it around from top to bottom to make a cylinder. When presented in this form, Information appears right next to Entertainment *and* Drama. So, during a story, a single Throughline might shift up or down or all around, as long as it stays within its Class column.

Taken together, all four Throughlines could shift from scene to scene into different relative positions, not unlike a combination lock, making the story all comedic at one time, serio-comic at another, and so on. By the end of the story, the progressive shift of Throughlines provides the combination for the unique Genre of a story.

SECTION II

The Art of Storytelling

Foundations

Introduction to Storytelling

All complete stories show evidence of two principal facets: An underlying dramatic structure contains the story's inherent meaning, and a secondary meaning created by the manner in which that structure is presented in words and symbols. In practice, neither aspect of story can exist without the other. Structure, which is not tangible in form, cannot be communicated directly, and similarly no mode of expression can be created without something to express.

The first half of this book explored *The Elements Of Structure*. Its purpose was to define the essential components that occur in the dramatic structure of all complete stories. These components fell into four principal categories: Character, Theme, Plot, and Genre.

This half of the book explores *The Art Of Storytelling*, which documents the process of conceptualizing and telling a story. This process passes through four distinct stages: Storyforming, Storyencoding, Storyweaving, and Story Reception.

An author might begin either with Structure or Storytelling, depending on his personal interests or style.

If you come to a word or idea that is unfamiliar or unclear, use the index to reference that topic in *The Elements Of Structure*. Also, don't forget to take advantage of the extensive appendices at the back of the book.

The Four Stages of Communication

There are four stages of communication that stand between an author and an audience. Stage one is Storyforming, in which the arrangement and sequence of dramatic story points are determined. Stage two is encoding (Storyencoding) where the storyform story points are translated into topics and events that symbolize the essential dramatic concepts in terms the author expects has meaning to an audience. Stage three is Storyweaving, where all the independent illustrations are woven together into an integrated whole that is the story as it will be presented to an audience. Stage four is Story Reception in which the audience assigns meaning to the work, hopefully decoding the intent of the author with some degree of accuracy.

In bringing a story to an audience, through any media, there are four distinct stages of communication through which the story will pass. When an author is developing a story or looking for ways in which to improve it, a good idea to evaluate how the story is working at each of these stages individually. Problems can exist in any single stage or bridge across into many. Seeing where the problem lies is half the work of fixing it.

The Four Stages are:

Stage 1: Storyforming—where the structural design and dynamic settings of an idea are created. This is where the original meaning of the story is born, the meaning that the author wants to communicate.

Stage 2: Storyencoding—where the symbols with which the author will work are chosen. Stories are presented through characters, setting, and other details that symbolize the meaning of the story. No symbols are inherently part of any storyform, so the choices of how a particular storyform is Storyencoded must be considered carefully.

Stage 3: Storyweaving—where the author selects an order and emphasis to use in presenting his encoded story to his audience in the final work. The way in which to deliver a story to an audience, piece by piece, involves decisions about what to present first, second, and last. The potential tactics are countless. You may start with the beginning, as in STAR WARS, or you my start with the end, as in REMAINS OF THE DAY, or with some combination, as in THE USUAL SUSPECTS. What you most want the audience to be thinking about will guide your decisions in this stage, because choices made here have the most effect on the experience of receiving the story as an audience member.

Stage 4: Story Reception—where the audience takes over, interpreting the symbols they've received and making meaning of the story. The audience is an active participant in its relationship with a story. It has preconceptions which affect how it will see anything put in front of it. The audience is presented with a finished, Storywoven work and hopes to be able to interpret the work's symbols and decipher the Storyforming intent of the authors behind the work. The accuracy with which this is carried out has a lot to do with how the story was developed in the other three stages of communication.

There are many ways to play with any one of these stages and many reasons for doing so. It all depends on what impact the author wants to make with his work.

Genre, Plot, Theme, and Character

In each of the four stages of story communication, authors have recognized four aspects of storytelling at work: Genre, Plot, Theme and Character. In other words, first there must be a Storyforming stage in which the author designs Genre, Plot, Theme, and Character as dramatic concepts. Next is the Encoding stage where the author symbolizes Genre, Plot, Theme, and Character into the language of the culture. Stage three, Storyweaving, sees the author blend the symbolic representations into a seamless flow that presents the symbols for Genre, Plot, Theme, and Character to an audience. The final stage of Reception puts the audience to work decoding the symbols to understand the author's intent as represented in Genre, Plot, Theme, and Character.

Naturally, with so many internal steps and story points, the opportunity for miscommunication is great. In addition, since the audience members are looking from stage four back to stage one, they are authors of their own Reception. In this role the audience may create meaning fully supported by the symbology, yet never intended by the author.

How Dramatica Fits In

The study of Reception theory is well documented in many books, articles, and essays. Many inspired teachers of the art, including Aristotle himself, brilliantly cover the process of storytelling. Dramatica provides a view of story never before seen so clearly: An actual model of the structure and dynamics that exists at the heart of communication—the Story Mind itself. By using the structure of story as a foundation, the process of communication becomes much more accurate, giving the author more control over the audience experience.

Author as Audience

With the author at one end of the communication chain and the audience at the other, it is not unusual for an author to cast himself in the role of audience to see how the story is working. In other words, many authors approach their story not so much as the creator of the work, but as its greatest fan. They look at the blended result of Storyforming, Storyencoding, Storyweaving and Story Reception and judge the combined impact even as they write it. This can be valuable in making sure that all stages of communication are working together, but it carries hidden dangers.

When an author adopts the audience perspective, he compresses all four stages together. Thus, Genre, Plot, Theme, and Character become complete, yet their components become indistinct and much harder to define. This makes it easy to tell if something is going wrong, but much harder to discover which part of the process is at fault.

To avoid this problem, Dramatica suggests first building a Storyform that spells out the dramatic story points necessary to fashion a complete argument in line with one's intent. Then, referring to this structure while encoding (or symbolizing) the storyform, an author can make sure that missing or inconsistent pieces of the storyform are not masked under clever storytelling.

Emphasis Where Emphasis is Due

Storyencoding simply creates scenarios and events that illustrate the Storyform's dramatic story points. In the Storyencoding stage, no illustration is more important than another. The nature of the illustration provides the emphasis. For example, a Goal of Obtaining might be encoded as the attempt to win a fifty-dollar prize or the effort to win the presidency of a country.

Further emphasis occurs in the third phase of communication, Storyweaving, when an author places the illustrated story points into the work, favoring some with extended coverage while de-emphasizing others with mere lip service. Portions of a Storyform structure more central to an author's personal interests rise to the surface of the work. Those story points of less interest sink to the bottom to form a complete but minimalist foundation for the story's argument.

In short, it is fine to stand back and admire one's handiwork, criticize it, and see if all its parts are working together. The audience point of view, however, is not a good perspective from which to fashion a work.

In keeping with this philosophy, this book began by outlining *The Elements Of Structure*. Now it is time to shift mental gears and outline the process of communication itself as expressed in *The Art Of Storytelling*.

The Art of Storytelling
STAGE ONE

STORYFORMING

Introduction to Storyforming

Inspiration

When an author begins work on a story, he seldom has the whole thing figured out in advance. In fact, he might start with nothing more than a bit of action, a scrap of dialogue, or perhaps only a title. The urge to write springs from some personal interest one wants to share. It could be an emotion, an experience, or a point of view on a particular subject matter. Once inspiration strikes, however, there is the compelling desire to find a way to communicate what one has in mind.

Another thing usually happens along the way. One creative thought leads to another, and the scope of what one wishes to communicate grows from a single item into a collection of items. Action suggests dialogue that defines a character that goes into action, and on and on. Eventually, an author finds himself with a bag of interesting dramatic elements, each of which is intriguing, but not all of which connect. It is at this point an author's mind shifts gears and looks at the emerging work as an analyst rather than as a creator.

Structure

The author as analyst examines what he has so far. Intuitively he can sense that some structure is developing. The trick now is to get a grip on the "big picture." Four aspects of this emerging story become immediately clear: Character, Theme, Plot, and Genre. An author may find the points of view expressed by certain characters are unopposed in the story, making the author's point of view seem heavy-handed and biased. In other places, logic fails, and the current explanation of how point A got to point C is incomplete. He may also notice that some kind of overall theme is partially developed, and the entire work could be improved by shading more dramatic elements with the same issues.

So far, our plucky author has still not created a story. Oh, there's one in there somewhere, but there's much to do to bring it out. For one thing, certain items he's developed may begin to seem out of place. They don't fit in with the feel of the work as a whole. Also, certain gaps have become obvious which beg to be filled.

In addition, parts of a single dramatic item may work and other parts may not. For example, a character may ring true at one moment, but turn into a clunker the next.

Having analyzed, then, the author sets about curing the ailments of his work in the attempt to fashion it into a complete and unified story. Intuitively, an author will examine all the logical and emotional aspects of his story, weed out irregularities and fill in cracks until nothing seems out of place in his considerations. Just as one might start with any piece of a jigsaw puzzle, so the story eventually fills the author's heart and mind as a single, seamless, and balanced item, greater than its parts. In the end, a larger picture emerges. The story takes on an identity all its own.

Communication

Looking at the finished story, we can tell two things right off the bat. First, there is a certain logistic dramatic structure to the work. Second, that structure is expressed in a particular way. In Dramatica, we call that underlying deep dramatic structure a *Storyform*. The manner in which it is communicated is the *Storytelling*.

As an example of how the Storyform differs from the Storytelling, consider ROMEO AND JULIET and WEST SIDE STORY. The dramatics of both stories are essentially the same, yet the expression of those dramatics is different. Storytelling dresses the dramatics in different clothes, couches the message in specific contexts, and brings added non-structure material to the work.

The structure of a story is like a vacant apartment. Everything is functional, but it doesn't have a personality until someone moves in. Over the years, any number of people might occupy the same rooms, working within the same functionality but making the environment uniquely their own. Similarly, the same dramatic structures have been around for a long time. Yet, every time we dress them up in a way we haven't seen before, they become new again. So, part of what we find in a finished work is the actual Grand Argument Story "form" and part is the Storytelling.

The problems most writers face arise from the fact that the creative process works on both storyform and storytelling at the same time. The two become inseparably blended, so trying to figure out what needs fixing is like trying to determine the recipe for quiche from the finished pie. It can be done, but it is tough work. What is worse, an author's personal tastes and assumptions often blind him to some of the obvious flaws in the work, while overemphasizing others. This can leave an author running around in circles, getting nowhere.

Fortunately, another pathway exists. Because the eventual storyform outlines all the essential feelings and logic produced by a story, an author can begin by creating a storyform first. Then, all that follows will work together because it is built on a consistent and solid foundation.

To create a storyform, an author needs to decide about the kinds of topics he wishes to explore and the kinds of impact he wishes to have on his audience. This can sometimes be a daunting task. Most authors prefer to stumble into the answers to these questions during the writing process, rather than deliberate over them in advance. Still, with a little consideration up front, much grief can be prevented later as the story develops.

If you're a non-structural writer, try writing first and create the storyform afterward.

Audience Impact

There are eight questions about a story that are so important and powerful that we refer to them as the *essential* questions. Determining the answers to these can instantly clarify an embryonic story idea into a full-fledged story concept. Four of the questions refer to the Main Character and four refer to the overall Plot. Taken together, they crystallize how a story feels when it is over, and how it feels getting there.

Choosing Without Losing

When given multiple choices in Dramatica, choosing an answer does not exclude the remaining choices. A grand argument story has all the pieces in every story. Making choices arranges the structural items with the story points. All dynamic choices appear in every story. Where they appear and how they relate to the story are controlled by the choices you make.

Character Dynamics

Both structure and dynamics can be seen at work in characters. We see structural relationships most easily in the Objective Characters who serve to illustrate fixed dramatic relationships that define the potentials at work in a story from an objective point of view. We see dynamic relationships more easily in the Subjective Characters who serve to illustrate growth in themselves and their relationships over the course of a story.

The Subjective Characters are best described by the forces that drive them, rather than by the characteristics they contain. These forces are most clearly seen (and therefore best determined) for the Main Character. There are four Dynamics that determine the nature of the Main Character's problem-solving efforts. The four Character Dynamics specify the shape of the Main Character's growth. Let's explore each of the four essential character dynamics and their impact on the story as a whole.

Main Character Resolve: Change or Steadfast?

The first Essential Character Dynamic determines if the Main Character is a changed person at the end of a story. From an author's perspective, selecting Change or Steadfast sets up the kind of argument made about the effort to solve the story's problem.

There are two principal approaches through which an author can illustrate the best way to solve the Problem explored in a story. One approach is to show the proper way of going about solving the Problem. The other is to show the wrong way to solve the Problem.

- To illustrate the proper way, your Main Character must hold on to his Resolve and remain Steadfast if he is to succeed, because he believes he is on the right path.

- To illustrate the improper way of dealing with a Problem, your Main Character must change to succeed, for he believes he is going about it the wrong way.

Of course, Success is not the only Outcome that can happen to a Main Character. Another way to illustrate that an approach for dealing with a Problem is proper would be to have the Main Character Change his way of going about it and fail. Similarly, a Main Character that remains Steadfast and fails can illustrate the improper way.

So, choosing Change or Steadfast has nothing directly to do with being correct or mistaken; it just describes whether the Main Character's final Resolve is to stay the course or try a different tack.

Just because a Main Character should remain Steadfast does not mean he doesn't consider changing. In fact, the alternative to give up or alter his approach in the face of ever-increasing opposition is a constant temptation.

Even if the Main Character remains steadfast despite difficulties and suffering, the audience may still not want him to succeed. This is because simply being steadfast does not mean one is correct.

If the audience sees that a character remains steadfast yet misguided, the audience will hope for his eventual failure.

Similarly, a Change Main Character does not mean he is changing all the time. Usually, the Change Main Character will resist change until he's forced to choose. At that point, the Main Character must choose to continue down his original path, or to jump to the new path by accepting change in himself or his outlook.

Regardless of the benefits to be had by remaining steadfast, the audience will want the Change Main Character finally to succeed if he is on the wrong path and changes. However, if he does not change, the audience will want him to lose all the benefits he thought he had gained.

Your selection of Change or Steadfast has wide-ranging effects on the dynamics of your story. Such things as the relationship between the Overall Story and Subjective Story Throughlines link to this dynamic. Even the order of exploration of your thematic points adjusts in the Dramatica model to create and support your Main Character's decision to change or remain steadfast.

Examples of Main Character Resolve:

Change Characters: Hamlet in HAMLET; *Frank Galvin in* THE VERDICT; *Wilber in* CHARLOTTE'S WEB; *Rick in* CASABLANCA; *Michael Corleone in* THE GODFATHER; *Scrooge in* A CHRISTMAS CAROL; *Nora in* A DOLL'S HOUSE

Steadfast Characters: Laura Wingfield in THE GLASS MENAGERIE; *Jake Gittes in* CHINATOWN; *Clarice Starling in* THE SILENCE OF THE LAMBS; *Chance Gardener in* BEING THERE; *Job in the* BIBLE.

The Impact Character Resolve

The Impact Character) has a Resolve that is the inverse of the Main Character's. When the Main Character is a Change character, the Impact Character remains Steadfast (such as the Ghosts in A CHRISTMAS CAROL, Viola De Lesseps in SHAKESPEARE IN LOVE, and the steadfast Impact of Ricky Fitts in AMERICAN BEAUTY). When the Main Character remains Steadfast, the Impact Character CHANGEs (such as Sam Gerard in THE FUGITIVE, Blanche Hudson in WHATEVER HAPPENED TO BABY JANE?, and Raymond Shaw in THE MANCHURIAN CANDIDATE). It is not important whether it's the steadfastness of one character that forces the change in the other, or the change in one that supports the steadfastness of the other. What is important is that the inverse relationship between the Main Character's Resolve and the Impact Character's Resolve provides a key point of reference for an audience's understanding of your story's meaning.

Examples of Impact Character Resolve:

Steadfast Characters: The Ghost of King Hamlet in HAMLET; *Laura Fischer in* THE VERDICT; *Charlotte in* CHARLOTTE'S WEB; *Ilsa in* CASABLANCA; *Kaye Corleone in* THE GODFATHER; *The Ghosts in* A CHRISTMAS CAROL; *Torvald in* A DOLL'S HOUSE

Change Characters: Jim O'Connor in THE GLASS MENAGERIE; *Evelyn Mulwray in* CHINATOWN; *Hannibal Lechter in* THE SILENCE OF THE LAMBS; *Dr. Allenby in* BEING THERE; *Satan in the* BIBLE.

Main Character Growth: Stop or Start?

The second essential question determines the direction of the Main Character's growth.

While the Main Character Resolve focuses on the results of the MC's response to his inequity, the part of Dramatica that focuses on the Main Character's "character arc" is call the Main Character Growth.

Like any well constructed argument, you must build to your conclusions—you can't just jump right to the end and expect anyone to accept it. The Main Character must go through the process of growth that gets him to a position where he can see the problem for what it is and deal with it directly.

Whether a Main Character eventually Changes his nature or remains Steadfast, he will still grow over the course of the story, as he develops new skills and understanding. This growth has a direction.

Either he will grow into something (Start) or grow out of something (Stop).

A Change Main Character grows either by adding a characteristic he lacks (Start) or by dropping a characteristic he already has (Stop). Either way, his makeup alters in nature. As an example we can look to Ebeneezer Scrooge in Dickens' A CHRISTMAS CAROL.

Does Scrooge need to Change because he is miserly or because he lacks generosity? Scrooge's problems do not stem from his active greed, but from his passive lack of compassion. It is not that he is on the attack, but that he does not actively seek to help others. This reflects a need to Start, rather than Stop. This difference is important to place the focus of conflict so it supports the overall argument of the story.

In contrast, Steadfast Main Characters will not add nor delete a characteristic, but will grow either by holding on against something bad, waiting for it to Stop, or by holding out until something good can Start.

For a Steadfast Character, growth is not a matter of Change, but a matter of degree. Change is still of concern to him but in his environment, not in himself. Conversely, a Change Character actually alters his being, under the influence of situational considerations. This helps clarify why it is often falsely thought that a Main Character MUST Change, and why Steadfast characters are thought not to grow.

To develop growth in a Main Character properly, one must decide whether he is Change or Steadfast and at the direction of the growth.

A good way to get a feel for this dynamic in Change Characters is to picture the Stop character as having a chip on his shoulder and the Start character as having a hole in his heart. If the actions or decisions taken by the character are what make the problem worse, then he needs to Stop. If the problem worsens because the character fails to take certain *obvious* actions or decisions, then he needs to Start.

Of course, to the character, neither of these perspectives on the problem is *obvious*, as he must grow and learn to see it. Often the audience sees another view the character does not get: The objective view. The audience can empathize with the character's failure to see himself as the source of the problem even while recognizing that he should or should not change. It is here that Start and Stop register with the audience as being obvious.

Essentially, if you want to tell a story about someone who learns he has been making the problem worse, choose Stop. If you want to tell a story about someone who has allowed a problem to become worse, choose Start.

A Steadfast Main Character's Resolve needs to grow regardless of Start or Stop. If he is a Start Character, he will be tempted by signs the wanted outcome is not going to happen or is unattainable. If he is a Stop Character, he will find himself pressured to *give in*.

Remember that we see Growth in a Steadfast Character largely in his environment. We see his personal growth as a matter of degree.

Examples of Main Character Growth:

Start Characters: *Laura Wingfield in* THE GLASS MENAGERIE; *Rick in* CASABLANCA; *Scrooge in* A CHRISTMAS CAROL; *Nora in* A DOLL'S HOUSE

Stop Characters: *Hamlet in* HAMLET; *Frank Galvin in* THE VERDICT; *Wilber in* CHARLOTTE'S WEB; *Jake Gittes in* CHINATOWN; *Clarice Starling in* THE SILENCE OF THE LAMBS; *Chance Gardener in* BEING THERE; *Job in* THE BIBLE; *Michael Corleone in* THE GODFATHER

Main Character Approach: Do-er or Be-er?

The third essential question determines the Main Character's preferential approach to problem solving.

By temperament, Main Characters (like each of us) have a preferential method of approaching Problems. Some would rather adapt their environment to themselves through action; others would rather adapt their environment to themselves through strength of character, charisma, and influence.

There is nothing intrinsically right or wrong with either Approach, yet it does affect how one will respond to Problems.

Choosing "Do-er" or "Be-er" does not prevent a Main Character from using either Approach, but merely defines the way they are likely to first Approach a

Problem. The Main Character will only use the other method if their preferred method fails. Having a preference does not mean being less able in the other area.

Do not confuse Do-er and Be-er with active and passive. If we see a Do-er as active physically, we see a Be-er as active mentally. While the Do-er jumps in and tackles the problem by physical maneuverings, the Be-er jumps in and tackles the problem with mental deliberations. For example, Harry Calahan in DIRTY HARRY is an aggressive Do-er. A bank robbery happens while he eats lunch. He walks out and shoots some bad guys, all the time munching on his hot dog—definitely an active Do-er. Hamlet, from William Shakespeare's HAMLET, is a classic Be-er. His approach to expose his murderous uncle is to change himself by pretending to be crazy. He's so aggressive with his "being" that it drives his girlfriend insane.

The point is not which one is more motivated to hold his ground but how he tries to hold it.

A Do-er would build a business by the sweat of his brow.

A Be-er would build a business by attention to the needs of his clients.

Obviously both Approaches are important, but Main Characters, just like the real people they represent, will have a preference.

A martial artist might choose to avoid conflict first as a Be-er character, yet be capable of beating the tar out of an opponent if avoiding conflict proved impossible.

Similarly, a schoolteacher might stress exercises and homework as a Do-er character, yet open his heart to a student who needs moral support.

When creating your Main Character, you may want someone who acts first and asks questions later, or you may prefer someone who avoids physical conflict if possible, then lays waste the opponent if they won't compromise.

A Do-er deals in competition, a Be-er in collaboration.

The Main Character's affect on the story is both one of rearranging the dramatic potentials of the story, and one of reordering the sequence of dramatic events.

Examples of Main Character Approach:

Do-er Characters: Frank Galvin in THE VERDICT; *Wilber in* CHARLOTTE'S WEB; *Jake Gittes in* CHINATOWN; *Clarice Starling in* THE SILENCE OF THE LAMBS; *Michael Corleone in* THE GODFATHER.

Be-er Characters: Laura Wingfield in THE GLASS MENAGERIE; *Rick in* CASABLANCA; *Scrooge in* A CHRISTMAS CAROL; *Hamlet in* HAMLET; *Chance Gardener in* BEING THERE; *Job in the* BIBLE; *Nora in* A DOLL'S HOUSE.

Main Character Mental Sex: Male or Female?

The fourth Essential Character Question determines a Main Character's problem-solving techniques to be linear or holistic.

Much of what we do as individuals is learned behavior. Yet, the basic operating system of the mind is cast biologically before birth as being more sensitive to space or time. Each of us has a sense of how things are arranged (space) and how things are going (time), but which one filters our thinking determines our Mental Sex as being Male or Female, respectively.

Male Mental Sex describes spatial thinkers who tend to use linear Problem solving as their method of choice. They set a specific Goal, determine the steps necessary to achieve that Goal, and then embark on the effort to carry out those steps.

Female Mental Sex describes temporal thinkers who tend to use holistic Problem solving as their method of choice. They get a sense of the way they want things to be, find out how things need to balance to bring about those changes, and then make adjustments to create that balance.

While life experience, conditioning, and personal choice can go a long way toward counterbalancing those sensitivities, underneath all our experience and training the tendency to see things chiefly in terms of space or time remains. In dealing with the psychology of Main Characters, it is essential to understand the foundation on which their experience rests.

How can we illustrate the Mental Sex of our Main Character? The following point-by-point comparison provides some clues:

Female: Looks at motivations	*Male:* Looks at purposes
Female: Tries to see connections	*Male:* Tries to gather evidence
Female: Sets up conditions	*Male:* Sets up requirements
Female: Determines the leverage points that can restore balance	*Male:* Breaks a job into steps
Female: Seeks fulfillment	*Male:* Seeks satisfaction
Female: Concentrates on "Why" and "When"	*Male:* Concentrates on "How" and "What"
Female: Puts the issues in context	*Male:* Argues the issues
Female: Tries to hold it all together	*Male:* Tries to pull it all together

In stories, more often than not, physical gender matches Mental Sex. Occasionally, however, gender and Mental Sex are cross-matched to create unusual and interesting characters. For example, Ripley in ALIEN and Clarice Starling in THE SILENCE OF THE LAMBS are Male Mental Sex women. Tom Wingo in THE PRINCE OF TIDES and Jack Ryan in THE HUNT FOR RED OCTOBER are Female

Mental Sex men. In most episodes of THE X FILES, Scully (the female F.B.I. agent) is Male Mental Sex and Mulder (the male F.B.I. agent) is Female Mental Sex, which explains part of the series' unusual feel. Note that Mental Sex has nothing to do with a character's sexual preferences or tendency toward being masculine or feminine in mannerism —it simply deals with the character's problem-solving techniques.

Sometimes stereotypes are spread by what an audience expects to see, which filters the message and dilutes the truth. By placing a female psyche in a physically male character or a male psyche in a physically female character, preconceptions no longer prevent the message from being heard. On the downside, some audience members may have trouble relating to a Main Character whose problem-solving techniques do not match the physical expectations.

Examples of Main Character Mental Sex:

Female Mental Sex Characters: *Laura Wingfield in* THE GLASS MENAGERIE; *Nora in* A DOLL'S HOUSE

Male Mental Sex Characters: *Frank Galvin in* THE VERDICT; *Wilber in* CHARLOTTE'S WEB; *Jake Gittes in* CHINATOWN; *Clarice Starling in* THE SILENCE OF THE LAMBS; *Michael Corleone in* THE GODFATHER; *Rick in* CASABLANCA; *Scrooge in* A CHRISTMAS CAROL; *Hamlet in* HAMLET; *Chance Gardener in* BEING THERE; *Job in the* BIBLE

Wrapping Up Character Dynamics

We have presented four simple questions. Knowing the answers to these questions provides a strong sense of guidelines for an author in framing his message. The one seeming drawback is that each of the questions appears binary in nature, which can easily lead to concerns that this kind of approach produces an excessively structured or formulaic story. One should keep in mind that this is just the first stage of communication. Storyforming creates a solid structure on which the other three stages can be built.

As we advance through this process, we shall learn how the remaining three stages bring shading, tonality, and more of a gray-scale feel to each of these questions. For example, the question of Resolve leads to other questions in each of the other stages. One question controls how *strongly* the Main Character has embraced change or how weakly he now clings to his steadfastness. Another controls how big the scope of the change is or how small the attitudes that didn't budge are. Yet another controls how much change or steadfast matters to the state of things in the story: Will it alter everything or just a few things in the big pond. In the end, the Character Dynamics firmly yet gently mold the point of view from which the audience receives its most personal experiences in the story.

Plot Dynamics

As with characters, both stucture and dynamics can be seen at work in Plot. Most of the plot dynamics center on the Overall Story, but affect all four throughlines. The following four questions decide the controlling events in the story, the "scope" of the story, the story's final resolution, and the plot's connection to the Main Character's outlook.

Overall Story Driver: Action or Decision?

Action or Decision describes how the story is driven forward. The question is: Do Actions precipitate Decisions or do Decisions drive Actions?

At the end of a story there will be an essential need for an Action to be taken and a Decision to be made. However, one of them will be the roadblock that must be removed first to enable the other. This causal relationship is felt throughout the story where either Actions would never happen on their own, except that Decisions keep forcing them, or Decisions would never be made except that Actions leave no other choice than to decide. In fact, the "inciting event" that causes the story's Problem will also match the kind of Driver required to resolve it. This "bookends" a story so its problem and solution are both precipitated by the same kind of Driver: Action or Decision.

Stories contain both Action and Decision. Choosing one does not exclude the other. It merely gives preference to one over the other. Do Actions precipitate Decisions, or do Decisions precipitate Actions?

This preference can be increased or nearly balanced out by other dynamic questions you answer about your story. It's a matter of the background against which you want your Main Character to act.

The choice of background does not have to reflect the nature of the Main Character. In fact, some interesting dramatic potentials emerge when they do not match.

For example, a Main Character of action (called a Do-er) forced by circumstance to handle a deliberation-type problem finds himself struggling for the experience and tools he needs to do the job.

Similarly, a deliberating Main Character (called a Be-er) would find himself whipped into turmoil if forced to resolve a problem needing action.

These mixed stories appear everywhere from tragedy to comedy and can add an extra dimension to an otherwise one-sided argument.

Since a story has both Actions and Decisions, it is a question of which an author wants to come first: Chicken or egg? By selecting one over the other, you direct

Dramatica to set up a causal order between dynamic movements in the Action line and the Decision line.

The Story Driver drives the Overall Story, not the Main Character (except in the Main Character's capacity as a player in the Overall Story throughline). The Main Character Approach moderates the Main Character's problem solving methodology.

The Story Driver appears in at least five instances in your story.

1. The inciting incident—this kicks off the Overall Story by setting things into motion.
2. The transition between Overall Story Signpost 1 and Overall Story Signpost 2—this event changes the direction of the story in a significant way and indicates the act break transition
3. The transition between Overall Story Signpost 2 and Overall Story Signpost 3—this event changes the direction of the story in a significant way and indicates the act break transition
4. The transition between Overall Story Signpost 3 and Overall Story Signpost 4—this event changes the direction of the story in a significant way and indicates the act break transition
5. The concluding incident—this event closes the story, or its absence indicates an open-ended story.

In each case, the nature of the event is consistent with the Story Driver. So, a story with a Driver of Action has an action as the inciting event, actions forcing Overall Story Act transitions, and an action to bring the story to a close. A story with a Driver of Decision has a decision (or deliberation) as the inciting event, decisions (or deliberations) forcing Overall Story Act transitions, and a decision (or deliberation) to bring the story to a close.

Consistency is important. Consistency sets up the temporal, causal logistics of the story. Consistency sets up whether actions drive decisions in the story, or decisions drive actions in the story. Order has meaning and the Story Driver controls the order and is part of the storyform dynamics.

ALL STORIES HAVE ACTIONS AND DECISIONS

Choosing the Story Driver does NOT eliminate the unchosen item from the story.

Choosing the Story Driver sets the order of cause and effect. The chosen driver describes the cause. The remaining driver describes the effect.

For example, imagine an American football game with the two teams on the field. The one with the ball is the offensive team. The one on the other side of the line of scrimmage is the defensive team.

In American football, the offensive team is driven by DECISIONS. At the start of each new play, the offensive team gathers together in a huddle and DECIDES what actions they are going to take. Based on their decision, they act accordingly. If you change the decision, the actions that follow necessarily change to accommodate the new decision.

The flip side is true for the defensive team. The defensive team is driven by ACTIONS (specifically, those of the offensive team). Once the offense acts, the defense can decide how best to respond to the actions. For example, if the offense moves all their team members to one side of the field, the defense may decide to change their plan of defense.

What Constitutes A Driver? Is There A Litmus Test?

Actions or Decisions are Story Drivers if they fundamentally change the course of the overall story, such as the five events described earlier. The closest thing to a litmus test is to think of the cause and effect relationship between the Driver and the unchosen driver. Ask yourself, "Would the effects still happen if the cause is removed?" If the answer is, "Yes, the effects still happen," then your driver does not stand up to the test. If the answer is, "No, the effects would not happen," then that's a good indication that it IS a driver.

Let's look at some examples.

STAR WARS (1977) has a Story Driver of Action. The inciting event is the theft of the Death Star plans by the Rebellion. What decisions follow that driver? The Empire decides to disband the Senate, kidnap Princess Leia, and take their secret weapon out of hiding before its completion. If the plans had not been stolen, would the Empire have decided to do the same things within the same time frame? No. The Death Star was not yet complete. The theft of the plans forced the Empire to change plans.

The concluding event in STAR WARS (1977) is the destruction of the Death Star. Does it end the overall story? Yes. Was there a decision that could have been made that might have stopped the Empire from destroying the Rebel base? No, none within the framework of the story as presented. (Anything is possible, but the story "rules" dictated an action must be taken to resolve the conflict in the story—not every conflict in the story's universe, but the one around which the story revolves.)

THE VERDICT has a Story Driver of Decision. The inciting event is the decision to give Frank the case. Since that happens before the film begins, let's say the "real" inciting event is the plaintiff's attorney's (Frank's) decision to bring the case to trial. Based on that decision, the defense attorneys send Frank's key witness to the Caribbean, hire a woman to act as a mole within Frank's camp, and otherwise stack the legal deck in their favor. Would the defense have done this if the plaintiff's attorney had chosen to settle? No, their actions would change accordingly.

The concluding event in THE VERDICT is...the *verdict*. A verdict is a decision. In this story, it is *the* decision that draws the OS throughline to a close. Is there an action that could have resolved this story? No. If the case was thrown out, the plaintiff's case would remain unresolved and the case could come back again in some other form. The verdict, ANY verdict, resolves the story and brings it to a conclusion.

Examples of Story Driver

Action Stories: HAMLET; THE SILENCE OF THE LAMBS; BEING THERE; A CHRISTMAS CAROL; RAIN MAN

Decision Stories: THE VERDICT; CHINATOWN; THE GLASS MENAGERIE; CASABLANCA; THE GODFATHER; THE STORY OF JOB; CHARLOTTE'S WEB; A DOLL'S HOUSE

Overall Story Limit: Timelock or Optionlock?

Limit determines the kind of constraints that bring a story to a conclusion.

For an audience, a story's limit adds dramatic tension as they wonder if the characters will complete the story's goal. In addition, the limit forces a Main Character to end his deliberations and Change or Remain Steadfast.

Sometimes stories end because of a time limit. Other times they draw to a conclusion because all options have been exhausted.

A Timelock forces the conclusion by running out of time. A Timelock is either a *specific deadline*, such as HIGH NOON, or a *specific duration of time*, such as 48 HRS. The conflict climaxes when the time is up.

An Optionlock forces the conclusion by running out of options. An Optionlock is either a specific number of options, such as three wishes, or a specific number of conditions, such as the alignment of the planets. The conflict climaxes when the options are exhausted.

Both of these means of limiting the story and forcing the Main Character to decide are felt from early on in the story and get stronger until the story's climax.

Optionlocks need not be claustrophobic so much as that they provide limited pieces with which to solve the Problem. They limit the scope of the Problem and its potential solutions.

Timelocks need not be hurried so much as they limit the interval during which something can happen. Timelocks determine the duration of the growth of the Problem and the search for solutions.

Choosing a Timelock or an Optionlock has a significant impact on the nature of the tension the audience will feel as the story progresses toward its climax.

A Timelock tends to take a single point of view and slowly fragment it until many things are going on at once.

An Optionlock tends to take many pieces of the puzzle and bring them all together at the end.

A Timelock raises tension by dividing attention, and an Optionlock raises tension by focusing it. Timelocks increase tension by bringing a single thing closer to being an immediate problem. Optionlocks increase tension by building a single thing that becomes a functioning problem.

One cannot look just to the climax to find out if a Timelock or Optionlock is in effect. Indeed, you may tag both Time and Option locks to the end of the story to increase tension.

A better way to gauge the limit at work is to look at the nature of the obstacles thrown in the path of the Protagonist or Main Character. If the obstacles are mainly delays, a Timelock is in effect. If missing essential parts causes the obstacles, an Optionlock is in effect.

An author may feel more comfortable building tension by delays or building tension by missing pieces. Choose the kind of lock most meaningful for you.

Examples of Story Limit

Optionlock Stories: SEVEN; HAMLET; THE SILENCE OF THE LAMBS; BEING THERE; THE VERDICT; CHINATOWN; THE GLASS MENAGERIE; CASABLANCA; THE GODFATHER; THE STORY OF JOB; RAIN MAN; A DOLL'S HOUSE

Timelock Stories: CHARLOTTE'S WEB; AMERICAN GRAFFITI; HIGH NOON; 48 HRS; A CHRISTMAS CAROL; AN AMERICAN PRESIDENT

Overall Story Outcome: Success or Failure?

Although easily tempered by degree, Success or Failure describes whether the Overall Story Characters achieve what they set out to achieve at the beginning of the story. If they do, it is Success. If they don't, Failure. There is no value judgment involved.

The Overall Story Characters may learn they don't want what they thought they did, and in the end not go for it. Even though they have grown, this is a Failure—they did not achieve what they originally intended.

Similarly, they may achieve what they wanted and succeed even though they find it unfulfilling or unsatisfying.

The point here is not to pass a value judgment on the worth of their Success or Failure. Simply decide if the Overall Story Characters succeeded or failed in the attempt to achieve what they set out to achieve at the beginning of the story.

For example, ROMEO AND JULIET is a Success story because the feud between the families is ended at the end of the play after the death of Romeo and Juliet:

> *A pair of star-cross'd lovers take their life;*
> *Whole misadventured piteous overthrows*
> *Do with their death bury their parents' strife.*
> *The fearful passage of their death-mark'd love,*
> *And the continuance of their parents' rage,*
> *Which, but their children's end, nought could remove*
>
> (ROMEO AND JULIET, *Prologue, William Shakespeare*)

By contrast, HAMLET is a Failure story. Hamlet is unable to protect his family from his murderous uncle and the entire family is destroyed.

Examples of Story Outcome

Success Stories: THE SILENCE OF THE LAMBS; BEING THERE; A CHRISTMAS CAROL; THE VERDICT; CHINATOWN; CASABLANCA; THE GODFATHER; THE STORY OF JOB; CHARLOTTE'S WEB

Failure Stories: HAMLET; THE GLASS MENAGERIE; RAIN MAN; A DOLL'S HOUSE

Main Character Judgment: Good or Bad?

Judgment determines whether the Main Character resolves his personal angst.

The rational argument of a story deals with practicality: Does the kind of approach taken lead to Success or Failure in the endeavor. In contrast, the passionate argument of a story deals with fulfillment: Does the Main Character find peace at the end of his journey?

If the Main Character's angst is resolved, then the Main Character is in a Good place on a personal level. If the angst is unresolved, then the Main Character is in a Bad place. It's important to evaluate the Judgment solely in terms of the Main Character's personal problems in this story. He may have other personal problems in other contexts, but those are not relevant to picking Good or Bad.

If you want an *upper* story, you will want Success in the Overall Story and a Judgment of *Good* in the Overall Story.

If you want a tragedy, you will want the objective effort to fail, and the subjective journey to end badly as well.

Life often consists of trade-offs, compromises, sacrifices, and reevaluations, and so should stories. Choosing Success/Bad stories or Failure/Good stories opens the door to these alternatives.

If we choose a Failure/Good story, we imagine a Main Character who realizes he had been fooled into trying to achieve an unworthy Goal and discovers his mistake in time. Or we imagine a Main Character who discovers something more important to him personally while trying to achieve the Goal. We call each of these examples of a "personal triumph."

A Success/Bad story might end with a Main Character achieving his dreams only to find they are meaningless, or Main Character who makes a sacrifice for the success of others but ends up bitter and vindictive. Each of these would be a "personal tragedy."

Because Success and Failure are measurements of how well specific requirements have been met, they are by nature objective. In contrast, Good and Bad are subjective value Judgments based on a story point of the Main Character's personal fulfillment.

What is interesting about the Story Outcome and the Story Judgment are how they work independently to provide meaning to the story argument, yet also work together to create additional meaning for the audience.

	Outcome: **Success**	Outcome: **Failure**
Judgment: **Good**	Triumph (Happy Ending)	Personal Triumph
Judgment: **Bad**	Personal Tragedy	Tragedy

Examples of Story Judgment

Stories with a Judgment of Good: BEING THERE; A CHRISTMAS CAROL; THE VERDICT; CASABLANCA; CHARLOTTE'S WEB; RAIN MAN; A DOLL'S HOUSE
Stories with a Judgment of Bad: HAMLET; THE SILENCE OF THE LAMBS; CHINATOWN; THE GODFATHER; THE GLASS MENAGERIE

Storyforming Structural Story Points

By answering the eight essential questions we refine our understanding of the way our story will feel to our audience. The next task is to clarify what it is we intend to talk about. In the Theme section of *The Elements of Structure* we were introduced to the various Story Points an audience will look for while experiencing and evaluating a story. Now we turn our attention to examining the issues we, as authors, must consider in selecting our Story Points. We begin with the Story Points that most affect Genre, then work our way down through Plot and Theme to arrive at a discussion of what goes into selecting a Main Character's Problem.

Selecting the Throughlines in your story

One of the easiest ways to identify the four Throughlines in your story (Overall Story, Subjective Story, Main Character, and Impact Character) is by looking at the characters that appear in each Throughline. Who are they? What are they doing? What are their relationships to one another? Clearly identifying the characters in each throughline will make selecting the thematic Throughlines, Concerns, Issues, and Problems for the throughlines easier.

For the Overall Story Throughline:

When looking at the characters in the Overall Story Throughline, identify them by the roles they play instead of their names. This keeps them at a distance, making them a lot easier to evaluate *objectively*. For instance, some of the characters in Shakespeare's HAMLET might be the king, the queen, the ghost, the prince, the chancellor, and the chancellor's daughter. Characters in THE FUGITIVE might be the fugitive doctor, the federal marshal, the dead wife, the one-armed man, and so on. By avoiding the characters' proper names you also avoid identifying with them and confusing their personal concerns with their concerns as Overall Story Characters.

Aren't the Main Character and the Impact Character also part of the Overall Story?

The Main Character and the Impact Character will each have a role in the Overall Story besides their explorations of their own throughlines. From the Overall Story point of view we see all the story's Overall Story Characters and identify them by the functions they fulfill in the quest to reach the Overall Story Concern. The

Overall Story throughline is what brings all the characters in the story together and describes what they do with one another to achieve this Concern.

It is important to be able to separate the Main Character throughline from the Overall Story throughline to see your story's structure accurately. It is equally important to make the distinction between the Impact Character and the Overall Story. Exploring these two characters' throughlines in a story requires a complete shift in the audience's perspective, away from the overall story that involves *all* the characters and into the subjective experiences that only these two characters have within the story. Thus, consider each of these throughlines individually.

The Main Character and the Impact Character will, however, each have at least one function to perform in the Overall Story as well. When we see them here, though, they both appear as Overall Story Characters. In the Overall Story all we see are the characteristics they represent in relation to the other Overall Story Characters.

So if your Main Character happens to be the Protagonist as well, then it is purely as the Protagonist that we will see him in the Overall Story. If your Impact Character is also an Archetypal Guardian, then his *helping* and *conscience* are all you should consider about that character in the Overall Story.

In every story, these two will at least engage in the Overall Story to represent the story's Crucial Element and its dynamic opposite. It is possible the Main and Impact Characters could have no other relationship with the Overall Story than these single characteristics. The importance of the Main Character and the Impact Character to the Overall Story is completely in terms of the Overall Story characteristics assigned to them.

For the Subjective Story Throughline:

When looking at the characters in the Subjective Story Throughline, it is best to look at the Main and Impact Characters by their relationship with each other instead of their names. The Subjective Story Throughline is the "We" perspective (that is first-person plural), so think in terms of the relationship *between* the Main and Impact Characters, not the characters themselves. Thus, "the relationship between Dr. Richard Kimble and Sam Gerard" is the focus of the Subjective Story Throughline in THE FUGITIVE, whereas THE VERDICT focuses on "the relationship between Frank Galvin and Laura Fischer."

For the Main Character Throughline:

When looking at the Main Character's Throughline, all other characters are unimportant and should not be considered. Only the Main Character's personal identity or essential nature is important from this point of view. What qualities of the Main Character are so much a part of him that they would not change even if he plopped down in another story? For example, Hamlet's brooding nature and his tendency to over-think things would remain consistent and recognizable if he were to show up in a different story. Laura Wingfield, in THE GLASS MENAGERIE by Tennessee Williams, would carry with her a world of rationalizations and a crippling inclination to dream if we were to see her appear again. These are the kinds of things to pay attention to in looking at the Main Character Throughline.

For the Impact Character Throughline:

When considering the Impact Character's Throughline, look at their identity in terms of their impact on others, particularly the Main Character. Think of the Impact Character in terms of his name, but it's the name of someone *else*, someone who can get under your skin. In viewing the Impact Character this way, it is easier to identify the kind of impact that he has on others. Obi Wan Kenobi's fanaticism (on *using the force)* in STAR WARS and Deputy Marshal Sam Gerard's tenacity (in *out-thinking his prey*) in THE FUGITIVE are aspects of these Impact Characters that are inherent to their nature. These qualities would continue to be so in any story in which they might be found.

Picking the proper Classes for the Throughlines in your Story

Which is the right *Class* for the Main Character *Throughline* in your story? For the Overall Story Throughline? For the Subjective Story Throughline? For the Impact Character Throughline? Assigning the appropriate Dramatica Classes to the Throughlines of your story is a tricky but important process.

There are four *Throughlines* in a story: The Main Character, the Impact Character, the Subjective Story, and the Overall Story. These throughlines provide an audience with various points of view from which to explore the story. The four audience points of view can be seen as *I*, *YOU*, *WE*, and *THEY*. The audience's point of view shifts from empathizing with the Main Character (I), to feeling the impact of the Impact Character (YOU). The audience's point of view shifts to experiencing the relationship between the Main and Impact Character (WE), and then finally stepping back to see the big picture that has *everyone* in it (all of THEM). Each point of view describes an aspect of the story *experience* to which an audience is privy.

There are four Classes containing all the possible kinds of problems that can be felt in those throughlines (one Class to each throughline): Situation (Universe), Fixed Attitude (Mind), Activity (Physics), and Manipulation (Psychology). These Classes suggest different areas to explore in the story.

In Dramatica, a story will contain all four areas to explore (Classes) and all four points of view (throughlines). Each Class is explored from one of the throughlines. Combining Class and point of view into a Throughline is the broadest way to describe the meaning in a story. For example, exploring a Main Character in terms of his situation is different from exploring a Main Character in terms of his attitude, the activities that occupy his attentions, or how he is being manipulated. Which is right for *your* story?

Pairing the appropriate Class with the proper throughline for your story can be difficult. An approach you may find useful is to pick a throughline, adopt the audience perspective that throughline provides, and from that point of view examine each of the four Classes to see which feels the best.

Each of the following sections present the four Classes from one specific audience perspective. For best effect, adopt the perspective described in the section and ask the questions as they appear in terms of your own story. One set of questions should seem more important or relevant from that perspective.

NOTE: Selecting a point of view/Class relationship (or Throughline) says a lot about the emphasis you wish to place in your story. No pairing is better or worse than another. One pairing will be, however, most appropriate to what you have in mind for your story than the other three alternatives.

Dynamic Pairs of Throughlines

Each of the throughlines in a story can be seen as standing alone or as standing with the other throughlines. When selecting which Classes to assign the throughlines of your story, it is extremely important to remember two relationships in particular among the throughlines:

The Overall Story and Subjective Story throughlines are always a dynamic pair. And....

The Main Character and Impact Character throughlines are always a dynamic pair.

These relationships reflect the kind of impact these throughlines have on each other in every story. The Main and Impact Characters face off throughout the story until one of them Changes (signaled by the Main Character Resolve). Their relationship in the Subjective Story will help precipitate either Success or Failure in the Overall Story (suggested by the Story Outcome).

What these relationships mean to the process of building the Throughlines in your story is that *whenever you set up one Throughline, you also set up its dynamic pair.*

For example, matching the Main Character throughline with the Situation class not only creates a Main Character Throughline of Situation in your story, it also creates an Impact Character Throughline of Fixed Attitude. Since Fixed Attitude is the dynamic pair to Situation in the Dramatica structure, matching one throughline to one of the Classes automatically puts the other throughline on the opposite Class to support the two throughlines' dynamic pair relationship.

Matching the Overall Story throughline with Manipulation to create an Overall Story Throughline of Manipulation automatically creates a Subjective Story

Throughline of Activity at the same time. The reasoning is the same here as it was for the Main and Impact Character throughlines. No matter which Class you match with one of the throughlines on the Dramatica structure, the dynamic pair of that class matches the dynamic pair of that throughline.

Who am I and what am I doing?

When looking from the Main Character's perspective, use the first person singular ("I") voice to evaluate the Classes.

- If the Main Character's Throughline is Situation (*for example Luke in* STAR WARS *or George in* WHO'S AFRAID OF VIRGINIA WOOLF?), questions like the following would arise: What is it like to be in my situation? What is my status? What condition am I in? Where am I going to be in the future? What's so special about my past?

- If the Main Character's Throughline is Activity (*for example Frank Galvin in* THE VERDICT *or Dr. Richard Kimble in* THE FUGITIVE), questions like the following would be more appropriate: What am I involved in? How do I get what I want? What must I learn to do the things I want to do? What does it mean to me to have (or lose) something?

- If the Main Character's Throughline is Fixed Attitude (*for example Scrooge in* A CHRISTMAS CAROL), you would consider questions such as the following: What am I afraid of? What is my opinion? How do I react to something? How do I feel about this or that? What is it that I remember about that night?

- If the Main Character's Throughline is Manipulation (*for example Laura in* THE GLASS MENAGERIE *or Frank in* IN THE LINE OF FIRE), the concerns would be more like: Who am I really? How should I act? How can I become a different person? Why am I so angry, or reserved, or whatever? How am I manipulating or being manipulated?

Who are YOU and what are YOU doing?

When considering the Impact Character's perspective, it is best to use the second person singular ("You") voice to evaluate the Classes. Imagine this as if one is addressing the Impact Character directly, where *"You"* is referring to the Impact Character.

- If the Impact Character's Throughline is Situation *(for example Marley's Ghost in* A CHRISTMAS CAROL), you might ask him: What is it like to be in your situation? What is your status? What condition are you in? Where are you going to be in the future? What's so special about your past?

- If the Impact Character's Throughline is Activity *(for example Jim in* THE GLASS MENAGERIE *or Booth in* IN THE LINE OF FIRE): What are you involved in? How do you get what you want? What must you learn to do the things you want to do? What does it mean to you to have (or lose) something?

- If the Impact Character's Throughline is Fixed Attitude *(for example Obi Wan in* STAR WARS *or Martha in* WHO'S AFRAID OF VIRGINIA WOOLF?): What are you afraid of? What is your opinion? How do you react to that? How do you feel about this or that? What is it that you remember about that night?

- If the Impact Character's Throughline is Manipulation *(for example Laura Fisher in* THE VERDICT *or Sam Gerard in* THE FUGITIVE): Who are you really? How should you act? How can you become a different person? Why are you so angry, or reserved, or whatever? How are you manipulating or being manipulated?

Who are WE and what are WE doing?

When considering the Subjective Story perspective, it is best to use the first person plural ("We") voice to evaluate the Classes. *We* refers to the Main and Impact Characters collectively.

- If the Subjective Story's Throughline is Situation *(for example The Ghost & Hamlet's pact in* HAMLET *or Reggie & Marcus' alliance in* THE CLIENT), consider asking: What is it like to be in our situation? What is our status? What condition are we in? Where are we going to be in the future? What's so special about our past?

- If the Subjective Story's Throughline is Activity *(for example George & Martha's game in* WHO'S AFRAID OF VIRGINIA WOOLF?): What are we involved in? How do we get what we want? What must we learn to do the things we want to do? What does it mean to us to have (or lose) something?

- If the Subjective Story's Throughline is Fixed Attitude *(for example Frank & Laura's affair in* THE VERDICT *or Dr. Kimble & Sam Gerard's relationship* in THE FUGITIVE): What are we afraid of? What is our opinion? How do we react to that? How do we feel about this or that? What is it that we remember about that night?

- If the Subjective Story's Throughline is Manipulation *(for example Obi Wan & Luke's relationship in* STAR WARS): Who are we really? How should we act? How can we become different people? Why are we so angry, or reserved, or whatever? How are we manipulating or being manipulated?

Who are THEY and what are THEY doing?

When considering the Overall Story perspective, it is best to use the third person plural ("They") voice to evaluate the Classes. *They* refers to the entire set of Overall Story Characters collectively (for example protagonist, antagonist, sidekick, and so on).

- If the Overall Story's Throughline is Situation *(for example* THE VERDICT, THE POSEIDON ADVENTURE, *or* THE FUGITIVE), consider asking: What is it like to be in their situation? What is their status? What condition are they in? Where are they going to be in the future? What's so special about their past?

- If the Overall Story's Throughline is Activity *(for example* STAR WARS): What are they involved in? How do they get what they want? What must they learn to do the things they want to do? What does it mean to them to have (or lose) something?

- If the Overall Story's Throughline is Fixed Attitude *(for example* HAMLET *or* TO KILL A MOCKINGBIRD): What are they afraid of? What is their opinion? How do they react to that? How do they feel about this or that? What is it that they remember about that night?

- If the Overall Story's Throughline is Manipulation *(for example* WHO'S AFRAID OF VIRGINIA WOOLF? or FOUR WEDDINGS AND A FUNERAL): Who are they really? How should they act? How can they become different people? Why are they so angry, or reserved, or whatever? How are they manipulating or being manipulated?

Selecting Plot Story Points

Plot Story Points come in two varieties: Static Story Points, and Progressive Story Points. Static Story Points are dramatic items such as Goal, Requirements, and Consequences, and may also include the Concerns of each throughline. Progressive Story Points deal with the order in which each Throughline's Types are arranged to become a throughline's Acts. In this section we shall first explore the issues involved in selecting the Static Plot Story Points, then turn our attention to what influence the order of Acts will have on our story's impact, and thus on our audience.

Static Plot Story Points

Story Goal

A story's Goal is most often found in the Overall Story Throughline for stories written in our culture. Apart from that bias, the story Goal might just as properly be in any of the four Throughlines. As we now consider how to select the Goal for our story, we need to know a little bit more about what a Goal does for an audience. What kinds of control over our audience we can exercise simply by choosing where we place the Goal?

An audience sees a story's Goal as being the central objective of the story. The goal will be of the same nature as the Concern of one of the four Throughlines. Which one depends on which throughline an author wants to highlight in his storytelling. For example, suppose your Main Character and his experiences are the most important thing to you, the author. Then you will most likely want to make the Main Character's Concern your story Goal as well. On the other hand, if your story is about a problem that is affecting everyone, you will probably want to make the Overall Story Throughline Concern your story Goal.

Each throughline will have its own Concern. When the audience considers each throughline separately, it will focus on that Concern as being the principal objective *from that point of view*. When the audience considers the story as a whole, however, it will get a feel for which throughline is most highlighted by the author's storytelling, and will see that throughline's Concern as the overall story Goal.

Since emphasis is a gray-scale process, the story Goal may be a highly focused issue in some stories and of lesser concern in others. In fact, you may stress all four throughlines equally which results in an audience being unable to answer the question, *what was this story about?* Just because no overall Goal is identifiable does not mean the plot necessarily has a hole. It might mean the issues explored in the story are more evenly considered in a holistic sense, and the story is simply not as Goal-oriented. In contrast, the Concern of each Throughline *must* appear clearly in a complete story. Concerns are purely structural story points developed through storytelling, but not dependent on it.

When selecting a Goal, some authors prefer to first select the Concerns for each Throughline. In this way, all the potential objectives of the story are predetermined and the author then simply needs to choose which one to emphasize. Other authors prefer not to choose the Goal at all, since it is not an essential part of a story's *structure*. Instead, they select their Concerns and then let the muse guide them in how much they stress one throughline over another. In this way, the Goal will emerge all by itself in a much more organic way. Still, other authors like to select the Goal before any of the Concerns. In this case, they may not even know which Throughline the Goal is part of. For these kinds of author, the principal question they wish to answer is, *what is my story about?* By approaching your story Goal from one of these three directions, you can begin to create a storyform that reflects your personal interests in telling this particular story.

There are four different Classes from which to choose our Goal. Each Class has four unique Types. In a practical sense, the first question we might ask ourselves is whether we want the Goal of our story to be something physical or something mental. By deciding this we are able to limit our available choices to Situation or Activity (physical goals), or Fixed Attitude or Manipulation (mental goals). Instantly we have cut the sixteen possible Goals down to only eight.

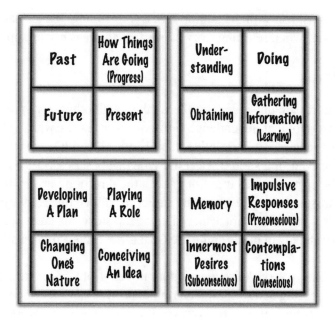

Next we can look at the names of the Types themselves. In Situation: Past, Progress, Present, and Future. In Activity: Understanding, Doing, Learning, and Obtaining. In Fixed Attitude: Memory, Impulsive Responses, Contemplation, and Innermost Desires. In Manipulation: Developing A Plan, Playing A Role, Conceiving An Idea, and Changing One's Nature. Some are easy to get a grip on; others seem more obscure. This is because our culture favors certain Types of issues and doesn't pay as much attention to others. Our language reflects this as well so even though the words used to describe the Types are accurate, many of them need a bit more thought and even a definition before they become clear. (Please refer to the appendices of this book for definitions of each.)

Whether you have narrowed your potential selections to eight or just jump right in with the whole sixteen, choose the Type that best represents the kind of Goal you wish to focus on in your story.

Requirements

Requirements are the essential steps or circumstances that must be met to reach the story's Goal. If we were to select a story's Requirements before any other appreciation, it would simply be a decision about the kinds of activities or endeavors we want to concentrate on as the central effort of our story. If we have already selected our story's Goal, however, much has already been determined that may limit which Types are appropriate to support that Goal.

Although the model of dramatic relationships set up in the Dramatica software can discover which are the best candidates to choose for a given appreciation, the final decision must rest with the author. "Trust your feelings, Luke," says Obi Wan to young Skywalker. When selecting story points that advice is just as appropriate.

Consequences

Consequences are dependent on the Goal, though other story points may change the nature of that dependency. Consequences may be what will happen if the Goal is not achieved, or currently suffered and will continue or worsen if the Goal is not achieved. You should select the Type that best describes your story's risk.

One of the eight essential questions asks if the direction of your story is Start or Stop. A Start story is one in which the audience will see the Consequences as occurring only if the Goal is not achieved. In a Stop story, the audience will see the Consequences already in place, and if the Goal is not achieved the Consequences will worsen.

Choosing the Type of Consequence does not control Start or Stop, and neither does choosing Start or Stop determine the Type of Consequence. *How the Consequence will come into play*, however, is a Start/Stop issue. Since that dynamic affects the overall feel of a story, it is often best to make this dynamic decision of Start or Stop before trying the structural one of selecting the Consequence Type.

Forewarnings

Forewarnings signal the imminent approach of the Consequences. At first, one might suspect that for a particular Type of Consequences, a certain Type of Forewarnings will always be the most appropriate. There are relationships between Forewarnings and Consequences that are so widespread in our culture that they have almost become story law. But in fact, the relationship between Forewarnings and Consequences is just as flexible as that between Requirements and Goal.

Can the Forewarnings be anything at all then? No, and to see why we need look no further than notice that Consequences and Forewarnings are both Types. They are never Variations, or Elements, or Classes. But, within the Types, which one will be the appropriate Forewarnings for particular Consequences depends on the impact of other story points.

When selecting the Type of Forewarning for your story, think of this appreciation both by itself and with the Consequences. By itself, examine the Types to see which one feels like the area from which you want tension, fear, or stress to flow for your audience or characters. Then, with the Consequences, decide if you see a way in which this Type of Forewarning might be the harbinger that will herald the imminent approach of the Consequences. If it all fits, use it. If not, you may need to rethink either your selection for Forewarnings or your choice for Consequences.

Driver and Passenger Plot Story Points

The eight static plot story points should be seen in relation to one another. Each of them affects how the others appear, and a rise in the presence of one will always begin a ripple in the presence of the others.

One way to predict their relationship with one another in your story is to arrange them into two quads and then explore the relationships that these quads create. The nature of these story points will be different for every story, however the story points will always have these *driver* and *passenger* quad arrangements.

Driver Plot Story Points

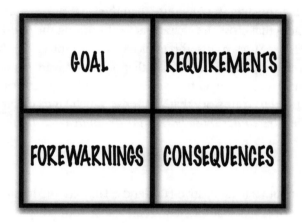

Passenger Plot Story Points

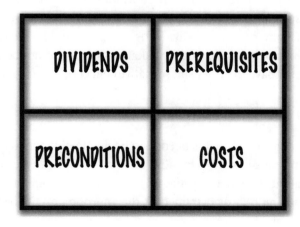

Dividends

Dividends are the benefits added bit by bit on the way to the Goal. Goal, Requirements, Consequences, and Forewarnings are all Driver Story Points in Plot. Dividends are the first of the Passenger Story Points. We see it used in storytelling more as a modifier than a subject to itself. Still, since authors may choose to stress whatever they wish, Dividends may be raised to the forefront in a particular story and take on significance far beyond their structural weight.

No matter what emphasis you give Dividends in your story, they are still modifiers of the Goal. When selecting the Type of Dividends for your story, consider how well your choice dovetails with your Goal. Sometimes Dividends are close in nature to the Goal, almost as natural results of getting closer to the Goal. Other times Dividends may be different in nature than the Goal, and are simply positive items or experiences that cross the characters' paths during the quest.

As with the Driver Story Points, this choice is not arbitrary. The dynamics that control it, however, are so many and varied that only a software system can calculate it. Still, when you answer the essential questions, it is likely your writing instincts become so fine-tuned to your story that you sense which kinds of Dividends seem appropriate to the Goal *under those particular dynamic conditions.*

Costs

Costs function much like negative Dividends. They are the harmful effects of the effort to reach the Goal. Look at the Requirements for your story and see what Type of Costs might make that effort more taxing. Look at the Consequences for your story and see what Type of Costs might seem like an indicator of what might happen if the Goal is not achieved. Look at the Forewarnings and determine the Type of Costs that increases the Forewarnings, or possibly obscures the Forewarnings from your characters. Finally, look at the Dividends and try to find a Type for Costs that balances the positive perks. To balance Dividends, Costs need not be an exact opposite, but simply have the opposite (negative) effect on the characters.

Prerequisites

Prerequisites determine what is needed to begin meeting the Requirements. When selecting Prerequisites, keep in mind they are in your story as *essential* steps or items that must be met or gathered to attempt a Requirement. The Type of Requirements much more heavily influences the appropriate Type of Prerequisites than the Type of Goal.

Prerequisites may open the opportunity for easy ways to bring in Dividends, Costs, or even Preconditions (which we shall discuss shortly.) Certain Types of

considerations may be more familiar to you than others because of your personal
life experience. They will likely be a better source of material from which to draw
inspiration. Choosing a familiar Type will help you later when it becomes time to
illustrate your story points in Storyencoding.

Preconditions

Preconditions are *non-essential* steps or items that become attached to the
effort to achieve the Goal through someone's insistence. A keen distinction here is
that while Prerequisites are almost always used with the Requirements in a story,
Preconditions are likely to apply to either Requirements or the Goal itself. Take both
Goal and Requirements into account when selecting Preconditions.

Think about the sorts of petty annoyances, frustrations, and sources of friction
with which your characters might become saddled, in exchange for help with some
essential Prerequisite. If you were one of your characters, what kind of Preconditions
would most irritate you?

Story Points of this level often appear as a background item in storytelling. Draw
on your own experiences while making this selection so the level of nuance required
can grow from your familiarity.

Plot Story Point Examples:

GOAL:

The Story Goal in HAMLET *is Memory:* Everyone wants to be comfortable
with the memory of King Hamlet. Most wish to do this by erasing the memory of his
unexpected death, but Hamlet wants to keep it alive and painful.

The Story Goal in THE GODFATHER *is Obtaining:* The Overall Story goal of
the Godfather is for the Corleone family to reclaim their place of power and find a
new "Godfather" to preserve this status.

REQUIREMENTS:

The Story Requirements in HAMLET *are Innermost Desires:* Hamlet must get
King Claudius to expose his true nature, his lust for power and Queen Gertrude,
before anyone will believe Hamlet's accusations.

The Story Requirements in THE GODFATHER *are Doing:* For a new Don
Corleone to regain his family's former stature and power, he must do things that
prove his superiority in the rivalry among the New York families. He succeeds with
the hits on Barzini, Tessio, and Moe Green on the day Michael "settles all family
business."

CONSEQUENCES:

The Story Consequences in HAMLET *are **The Past***: If the characters forget King Hamlet's murder, a repetition of the past murder will (and does) occur. King Claudius kills Hamlet to preserve his position as king.

The Story Consequences in THE GODFATHER *are **Changing One's Nature***: If the Corleone family fails to reclaim their power they will be forced to become one of the secondary families in the New York crime scene.

FOREWARNINGS:

The Story Forewarnings in HAMLET *are **Changing One's Nature***: Hamlet starts becoming the crazy person he is pretending to be. This alerts everyone, including King Claudius who plots against Hamlet, that Hamlet will not let the memory of his father die peacefully.

The Story Forewarnings in THE GODFATHER *are **Progress***: When Don Corleone realizes that it was the Barzini family orchestrating his downfall, the Barzini's have already made progress towards becoming the new top family in New York. The progress of the loyalty of other families falling in line with Barzini threatens to cut off Michael's chance to reestablish his family's stature.

DIVIDENDS:

The Story Dividends in HAMLET *are **Developing A Plan***: There is a general sense of creative freedom among the members of King Claudius' court typified by Polonius' advice to Laertes on how to take advantage of his trip abroad. Hamlet finds that suddenly many ordinary things help in his objective of manipulating the truth out of King Claudius, and he takes pleasure in them. The play becomes a trap; every discussion becomes an opportunity to find out people's true opinions. These are all dividends of the efforts made in this story.

The Story Dividends in THE GODFATHER *are **The Future***: The struggle in organized crime over how distribution is costly, but it lays the groundwork for what will one day be their biggest moneymaking industry. Michael's choice of murders make him New York's new "Godfather" and ensures his family a safe move to Las Vegas in the future.

COSTS:

The Story Costs in HAMLET *are **Understanding***: In HAMLET, understanding is a high price to pay—sometimes too high. King Claudius comes to the understanding that Hamlet is on to him and won't stop pushing until Hamlet avenges his father's death. Ophelia comes to the understanding that Hamlet does not love her and is also responsible for her father's death, so she loses her mind. Queen Gertrude comes to the understanding that her son likely is insane and her new husband is a murderer, and so on.

The Story Costs in THE GODFATHER *are **Innermost Desires**:* As the struggle for power in New York's underground continues, all the people involved suffer emotional damage which hits them in their subconscious. For example, Sonny's death aggravates Tom's pain not being the Don's son. Don Corleone suffers for the future of his family as his sons die or become criminals like himself. Sonny suffers the insult of living with a brother-in-law who beats Sonny's sister. The "Turk" realizes his fears when the murder attempt on the Don only wounds him. Kaye buries her suspicions that her husband is in organized crime.

PREREQUISITES:

The Prerequisites in HAMLET *are **Future**:* Before Hamlet can begin the work of exposing Claudius, he must know when the appropriate people will be around so he can put his plans (such as the play) into place.

The Prerequisites in THE GODFATHER *are **Playing A Role**:* Because Michael avoids being in his family's business, others must fill in the temporary vacancy left by his wounded father. Michael himself believes his involvement with the Mafia is temporary until the point when he has become the new "Godfather."

PRECONDITIONS:

The Preconditions in HAMLET *are **Obtaining**:* Hamlet needs hard evidence of his uncle's murderous actions—his own preconditions are that he cannot allow himself to go on the word of the Ghost alone.

Preconditions in THE GODFATHER *are **Impulsive Responses**:* For someone to be a good Don, they have to have the correct kinds of immediate responses. Sonny was "not a good Don," because he was too hotheaded. Fredo isn't a good candidate because fumbles and drops his gun during his father's shooting. A precondition, which Michael fulfills, is that he has the instincts to guide the family well. He displays these when he has no frightened responses while protecting his father at the hospital and when he immediately insists on killing the "Turk" himself. He shows this once again when he accepts the news of Tessio's betrayal without blinking an eye or betraying himself at any point through Impulsive Responses. When Sonny's hotheaded attempts to muscle the Corleone's back to the top failed, it became clear there are preconditions set about whom could be the next "Godfather." Only someone with a steel control over his Impulsive Responses is cool enough to lead the Corleone family successfully back to prominence.

Summary On Selecting Static Plot Story Points

We have examined some of the considerations that go into selecting Static Plot Story Points. Independent of any other dramatics, any Type might be selected for any of these story points. When more structural story points already are chosen, however, one must consider their impact as well in making a selection.

In Western culture, the Goal is most often found in the Overall Story Throughline; however, it might be equally appropriate in any of the four Throughlines. With the eight essential questions the relationship between the Static Plot Story Points may place them evenly throughout the Throughlines, or may favor some Throughlines more than others.

These eight Static Plot Story Points are not solely structural items (though grounded in structure). Modulating their emphasis in the storytelling also affects them.

Static & Progressive Plot Story Points

There are two kinds of plot story points, *Static* ones which do not change and *Progressive* ones that transform as the story continues. To see each kind of appreciation in your story you need to alter your point of view.

Static plot story points are *Goal, Requirements, Consequences, Forewarnings, Dividends, Costs, Prerequisites,* and *Preconditions.* Since these static plot story points remain constant in nature from the beginning of the story to the end, look at them as they relate to the story as a *whole*, as if the story is one single thing. These story points should be in effect no matter what part of the story you look at. The Goal will always be present and identifiable, the Consequences will always be looming. Their presence at any point in the story may be understated or right up front, but the clearer they remain throughout the story, the stronger the story's plot will be from this point of view.

Progressive Plot story points are *Acts, Sequences, Scenes,* and *Events*. These story points describe the experience of moving *through* the story so it is important to look at them in sequence. Whichever kind of progressive appreciation you are looking at, how they flow from one item to the next is the most important quality.

Progressive Plot Story Points

The structure of a Grand Argument Story can be thought of as a house the characters need to explore. The Overall Story Characters look for clues to a treasure. The Main Character thinks of buying the house and the Impact Character tries to sell it to him. The plot is like a sightseeing tour through this story house. The house itself has three floors, each separated into two wings. Each wing has four rooms. This is like a story with three acts, each act separated into two sequences, and each sequence has four scenes.

Our characters begin on the ground floor and enter the first room in the first wing. This room is like the first scene in the first sequence (wing) of the first act (floor) of the story. Here, they look around, opening drawers, checking under the furniture and peering out the windows, if any. Each little area of investigation is an event in the first scene.

The Overall Story Characters are trying to discover a treasure map. The Main Character is looking for termites and problem plumbing and the Impact Character is pointing out the conveniences. When they have all finished, they have a good idea about the value of this room, either as a source of clues to the treasure or as a place to live. Still, they have learned all they can here, and it is time to move on.

The characters now enter a second room, which is still in the same wing on the same floor. This is like the second scene in the first sequence (wing) in the first act (floor). Again, they explore. They may find this room geared more to function than the last. Or, it might be designed more for entertainment. It may or may not have windows or more than one doorway to other rooms. In fact, part of the interest (and possibly suspense) for them is which room they visit next.

When they have fully explored four rooms (scenes), it is time to move on to the next wing (sequence). Some of the rules of our tour is the characters cannot leave a room (scene) until they explore it fully. They cannot leave a wing (sequence) until they explore all the rooms (scenes) on that floor of the wing. And, they cannot leave a floor (act) until they explore all the rooms (scenes) on that floor in both wings (sequences).

In the second wing, our characters also find four rooms and explore them one after another. Once they have finished, the entire first floor (act) has been examined in its entirety. Now it is time to go up to the next floor and continue their tour of the house. On the second floor they look through the four rooms in the first wing, the four in the second, complete that level and move up one more to the third and final floor. Here they repeat the same procedure until, at last, the entire house has been fully explored.

At this point, the characters have gathered all the information about the house they are going to find. If the Overall Story Characters have gathered enough clues to find the treasure, they solve their problem. If the Main Character buys the house, he is a change character. The question then remains, is he solving his problem of having a place to live or buying into even more problems with the faulty plumbing?

We can see the Main Character's decides based partly on what was in the house and partly on the order in which things were presented. We know that first impressions are powerful, even if they are later proven to be inaccurate. How the Main Character decides must conform to both these influences.

Similarly, the order in which the Overall Story Characters gather clues will have an influence on whether they are able to put the pieces together or not. Assumptions easily made would differ when presented with the information in a different order.

In the end, an audience will reject our story's argument either if there are rooms missing (static) or visited in an order that doesn't reflect the outcome (progressive). It is important, therefore, to pay as much attention to the Progressive Plot Story Points as the Static ones. Because Acts are the largest resolution of the Progressive Story Points they have the greatest influence on the flow of a story's plot, and therefore deserve significant attention.

ACTS

Each throughline has its own four structural acts, which are like the three floors and the roof of our story house. Each of the dynamic acts is like the journey that explores the rooms on one of the three floors. As already discussed, when we choose a Class to be a particular Throughline, the four Types in that Class become the names of the four structural acts. We might write those names on cards and place them in front of us. We can then rearrange those cards to set up an order that reflects the concern with which we want that throughline to begin, the intermediate concerns, and the concern of interest when that throughline ends. Most likely, we will base our decision not only on the logistics of our story, but just as heavily on how this order feels, both to us and we hope to our audience. When we have settled on an order, we can be confident that throughline reflects the proper journey to reach the conclusion we have imagined for it.

If we set up an order for each of the throughlines, we might feel our act level work is done. That would be true if the throughlines were independent. As we already know, however, there is a strong connection between the four throughlines, for each represents only one angle on the same overall story. All four throughlines happen simultaneously, just as the characters in our story house all take the tour at the same time. To truly understand the impact of our decisions for act order, we must lay out all four sets of our cards in parallel rows, side by side, and compare what is happening in the same act in all four throughlines.

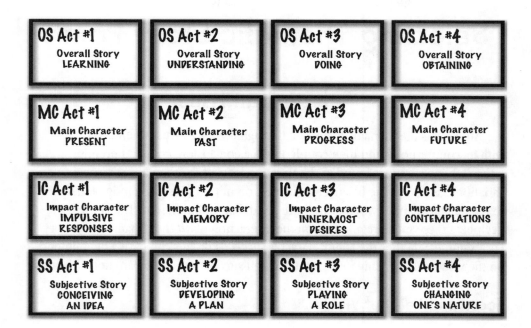

As we can see in the illustration above, the flavor of our story as a whole depends both on the order of acts within each throughline and the combination of the acts from all four throughlines. When we lay our plot in this manner, we may elect to make a few changes in one or more throughline's order to more accurately represent the overall concerns of our story's progression as we imagine it.

It is important to remember the order we're talking about reflects only the *internal* logic of the story, not necessarily the order in which we reveal it to the audience. How we present exposition to the audience is a whole different area of concern covered extensively in Storyweaving. Here we simply want to make sure the act progression in each of the throughlines supports the outcomes, judgments, and conclusions of our story both from a logical and emotional perspective.

Obviously, such considerations must rely heavily on intuition. That is why it is often best to select all the static story points before determining the progressive story points. That extra familiarity with your story will go a long way toward clarifying your intent, providing a more solid foundation for your intuition. In addition, for those who find setting up act order a daunting task, the Dramatica software model is able to *calculate* the best progression for each throughline's acts, based on your selection of static story points. In this manner, authors who would like some guidance in designing their plots can approach their stories by subject matter and have that input translated into the key stages of plot development and character growth.

Selecting Thematic Story Points

Selecting an Issue

An Issue is the thematic focus of a throughline. The focus, when explored with its counterpoint and then coupled with a conclusion, *creates* a premise. A throughline's Issue is found at the Variation level of the thematic structure. Variations, as part of the balanced structure, do not provide value judgments to thematic foci about whether they are good, bad or indifferent. The audience deciphers these interpretations from the interaction of *all* the dynamics of a story. For example, whether the Main Character succeeds or fails can have a big influence on the value of a thematic focus, even though success and failure are not Variations.

Focus and Point of View

An author might select the Variation "Morality" as the thematic focus, making the thematic conflict Morality vs. Self-Interest. But which is better between the two? It depends on the context. The author's message might be to speak out in favor of putting others first, or that one must first take care of oneself before one can help others. Either point of view is arguable, as long as the argument is complete and makes sense in context.

Because it is simply the point of focus, one might argue for an Issue of Morality by either showing that Morality is a good thing or that Self-interest is bad. Of course, both Variations will take their turn at the forefront in exploring the pair, yet one will be the pivot point around which the throughline revolves. Is the throughline's message *about* Morality or *about* Self-Interest? The answer to that question determines the thematic Issue.

Thematic Quads

Although exploring a thematic focus will develop nuance and detail, the focus itself (as well as the thematic counterpoint) must be pure so the issues at stake are clear. This provides a balanced, defined argument at the heart of the thematic exploration, much as there must be a clear storyform at the heart of the storytelling. To allow this need for clarity, one must zero in on the specific Issue at the heart of a throughline's argument. With so much balance involved, choosing the right one for your story is not always an easy thing to do. There is a method one can apply, however, that makes it a bit easier and even rather fun.

As described earlier in the section on Theme, there are 64 Variations, grouped into four sets of 16. Each set has four quads as illustrated below. We can start by selecting a set, then a quad, then a conflict and finally an Issue. We do this by adopting a manner similar to that which we originally explored the thematic structure by starting with the broad stroke Classes and then subdividing each into Types, then Variations, and finally Elements.

Dramatica's 64 Thematic Variations

Situation Variations   *Activity Variations*

Fate	Prediction		Fact	Security		Instinct	Senses		Wisdom	Skill
Interdiction	Destiny		Threat	Fantasy		Interpretation	Conditioning		Experience	Enlightenment
Openness	Delay		Work	Attract		Approach	Self Interest		Prerequisites	Strategy
Choice	Destiny		Repel	Attempt		Morality	Attitude		Analysis	Preconditions
State of Being	Situation		Knowledge	Ability		Truth	Evidence		Value	Confidence
Circumstances	Sense of Self		Desire	Thought		Suspicion	Falsehood		Worry	Worth
Rationalization	Commitment		Permission	Need		Closure	Hope		Investigation	Appraisal
Responsibility	Obligation		Expediency	Deficiency		Dream	Denial		Reappraisal	Doubt

Manipulation Variations   *Fixed Attitude Variations*

Perhaps the easiest way to get a *feel* for one's theme is to take each quad by itself, and experience the four Variations all at once to get a sense of the relationships between them. In the Morality/Self-Interest quad, for example, the other two Variations are Approach and Attitude. It is the nature of these Variations that the other pair measures the good or bad nature of one pair. In this case, if we select either Morality or Self-Interest as the focus, we measure the contrast between them in terms of Attitude and Approach. If we explore Attitude and Approach, they would be measured by Morality and Self-Interest.

Grazing for Themes

Let's assume you have not yet selected any other story points. Begin by picking the throughline you want to work with, that is, Overall Story or Main Character, for example. Don't consider to what Class that throughline is attached. Then, keeping that throughline in your mind, get a feel for the Variations in each Class by simply letting your eyes wander over each set of sixteen and treating them as a single item. Eventually one set should emerge as having the best overall feel for that throughline. In other words, the Variations in that set best express the kinds of thematic issues you will want to explore in that throughline.

Now, think of the sixteen Variations in that set as four groups of four. Each group is a *quad*, and has a unique flavor that defines the four Variations in it as being part of the same family. Consider all four quads in the set, getting a feel for each one. Then zero in on the quad that best typifies the family of subject matter you wish to address in that throughline.

In the quad you have selected there are two different diagonal pairs of Variations. Pick the diagonal pair (dynamic pair) of Variations that illustrates the thematic conflict you wish to explore. Finally, choose one of the two Variations in the pair to be the focus of your theme, and you have your Issue. The other Variation in the pair is your thematic counterpoint.

In this manner, you can begin with a feeling and end up with a specific dramatic choice that will affect not only theme, but character and plot as well.

Selecting Character Story Points

A Bridge between Subjective and Objective...

What is so special about the Main Character? The Main Character is uniquely qualified to illustrate both the Overall Story and Subjective problems. This is because he contains the one character Element that is central to both the Overall Story and Subjective problems. As a result, neither problem can be resolved without his participation. Therefore, selecting the Main Character's Problem requires considering other Elements as well.

The Main Character need not be the source of the problem, but might contain the Element crucial to the solution. This is why it is so easy to make the Protagonist the Main Character. The Protagonist is pursuing the Overall Story goal already; why not have him pursue the subjective one as well? If he is taking the correct approach in the author's view, he contains the solution. If he is taking the wrong approach, he contains the problem. Either way, the Main Character, as Protagonist or not, is the linchpin that holds the Objective and Subjective Stories together.

The act of pursuing a goal and being crucial to achieving it are two different things. For example, it might be the Main Character's insight or resolve that spurs the Protagonist on to success or distracts it into failure. Either way, the Main Character *precipitates* the outcome of the story by changing or by remaining steadfast on that crucial Element.

The Problem Quad

PROBLEM	SYMPTOM
RESPONSE	SOLUTION

In the quad of Elements containing the Problem Element, there is also its counterpart, the Solution Element, which is indeed the solution to that particular problem. There are also two remaining Elements in the quad: The Symptom and the Response. If the Problem is a disease and the Solution the cure, then the Symptom is the primary symptom of the story's problem and the Response is that symptom's most appropriate treatment.

As suggested, Main Characters do not have to contain the Element that is the cause of the problem. But if they do not contain the Problem Element, they will contain one of the other Elements in this crucial quad.

For example, we might decide that we want the problem and solution to be in the quad containing Logic, Feeling, Control and Uncontrolled. Any one of these can be the problem. If we select Feeling as the problem, then Logic will be the solution. If we select Control as the problem, then Uncontrolled will be the solution. Once we decide one pair to be the Problem-Solution pair, the other pair is the Symptom-Response pair.

Symptom is simply descriptive of what the Main Character believes the problem to be; Response is what he feels the solution is. So, for every actual Problem and Solution, there is a matching Symptom and Response. Which Element is symptom and which is response is determined by other dynamics at work in the story.

Change Characters and the Crucial Element

With a *Change* Main Character, he will either contain the Problem or Solution Element. With a *Steadfast* Main Character, he will either contain the Symptom or the Response Element.

Why would a Change Main Character contain the problem or solution? In a sense, the inequity of the story is not just in the Main Character or in their environment, but exists between the two. It grows from an imbalance in the distribution of Elements. When a Main Character solves a problem by changing, he restores balance either by taking an Element from himself and placing it back in the environment where it belongs, or by grabbing an Element out of the environment and putting it within himself where needed. If he must give up an Element, he contains the solution to the problem. If he must receive an Element, he contains the problem. Either way, the Main Character must change his internal make-up—his very nature.

Steadfast Characters and the Crucial Element

For a Steadfast Main Character, the imbalance is not seen by him to be between himself and the environment, but wholly within the environment. In this case, the Main Character takes an Element from one place and moves it to another to restore balance. If the story is built around the Element that needs to be moved, the Main Character contains the Symptom. If the story is built around the hole that needs to be filled, the Main Character contains the Response.

The real essence of the Crucial Element is that the Main Character is responsible for either getting rid of something undesirable or obtaining something desirable, either within himself or in his environment. If carried out, the Main Character restores equilibrium and resolves both the Objective and Subjective problems.

Wrapping Up The Selection Of Story Points

We could write endlessly on how to evaluate each story point. But in truth, there is no mechanical way to make these choices. Any choice is just as good as any other. It is only when the author's feelings and intents come into play that one selection proves better than another.

When previous selections have already been made, however, the logistics of the story's argument begin to take a degree of control. The more selections made, the greater that control becomes until all remaining selections are predetermined by the author's earlier choices.

Understanding which story points have the greatest influence on others goes a long way to helping an author make appropriate choices that keep his message and the feelings produced by his story's structure consistent. Still, such considerations are intuitive in nature, and when intuition fails, it helps to employ the model of the relationships between story points contained in the Dramatica software.

The Art of Storytelling
STAGE TWO

STORYENCODING

Introduction To Storyencoding

Storyencoding is simply the process of turning the *raw* story points of a storyform structure into the flesh and blood people, places, and events of a story that can be told.

As an example, suppose in our storyform we have selected an Overall Story Throughline of Situation. As we have learned, this means the Overall Story throughline revolves around an external situation. Now, when it comes to writing our story, we are not going to put down on paper, "The Overall Story throughline revolves around an external situation." Our audience would have trouble getting involved with that! Instead, we're going to connect that bare story point to something concrete so the audience can relate to what we're talking about.

To make this story point real, we ask ourselves, "What kind of a situation is it?" One author might choose to say, "A group of travelers trapped in a sunken ship." That fulfills the dramatic function called for by placing the Overall Story Throughline in a Situation.

Another author might choose to encode an Overall Story Throughline of Situation by saying, "The death of the parents of five children in a car crash leaves the children to fend for themselves."

Clearly, each story point might be encoded in any number of ways. Which way you choose depends only on the kinds of subject matter you wish to explore. How you encode each story point influences much of the setting of your story in a Genre sense. Encoding also influences the events that happen in your plot, the thematic issues that rise to the surface, and the nature of the people populating your story.

Once you understand encoding, another issue often comes up: "Storyforming and then Storyencoding doesn't seem like an organic way to go about creating a story." Well, we can't argue with that. Most authors are attracted to a story by both the underlying structure and by some element of storytelling. It could be a setting or a character or a bit of action—anything that stimulates the imagination. In fact, *most* authors don't even think about a message at this stage. What inspires them is some intriguing concept, and the rest of their effort in developing that concept is to try to build a story around it.

At first, things go smoothly. But at some point along the way there is a hole and no inspiration to fill it. Or, there are some incompatibilities or inconsistencies and no idea how to fix them. It is at this point that authors beat their heads against the wall, run in circles screaming and shouting. They tell their story to every remaining friend they have in hope of getting some comment that will clear the creative skies.

It is a lot easier if you have a storyform.

If you already *know* what your story is about, then all you need to do is illustrate it. Rather than being constraining, this process is freeing. You can let your imagination run wild, then hold up each new inspiration to the storyform and see if there is a story point that idea will encode. You may have to tweak it a bit to make sure it will communicate the story point accurately. If your intuition is on the mark, then just about anything you come up with is likely to be a part of the puzzle. It simply needs to be nuanced a bit to slip it into the job it ought to be doing.

Some of the story points in your storyform will already be encoded. In fact, they were encoded before you created the storyform; that's how you knew which story points to select. If you are using the Dramatica software, after making a limited number of selections (perhaps twelve or even fewer!) the Story Engine will select all the remaining story points. In other words, the model of story programmed into the software has calculated the dramatic influence of the selections you've made and determined the remaining story points necessary for a balanced and complete story structure.

In the case above, many of the story points predicted by the Story Engine may not yet connect with anything you have already developed. Rather, you find in your Storyform a Goal of Obtaining, for example, and wonder, "Obtaining *what*? What are my characters after?" This is when you think about what you *do* know about your story. Maybe it takes place in a circus. Then a Goal of Obtaining could be getting to perform in the center ring, or winning a place as a permanent attraction in a new mega-amusement park. Your story might be about a mountain man, and his Goal of Obtaining might be to find a wife, or to get a ranch of his own. It doesn't matter *how* you encode a story point, as long as the encoding carries the message of the story through one more stage of communication between author and audience.

Finally, if you are not using the Dramatica software, you will have selected your story points by feel or topic. Some may have been chosen as appropriate to specific ideas you are working with, but the rest just seemed appropriate to the story you have in your mind or in your heart. We're back to intuition again here. And once again, you will need to examine those story points that do not yet have specific encoding in your story and ask your muse to suggest something.

In the end, even if the storytelling may be atrocious it will at least make sense if built on a sound storyform.

The rest of this section presents hints and tips for encoding all four aspects of story: Character, Theme, Plot, and Genre. By far, Character is the most complex of these for it requires the greatest subtlety and nuance to fashion believable people who still manage to fulfill their dramatic functions. As a result, you will find the character section the longest of the lot, and, because of its importance, the first one we address.

Encoding Overall Story Characters

Although encoding places the argument of a story about real life, the storyform itself is not real life at all. It is an analogy to the mind's problem-solving process. We know what it is like to face problems in our own lives. However, we have no way of knowing what our manners of dealing with problems looks like from the outside from a more objective viewpoint. Storyforms deal with only one problem seen from two principal directions: The inside *and* the outside. When we look at the problem from the inside, we can connect with experiences we have had. The view is familiar and we connect emotionally to situations that touch our personal nerves. In fact, we tend to substitute our own experiences in place of what we see in the story. This subjective view holds our feelings and gives credibility to the objective view.

Out of Body Experiences

When we take an external view of a story, however, we no longer identify with the Story Mind directly but view it more like we would in an "out of body" experience. It is if we had stepped out of our own heads, then turned around to see what we were thinking. From this view the author makes his rational argument, telling the audience, "If it feels like *this* from the inside, you'll want to be doing *that*."

Even this simple message carries value for an audience since the audience members can benefit from good advice born of experiences they have not had to suffer personally. In this way, when similar situations occur to them subjectively they can recall the objective dictum from the story giving them at least one plan to try.

Characters as the Author's Positions

A story's characters represent all the ways of considering each problem. Because they represent parts of the argument, Overall Story Characters must be called in the proper order and combination to support each of the author's positions. This all sounds complex and manipulative. It is. But as authors, when we are on a roll we don't stop to consider each aspect of what we are doing. Rather, it all blends into the smooth flow of creativity that we "feel" through our writer's instincts. If the complexity is not there beneath it all, however, there will be noticeable holes in our plot and inconsistent characters.

Dramatica identifies every point of view that is essential to the objective argument. It allows an author to divvy them up among his characters, and then tracks the progress of the characters through the story. In this way, an author can cut loose with creative fervor until the muse fails. Then he can call on Dramatica to find the end of the thread so he can begin to weave it again.

Archetypal Characters

Just because characters are Archetypal does not mean they cannot be fresh and interesting. Archetypal Characters have just as many diverse characteristics as Complex Characters. The only difference is how these characteristics are distributed among your story's characters. When each character has an equal number, and when the elements making up each character are from a single "family" of elements, Archetypal Characters are created. In this sense, an Archetypal Character set is like an alignment of the planets: Each individual orbit is complex, but we choose to view them when they are all lined up in a clear and simple pattern.

Nonetheless, we must still explore all aspects of each character to make the Story Mind's argument fully. However, since there is such consistency to the way the elements are divided, the audience presumes the content of each character. This allows an author the luxury of using shortcuts to describe them. In fact, once a character is outlined enough to show its Archetypal tendency, an author can leave out the rest of the information since the audience will fill it in anyway. In a sense, a character is guilty of being an Archetype until proven otherwise.

A Sample Story Using Archetypes

When an author wishes to concentrate chiefly on action or entertainment, it is often best to take advantage of the Archetypal arrangement to make the story's argument fully and with a minimum of exposition. The characters still need to be interesting to involve an audience in their story. To illustrate how even Archetypal characters can be intriguing, let's create story using only Archetypes and dress them up in some attractive storytelling.

Creating a Protagonist

We want to write a simple story using Archetypal Characters. We can create a PROTAGONIST called Jane. Jane wants to... what? Rob a bank? Kill the monster? Stop the terrorists? Resolve her differences with her mother? It doesn't matter; her goal can be whatever interests us as authors. So we'll pick "stop the terrorists" because it interests us. All right, our Protagonist—Jane—wants to stop the terrorists.

Creating an Antagonist

Dramatica says we need an ANTAGONIST. Antagonist by definition is the person who tries to prevent achievement of the goal. So, who might be diametrically against completing the task Jane wants to do? The Religious Leader whose dogma is the source of inspiration that spawns the acts of terror? The multinational business cartel that stands to make billions if the terrorists succeed in their scheme? Her former lover who leads the elite band of criminals? We like THAT one! Okay, we have our Protagonist (Jane) who wants to stop the terrorists led by her former lover (Johann).

Creating a Skeptic

Two simple Characters down, six to go. Dramatica now tells us we need a SKEPTIC. Who might oppose the effort and disbelieve in the eventual success of good Jane? A rival special agent who doesn't want to be left in the dust by her glowing success? Her current love interest on the force that feels Jane is in over her head? Her father, the Senator, who wants his daughter to follow him into politics? Good enough for us. So we have Jane who wants to stop the terrorists, pitted against her former lover Johann who heads the criminal band, and opposed by her father, the Senator.

Creating a Sidekick

To balance the Skeptic, we're going to need a SIDEKICK. We could bring back her current lover but *this* time have him knowing how much ridding the world of scum-sucking pigs appeals to Jane so he remains steadfastly behind her. Or we might employ her Supervisor and mentor on the force that knows the depth of Jane's talent. Perhaps he wants to inspire other young idealists to take action against threats to democracy, or prove his theories and justify his name in the undercover world... We'll use the Supervisor. So here's Jane who wants to stop the terrorists, pitted against her former lover Johann, the head of the band who wants to stop her, opposed by her father, the Senator, and supported by her Supervisor.

Creating a Contagonist

Let's bring in a CONTAGONIST: The Seasoned Cop who says, "You have to play by the rules" and thwarts Jane's efforts to forge a better way of working? Or, the Ex-Con with a heart of gold who studies the classics and counsels her to base her approach on proven scenarios? Or, her friend Sheila, a computer whiz who has a bogus response plan based on averaging every scenario every tried? Computer whiz it is. So Jane wants to stop the terrorists, is pitted against the head of the band (her former lover Johann) who wants to stop her, opposed by her father, the Senator, supported by her Supervisor, and tempted by her friend Sheila, the computer whiz.

Creating a Guardian

Keeping in mind Dynamic Pairs, we are going to want to balance the Computer Whiz with a GUARDIAN. The Master of the Oriental martial arts who urges her to "go with the flow" ("Use The Force, Jane!")? The Ex-Con again who urges, "Get back to basics"? Or perhaps the Seasoned Cop who clears his way through the undercover jungle? We like the Seasoned Cop. Note how we could have used him as Contagonist, but elected to use him as Guardian instead. It's totally up to us as authors to choose which characteristics go into which players. Jane wants to stop the terrorists, is pitted against the head of the band (her former lover Johann) who wants to stop her, is opposed by her father, the Senator, supported by her Supervisor, tempted by her friend Sheila the computer whiz, and protected by the Seasoned Cop.

Creating Reason and Emotion Characters

Since we like some of our earlier concepts for Characters, let's use the Ex-Con as REASON, stressing the need to use classic scenarios. We'll balance her with the Master of the Oriental martial arts, who argues Jane's need to break with the Western approach by letting loose and following her feelings.

Well, that covers all eight Archetypal Characters: Protagonist, Antagonist, Skeptic, Sidekick, Contagonist, Guardian, Reason and Emotion. Finally, we have Jane who wants to stop the terrorists and is pitted against the head of the band (her former lover Johann) who wants to stop her, is opposed by her Father, the Senator, is supported by her Supervisor, tempted by her friend Sheila the computer whiz, protected by the Seasoned Cop, urged by the Ex-Con to copy the classics, and counseled by the Master of Oriental martial arts to let loose and follow her feelings.

The Same Old Story?

This is beginning to sound like many stories we've seen before. Why have we seen this so many times? Because it is simple and it works. Of course, we have limited ourselves in this example to the Archetypal Characters, not even taking advantage of the Complex Characters we could also create.

When you keep in mind the Dramatica rules for mixing and matching characteristics to create Complex Characters, you have an astronomical number of possible people (or non-people) who might occupy your story. Because of the structure of interrelationships Dramatica provides, they fit together to the greatest potential with nothing repeated or missed. As a result, the Story Mind will be fully functional; the argument fully made.

Complex Characters

It is not the content that makes characters complex, but the *arrangement* of that content. We know people who have one-track minds or are so aligned to be predictable (and often, therefore, boring!) People who are more diverse contain conflicting or unlike traits and are much more interesting to be around. So it is with characters.

Imagine building characters to be like playing Scrabble. There are a given number of letter tiles, no more, no less. The object is to create words using all the tiles. The game won't feel "complete" if any unused tiles remain. Now imagine a set of words that are all the same length and use up all the letters so none are remaining. Suppose there is only one combination of letters that will do this. If we build characters that way, we get the one and only Archetypal set. There's nothing wrong with playing the game that way, but after a few zillion times, seeing the same limited set of words over and over wears thin. It is much more interesting to create a wide vocabulary of all kinds and sizes of words.

Archetypes Have Their Place, But....

Archetypal Characters have their place, mind you. If an author's focus is on Plot or Theme, he may want to create easily identifiable Archetypes as shorthand to save space and time. As soon as the edges of an Archetypal Character are sketched out, audiences (who have seen these Archetypes time and again) will fill in the rest, waiting for information to the contrary. In this way, an author can free up time or pages for aspects of the story that may be much more interesting to him.

As a result, Complex Characters are often the first things torn down to conserve media real estate. This leads to a glut of action-oriented stories populated by stick figure people. Whenever there is a glut in one place, you will find a shortage somewhere else. The imbalance between glut and shortage creates demand. Box office is directly proportional to demand. No more need be said.

Four-Dimensional Characters

All characters, Archetypal or Complex, have four levels or Dimensions in which they may contain characteristics. These are:

1. Motivations
2. Methodologies
3. Means of Evaluation
4. Purposes

Archetypal Characters contain one characteristic in each of these areas that describes how they deal with external problems. They also contain one each that describes how they deal with internal problems. All together they possess eight characteristics.

Swap Meet

The easiest way to create Complex Characters is to swap a few Elements between one Archetypal Character and another at the same level. This results in evenly balanced characters that are not nearly as predictable as Archetypes. When the points of view are mixed, the manner in which a character responds might also shift dramatically. For example, the focus of a scene or act may change from Methodologies to Motivations.

Even more Complex Characters can be built by giving more characteristics to some and fewer to others. For example, one character might have two Motivations, three Methodologies and so on. Another character might only have Purposes but no Motivations or any of the others. Those characters having the most characteristics appear more often, strengthening their presence with an audience.

A Character Cannot Serve Two Masters

An author can create characters for any purpose, to be played like cards at particular points in the hand. The only "rules" of character construction caution against any character containing more than one Element of a dynamic pair. In addition, it is best to avoid assigning a character more than one Element from the same quad as the character would then represent conflicting points of view on the same issue.

At first, this might seem desirable since it would create internal conflict. But with Overall Story Characters, we see them from the outside. We cannot see their internal deliberations. Any internal conflict simple weakens their objective function. However, it's sometimes unavoidable because of Storyforming choices you make.

Overall Story Throughline Characteristics

Elements are the most refined resolution of the problem in a story. Beneath each Variation are four Elements that make up the parts of that Variation and are also defined by its umbrella. One of the four elements under the Issue is the Problem of the story in its most essential form. Another of the four will prove to be the Solution. A third element is the Symptom of the story, where the Problem principally reveals itself as symptoms of the Problem. The final element represents the Response taken in response to the Symptom.

Each of these elements has a specific and recognizable function even in traditional story theory. For example, we know that characters often do not work toward the real solution but to an apparent solution. And characters often grapple with a problem that is eventually recognized as only a symptom of the real problem.

The "Crucial" Element

As pointed out elsewhere, stories are about inequities and their resolutions. When you consider the four principal elements in this light, the Problem element appears more like the essence of the inequity. The Solution becomes the essence of what is needed to restore balance. Depending on the dynamics of the story, one of the four elements is "lifted up" as the prominent point of view. It becomes the *Crucial Element* on which all other lesser inequities in the story center. It is Crucial because if it comes into balance all the remaining inequities of the story balance themselves as well. If not balanced, none of the others can be resolved.

Overall Story Elements and the Subjective Characters

Elements serve to show what the inequity looks like from all possible points of view and hone in on the source: The one bad apple in the basket. All 64 Elements in this level must be represented in character form to explore the story's inequity fully. Of all these, two special characters bare special attention: The Main Character and Impact Character.

The Main and Impact characters do double-duty by carrying the Subjective Story throughline and playing an Overall Story role by being assigned to two different players that contain an Overall Story function. The player containing the Main

Character always contains the Crucial Element in its Overall Story role. However, that element does not always have to be the Solution. It might be the Problem, Symptom, or Response Element, depending on the dynamics. It is this duality that makes those two players the linchpins of the story: The hinge on which the Overall Story AND Subjective Problems and throughlines converge.

The player containing the Impact Character also contains the Element diagonal to the crucial element: The other half of the dynamic pair. In this way as a Main Character or Impact Character eventually comes to change or remain steadfast, The subjective problem influences how each player responds based on the Overall Story Element it also contains. Like magnets with North and South poles, what happens on the Subjective side will influence the Overall Story stand, and when pressures force a change in the Overall Story stand, it will influence the Subjective point of view. It is no surprise that this relationship between Overall Story and Subjective dynamics in characters has seemed so indefinably obscure for so long.

Encoding Subjective Characters

Although authors use Subjective Characters all the time they unfortunately view the Subjective functions simply as other aspects of Overall Story Characters. In fact, the two functions are most often blended into a single concept of character that does double-duty. This is dangerous since every aspect of the argument must be made twice: Once Objectively and once Subjectively. If both roles are blended, this can appear redundant. As a result, important points in the separate arguments may be missing. In a temporal medium such as motion pictures, it is often the Subjective argument that suffers as the focus is on more objective action. In novels, the Overall Story is often flawed as the spatial nature of a book favors the Subjective view.

Just because a medium favors one view over the other does not mean you can neglect anything. All parts of both arguments must be present to create an effective synthesis in the mind of the audience regardless of the emphasis a medium may place on each view.

The Main Character is Not Necessarily the Protagonist

Many authors are not aware that a Protagonist does not have to be the Main Character. When we stop to think about it, many examples come to mind of stories in which we experience the story through the eyes of a character other than a Protagonist. Many Sherlock Holmes novels are told from the perspective of Dr. Watson who is sidekick to the protagonist, Sherlock Holmes. TO KILL A MOCKINGBIRD is told from the perspective of the young girl, Scout, while the protagonist and defense attorney in the story's trial is her father, Atticus. Yet when it comes to writing our own stories, many of us never diverge from a Protagonist/Main Character combination.

There is nothing wrong with this combination. In fact, as long as you represent both characters in the single player, such a blend is a fine Archetypal Character. The point is: There are other ways.

Subjective Characters range from the Main Character with whom we identify to all the "other soldiers in the trenches" around us as we experience the battle together. They are friends and foes, mentors and acolytes. We see in them characteristics of Worry, Instinct, Experience and Doubt. Rather than functioning as approaches the way the Overall Story Characters do, the Subjective Characters function as attitudes.

"We're Both Alike, You and I..."

The Main and Impact Characters are counterparts. They represent the two principal sides to the argument of the story. Because they are dealing with the same issues, they are not too far apart. This often results in such familiar lines as "We're both alike," "We're just two sides of the same coin," "I'm your shadow self," and so on. In contrast, though the same things concern them, they are coming at them from completely opposing views. This leads to common line such as "We're nothing alike, you and I," or "We used to be friends until you stepped over the line."

Evil Twins?

Many authors picture the Impact Character as a negative or evil twin. Although this can be true, it has little to do with the Impact Character's dramatic function. For example, if a Main Character is evil and needs to change, their impact might be a virtuous steadfast character. Or *both* characters might be evil, with the resolve of one contrasting the change in the other. Anyway, the function of the Main and Impact Characters is to show two opposing sides of the same issue. That is their story function: To show what happens when one changes and the other remains steadfast on a particular issue.

Encoding Mental Sex

Both Males and Females use the same problem-solving techniques, but in different contexts. As a result, what is problem solving for one may be justification for the other. In fact, for the four perspectives in any given story, in one Throughline both male and female mental sex characters will see a given approach as problem solving, while in another Throughline both will see it as justification. The third Throughline would be problem solving for one mental sex and justification for the other and the fourth just the reverse.

Men *tend* to use linear problem solving as their first method of choice. In linear problem solving, they set a specific goal, determine the steps necessary to achieve that goal, and embark on the effort to carry out those steps. Gathering facts, or successfully achieving requirements all deal with seeing several definable items that must be brought together to make the mechanism work in the desired manner.

This is a spatial view of problem solving, as it sees all the parts that must be accomplished or brought together to resolve the problem or achieve the goal.

Women TEND to use holistic problem solving as their first method of choice. In holistic problem solving, steps are not important and there may not even be a specific goal to achieve but simply a new direction wanted. As a result, the *relationships between* things are measured and adjusted to create a change in the forces that decide that direction. Unlike male problem solving, there is no causal relationship stating that *this* leads to *that*. Instead, *combinations* of changes in the way things relate alters the dynamics of the situation rather than the structure, and changes context rather than meaning.

This is a temporal view of problem solving, as it looks at the way things are going and tries to alter relationships so to deflect the direction of the forces that create the problem.

Men and women use both problem-solving techniques. Also, women may become trained to use the linear method first, and men may develop a preference for the holistic method as their primary problem solving approach. These are preferences made through conscious choice, training, or experience. Underneath it all, the brain's operating system for problem solving will either be linear or holistic. This is what sets men and women apart from one another. No matter how much common ground they come to from training, experience and conscious choice, there is always that underlying level in which they can rarely see eye to eye, because they have intrinsically different outlooks.

So, when choosing male or female mental sex, we are not concerned with the up front and obvious. What concerns us is the hidden level at the foundation of the Main Character's psyche that dictates a linear or holistic approach to the problem regardless of what is done consciously.

That's why the issue becomes vague—because it is not cut and dried in the Main Character nor is it up front. It is just their tendency at the lowest most basic part of their mind to go linear or holistic.

How can we illustrate this in a Main Character? The following point-by-point comparison can help:

Female: Looks at motivations	*Male:* Looks at purposes
Female: Tries to see connections	*Male:* Tries to gather evidence
Female: Sets up conditions	*Male:* Sets up requirements
Female: Determines the leverage points that can restore balance	*Male:* Breaks a job into steps
Female: Seeks fulfillment	*Male:* Seeks satisfaction
Female: Concentrates on "Why" and "When"	*Male:* Concentrates on "How" and "What"
Female: Puts the issues in context	*Male:* Argues the issues
Female: Tries to hold it all together	*Male:* Tries to pull it all together

As we can see, though both men and women will use both techniques depending on context, one kind comes first or takes priority. Mental Sex determines which one is the principal technique. So, if you keep in mind that this all may be overshadowed by other learned techniques, you can illustrate male and female problem solving techniques as a *tendency* to employ those listed above, all other things being equal.

Building a Mind for the Audience to Possess

When an audience looks at the Overall Story Characters, they see the Story Mind from the outside in. When an audience empathizes with the Main Character, they see the story from the inside out. For the audience to be able to step into the shoes of the Main Character and look through his eyes, he must have a complete mind for the audience to take over. And that perhaps is the best way to look at it: The audience takes possession of the Main Character's mind. That's why you hear people in a movie yelling, "NO.... Don't do that!!!" to a Main Character who is about to enter the shed where the slasher is waiting, or break up with a lover over inaccurate gossip.

However, the question arises: Who is taking possession of whom? As authors we direct our Main Character to take control of the audience's hearts and souls. We make them feel what the Main Character feels, experience what he experiences. It's a sinister occupation we engage in. But that is how a story stops being a spectacle and worms its way into the heart.

Encoding Theme

The trick in Storyencoding theme is to make sure the audience knows what the argument is about without coming right out and saying it. It's also to make sure you make the argument without the audience ever feeling manipulated or the point made in a heavy-handed fashion. In this section we will explore methods of achieving these purposes for theme in general and suggest tips and considerations specific to the themes of each of the four throughlines.

What Are You Talking About?

Without theme, a story is just a series of events that advances logistically and ends up one way or another. Theme is what gives it all meaning. When encoded, theme will not be a universal meaning for all things, but a smaller truth about the *proper* way of dealing with a *particular* situation. In a sense, the encoding of theme moves the emotional argument of the story from the general to the specific. It you make the argument strongly enough, it may influence attitudes in areas far beyond the specific, but to be made strongly, it must limit its scope to precise encoding.

If our thematic conflict were Morality vs. Self-Interest, for example, it would be a mistake to try to argue that Morality is *always* better than Self-Interest. In fact, most people's life experience would tell them that sometimes Self-Interest is the better of the two. Keep in mind here that Dramatica defines Morality as "Doing for others with no regard for self" and Self-Interest as "Doing for self with no regard for others." This doesn't mean a Self-Interested person is out hurt to others, but simply that what happens to others, good or bad, is not even a consideration.

As an example, Morality might be better if one has plenty of food to share during a harsh winter and does so. Morality might be worse if one subdues one's life rather than displease one's peers. Self-Interest might be better if a crazed maniac is charging at you and you kill him with an ax. Self-Interest might be bad if you won't share the last of the penicillin in case you might need it later. It all depends on the context.

Clearly, the first step in encoding thematic story points is to check the definitions first! Dramatica is extremely precise in its definitions to make sure the thematic structure represents all the shades of gray an audience might expect to see in a thematic argument. So, before you even consider the conflict, read the definition that will help define where the real conflict lies.

A good rule of thumb is that each conflict should be explored at least once each act. In this way, the balance between the two sides of the conflict can be examined in all contexts appropriate to story's message.

Further, it is clumsy to encode the entire conflict. It is much better to show one side of the conflict, and then later show the other side in a similar situation. In this manner, you show the relative value of each side of the thematic conflict without directly comparing the two. In each act, then, what are some methods of encoding the two sides of the thematic conflict? This depends on which throughline is in question.

Encoding the Overall Story Theme

The Overall Story theme is an emotional argument that is story wide. Its connection to the Overall Story makes this theme "objective", *not* any unemotional feeling possibly implied by the title. To encode the Overall Story theme, one must come up with scenes, events, comments, or dialogue that involves the thematic conflict. They must also imply that this particular issue represents the central imbalance in value standards that affects *everyone* in the story. In fact, it is often better if you encode the Overall Story theme through incidental characters or background incidents so association with any other dynamics in the story does not taint the message.

For example, our Protagonist is walking down the hall of a ward in a Veteran's hospital with an elderly doctor who is an incidental character whose purpose in the story is only to provide exposition on a particular point. While they are walking, the doctor notes that he is out of breath trying to keep up with our Protagonist. The doctor says, "I can't keep up with you young guys like I used to." Moments later, a double amputee wheels across their path, stops, says cheerfully to the Protagonist, "As soon as they fix me up, I'm going to be a dancer again!" and wheels off. The doctor then remarks, "He's been like that since they brought him here." The Protagonist asks, "How long?" The doctor says, "Nineteen sixty-eight."

What thematic conflict is at work here? The doctor's comments represent Closure (accepting an end). The patient's comments reflect Denial (refusing to accept an end). By itself, this short thematic encoding will not make the conflict clear. But as the story continues to unfold, several different encodings will eventually clarify the item they all share in common.

Theme encoding is an effort of subtle balance. Simply shifting a word or a reaction, even slightly, can tip a well-balanced argument. That is why many authors prefer more black-and-white thematic statements than a gentle thematic argument. In truth, it is the ability to get away from the binary that brings richness and depth to the emotional content of a story.

One other thing we might notice about our example is that we might evaluate whether Closure or Denial is better by seeing how each camp fared with reference to Hope and Dream. Why Hope and Dream? They are the other two Variations in the same quad as Closure and Denial. We can see the doctor has no Hope, but the patient still has Dreams. By showing that lack of Hope causes misery and an abundance of Dreaming bring joy, the case is made that the doctor who represents Closure does not achieve as favorable a result as the patient who represents Denial.

Clearly this thematic message is not true in every situation we might encounter in real life. For our latter example, however, we may say that for this particular kind of problem (the Overall Story Problem) Denial is a better way to go.

Our next concern is that even with a more balanced argument, it still seems one-sided. The way to soften this quality is to have some thematic moments occur in which Closure turns out to be better than Denial. By so doing, we admit to our audience that even for the kind of Overall Story Problem we are dealing with, neither Closure nor Denial is a panacea. As a result, the audience begins to draw excitedly toward the end of the story. Only then can it average out all the incidents of Closure and Denial and see which one came out on top and by how much.

Theme encoding requires skill and inspiration. Because we approach it by feel, rather than by logic, it is hard to learn and hard to teach. But by understanding the nature of the gentle balance that tips the emotional argument in favor of the Issue or its counterpoint, one can consciously consider when and where and how to encode the theme. This is better than simply winging it and hoping for the best. Knowing the storyform for your theme makes it far easier to draw the audience into feeling as you want them to.

Encoding Theme for the Other Throughlines

The Main Character theme follows many of the same guidelines as the Overall Story theme. In fact, the basic approaches of illustrating the conflict by indirect means are good rules of thumb for all four throughlines. We do this by calling on the other two Variations in the thematic quad and having the balance between Issue and counterpoint shift back and forth. The principal difference in theme encoding from one throughline to another is where you direct the conflict.

For the Main Character Throughline, only the Main Character will be aware of the thematic conflict in that Throughline. It might still be illustrated by contrasts between incidental characters or in non-essential actions or events, but no one will notice but the Main Character. For example, our Main Character in a motion picture might be sitting in a diner and look out the window to see a hungry man sifting through a trashcan for some food. The focus shifts (as the Main Character ostensibly shifts his attention) to bring to clarity another man sitting in front of the window getting up to leave from his plate of half-eaten food. No one else is able to see this except our Main Character (and through him, the audience).

The example would be a subtle beginning of an argument about Morality vs. Self-Interest. In and of itself, there is not enough to say which is the Issue and which is the counterpoint. Also, this example merely sets up the haves and have-nots, but does not yet place a value judgment, for we do not even know which of the two men represents Morality and which represents Self-Interest.

An interesting turn would be to have a Maitre'd notice our Main Character looking at the hungry man through the window and run over to say, "I'm sorry, Monsieur, I'll have my waiter tell him to leave." Our Main Character says, "No, wait..." He reaches into his pocket, pulls out his last hundred francs and, giving it to the Maitre'd says, "Bring him some food instead."

Still watching from the window, our Main Character sees the waiter taking a plate of food to the hungry man. As soon as he arrives, the hungry man beats the waiter over the head, takes his wallet, and runs off. The food has fallen into the garbage. Now, what have we said through our encoding about the relative value of Morality vs. Self-Interest as experienced by the Main Character? Also, which one is the Issue?

In our Main Character example, we did not feel like we were judging the Main Character himself because of the results of his actions. Rather, we were judging the relative value of Morality and Self-Interest. In contrast, the Impact Character theme encoding is designed to place a value judgment on the Impact Character himself.

Impact Characters are looked AT, not from. We want to evaluate the appropriateness of their actions. Part of this is performed by showing whether the Impact Character's influence on the balance between Issue and counterpoint results in positive or negative changes.

Suppose we keep everything from our Main Character example in the diner the same, except we substitute the Impact Character instead. All the events would happen in the same order, but our point of view as an audience would have to shift. The question for the audience would no longer be, "How am I going to respond in this situation?" but would become, "How is *he* going to respond in this situation?"

If this is a film, the point of view shot through the window might no longer be appropriate. Instead, we might shoot from over the shoulder of the Impact Character. Further, we would want to make sure the audience does not get too drawn in toward the Impact point of view. So, we might have another customer watching the whole thing. Or, we might simply choose camera positions outside the diner to show what happens, rather than staying in the whole time looking out as we did with the Main Character.

Novels, stage plays, and all different media and formats present their own unique strengths, weaknesses, and conventions in how one can suitably encode a given throughline. Knowing which ones to use and inventing new ones never used before comprises a large part of the craft and art of storytelling.

Finally, let us briefly address thematic encoding for the Subjective Story Throughline. Theme in the Subjective Story Throughline describes the meaning of the relationship between the Main and Impact Characters. There are two distinct ways to evaluate everything that goes on in the relationship and these two ways don't lead to the same conclusions. The thematic Issue and counterpoint reflect these two different means of evaluation.

In most relationships, everyone involved has an opinion about what's best to do. That's the way it always is in a story. As the Impact Character Throughline and the Main Character Throughline have an impact on each other, so do the Overall and Subjective Story Throughlines. Therefore, both Objective and Subjective Characters will have opinions to express about how the *relationship* between the Main and Impact Characters is going. Remember, it's this *relationship* that makes the Subjective Story.

The variety of places to find opinions about the Subjective Story relationship means the Issue and Counterpoint in the Subjective Story need not come only from the Main and Impact Characters. They can be brought up and argued without the presence of either the Main Character or Impact Character.

Of course, these two characters will be involved at some point as well. When they're together, they're likely to be arguing the two sides of the Subjective Story's Thematic issue and providing the Thematic Conflict. When they do, however, it is a good idea to avoid just giving one character the Issue and the other character the Counterpoint. That would lead to a simple face off over the issues without exploring them. Instead, have them swap arguments, each using the Issue, then the Counterpoint as their *weapon*. Neither of them is solely a villain or a good guy from this personal point of view.

Giving your Overall Story Characters conversations about this relationship is a good way to express Issue vs. Counterpoint without involving the Main or Impact Characters. This will help avoid unintentionally biasing the audience against either of them.

The real issue is, which is the best way to look at the relationship?

We all know stories involving newlyweds where the father of the bride argues that his daughter's fiancée is not good enough for her since the boy has neither job nor means to provide for her. In these stories, the mother will often counter the father's argument by saying the two kids love each other, so what could be better?

In that example, father and mother may be Overall Story Characters arguing about the best way to look at the Subjective Story between the Main and Impact Characters (the daughter and son-in-law). In the end, one way of seeing the kids' romance will prove to be the better way of evaluating the relationship.

The thematic resolution may be that the Subjective Story relationship appears terrible from one standard of evaluation and only poor from the other, in which case these people haven't got much of a relationship. Or, a relationship may appear mundanely workable from one standard and thrilling from the other. Or, one may see it as highly negative and the other sees it as highly positive. These are all potential conflicting points of view about a relationship and these differences give the Subjective Story theme its depth.

The important job of the writer is to balance the argument so there is a real question about which way of seeing the relationship is using the best standard of evaluation. Don't' sell the audience a biased bill of goods. Present them a much more realistic tableau.

Encoding Plot

Encoding Static Plot Story Points is simple. One need only figure out what it is. How and when it is going to show up in the story is a different issue and is part of Storyweaving.

The way to approach the encoding of Static Plot Story Points is more or less the same for all of them. As an example, let us consider something conventional: A Goal of Obtaining. Obtaining what? That is what encoding determines. The Goal might be to Obtain the stolen diamonds, a diploma, or someone's love. In each case, Obtaining has been effectively encoded. Which one you might choose is dependent only on your personal muse.

Interestingly, there are many ways to stretch a story point to fit preconceived story ideas. Suppose that we want to tell a story about a woman who wants to be President. It might be he wants to be elected to the office. That would encode a Goal of Obtaining. Or, he might want to have people believe he was the President on a foreign trip. That would be a Goal of Playing A Role. He might already hold the office but feel that he is not authoritative enough and wants to Become presidential. That would encode a Goal of Changing One's Nature.

Clearly, there are ways to bend a story to fit almost any story point. And, in fact, that is the purpose of encoding—to create symbols that represent a story point's particular bend. So, going around the remaining Types, we might also have:

- A Goal about discovering a president's Past

- How much legislative Progress a president is able to make

- The Future of the presidency

- Whether the president is able to address Present concerns

- To Understand the president's vision

- Doing what is necessary regardless of chances for reelection

- Learning the President's hidden agenda,

- Developing A Plan for strengthening the presidency

- Conceiving An Idea a new kind of political leverage

- Trying to evoke the Memory of a past president's greatness

- Responding with Impulsive Responses should the president be attacked

- Trying to curb a president's subconscious drives until after the election

- Making the president Conscious of a problem only he can solve

Each of these encodings deals with the presidency, but in a different way. This allows an author to stick with the subject matter that interested him first, yet still accurately encode the Story Goal. And why even bother? Because the wrong perspective creates the wrong meaning. Anything not properly encoded will work against the dramatics of your story, rather than with them, and weakens your story's overall message and audience experience.

Encoding Progressive Plot Story Points

Progressive Plot Story Points are also fairly straightforward. At act resolution there is a simple method for encoding Signposts and Journeys that also sets up the plot aspects of your story's scenes.

Signposts and Journeys

When we develop a plot, we are in effect planning a journey for our characters. We might imagine our plot as a road. We have already discussed how that road might be thought of as containing four signposts that define three journeys. The Type at Signpost #1 marks our characters' *Point of Departure*. This Type is the name of the town at which we are beginning our Journey. In our example, the characters are in the good borough of Learning.

We have also planned a destination for our characters. Again, in our example, we wish our characters to arrive at the village of Obtaining. Signpost #4 marks Obtaining's city limits.

For our characters to experience the Journey we intend, we also want them to pass through the towns of Understanding and Doing along the way. Once they have arrived at Obtaining, they will have covered all the ground we want them to.

Our Plot consists of Signposts plus the experience of traversing the road *between* the Signposts.

If we have four Signposts, we can see three Journeys between them. The Signposts merely provide our audience with an unbiased map of the checkpoints along the way. It is the Journeys, however, that involve our audience in the experience of crossing that ground.

Some writers have learned to create stories in a Three-Act *Structure*. Others have worked in a Four-Act *Structure*. In fact, we need *both* to map out the terrain *and* involve the audience.

Now that we know the names of the Signposts in our Overall Story, it is time to describe the kinds of Journeys that will take place on the road between them.

Example:

In our example, the three Journeys are:

Topic 1. Learning ———————— >Topic 2. Understanding

Topic 2. Understanding ———————— >Topic 3. Doing

Topic 3. Doing ———————— >Topic 4. Obtaining

For a hypothetical story, we might then encode each Signpost and Journey as follows:

Signpost #1

Type 1. Learning

Our characters Learn that several robberies have occurred involving diamonds.

Journey #1

Type 1. Learning- ———————— > **Type 2.** Understanding

As our characters Learn about the robberies that have occurred, they become aware of similarities in the crimes. Eventually, the similarities are too much to be coincidental.

Signpost #2

Type 2. Understanding

Our characters arrive at the Understanding that there is one multinational consortium involved in the heists.

Journey #2

Type 2. Understanding ———————— >Type 3. Doing

The more our characters Understand about the consortium, the more they are able to figure out which smaller organizations are involved, as well as the names of specific individuals. Eventually, the characters Understand enough of the organization of the consortium to try to put someone on the inside.

Signpost #3

Type 3. Doing

Our characters track down and infiltrate the consortium.

Journey #3

Type 3. Doing ———————— > **Type 4**. Obtaining

Our characters get in tighter and tighter with the consortium until they are finally trusted enough to take part in the heist. Through a series of dangerous maneuvers, our characters are able to get word of the heist back to their organization, which alert the authorities.

Signpost #4

Type 4. Obtaining

Our characters recover the stolen diamonds.

As you can see, the Signposts outline the direction events will take. The Journeys help bring them to life.

Main Character Throughline Plot Progression

By now you should be familiar with the idea that the Main Character represents a point of view for the audience. In fact, the audience stands in the shoes of the Main Character and sees what he sees and feels what he feels.

In the Overall Story Throughline, the Plot Progression concentrates on the kinds of activities involving Overall Story Characters. In the Main Character Throughline, Plot Progression describes the stages of the Main Character's Growth.

Each Type in the Main Character Throughline reflects the Main Character's primary concern at that point in his development. Eventually, he will grow enough to deal with the issue closest to his heart: The Main Character Concern. Let's look at an example of how you might encode this by continuing to develop the story we presented for Type Order Plot Progression of the Overall Story.

Example:

In this fictitious story example, the Main Character Throughline is a Situation. The Type order selected for the Main Character is as follows: Past, Progress, Present, and lastly Future.

Signpost #1

Type 1. Past

The Main Character is a law enforcement agency Department Chief with political ambitions. He has zero tolerance for officers of the law who have accepted payoffs from organized crime. As the story opens, his chief Concern of the moment is the history of graft in his department.

Journey #1

Type 1. Past ——————————— > **Type 2**. Progress

The Main Character looks into Past instances of Consortium influences in his department. Using this historical information, he gets closer to infiltrating the Consortium.

Signpost #2

Type 2. Progress

The Main Character decides his agents are too weak to resist stealing money from the Consortium. Therefore, he takes the case himself, going undercover and slowly snaking his way into the heart of the Consortium over some months.

Journey #2

Type 2. Progress ——————————— > **Type 3**. Present

The more the Main Character gets deeper into the Consortium, the more he is trusted with the Consortium's funds. Also, he finds himself in something of a Godfather position in which local businesses and organizations come to him for help. For a while, he is able to either deny them or calm them.

Signpost #3

Type 3. Present

Now, well settled in the Consortium, the Main Character is faced with a situation in which an important Children's Hospital will be closed unless he uses some of the Consortium's ill-gotten gains to provide the necessary funding.

Journey #3

Type 3. Present ──────────── > **Type 4.** Future

The Main Character gives in to the needs of others, violating his own zero tolerance code of ethics because of the serious needs of the children. Still, he is able to get the goods on the Consortium enough to stop some of their local plans, though not enough to damage the consortium at core level. When he is "brought in from the cold" by his agency, they treat him as a hero for his success. In contrast, his own ethical failings trouble him. He gave in to the temptation to take the money.

Signpost #4

Type 4. Future

Though he is in a better position than ever to break into the political scene and demand strict adherence to a code of ethics, his grand words about his Future are now just ashes in his mouth. He sits miserably in his office pondering his failings, drained of ambition.

Impact Character Throughline Plot Progression

The Impact Character in a story never stands alone, but is always evaluated in terms of his impact on the Main Character. When encoding the Impact Character Throughline Plot Progression, this is equally true. Unlike the Main Character Type Order, which reflects the Main Character's Growth from one concern to another, the Impact Character Type Order reflects the progression of the Impact Character's impact on the Main Character. In other words, each of the four Impact Character Types describes a chink in the Main Character's armor, a weakness exploited by the Impact Character. This forces the Main Character to consider issues that will eventually bring him to Change or remain Steadfast.

For example, in our sample story, the Impact Character Throughline is in the Fixed Attitude Class. As a result, the Impact Character Throughline Types are Memory, Impulsive Responses, Contemplation, and Innermost Desires. This means the Impact Character will (in some order) force the Main Character to remember (Memory), to respond differently when there is no time for consideration (Impulsive

Responses), to become aware of something (Contemplation), and to desire something (Innermost Desires).

Encode the Impact Character's Types by the impact the Impact Character has in that area of concern on the Main Character. In this way, your Impact Character will *force* your Main Character to grow to a point of potential Change. That is the function and purpose of the Impact Character in a story.

Impact Character Throughline Type Order Encoding

Example:

In this fictitious story example, the Impact Character Throughline has a Fixed Attitude (Mind). The Type order selected for the Impact Character is as follows: Impulsive Responses [Preconscious], Contemplation [Conscious], Memory, and lastly Innermost Desires [Subconscious].

Signpost #1

Type 1. Impulsive Responses

The Impact Character is a happy-go-lucky kind of guy. He sees justice and honor as being flexible, dependent on the situation. His attitude causes unthinking responses (Impulsive Responses) in the Main Character, who reacts to every instance of the Impact Character's sliding scale of values as if he was shocked with an electric prod. The Impact Character's actions force the Main Character to lose his temper, make threats he later regrets, and smash things in a fit of self-righteous rage.

Journey #1

Type 1. Impulsive Responses ———— > **Type 2.** Contemplation

As the Main Character becomes more obsessed with infiltrating the Consortium and edges toward putting himself under cover, the Impact Character's flexible ways enrage him more and more. Eventually, the Impact Character has had enough of this, and intentionally begins to show his easy attitude in front of the Main Character, so he can make him aware of situations in which rigid views just won't work.

Signpost #2

Type 2. Contemplation

The Impact Character carries the argument to the Main Character that no one is immune to temptation. Going under cover in the Consortium will surely cause the Main Character to break if he does not learn to bend. Prophetically, the Impact Character makes the Main Character aware (Contemplation) of some situations in which a fixed code of ethics creates a paradox where one must reexamine one's ideals.

Journey #2

Type 2. Contemplation ——————— > **Type 3.** Memory

Coming to see that even though the Main Character is now aware of the issues involved, he still does not relent in his plans. The Impact Character begins to bring up "the old days" when they were both beat cops together, fresh out of growing up in the same neighborhood. The Impact Character uses the Main Character's memories to drive home the point that the Main Character was also flexible in those days, and they laughed at the stiffs who usually ended up getting killed or going crazy.

Signpost #3

Type 3. Memory

The Main Character has gone so deeply under cover that no one at the agency has heard from him in days. The Impact Character contacts and meets with the Main Character, finding him caught in a web of self-doubt, unable to choose between sticking with his code and helping the children's hospital. The Impact Character forces the Main Character to remember their days growing up together in the same neighborhood. Recalling how the Main Character's thinking was not always so black and white, he urges the Main Character to learn a lesson from those memories and bend with the wind, rather than snap under the pressures that are on him.

Journey #3

Type 3. Memory ————————— > **Type 4.** Innermost Desires

Unable to be in further contact with the Main Character who remains under cover, the Impact Character gets a few old friends from the early days to cross paths with the Main Character in the attempt to loosen him up. Each has been told by the Impact Character to remind the Main Character about "the old days" and how much fun they used to have, how many dreams they shared before they got "locked-in" to the system.

(Note to authors: The Impact Character need not be physically present for his impact to be felt!)

Signpost #4

Type 4. Innermost Desires

With the Main Character back in the agency, the Impact Character passes judgment on him. He tells the Main Character to look to his heart—look to all the noble things the Main Character had hoped to do in the political realm. The Impact Character asks the Main Character how he feels now, knowing that he has violated the ideals he had intended to run on. "What does your heart tell you now?" he asks of the Main Character, and then walks out leaving the dejected Main Character alone.

Subjective Story Throughline Plot Progression

It is always best to work on the Subjective Story Throughline last since it describes the growth of the relationship between the Main and Impact Characters, and therefore needs to call on what was determined previously for them.

Imagine for a moment the Main Character is a boxer. As an audience we stand in his shoes, effectively becoming him during the story. We look in the far corner and see our opponent, the Impact Character warming up for the bout. As the fight begins, we pass through changing concerns represented by the Main Character Throughline Type Order. As the fight progresses, the Impact Character lands some telling blows. The Impact Character Type Order describes these.

Outside the ring sit the judges. They do not stand in the shoes of the Main Character, nor are they concerned, fearful, or affected by the Impact Character's attack. Rather, the judges watch two fighters circling the issues—preserving the same relationship between them as opponents, but covering different ground in the ring.

So it is with the Subjective Story Throughline Type Order. As the first round begins, the Main and Impact Characters converge on a particular issue. They argue the issue, each from his own point of view. Once they have thrashed that topic into submission, they move on to another area of friction and continue sparring.

Example:

In this fictitious story example, the Subjective Story Throughline is Manipulation. The Type order selected for the Subjective Story is as follows: Developing A Plan, Conceiving An Idea, Playing A Role, and lastly Changing One's Nature.

Signpost #1

Type 1. Developing A Plan

Developing A Plan means working out a plan, model, belief system, or paradigm. In the Subjective Story, the Main and Impact Characters quickly come into conflict about how to look at the relationship between organized crime and law enforcement. The Main Character argues that law enforcement is like a breakwater, holding back an ocean of anarchy. The Impact Character sees the system more like an ecology, where each kind of activity has its place in an ever-changing environment.

Journey #1

Type 1. Developing A Plan —————— > **Type 2**. Conceiving An Idea

As new information about the increasing number of diamond heists builds, both the Main and Impact Characters approach the problem, arguing over how to put the clues into a meaningful pattern. When they discover the international Consortium, the Main Character looks for ways to stop it, while the Impact looks for ways to divert it. Based on his views, the Main Character Conceives of the need to place one of his agents deep within the Consortium as a mole. The Impact Character argues that the Main Character is thinking about it all wrong. They should be working out how to make the heists too difficult and costly a venture so the Consortium will go elsewhere to greener pastures.

Signpost #2

Type 2. Conceiving An Idea

Conceiving An Idea means coming up with an idea or discovering a need. They finally come up with the idea of using the Main Character as the mole in an undercover operation, agreeing that this will be the best way to continue given their two points of view. They both believe that this plan will not only achieve their purposes, but will also make the other see the error of his ways. The Main Character believes he will be able to prove that he can stop the Consortium dead in its tracks, and the Impact Character believes the Main Character will be forced to compromise and change his point of view.

Journey #2

Type 2. Conceiving An Idea ───────── > **Type 3**. Playing A Role

As the Main and Impact Character come up with more ideas to help him rise among the Consortium, they realize they are still not agreeing on how to run this operation. The Main Character starts acting more and more impatient with the Impact Character, being more and more like the role he is playing to be in among the sting. The Impact Character starts taking on a different role, that of the Main Character's nagging conscience.

Signpost #3

Type 3. Playing A Role

Playing A Role [Being] means acting a role or playing a part. With the Main Character now within the Consortium, he adopts the role of an up-and-coming organized crime boss. The Impact character is only allowed to see him while playing the role of his longtime friend and priest. Having to meet under the gaze of criminals, their relationship becomes one of playacting.

Journey #3

Type 3. Playing A Role ─────── > **Type 4.** Changing One's Nature

In their meetings, the Impact Character argues that if the Main Character is to become a mole in the Consortium successfully, the

Main Character needs to play the role better than he has been. This will mean acting ruthlessly and letting a few people get hurt. The Main Character argues that he will not cross his personal line, even if that choice blows his cover: If he acted like them, he says he would be no better than they are. The Impact Character points out that if the Main Character doesn't bend his own code a little more, they will both become suspected narcs and probably will be exposed. This comes down to the choice between using crime money to save the children's hospital or shutting down the hospital. The Main Character chooses to save it.

Signpost #4

Type 4. Changing One's Nature

Changing One's Nature [Becoming] means truly transforming one's nature. The Impact Character points out to the Main Character that The Main Character is no longer the self-assured champion of virtue he once was. He points out there was no escaping the change the Main Character made in his personal code to be able to bring the Consortium to some measure of justice. The Main Character says the angst he is suffering is a test of his moral fiber. Those who stand against the pressure and survive Become stronger for it. He throws the Impact Character out of his office yelling that they will never work together again. It is clear the Main Character has seen too much in himself and has become convinced that his moral ethics are no longer as powerful as they used to be.

Encoding Genre

As previously discussed, Genre is only slightly influenced by a storyform. This is because only four story points have a structural influence on Genre: The four Throughlines. Once each Throughline has been encoded, all the rest of the indistinct realm called Genre consists of storytelling preferences.

We have already explored the meaning of each Throughline story point in the Genre portion of *The Elements of Structure*. In the next section on Storyweaving, we will touch on many writing techniques that help to fashion Genre.

For now, let us simply recall that a story's Genre does not spring forth full-grown from the first word. Rather, it begins as a generalization and gradually evolves into a more and more refined overall feel and tone until it becomes a unique Genre represented only the this single story.

As a caution, keep in mind that trying to be completely unique up front often alienates an audience. Conversely, failing to develop enough unique refinements over the course of a story makes it less than memorable. A safer approach is to start with the same general nature as any one of thousands of other stories and then slowly mold a new realm. This is much more audience-friendly and will still create a one-of-a-kind experience.

Another consideration is to be aware of genre-specific storytelling conventions. Using genre conventions smartly and sparingly often satisfies an audience's expectations. Overusing genre conventions often works against a story's success by making it overly familiar and predictable. For example, putting your horror story in a dark, rainy location is consistent with genre conventions. However, having a cat unexpectedly jump out from somewhere is a tired convention. It may work to startle your audience, but it often produces as many groans and giggles as it does gasps.

Medium and Format

Up to this point, we have explored the encoding process as if storyform and storytelling were the only concerns. This is only true in a theoretical sense. In practice, you cannot relay a story from author to audience except across a medium. The medium in which a story is presented both limits the tools available to the author, and provides uniquely useful tools. For example, motion pictures are not known for the capacity to present stories told in taste or touch or smell. Stage productions, however, have made effective use of all three. Also, a novel allows a reader to jump ahead if he desires, and examine aspects of the story out of order, something one cannot do as easily in a movie.

Stories in many media are recorded to play back directly to the audience. Others are recorded as cues to performers and translated through them to the audience.

Still others are not recorded at all and simply told. There can be as many media as there are means of transferring information.

Even within a single medium there may exist several formats. For example, in television there are half-hour, three-camera formats, half-hour, single-camera formats, one-hour and two-hour and miniseries formats. Also, time is not the only quality that defines a format. Soap operas, episodic series, and multi-throughline episodic series are but a few variations. Each of these formats offers dramatic opportunities and each works under constraints. By exploring their demands and benefits, the process of encoding can be related to best advantage in each.

The Art of Storytelling
STAGE THREE

STORYWEAVING

Introduction To Storyweaving

Of the Four Stages of Communication, Storyweaving is most like what authors usually think of as the writing process. It is here that we gather everything we know about our story and decide how to present it to our audience.

Some authors are *planners* and like to work out everything before they write a word. For them, the Storyweaving process is simply deciding the most interesting way to tell a story that, for them, is already complete in their minds. Another breed of author consider themselves *organic* writers, and jump headlong into the writing process, only discovering what their stories are about along the way. Most authors fall somewhere between these two extremes, working out portions of their stories to varying degrees, then jumping in with the intent to become inspired by the writing process to fill in the gaps.

Which technique is best? Whichever works for you. Writing should be a positive experience, not drudgery. If you are having headaches instead of triumphs, you might want to consider changing the balance between your degree of preparation and your spontaneous exploration. For anyone destined to write, find the best mix of the two.

Of course, the proper mix of structure and stream of consciousness may change for an author from day-to-day. Some days may be good for working on the framework of a story. Other days it may be best simply to dive in and write. And the best mix can also change depending on the subject matter or even the medium or format. Writing is not a science but an art. Still, like any art, science can improve the tools of the trade making artistic expression more enjoyable and the finished product more reflective of the author's intent. This is where Dramatica can help.

As aids to structure, the Storyforming and Storyencoding stages of communication describe everything necessary to form a complete argument. As tools for organic writing, Storyweaving and Story Reception provide techniques that create results. As you approach a story, you will likely want to draw on many of these tools to fashion the story you have in mind in the manner that brings the most creative fulfillment.

Having now set the stage, as it were, of how Storyweaving fits into the writing process, let's explore some of the tricks of the trade.

Storyweaving and Structure

Part of the purpose of Storyweaving is to communicate the underlying dramatic structure or message of a story. The other part is to make that process of communication as interesting and effective as possible. In addition, the manner in which you express the structure has a great impact on how the audience receives the message that extends far beyond simply understanding the message.

Our first job then is the mundane task of describing how to communicate a structure through exposition. Once we have laid this foundation, we can cut ourselves free to consider the enjoyable aspects of using weaving techniques to build suspense, create comedy, shock an audience, and generally have a good time putting the frosting on the cake.

Space and Time Together Again

By now, you should be familiar with the idea that part of a story's structure is made up of Static Story Points and part consists of Progressive Story Points. It is here in Storyweaving that we must find a way to blend the two together so all aspects of our story can unfold in concert.

In the Plot section of Storyencoding, we learned how the four structural and three dynamic acts of each throughline work as four signposts that defined three journeys. Although there are many ways we might weave all of this into a story, there is one straightforward method that is useful to illustrate the basic concepts.

First, think of each signpost and each journey not as an act, but as a Storyweaving scene. From this perspective, we can see there will be twenty-eight scenes in our story (four signposts and three journeys in each of four throughlines). If we write the Type of each signpost on a card and then write the Types that describe the beginning and ending of each journey on a card, we end up with twenty-eight cards. Each card represents a Storyweaving scene. (It is a good idea to put all the signposts and journeys from each throughline on a different color card to tell them apart easily.)

Now, we have in front of us twenty-eight scenes. Each one has a job to do, from a structural point of view. Each one must express to an audience the story point it represents. This is the process of encoding the signposts and journeys as we did in the Plot section of Storyencoding. We might write that encoding right on each card so we can tell at a glance what is going to be happening in that scene.

It is at this point we can begin to Storyweave. What we want to decide is the order in which those twenty-eight scenes will be played out for our audience.

A good rule of thumb for a straightforward story is to keep the scenes in each throughline in order. So, Signpost 1 will be followed by Journey 1 which is in turn followed by Signpost 2 and Journey 2, and so on.

Now we run into a bit of a sticky wicket. Since all four throughlines are happening simultaneously from a structural point of view, all four Signposts 1 from all four throughlines occur at the same time! Of course, this might be difficult unless we were making a movie and used a four-way split screen. Still, some of our most sophisticated authors find ways to use a single event to represent more than one dramatic point at a time. This technique requires experience and inspiration.

A much more practical approach for those using Dramatica for the first time is to put one of the Signposts 1 first, then another, a third, and finally the last. Which of the four Signposts 1 goes first is up to our personal tastes, no limitations whatever. Although this is not as complex as describing all four throughlines at once, it is a much easier pattern to weave and has the added advantage of providing better clarity of communication to our audience.

Next, we will want to Storyweave all four Journeys 1. We might decide to move through them in the same order as the Signposts or to choose a different sequence. Again, that has no structural impact at all, and is up to our creative whims.

Just because we have absolute freedom, however, does not mean our decision has no affect on our audience. In fact, the order in which each scene crops up determines which information is a *first impression* and which is a *modifier*. It is a fact of human psychology that first impressions *usually* carry more weight than anything that follows. It takes much undoing to change that first impact. This is why it is usually better to introduce the Main Character's Signpost 1 before the Impact Character Signpost 1. Otherwise, the audience will latch onto the Impact Character and won't switch loyalty until farther into the story. Clearly, if our weaving has brought the audience to think the Impact Character is the Main Character, we have failed to suggest the real structure and meaning of our story. So, just because we have freedom here doesn't mean are not accountable.

Using these techniques, we could order all the Signposts and Journeys for all four throughlines until we set up a Storyweaving sequence for all twenty-eight scenes.

Storyweaving the 28 simple scenes with minimal "weaving"

Before we move on to the next step of this introduction to building
Storyweaving scenes, we can loosen up our constraints even a bit further. We
don't have to present all four Signposts and then all four Journeys. Together, each
Signpost and Journey pair moves a throughline from where it starts right up to the
edge of the next act break. Each pair feels to an audience as if they belong in the first
act for that throughline. Therefore, as long as the Signposts precede their matching
Journeys, the order of exposition can stick with one throughline for both Signpost
and Journey or jump from a Signpost to another throughline before returning to the
matching Journey.

Taking this more liberal approach, we might begin with Main Character Signpost 1 and Journey 1 (as illustrated below), then show Overall Story Signpost 1, then Impact Character Signpost 1, Overall Story Journey 1, Subjective Story Signpost 1 and Journey 1, and end with Impact Character Journey 1. In this manner, the Signposts and Journeys in each throughline stay in order, but we have much more latitude in blending the four throughlines together.

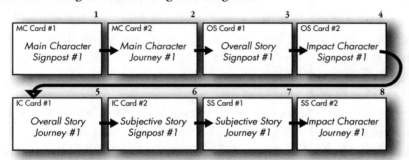

This still may be too "chunky" for our taste. If we want, we can break Signposts and Journeys into multiple parts. Each part explores only a portion of the Signpost or Journey. In this way we can weave the throughlines together more tightly than using whole Signposts and Journeys. When you subdivide Signposts and Journeys into smaller pieces, you allow for greater freedom in your storyweaving.

In practice, subdividing Signposts and Journeys into multiple pieces is a more commonly used approach than leaving entire Signposts and Journeys intact.

Storyweaving Static Story Points

By now, we have let our feelings be our guide in setting up a sequence for the twenty-eight Storyweaving scenes. Our next task is to figure out how to illustrate all of our remaining story points within those scenes.

One of the first things we might notice is the nature of each throughline is already expressed in the kinds of material we encoded for each Signpost and Journey. That is because the Types are simply a more detailed breakdown within each Throughline. All the remaining story points, however, will probably have to be addressed directly.

Since we have already woven all the crucial Progressive Story Points into our scenes, what remains is for us to weave the Static Story Points. Static Story Points *all* share one common quality: They must show up at least once, but can show up as many more times as you like. Again, we have freedom here. As long as we illustrate each story point somewhere, we have fulfilled our obligation to our structure. Anything beyond that is just technique that may make the story experience for our audience a more involving one.

So, let's take Goal. We might spell out the Goal in the first Storyweaving scene and never mention it again. Hitchcock often did this with his famous "MacGuffin", which was an excuse to get the chase started. Or, we might bring up the Goal once each act to make sure our audience doesn't lose sight of what the story is all about. In fact, that is another good rule of thumb: Even though once will do it, it is often best to remind the audience of each Static Story Point once each act. As we shall later see, this idea forms the basis of *The Rule of Threes*, which is a handy writer's technique.

Another thing we might do with a Static Story Point is hint at it, provide pieces of information about it, but never come out and say it. In this manner, the audience enjoys the process of figuring things out for itself. Since we are obliged to illustrate our structure, however, we better make sure that by the end of the story the audience has enough pieces to get the point.

For each kind of Static Story Point, authors have created many original ways in which to weave them into a scene through action, dialogue, visuals, even changing the color of type in a book. We suggest making a list of all your story points and then peppering them into your scenes in the most interesting and non-cliché manner you can. Even if you are not excessively clever about some of them, at least the structure has been served.

Storyweaving Characters

Lastly, a word about weaving characters into your story. There is a huge difference between weaving a Subjective Character and an Objective Character. In fact, now the weaving of Subjective Characters is much easier. Just through creating scenes based on the Signposts and Journeys in the Main and Impact Character Throughlines, much of their character has been woven into the story. Then, by illustrating these character's Static Story Points (such as Problem and Issue) the job almost finishes itself.

Objective Characters, however, are another matter altogether. Objective Characters have functions, and therefore to be woven into the Overall Story throughline they must exercise those functions. With archetypes it is an easy affair. There are eight archetypes. Each must be *introduced* so the audience knows what functions they represent. Each must be *dismissed* so the audience knows how they ended up. And, each must *interact* to show the audience which problem-solving techniques work better than others. Introductions, Interactions, and Dismissals: Another Rule of Threes again.

The most obvious and important interactions between archetypal characters occur between dynamic pairs, such as the Protagonist and Antagonist or Reason and Emotion. The two sides of each argument between functions must be played against each other to show which archetype fares better.

In addition, each interaction must go through the three steps of development: Set-up, conflict, and resolution. This means you must first establish the argument over the functions between each dynamic pair of archetypes. Then, the approaches must come into conflict. Finally, one of the two opponents must be shown to be better than the other.

Putting all this together, we have eight introductions, eight dismissals, and four interactions with three steps in each. This amounts to twenty-eight character *events* that must occur in a story using archetypes. As one might suspect, with twenty-eight character events and twenty-eight Storyweaving scenes, it dovetails nicely to put one character event in each Storyweaving scene. Now, you don't have to do this. It's just one simple way of getting the whole job done.

In keeping with this kind of approach, you might choose to touch on theme in each of the scenes, and explore at least one aspect of a Static Story point in every scene as well. This makes sure the entire structure relates. But it also runs the risk of creating a monotonous feel to your story.

Loading up one scene with many story points, then clearing the boards to concentrate on only one story point in the next scene, can liven up your storyweaving. In addition, all of this is based on an assumption of one Signpost or

Journey for each Storyweaving scene. Although that is the simple way to Storyweave, there are many more ways to communicate the structure of a story.

Storyweaving complex Objective Characters is a little more involved but follows the same pattern. Instead of relying on the combination of functions represented by each archetype, we must storyweave the introduction, interaction, and dismissals of each character element individually. For example, the motivation element of Pursuit must be introduced, interact with the other elements, most notably Prevent/Avoid, and then dismissed.

As with archetypal characters, each element interaction should include a set-up, conflict, and resolution. With sixty-four elements to explore, one can begin to see the attraction of the simplicity of archetypal characters. Conversely, the diversity of complex objective characters allows for nuances unavailable in archetypes. Fortunately it's your choice as to how you wish to build your Objective Characters. Find the right combination of complex characters and archetypes that works best for your story.

Complex Characters require more consideration when peppering their *events* in your scenes. There are far more than the twenty-eight character events created by the character archetypes. Here is a useful trick to storyweaving complex characters: Limit the elements you explore in a given scene—do not explore all of a complex character's characteristics in every scene in which it appears.

For example, Character A is a complex character with the following characteristics: Faith, Control, Proaction, and Chaos Character B is a complex character with the following characteristics: Disbelief, Feeling, Trust, Acceptance, and Order. Imagine a scene in which both Character A and Character B interact. We can choose to illustrate every one of each of their functions, or we can choose to limit the interactions. A limited interaction might show Character A and Character B conflicting over Faith vs. Disbelief. Character A might also discuss the value of being proactive. Character B might suggest acceptance and a the value of trust. This leaves Character A's elements of Control and Chaos and Character B's elements of Feeling and Order open for exploration in some other scene.

Storyweaving and Storytelling

There are two kinds of storytelling techniques: Those that affect the arrangement and relationships of things (spatial), and those that affect the sequence of things (temporal). In Dramatica theory, we have cataloged four different techniques of each kind.

Spatial techniques:

Building size *(changing scope)*

This technique holds audience interest by revealing the true size of something over the course of the story until you show it to be either larger or smaller than it originally appeared. This makes things appear to grow or dwindle as the story unfolds.

Conspiracy stories are usually good examples of increasing scope, as only the tip of the iceberg first comes to light and the full extent is ultimately much bigger. The motion picture THE PARALLAX VIEW illustrates this nicely. Stories about things being less extensive than they originally appear are like THE WIZARD OF OZ in which a seemingly huge network of power turns out to be just one man behind a curtain. Both of these techniques are used almost as a subgenre in science fiction stories, notable in the STAR TREK: THE NEXT GENERATION television series.

Red herrings *(changing importance)*

Red herrings make something appear more or less important than it really is. Several good examples of this technique can be found in the motion picture THE FUGITIVE. In one scene a police car flashes its lights and siren at fugitive-from-the-law Dr. Kimble, but only to tell him to move along. In another scene, Kimble is in his apartment when an entire battalion of police shows up with sirens blazing and guns drawn. It turns out they are after the son of his landlord and have no interest in him at all. Red herrings can inject storytelling tension where more structurally related weaving may be less interesting. (Note the difference from changing size, which concentrates on the changing extent of something, rather than reevaluations of its power.)

Meaning Reversals *(shifting context to change meaning)*

Reversals change context. In other words, part of the meaning of anything we consider is because of its environment. The phrase, *guilt by association*, expresses this notion. In Storyweaving, we can play on audience empathy and sympathy by making it like or dislike something, only to have it find out it was mistaken. There is an old Mickey Mouse cartoon called MICKEY'S TRAILER that displays this nicely. The story opens with Mickey stepping from his house in the country with blue skies and white clouds. He yawns, stretches, and then pushes a button on the house. All at once, the lawn rolls up, the fence folds in and the house becomes a trailer. Then, the sky and clouds fold up revealing the trailer is parked in a junkyard. This is a reversal from our original understanding.

Message Reversals *(shifting context to change message)*

In the example above, the structure of the story changed from what we thought it was. In contrast, when we shift context to create a different message, the structure remains the same, but our understanding of it changes. This is clearly illustrated in a TWILIGHT ZONE episode entitled, INVADERS, in which Agnes Moorhead plays a woman alone on a farm besieged by aliens from another world. The aliens in question are only six inches tall, wear odd space suits and attack the simple countrywoman with space-age weapons. Nearly defeated, she finally musters the strength to overcome the little demons, and smashes their miniature flying saucer. On its side we see the American Flag, the letters U.S.A. and hear the last broadcast of the landing team saying a giant has slaughtered them. Now, the structure didn't change, but our sympathies sure did, which was the purpose of the piece.

Temporal techniques:

Building importance *(changing impact)*

In this technique, things not only appear more or less important, but also actually become so. This was also a favorite of Hitchcock in such films as NORTH BY NORTHWEST and television series like MACGUYVER. In an episode of THE TWILIGHT ZONE, for example, Mickey Rooney plays a jockey who gets his wish to be big, only to be too large to run the race of a lifetime ("THE LAST NIGHT OF A JOCKEY," Episode #5.5).

Non-causality

There is often a difference between what an audience expects and what logically must happen. A prime example occurs in the Laurel and Hardy film, THE MUSIC BOX. Stan and Ollie are piano movers. The setup is their efforts to get a piano up a long flight of stairs to a hillside house. Every time they get to the top, one-way or another it slides down to the bottom again. Finally, they get it up there only to discover the address is on the second floor! So, they rig a block and tackle and begin to hoist the piano up to the second floor window. The winch strains, the rope frays, the piano sways. And just when they get the piano up to the window, they push it inside without incident.

After the audience has been conditioned by the multiple efforts to get the piano up the stairs. Pushing it in the window without mishap has the audience rolling in the aisles, as they say.

Out of sequence experiences *(changing temporal relationships)*

With this technique, the audience is unaware they are being presented things out of order. Such a story is the motion picture, BETRAYAL, with Ben Kingsley. The story opens and plays through the first act. We come to discover whom we side with and whom we don't: Who is naughty and who is nice. Then, the second act begins. It doesn't take long for us to realize that this action actually happened *before* the act we have just seen. Suddenly, all the assumed relationships and motivations of the characters must be reevaluated, and many of our opinions have to be changed. This happens again with the next act, so only at the end of the movie are we able to be sure of our opinions about the first act we saw, which was the last act in the story.

Other examples are PULP FICTION and MEMENTO in which we are at first unaware that things are playing out of order. Only later in the film do we catch on to this, and are then forced to alter our opinions.

Flashbacks and flash-forwards *(sneak previews and postviews)*

There is a big difference between flashbacks where a character reminisces and flashbacks that simply transport an audience to an earlier time. If the characters are aware of the time shift, it affects their thinking, and is therefore part of the story's structure. If they are not, the flashback is simply a Storyweaving technique engineered to improve the audience experience.

In the motion picture and book of INTERVIEW WITH THE VAMPIRE, the story is a structural flashback. Our concern centers on how Louis will react once he has finished relating these events from his past. In contrast, in REMAINS OF THE DAY, the story is presented out of sequence to compare aspects of the characters lives in ways only the audience can understand. Even PULP FICTION employs that technique once the cat is out of the bag that things are not in order. From that point forward, we are looking for part of the author's message to be *outside* the structure, in the realm of storytelling.

Technique Wrap-up

As long as the audience is able to make out the story's structure when the Storyweaving is completed, the underlying argument will be clear. Beyond that, there is no law that says if, when, or in what combinations these Storyweaving techniques can be brought into play. That is part of the art of storytelling, and is best left to the muse.

The one area we have not yet explored is the impact medium and formats have on Storyweaving techniques. Not to leave a stone unturned, Dramatica has a few tips for several of these.

Tips for Short Stories

How to Make Short, a Story

The Dramatica model contains an entire Grand Argument Storyform. There is simply not enough room in a short story, however, to cover all aspects of a Grand Argument. The worst thing to do is arbitrarily hack off chunks of the Grand Argument Story in an attempt to whittle things down. A better solution is to limit the *scope* of the argument. This can best be done by focusing on a single Class or removing a level of resolution (such as Overall Story Characters or Theme).

Two Ways to Limit Scope

When limited to one Class, the story will be told from only one point of view: Main Character, Impact Character, Overall Story Throughline, or Subjective Story Throughline. Because storyforms are holographic, the gist of the argument is made but only "proven" within that point of view.

When limiting to fewer resolutions, we remove a whole level of examination, effectively obscuring a portion of the exploration and leaving it dark. Again, we explore the gist of the topic but only in the clarified areas.

With a single-Class story, the argument appears one-sided, and indeed it is. In the limited-resolution story, exploring the topic seems shallow but is complete as deep as it goes.

Ultra-Short Stories

When writing VERY short stories, these two methods of "paring down" the information are often combined, resulting in a loss of perspective AND detail. So how small can a story be and still be considered a story? The minimal story consists of four dramatic units in a quad. This is the tiniest story that can create an interference pattern between the flow of space and time, encoding both reason and emotion in a way than can be decoded by an audience. However, ANY quad will do, which leads to a great number of minimal stories.

Tips for
Episodic Television Series

Characters in Episodic Series

Keeping Characters Alive

Unlike single stories told from scratch, television stories have "carry-over." That which is established becomes embedded in the mythical lore of the series, creating an inertia that strangles many fine concepts before their time. This inertia can be a good thing if it forms a foundation that acts as a stage for the characters rather than burying the characters under the foundation.

To keep a limber idea from succumbing to arthritis in this concrete jungle, create characters that can portray the full Element level of the structural storyform. Make choices that shift the dynamics from episode to episode. That keeps things lively.

Archetypal Characters

Many episodic series rely on Archetypal Characters who can be counted on to respond in the same way from episode to episode. This caters to the strengths of television series with a loyal audience: The ability to create friends and family on which one can rely.

The first few episodes of a series usually bring in the "Villain of the Week" (essentially a new Archetypal Antagonist each time) while establishing the Archetypal roles for the regular cast and outlining the mythical lore. This formula wears thin rather quickly as the characters fall into predictable relationships with one another. They assume standard roles from which they never vary until the series loses its ratings and is canceled.

Swapping Roles

A solution to this growing inflexibility is to change the formula after a few "establishing" episodes. If one keeps the Overall Story Characters the same for stability but swaps the Subjective Character roles, the dynamics of the character interrelationships change even while the structure remains the same. This means the Protagonist is still the Protagonist, Reason is still Reason and so on, but Reason may be the Main Character of the week and Protagonist the Impact Character. By shifting Subjective Character roles, several season's worth of character variations can be created without any repeats and the loyal audience's attention is held.

To further break up the routine, occasional stories can focus on one of the Overall Story Characters as Protagonist and Main Character in his own story, without the other cast members. For this episode only, assemble a whole new ensemble as if it were a story independent of the series. Obviously, too much of this weakens the mythical lore, so use this technique sparingly.

Characters of the Week

On the other hand, many successful series have been built around a single character that travels into new situations from week to week, meeting a whole new cast of characters each time. This forms the equivalent of an anthology series, except the Main Character recurs from week to week.

A means of creating character variety is to assign this recurring character occasionally to roles other than that of Protagonist. Instead of telling every episode as revolving around the recurring character, have that character be Guardian or Antagonist or Skeptic to some other Protagonist. This technique has allowed many "on the road" series to remain fresh for years.

Plot in Episodic Series

Plot is the aspect of episodic series most plagued with formula. This is because of a predictable *Dramatic Circuit*. A Dramatic Circuit consists of a Potential, Resistance, Current, and Outcome. Each of these aspects must be present to create the flow of dramatic tension.

Storytelling conventions often follow the order suggested above. Each episode begins with the potential for trouble either as the first act in a half hour series or as the teaser in an hour series. In half hour series, the next act brings in a Resistance to threaten conflict with the Potential. Hour-long series present an act setting up the status quo the Potential is about to disrupt, then present an act on the Resistance. Next follows the Current act in which Potential and Resistance conflict. In the final act, Potential and Resistance "have it out" with one or the other coming out on top. Some series favor the Potential winning, others the Resistance; still others alternate depending on the mood of the producers, writers and stars.

Some feel this kind of formula is a good pattern to set up because the audience becomes comfortable with the flow. Sometimes this is true, but unless the Character, Theme, and Throughline of each episode vary the audience will wind up getting bored instead. More interesting approaches vary which function of the Dramatic Circuit comes first and jumble up the order of the others as well. Starting with an

Outcome and showing how it builds to a Potential, then leaving that Potential open at the end of the story can make plots seem inspired. Many a notable comedy series has its occasional bittersweet ending where all the pieces don't come together.

Theme in Episodic Series

Often in episodic series, "themes" are replaced with "topics." Although Dramatica refers to the central thematic subject as a Topic, common usage sees topics as hot subjects of the moment. This makes topics an element of storytelling, not storyform. Often, the actual thematic topic is missing or only hinted at in exploring a news topic.

For example, the "topic of the week" in a typical series might be "Babies for Sale." But is that a Theme? Not hardly. What is interesting about Babies for Sale? Are we exploring someone's Strategy or Worry or Responsibility or Morality? Any of these or any of the 60 other Variations could be the thematic topic of "Babies for Sale."

To involve the audience emotionally, the theme of each episode must be distinct, clearly defined and fully explored in essential human ways—not just revolving around a news item.

Genre in Episodic Series

Series can be comedies, action stories, love stories—whatever. The key point to consider is that Dramatica Throughlines work in any Genre. To keep a "high" concept from bottoming out, rotate through the Throughlines, using a different one each week. There are only four Throughlines: A Situation, an Activity, Manipulation and a Fixed Attitude. A Situation Comedy (Situation) is different from a Comedy of Errors (Manipulation). Whatever Genre the series is cast in, bouncing the episodes through the Throughlines keeps the Genre fresh. In addition, jumping among genres can spice up the flavor of a series that has begun to seem like leftovers from the same meal, week to week.

Tips for Multi-Story Ensemble Series and Soap Operas

Subplots

The least complex form of the Multi-Story Ensemble Series employs the use of subplots. Subplots are tales or stories drawn with less resolution than the principal story. They hinge on one of the principal story's characters other than the Main Character. This hinge character becomes the Main Character of the subplot story.

Subplots are never essential to the progression of the principal plot and only serve to more fully explore issues tangential to the principal story's argument. "Tangent" is a good word to use here, as it describes something that touches on yet does not interfere with something else.

Subplots may begin any time during the principal story, but should wrap up just before the principal climax, or just after in the denouement (author's proof).

Relationships of Subplots to Plot

Since subplots are essentially separate stories, they may or may not reflect the values and concerns of the principal story. This allows an author to complement or counterpoint the principal argument. Often a subplot becomes a parallel of the principal story in another storytelling context, broadening the scope of the principal argument by inference to include all similar situations. In contrast, the subplot may arrive at the opposite conclusion, suggesting the solution for one storytelling situation is not universally appropriate.

There can be as many subplots in a story as time allows. Each one, however, must hinge on a character that is essential to the principal story (as opposed to a character merely created for storytelling convenience). Each character can only head a single subplot, just as the Main Character of the principal story cannot carry any more subplots. However, the Main Character can (and often does) take part in a subplot as one of its objective characters.

Multi-Story Formats

Other than subplots, Multi-Story Series can contain several unrelated stories. In this case, there may be two or more independent sets of characters that never cross paths. Or an author may choose to interweave these independent stories so the characters come into contact, but only in an incidental way. In a sense, this form is a "spatial anthology" in which multiple stories are not told in succession but simultaneously.

Perhaps the most complex form of the Multi-Story Ensemble Series is when both subplots and separate stories are employed. Often, the subplots and the separate stories both use the principal story's characters as well as characters that do not come into play in the principal story.

Stretching Time

An overabundance of storytelling becomes difficult to finish within the limits of even a one-hour show. Therefore, single episodes can be treated more like acts with stories sometimes running over four or more episodes. Each episode might also contain subplots staggered in such a way that more than one may end or begin in the middle of another subplot which continues over several episodes.

Obviously, many cross-dynamics can be going on here. It is the author's job as storyteller to make sure the audience always is aware which story or subplot they are seeing and what the character's roles are in each context. This is essential, since no internal storyform controls all the independent stories. The connective tissue of storytelling holds them together.

Tips for Novels

Novels, like all forms of prose, employ "stretchy time" where (unlike plays) individual audience members can advance through the work at their own pace. They can also reexperience important or personally meaningful sections and skip sections. As a result, in novels an author can play with storytelling in ways that would be ineffective with the audience of a stage play.

More than most formats, the author can meander in a novel without losing his audience. This is a wonderful opportunity to explore areas of personal interest, develop an intriguing character, harp on a message or engage publicly in a fantasy.

Of course, if you intend to tell an actual story in your novel, then the storyform has to be in there somewhere. However, with stretchy time in effect, time is not of the essence and one can afford to stray from the path and play in the fields on the way to Grandmother's house.

Tips for Motion Pictures

The Rule of Threes

Many rules and guidelines work fine until you sit down to write. As soon as you get inspired, creative frenzy takes over and the muse bolts forward like a mad bull. But there is one rule of thumb that sticks out like a sore thumb: The Rule of Threes.

Interactions and the Rule of Threes

Overall Story Characters represent dramatic functions that need to interact to reflect all sides of solving the story problem. The first interaction sets the relationship between the two characters. The second interaction brings them into conflict. The third interaction shows which one fares better, proving one as more appropriate than the other.

This is true between Protagonist and Antagonist, Protagonist and Skeptic, Skeptic and Sidekick—in short, between all essential characters in a story. A good guide while writing is to arrange at least three interactions between each pairing of characters. In this manner, the most concise, yet complete portrayal can be made of essential storyform dynamics.

Introductions

You must introduce each of the characters before the three interactions occur, and dismiss them after the three interactions are complete. These two functions set up the story and then disband it, much like one might put up a grandstand for a parade and then tear it down after the event is over. This often makes it feel like there are five acts in a story when three are dynamic acts and two have been "borrowed" from the structure.

Introducing characters is so well known that the author often forgets it. A character's intrinsic nature must be illustrated *before* he interacts with any of the Overall Story Characters. This is so basic that half the time it doesn't happen and the story suffers right from the start. (Keep in mind that an author can use storytelling to "fool" his audience into believing a character has a given nature, only to find out it made assumptions based on too little information in the wrong context.)

Introductions can be on-camera or off. They can be in conversation about a character, reading a letter that character wrote, seeing the way they decorate their apartment—anything that describes their natures.

Dismissals

The Rule of Threes should be applied until all the primary characters are played against one another to see what sparks are flying. Once we understand how they interact, it is time to dismiss the company. Dismissals can be as simple as a death or as complex as an open-ended suggestion of the future for a particular character. When all else fails, just before the ending crawl a series of cards can be shown: "Janey Schmird went on to become a New Age messiah while holding a day job as a screenplay writer."

The point is the audience needs to say good-bye to their new friends or foes.

Handoffs

Handoffs and Missing Links

Often we may find that a particular point of view needs to be expressed in a given scene but the character that represents that view has gone off to Alaska. Why did we send him to Alaska? Well, it seemed like a good idea at the time. But now... Do we go back and rewrite the entire plot, have him take the next flight home or blow it off and let the lackluster scene languish in his absence?

None of the above. We could do those things, but there are two other choices that often prove much more satisfying as well as less destructive to what has already been written. One method refers to absent characters; the other is the handoff.

Characters in Absentia

The function of characters in a scene is not to show their physical presence, but to represent their points of view on the topic. As long as they fulfill that mandate and throw their two-cents into the mix, their actual presence is not required.

As authors, how can we represent a character's point of view in a scene without having to haul him in and place him there? Perhaps the easiest way is to have other characters talk about the missing character and relay the opinion that character would have expressed if he had been present. For example, one character might say, "You know, if Charlie were here he'd be pissed as hell about this!" The conversation might continue with another character taking a contrary position on what old

Charlie's reaction might be until the two have argued the point to some conclusion much as if Charlie had been there in spirit.

Other techniques might use an answering machine message, a letter, diary or video interview from the character in question that is examined during a scene. Many current stories use a murder victim's videotaped will to include him in scenes involving his money-grubbing heirs. More subtle but potentially even more effective is for one character to examine the apartment, studio, or other habitat of a missing character and draw conclusions based on the personality expressed in the furnishings and artifacts there. Even the lingering effect of processes a character started before he left, or other characters' memories of the missing character can position him amid intense dramatic discussions without his actual attendance.

Still, for some storytelling purposes, you need a live body to uphold and represent a point of view. If there is just no way to bring the character that contains those characteristics into the scene personally, an author can assign a proxy instead. Do this by temporarily transferring the dramatic function from one character to another. We call this a handoff.

What is a Handoff?

A handoff occurs when one *player* temporarily takes on the story function of a missing *player*. This new player carries the dramatic flag for the scene in question, and then hands it back to the original player on his return.

Doesn't this violate the Dramatica guideline that every Objective Character is the sole representative of his unique characteristics? Not really. Having one character be the sole representative of a characteristic is a guideline, not a law. The essential part of that guideline is that a character does not change his internal inventory of characteristics during the story. A *player*, however, is not bound by that restriction.

In a handoff the player is not actually giving up a characteristic because he isn't around when another character is using it, so technically the first player is never seen without it. But because of this, he cannot share characteristics with other players *at the same time*. If he did, two characters might be trying to represent the same point of view in the same scene, making dramatic tension just go limp.

How to Do Handoffs

When we employ the handoff, we create two players to represent the same trait at different times. It is reminiscent of time-sharing a condo. In any given scene, a single point of view might be represented by character "A" or by character "B," but never by both in the same scene.

Most often, one of the players will be a *major* player and the other just a "plot device" player of convenience who appears for one scene and is never heard from again. Such players just fill in the gaps. Sometimes, both players prove intriguing to the author and each becomes a major player. The difficulty then arises that at the climax of the story, both players might still be alive and kicking and therefore suddenly converge in an awkward moment. No matter what you do, it's going to be clunky. Still, if you must have both present, it's best to either make a statement in the story that they have the same characteristics, binding them in the mind of the audience, or deal with them one after another.

A special case exists when (for whatever reason) an author decides to remove a player from the story. This can be a result of sending the player to its death, to the Moon or just having it leave at some point and not return. Often, this technique is used to shock an audience or throw them a red herring. Unless the functions represented by the eliminated player reappear in another player, however, part of the story's argument will disappear at the point the original drops out. In the attempt to surprise an audience by killing off a major player, many an author has doomed an otherwise functional storyform.

There are two primary ways in which an eliminated player's functions can continue without him. The easiest is to bring in a new player who is dramatically identical with the first, although its personal qualities are usually different. Often the storytelling requirements of a plot judge one player more suited to part of a story and another player to be more in line with the rest. Killing off the first player but continuing its dramatic function through a new player can serve both purposes and provide the best storytelling effect without a loss of dramatic continuity. The major condition is the audience must be made aware that this "deadman handoff" has occurred so it does not suddenly sense a vacuum in the story's argument. This may require a fair amount of introduction to place the new player solidly in the old role.

The second technique for replacing a player yet continuing the character's functions is to divide the functions among several new players, each representing only a portion of what had previously been contained in one. Naturally, these new players would be less complex than their predecessor, which may decrease nuance at certain levels of the story. On the plus side, this method scatters the functions into new bodies, allowing for external conflicts between functions previously blended into a single individual. Once again, telling the audience who got what is essential to the smooth progression of this type of handoff.

The Art of Storytelling
STAGE FOUR

STORY RECEPTION

About the Audience

What do you have in mind?

Few authors write stories without at least considering what it will be like to read the story or see it onstage or screen. As soon as this becomes a concern, we have crossed the line into Story Reception theory. Suddenly, we have more to consider than our story's message. We now must try to predict how that message is received.

One of the first questions then becomes, how do we *want* it to be received? And from this, we ask, what am I hoping to achieve with my audience? We may wish to educate our audience, or we may simply want to bias them. Perhaps we are out to persuade our audience to adopt a point of view, or simply to pander to an existing point of view. We might provoke our audience, forcing them to consider some topic or incite them to take action about a topic. We could openly manipulate them with their informed consent, or secretly propagandize them, changing their outlook without their knowledge.

No matter what our author's intent, it is shaped not only by who we are, but also by the audience we are trying to reach.

Who are you talking to?

You are reading this book because you want to use the Dramatica theory or software to help you record something you are thinking about or feeling. For whatever reasons, you have decided you want to record something of yourself in a communicable form.

A primary question then becomes: To whom do you intend to communicate? You might simply wish to communicate to yourself. You may be documenting transient feelings that you wish to recall vividly in the future. Or you may want to capture the temporal ramblings of your chain of thought and then stand back to see what pattern it makes. Self-searching is often a primary objective of an author's endeavor.

Writing for Someone Else

What if you are writing not for yourself but to reach someone else? It might be that you hope to reach a single individual that can be done in a letter to a friend, parent, or child. You might be composing an anecdote or speech for a small or large group, or you could be creating an industrial film, designing a textbook, or fashioning a timeless work for all humanity.

In each case, the scope of your audience becomes more varied as its size increases. The opportunity to tailor your efforts to target your audience becomes less practical, and the symbols used to communicate your thoughts and feelings become more universal and simultaneously less specific.

The audience can thus range from writing for you to writing for the world. In addition, an author's labors are often geared toward a multiplicity of audiences, including both him and others as well. Knowing one's intended audience is essential to deciding form and format. It allows one to select a medium and embrace the kind of communication that is most appropriate—perhaps even a story.

Dramatica and Communication Theory

Exploring all avenues of communication is far beyond the scope of this early implementation of the Dramatica Theory. To be sure, Dramatica (as a model of the mind) has much to offer in many diverse areas. However, for the practical purposes, we cannot cover that much ground. Rather, we will briefly touch on major perspectives in the author/audience relationship that can also serve as templates for translation of the Grand Argument Story perspective into valuable tools for other forms of communication. In this manner, the usefulness of this specific software implementation can extend beyond its immediate purpose. (What does this say about OUR intended audience?)

Writing for Oneself

In the Great Practical World of the Almighty Dollar Sign, it might seem trite or tangential to discuss writing for oneself (unless one expects to pay oneself handsomely for the effort). In truth, the rewards of writing for oneself DO pay handsomely, and not just in personal satisfaction. By getting in touch with one's own feelings, by discovering and mapping out one's biases, an author can grow to recognize his own impact on the work as being an addition to the structure of the work itself. An author can also become more objective about ways to approach his audience. (And yes, one can gain personal insights and satisfaction as well.)

The Author as Main Character

As an experiment, cast yourself in a story as the Main Character. Cast someone with whom you have a conflict as the Impact Character. Next, answer all the Dramatica questions and then go to the Story Points window in the Dramatica Pro software. Fill in as many of the story points as seem appropriate to you. Print out the results and put them aside.

Now, go back and create the same story again—this time with your "opponent" as the Main Character and YOU as the Impact Character. Once again, fill in the story points and print them out. Compare them to the first results. You will likely find areas in which the story points are the same and other areas in which they are different.

These points of similarity and divergence will give you a whole new perspective on the conflicts between you and your adversary. Often, this is the purpose of an author when writing for himself. Thoughts and feelings can be looked at more objectively on paper than hidden inside your head. Just seeing them all jumbled up together rather than as a sequence goes a long way to uncovering meaning that was invisible by just trotting down the path. After all, how can we ever hope to understand the other person's point of view while trying to see it from our perspective?

A wise woman once said, "Don't tell me what you'd do if you were me. If you were *me*, you'd do the same thing because I AM ME and that's what I'm doing! Tell me what *you'd* do if you were in my situation."

Documenting Oneself

Another purpose in writing for oneself is simply to document what it is like to be in a particular state of mind. In a sense, we jot down the settings of our minds so we can tune ourselves back into that state as needed later. The images we use may have meaning for no one but ourselves, and therefore speak to us uniquely of all people. The ability to capture a mood is extremely useful when later trying to communicate that mood to others. To bring emotional realism to another requires being in the mood oneself. What better intuitive tools than emotional snapshots one can count on to regenerate just the feelings one wants to share. To make an argument, *accept* the argument. To create a feeling, *experience* the feeling.

Who is "Me"?

A simple note sticks to the refrigerator door: "Call me when you get home." Who is "me?" It depends on whom you are asking. Ask the author of the note and he would say it was "myself." Ask the recipient of the note and they would say, "It's him." So the word "me" has different meanings depending on who is looking at it. To the author, it means the same when they wrote it as when they read it as an audience. To the intended audience, however, it means something different.

In life, we assume one point of view at a time. In stories, however, we can juxtapose two points of view, much as we blend the images from two eyes. We can thus look AT a Main Character's actions and responses even as we look through his eyes. This creates an interference pattern that provides much more depth and meaning than either view has separately.

My "Me" is Not Your "Me"

When writing for others, if we *assume* they share our point of view, it is likely that we will miss making half of our own point. Far better are our chances of successful communication if we not only see things from our side but theirs as well. Overlaying the two views can define areas of potential misunderstanding before damage is done. Still, "Call me when you get home" is usually a relatively low-risk communication and we suggest you just write the note without too much soul-searching.

Writing for Groups

What Binds a Group?

Groups are not clumps. They are conglomerations of individuals, bound (to various degrees) by an aspect of shared interests or traits. Sometimes the common theme can be an ideology, occupation, physical condition, or situation. Sometimes the only thread of likeness is that they all gathered to be an audience.

Do readers of novels "group" as an audience? Not in the physical sense, yet fans of a particular writer or genre or subject matter are bound by their common interest. Regular viewers of a television series start out as individuals and become a group through bonding of experience. They know the classic "bits" and the characters' idiosyncrasies. In fact, the series' audience becomes a group representing a fictional culture that eventually becomes one more subcultural template in actual society. Works can indeed *create* groups as well as attract them.

What Binds Us All Together?

What of the "captive" audience that has no sense of what they are about to experience, yet are gathered in a classroom or reception room or boardroom or theater? What of the audience attending the first telecast of a new series, knowing little of what to expect?

Underneath all the common threads binding an audience together is a group of individuals. Each one is responsive to the same essential mental processes as the next. It is this intrinsic sameness—not of ideas but of the way in which ideas are formed—that makes us all part of the group we call humans. At this most basic level, we are all part of the same group.

Symbolic Identification

Throughout this book we have stressed the difference between story*forming* and story*telling*. A clear communication requires succinct storyforming. Communicating clearly requires appropriate storytelling.

What makes storytelling appropriate? The symbols used to encode the storyform are both understood in denotation and connotation by the intended audience. If the audience misreads the symbols, the message will be weakened, lost, or polluted.

Identifying with one's audience is not enough: One must also *identify* one's audience. It is fine to feel part of the group. But it can be a real danger to assume that identification with a group leads to clear communication in appropriate symbols or clear reception by all audience members.

A Quick Lesson in Propaganda

Propaganda, n. 1. any organization or movement working for the propagation of particular ideas, doctrines, practices, etc. 2. the ideas, doctrines, practices, etc. spread in this way. **(Webster's New Twentieth Century Dictionary)**

Propaganda: 3. a storyforming/storytelling technique used to impact an audience in specific ways, often employed to instigate deliberation and/or action. **(Dramatica)**

Propaganda is a wonderful and dangerous story device. Its primary use in stories is as a method for an author to influence an audience long after they have experienced the story itself. By using propaganda, an author can inspire an audience to think certain ways, think about certain things, behave certain ways, and take specific actions. Like fire and firearms, propaganda can be used constructively and destructively and does not contain an inherent morality. Any morality involved comes from the minds of the author and his audience.

This section is not about the morality of propaganda. It is designed as a primer on how to create and employ propaganda in stories. With that in mind, let's get down to the nitty-gritty.

The Basics of Propaganda

The human mind seeks to understand itself and the world around it. It does this through various ways including organizing information into meaningful patterns. Depending on the quantity of the information and the accuracy of its interpretation, a mind will identify a pattern (or several potential patterns) and supply the seemingly "missing" pieces to make the pattern, and therefore meaning, complete. This pattern matching and filling in of missing pieces is intrinsic to the processes that create the human "mind." By choosing which pieces of the storyform to omit, authors can manipulate the impact a story will have on the minds of their audiences.

In its most basic form, propaganda is a way for authors to have an audience share their point of view. Closed (or complete) stories allow authors to present their points of view in the form of an argument that the audience can then take or leave. Open (or incomplete) stories require their audiences to supply the missing pieces to get meaning from the story. Just creating an open story, however, does not create propaganda. There must be a pattern to what is missing.

The amount and nature of the missing pieces have an effect on the story's propagandistic impact. If you leave too much out of your story, an audience may not make the effort to "fill-in-the-blanks." The audience may then interpret the story as meaningless. If, however, you selectively leave out specific pieces of the storyform, the audience may unknowingly fill in those holes with aspects of its personal experience. In this way, the story changes from an argument made by the author **to** the audience, to an argument made by the author **and** the audience. Unwittingly, the audience begins to share the author's point of view and perhaps even becomes a coconspirator in its propagation: Therefore, propaganda.

Since a propaganda story is based on a fragile relationship between an audience and an author, both perspectives should be considered to understand the techniques that can be used and the results that can be achieved.

The Audience

Knowing (or preparing) your audience can have a tremendous effect on how your propaganda will impact them. Here are some rules of thumb:

- The more specific the symbols you use to encode your story, the more limited an audience it will affect. The less specific the symbols, the greater potential audience.

- The more specific the symbols used to encode the story, the greater the likelihood it will influence the portion of the audience that understands the symbols. The less specific the symbols, the less impact the story will have.

- The more familiar an audience is with the symbols used to encode a story, the more susceptible they are to propaganda. The less familiar, the less susceptible.

The Author

Here are the things an author should consider while creating a propaganda story:

1. Nature of Impact

How do you want to influence your audience? Do you wish to play with your audience's:

- Motivations (what drives them)?
- Methodologies (how they go about doing things)?

- Purposes (what they are striving for)?

- Means of Evaluation (how they measure their progress — their personal yardsticks)?

Pick only one as the area of primary impact. This will become the area of the storyform that you purposely omit when storytelling. The remaining three areas will be used to support your intent by drawing attention away from the missing pieces.

2. Area of Impact

What part of your audience's world-view do you wish to influence?

- View of the world around them — "objective reality" (Overall Story)

- View of relationships (Subjective Story)

- View of themselves (Main Character)

- View of others (Impact Character)

Choose one of the perspectives. This will be the domain in which to place the "hole" in the storyform. The area of impact determines which part of your audience's world-view the propaganda will "infect."

3. Type of Impact: Specific vs. General

Do you want the impact on your audience to be of a specific nature, or of a broader, more general nature?

The more specific you make the propaganda, the more specific and predictable its impact will be on an audience. The upside (from an author's point of view) is that specific behavior (mental or physical) can be promoted or changed. The downside is that specific propaganda is more easily identifiable and therefore contestable by the audience.

Specific propaganda is achieved by intentionally not encoding selected story points, such as the Main Character's motivation or the story Outcome (Success or Failure). The audience will supply the missing piece from its own experiences, for example, the Main Character's motivation in THELMA AND LOUISE. What happened to Louise in Texas that prevents her from ever going back is specifically *not* mentioned in the film — that blank is left for the audience to fill.

The more general you make the propaganda, the less specific but all pervasive its impact will be on an audience. Instead of focusing impact on the audience's motivations, methodologies, purposes, or means of evaluation, generalized propaganda will tend to bias the audience's perspectives of their world. The upside (from an author's point of view) is that generalized propaganda is difficult for an audience to identify and therefore more difficult to combat than the specific form of propaganda. The downside is that it does not promote any specific type of behavior or thought process and its direct impact is less recognizable.

General propaganda is achieved by intentionally not encoding entire areas of the story's structure or dynamics. For example, by leaving out almost all forms of the story's internal means of evaluation, NATURAL BORN KILLERS forces its audience to focus on the methodologies involved and questions its own (the members of the audience) means of evaluation.

4. Degree of Impact

To what degree do you wish to influence your audience? The degree to which you can influence an audience is dependent on many variables not the least of which are your storytelling skills and the nature of the audience itself. There are some basic guidelines, however, that can mitigate and sometimes supersede those variables when skillfully employed.

Shock as Propaganda

One tried-and-true method is to control what an audience knows about the story before experiencing the storytelling process so you can shock them. Within the context of the story itself (as opposed to marketing or word-of-mouth), an author can prepare the audience by setting up certain *givens*, and then purposely break the storyform (destroy the givens) to shock or jar the audience. This hits the audience at a preconscious level by inviting an instantaneous, knee-jerk reaction. This type of propaganda is the most specific and immediately jarring on its audience. Two films that employed this technique to great effect are PSYCHO and THE CRYING GAME.

PSYCHO broke the storyform to shock the audience's preconscious by killing the main character twenty minutes or so into the film (the "real" story about the Bates family then takes over). The *shock* value was strengthened through marketing by having the main character played by big box office draw Janet Leigh (a good storytelling choice at the time). They used a marketing gimmick to help set up the shock. No one was allowed into the movie after the first five or ten minutes. This "gimmick" was essential for the propaganda to be effective. It takes time for an audience to identify on a personal level with a main character. Coming in late to the film would not allow enough time for the audience member to identify with Janet Leigh's character and her death would have little to no impact.

THE CRYING GAME used a slightly different process to achieve a similar impact. The first twenty minutes or so of the film are used to set up a bias to the main character's (and audience's) view of reality. The "girlfriend" is clearly established except for one important fact. That "fact," because it is not explicitly noted, is supplied by the mind of the main character (and the minds of the audience members). By taking such a long time to prep the audience, it comes as a shock when we (both main character and audience) find out that *she* is a *he*.

Awareness as Propaganda

Another method is to be frank about the nature of the propaganda, letting your audience know what you are doing as you do it to them. This impacts an audience at a conscious level where they must actively consider the pros and cons of the issues. The propaganda comes from controlling the givens on the issues being discussed, while the audience focuses on which side of the issues they believe in.

A filmic example of this technique can be seen in JFK. By choosing a controversial topic (assassinating President Kennedy) and making an excessively specific argument about what parties were involved in the conspiracy to carry out and cover-up the assassination, Oliver Stone was able to focus his audience's attention on how "they" got away with it. The issue of who "they" were was suspiciously controversial as the resulting media bru-ha-ha over the film showed. Who "they" were, however, is not the propaganda. The propaganda came in the form of the story's *given* which is that Lee Harvey Oswald had help. By the end of the story, audiences were arguing over *which* of the parties in the story were or were not participants in the conspiracy, accepting the possibility that people other than Oswald may have been involved.

Conditioning as Propaganda

Presenting an audience with an alternative life experience is yet another way to influence your audience. By ignoring (or catering to) an audience's cultural bias, you can present your story as an alternative reality. This impacts an audience by undermining or reinforcing their personal Memories. By experiencing the story, the message or meaning of the story becomes part of the audience's memory base.

The nature of the propaganda, however, is that the story lacks context, which must be supplied by the audience. Thus personalized, the story memory is triggered automatically when an experience in the audience's real life summons similarly stored memories. Through repeated use, an audience's "sensibilities" become conditioned.

In Conditioning propaganda, audience attention is directed to causal relationships like *When A also B* (spatial), and *If C then D* (temporal). The mechanism of this propaganda is to leave out a part of the causal relationships in the story, such as *When A also B* and *If ?? then D*. By leaving out one part, the objective contextual meaning is then supplied automatically by the audience. The audience will replace *??* with something from its own experience base, not consciously considering that a piece is missing because it will have emotionally arrived at the contradiction: *When A also B and then D.*

This type of propaganda is closest to the *traditional* use of the term used with stories, entertainment, and advertising. For example, look at much of the tobacco and alcohol print advertising. Often the Main Character (the type of person to whom the advertisement is supposed to appeal) is attractive, has someone attractive with them, and appears to be well placed in life. The *inference* is that when you smoke or drink, you are also cool, and if you are cool then you will be rich and attractive. The connection between "cool" and "rich and attractive" is not really in the advertisement but an audience often makes that connection for itself. In Conditioning propaganda, more than in the other three forms of propaganda, the degree of impact on your audience is extremely dependent on your audience's life experience outside the story experience.

CRIMES AND MISDEMEANORS is a film example that employs this conditioning technique of propaganda. The unusual aspect of the film is that it has two separate stories in it. The "CRIMES" story involves a self-interested man who gets away with murder and personally comes to peace with it (a Success/Good story). The "MISDEMEANORS" story involves a well-meaning man who loses his job, his girlfriend, and is left miserable (a Failure/Bad story). By supplying two competing stories instead of one, the audience need not supply its own experiences to arrive at a false context while viewing this work. Audiences will come to stories, however, with a particular cultural bias. In our culture, Failure/Bad stories which happen to nice people are regrettable, but familiar; Success/Good stories about murderers are uncommon and even "morally shameful."

The propaganda comes into effect when the audience experiences in its own life a Failure/Bad scenario. The experience triggers a recollection of the Success/Good story about forgetting the grief of having murdered. This is an alternative the audience would not normally have considered. Lacking an objective contextual meaning that sets one over the other, both stories are given equal consideration as solutions. Thus, what was once unthinkable because of a cultural or personal bias is now automatically seen as a possible avenue for problem solving.

Misdirection as Propaganda

The most subtle and possibly most effective form of propaganda from a single exposure is the use of misdirection as a way to influence an audience's Subconscious. Like "smoke and mirrors" used by magicians, this form of propaganda requires focusing the audience's Conscious attention in one place while the real impact is made in the Subconscious. Fortunately for propagandistic-minded authors, this is one of the easiest forms of propaganda to create.

This technique comes from omitting parts of the storyform from your storytelling. What you leave out becomes the audience's blind spot, and the dynamic partner to the omitted storyform piece becomes the audience's focus. The focus is where your audience's attention will be drawn (the smoke and mirrors). The blind spot is where your audience personalizes the story by "filling-in-the-blank." The story's argument is thus linked directly to the audience's subconscious, based on the context in which the story is presented.

Let's look at some dynamic pairs of partners that appear in a storyform. The following pairs concern the *nature* of the impact on your audience:

$$\begin{array}{ccc} \text{Motivation} & <-> & \text{Purpose} \\ \text{Means of Evaluation} & <-> & \text{Methodology} \end{array}$$

Should you wish to influence your audience's motivations, omit a particular motivation in the story. The audience, then, focused on the purpose they can see will automatically supply a motivation that seems probable to them (for example: THELMA AND LOUISE).

Here are the storyform dynamic pairs that relate to story/audience *perspectives*:

$$\begin{array}{ccc} \text{Overall Story Perspective} & <-> & \text{Subjective Perspective} \\ \text{Main Character Perspective} & <-> & \text{Impact Character Perspective} \end{array}$$

Combining a *nature* with a *perspective* gives an author greater control over a story's propaganda. For example, if you wish to influence your audience in how they view the means of evaluation employed by the world around them, omit the Overall Story means of evaluation elements and the audience's attention will be distracted by focusing on the methodologies employed (such as in NATURAL BORN KILLERS).

A Word Of Warning

Propaganda is powerful but using it involves risks. It is like a virus or engaging in germ warfare. Once an audience is exposed to a propagandistic message, the only way they can neutralize it is to balance it with an equal but opposite force. Audiences often don't like to think they are being manipulated. If the audience becomes aware of the nature of your propaganda, the equal but opposite force can take the form of a backlash against the author and the propaganda itself. Look at the strong reaction against advertisers who "target" their advertising to specific demographic groups (for example African-Americans, women, Generation X, and so on). Strong reactions occur particularly when vendors try to sell liquor, tobacco products, or other items considered "vices" in America.

Once released, propaganda is difficult to control and often becomes subject to real world influences. Sometimes propaganda can benefit from real world coincidences. THE CHINA SYNDROME's mild propaganda about the dangers of nuclear power plants got a big boost in affecting its audience because of the Three-Mile Island incident. The media coverage of the O.J. Simpson murder case may not have tainted potential jurors, but NATURAL BORN KILLERS' propaganda against the media's sensationalization of violence got a little extra juice added to its punch. Often real life or the passage of time can undermine the effectiveness of propaganda. REEFER MADNESS may have been effective when it first came out, but audiences today find its propaganda against drug use obvious, simplistic, laughable and, more importantly, ineffective.

A Word About Adaptation

"Read the book; see the movie!" "Now a major motion picture!" "A novelization..." "A new musical based on the stage play..." "...based on the book..." "...based on the hit movie!" "The timeless story of..." "...a classic tale..." "...updated for today's audience..." "...colorized..." "...reformatted to fit your screen..." "edited for television."

It's the same old story. Or is it? Is a story the same when translated from one medium to another and if not, how is it different? What qualities *must* be changed to preserve a story's integrity? To adapt adeptly an author needs to know the answers to these questions.

Before we can find out answers, it would be prudent to define some terms. First, what do we mean by "adaptation?" Simply, adaptation is the process of translating a story from one medium to another. What is a "medium?" A medium is a physical facility for storing information *and* the processes involved in recovering it. Finally, what is "story?" For our purposes we shall define story as any information an author wishes to communicate to an audience (including considerations, experiences, and feelings).

So, putting it all together, *adaptation* is the process of translating information from one physical facility for storage and retrieval to another in such a way that it can be communicated to an audience. Sounds cold, doesn't it. That's because this is simply the logistic description of adaptation.

A more organic description might be: Adaptation is the process of reproducing an audience experience in another medium. That has a better feel to it, but is much less precise. Also, we can clearly see a difference in the purpose of each approach, as pointed out above when we spoke of the new story's identity versus its integrity. One seeks to preserve the parts, the other to be true to the whole. And that is the paradox at the heart of the adapter's dilemma: Should authors strive to recreate the structure accurately or to reproduce the dynamics faithfully? More to the point, why can't we do both?

The answer lies with the media themselves. Every medium has its own strengths and weaknesses. Often what can be easily carried out in one medium is either difficult or even impossible to achieve in another. Books are not very good at directly communicating sounds or visual atmospheres. The motion picture, on the other hand, is a poor medium for directly communicating a character's inner thoughts and feelings.

In each case, indirect means must be employed to accomplish what might be directly communicated in the other medium. To adapt a work successfully, an author must determine what to add or remove to achieve the same effect as the original medium.

It would seem that adaptations always fail to capture some aspect of the original, either in substance or essence. That is true, but it does not have to be a fatal problem. An audience tends to regard certain aspects of a story as being essential. As long as an adaptation keeps or recreates those essential elements, the audience will find the effort successful.

Beyond the essential, other elements may be more or less fully developed than in the original, providing something of the same flavor while allowing the latitude to tailor the piece for the new medium. The question then becomes how to decide which items are essential and how deeply they need to be developed, on a case-by-case basis.

The first step is to do a <u>complete</u> analysis of the original work. Just reading the book a hundred times or watching the movie until images are imbedded on your retina is not good enough. You don't want to know a work just from the inside out, but you want to know it from the outside in as well—the way the audience sees it. To develop both an understanding and empathy for the story, it helps to examine it in terms of the Four Stages of Communication.

The Four Stages of Communication describe the manner in which the author's original intent makes its way from his mind into the minds of his audience. Stage one is Story *forming*, in which the author first defines the message for himself. Stage two is Story *encoding*, where the author comes up with images and events to symbolize the message. Stage three is Story *weaving*, which is the process of arranging these images into scenes and acts. Stage four is Story *Reception,* which describes the relationship of the audience to the work. By analyzing how each of these stages functions in a story, an author can make sure the adaptation will connect at *all* levels of appreciation.

Storyforming

A key concept of traditional narrative theory is that the narrative itself is transportable among media. The narrative is not the complete story, but simply the essential dramatics of the deep structure. In Dramatica, we call this the Storyform. Dramatica is precise about what this underlying dramatic argument contains.

Each of the elements that must appear in a complete storyform is called a story point, because it is necessary for the audience to *understand* the story from that perspective to prevent a hole in the dramatic argument. Some story points are structural in nature, such as the story's *goal,* or the Main Character's *unique ability*. Others are more dynamic, such as the Main Character's *mental sex,* or the story's *limit* through imposing a *timelock* or an *optionlock.*

When analyzing a work to be adapted, it is sometimes difficult to separate the storyform from the storytelling. A good rule of thumb is to think of the storyform as the author's logistical argument and the storytelling as the *emotional* argument.

A good example of this can be seen by comparing ROMEO AND JULIET to WEST SIDE STORY, CYRANO DE BERGERAC to ROXANNE, or HEART OF DARKNESS to APOCALYPSE NOW. In each pair, the storyform is nearly the same, while the storytelling is different.

An example of a poor adaptation that failed in the storyforming was the translation of A CHRISTMAS CAROL into the motion picture SCROOGED, starring Bill Murray.

In the original Dickens story, Scrooge is a character who must *start* doing something, rather than *stop* doing something. Scrooge does not proactively hurt people. Scrooge allows suffering to continue because of his lack of action. He has a hole in his heart. The ghost of Christmas Present presents him with two children, *Ignorance* and *Want.* They serve to illustrate the problems Scrooge perpetuates through his lack of generosity.

In the modern adaptation, Bill Murray's character is someone who must *stop* doing something. He proactively harms several people. But when the argument is made for him to change, he is still presented with those who want and are needy. That argument is simply not appropriate to a character that needs to stop. As a result, the attempt to make a more proactive villain, updated for our time, failed because the supporting argument contained in the balance of the storyform was not adjusted to support the change.

Use your Dramatica software to arrive at the single storyform that best describes the work you are adapting. Make sure that if you decide to change anything, you run another storyform to learn what else must be changed as well. You may discover that you need to make only minor adjustments. Or you may find out the storyform requires so much altering that the item you intended to change would scuttle any sense of familiarity with the original.

Storyencoding

If the storyform is the skeleton, the storyencoding is the meat. Let's take a single storyforming story point and see how encoding can flavor its meaning. Suppose the goal of the original story is to obtain the stolen diamonds. Without changing the storyform, we might adapt that to obtaining the stolen gold. We could also change it to obtaining a diploma, obtaining someone's love, or obtaining the office of President of the United States. Each and every one of these examples has a goal of obtaining, but each also has a different flavor depending solely on the encoding.

Often, encoding is more important to an audience than anything else. Encoding determines the setting, the subject matter, the size and scope of the issues. Substituting stolen gold for stolen diamonds would probably be interchangeable to most audience members. Substituting obtaining a diploma would not.

Encoding is the first stage that is open to authors' interpretation. It is important to illustrate the original story's storyform completely, so all the specific symbols used by the original author can be documented. Then, the process is to sort through the list, see which are essential, which are secondary but must be given lip service, and which can or even should be cut because of the specifics of the new medium.

When delving into this much detail, it is easy to miss the forest for the trees. For example, if we elected to change "stolen diamonds" to "stolen gold" but still had our Main Character working for DeBeers, we might have created a problem.

This is not to say that every encoding story point must be consistent with all the others in flavor. In fact, many stories are appealing simply because the juxtaposition of contrasting symbols. The key is to make sure you preserve the same relationship *between* the flavors. Much like adapting a recipe for a culinary feast, you might substitute salt for sugar, but then you must also substitute vinegar for sour cream. The overall flavor would be different, but the relationship between flavors is upheld. That level of pattern-recognition is well within the grasp of most audiences. How many times has THE SIMPSONS reproduced famous scenes from famous movies in a completely different context? This works because the *internal* relationships remain consistent.

Storyweaving

Storyweaving is the process of unfolding the symbols of your story for the audience. It is where we create suspense, tension, mystery, and surprise. When adapting genres such as horror, thriller, and murder mystery, the experiential mood is almost storyform and storyencoding dependent. It is the weaving that takes center stage, and is therefore the most crucial characteristic to preserve in an adaptation.

With murder mysteries, the manner in which the cat is let out of the bag defines the audience experience. Much of the appeal of a Sherlock Holmes mystery, for example, is because of the steps through which the chase becomes afoot. Holmes has been successfully translated to almost every time and place in human history changing both storyform and storyencoding until nothing remains of the original because the *feel* remains the same because of the way the case unravels. In many respects, the Holmes stories are identified by their exposition template, and that is why the audience comes to the work.

This same stage of communication is highlighted in THE TWILIGHT ZONE (the first series, the movie adaptation, and the adapted second series). It is also used in THE OUTER LIMITS (first series and adapted series), and almost every Stephen King book and movie. Did you ever wonder *why* some of King's best works don't translate well to the screen? The adaptations that don't work change the storyweaving, which is the identifying trademark of the King experience.

Make sure you examine the manner in which the audience is let in on the secrets of the story to be adapted. Is the story an Extrovert that lets it all hang out from scene one? Is it a Flirt that flaunts it but takes its time in delivering? Is your story an Introvert that must have its secrets coaxed out one at a time, or is it a Liar that fools us with red herrings and misdirections?

Unless you strive to keep the original's personality, much of the charm may be lost in the translation. An example of this kind of mistake occurred in bringing THE BEVERLY HILLBILLIES to the big screen. In the original series, the storyweaving personality was much like a British comedy of manners in which the cultured and proper are forced by circumstances to accommodate unsophisticated bumpkins. Enter Politically Correct storyweaving. Suddenly, the focus of comedy shifts from manners to physical comedy.

The slapstick gags are funny enough, but that is not what the audience expected. THE BEVERLY HILLBILLIES, with whom the audience grew up, was nowhere to be found in this movie. The personality associated with the title was not maintained. Interestingly, if there had been no original series, the motion picture would likely have been much funnier to an unbiased audience. When creating an original work, storyweaving considerations can be limited to exposition of the storyform. When adapting a work, storyweaving must also consider the expectations of the audience, described in the fourth stage of communication, Story Reception.

Story Reception

We started in Storyforming with the message, encoded it into symbols, relayed those symbols through storyweaving, and now that multiplexed signal arrives at the receiver: Your audience. Problem is, they all might be tuned to a different channel!

Some members of your audience will be familiar with the original work itself. Some may have experienced it many times. Others will have heard about it from a friend, but never saw or read the original. Many have only seen the advertisements, or the book review, or the trading cards, or the lunch box. A few have never heard of it at all and just stumbled on your adaptation. You may want to play on in-jokes and setups that require prior knowledge. How about that scene in SUPERMAN: THE MOVIE when Clark runs up to the phone booth to change and there's somebody using the phone? It would not be funny to someone who does not recognize it as a twist on the expected pattern.

In addition, there is no such thing as an audience, except when defined as a collection of individuals who experience a work. They may have nothing else in common, so you can't expect them to respond as a single unit. What buzzwords can you safely use? Which obscure buzzwords do you want to use anyway because you expect they will catch on and become all the rage? How much biased, special-interested, politically correct, atheistic, agnostic, faithful, black, brown, white, red, yellow, young, old, middle-aged, female, male, gay, straight, bi, Republican, Democrat, Independent, Catholic, Protestant, Jewish, Buddhist, brilliant, stupid, insane, and emotionally challenged baggage are audience members going to carry to your adaptation?

Part of the adapter's job is to identify the audience. An equally important job is to identify *with* the audience. This puts a burden on the author of an adaptation that the author of an original work usually does not share.

When creating an original story, one often has the luxury of writing whatever one wants, and then hoping the finished piece finds its audience. In contrast, the adept adapter must consider the full spectrum of the *new* audience. Usually, if a work is being considered for adaptation, it is because there is some following for the original. The adaptation is intended to not only appeal to that audience but also exceed it and attract a wider crowd.

How do you adapt a work for the masses? Simple. Make sure the story works not only as an adaptation, but on its own merits as well. Never violate dramatic integrity solely for the sake of adaptive integrity. Better to disappoint a few diehard fans than to disappoint the potential legions of new fans.

Conversely, there are those projects where the size of the new audience is unimportant. The purpose of this kind of adaptation is to supply those few diehard fans with a new medium of enjoyment for their favorite story. In this case you must be faithful to every detail, even if it turns out a work that can't stand on its own merit.

Either approach is reason enough to shape the nature of the adaptation. Seldom can both be done at the same time. More than anything, Story Reception is where the author decides for whom they wish to write. Once you have identified that group, you must get into their heads, to get into their hearts.

In Summary

Adaptation is no simple task. It requires familiarity with both the logistics and passion of the original, from the inside out and the outside in. To achieve this familiarity, one must resonate with the original on many levels, best examined through the Four Stages of Communication.

- **Storyforming**: Storyform the original and then create a new storyform to reflect any changes you make in the adaptation.

- **Storyencoding**: Delineate the original encoding and determine what must be lifted verbatim, what might be altered, and what could or should be removed or added.

- **Storyweaving**: Reproduce the storyweaving personality to reproduce the dramatic flavor faithfully.

- **Story Reception:** Determine the prior knowledge and expectations of your audience.

In conclusion, and above all, to your new audience be true, for then how canst thee be false to the original?

Epilogue

THE LEFTOVERS

Is That All There Is?

Dramatica is a theory of Story. But behind Dramatica is a whole new understanding of the mind's problem solving and justification processes. In fact, the model of the mind drawn from the intrinsic relationships inherent in stories form the basis of a theory of psychology called Mental Relativity.

Mental Relativity describes the mind's pattern making capability and explains in detail how and why we see such things as spirals in a seashell, a galaxy, or strands of DNA. Mental Relativity outlines the structural and dynamic relationships that form the matrix of self-awareness. Mental Relativity connects with low-level neurology at one end and high-level psychology at the other, bridging the gap between the biochemical functioning of the brain and the elusive essence of self.

Through Mental Relativity, insights are provided not only into story, but many other areas as well such as:

- Music: Predictive in controlling the emotional impact of melodies, harmonies, rhythm, and meter.

- Personal Problem Solving: Aids in prioritizing concerns and choosing a consistent perspective for all considerations.

- Interpersonal Relationships: Allows for adopting a truly objectified view of differences between individuals.

- Psychology: Provides an understanding of the exact mechanism for the creation and dissolution of Justifications.

- Quantum Physics: The mathematical equations and formulas by which the model operates hold meaning for the Uncertainty Principle, Tendency Theory, Synchronicity, and the connection between packets of energy and particles of mass.

- Biology/DNA: By providing a dynamic model based on *frictals*, a clear view can be provided of the *processes* involved in DNA triggering, and neural processing.

- Social Systems/Trends: All large-scale patterns that ebb and flow come into greater focus through frictal ordering.

- Astrophysics: Black holes and Quasars can be modeled in great detail using the same processes that describe the mental acceptance of givens in relationship to spontaneous creative thought.

Obviously many of these potential applications have not been fully developed. Some are only the promise of a theory that describes the mind's pattern making process. It is our hope that others more versed in these disciplines than us will see the potential as implemented in Dramatica and apply it to their specific areas of interest.

CONSTRUCTIVE CRITICISM

Analysis of JURASSIC PARK

Building a Better Dinosaur

(The following analysis provides a glimpse of how some of Dramatica's basic concepts can be employed to improve a story. Use this as an example of how many aspects of the theory can be brought together in a practical sense.)

The film JURASSIC PARK is wonderfully entertaining. The concepts are intriguing, the visuals stunning. Everything it does, it does well. Unfortunately, it doesn't do enough. There are parts missing, little bits of "story DNA" needed to complete the chain. To be fair, these problems largely result from the mostly faithful adherence to the dramatic structure of the book on which the movie is based.

Storyform, the structure and dynamics of a story, is not medium dependent. What works in one medium will work in all others. Storytelling, however, must vary significantly to take advantage of the strengths and avoid the weaknesses inherent in any format. JURASSIC PARK effectively makes this storytelling translation, but the flawed dramatics were nearly lifted intact, shackling the movie just like the book with a Pterodactyl hanging 'round its neck.

Criticisms are a dime a dozen. Suggestions for improvement are much more rare. Fortunately that is the strong suit of the Dramatica theory. Here is one plan for building a better dinosaur.

Dramatica Background

As a starting point, Dramatica notes a difference between a Tale and a Story. A Tale describes a series of events that lead to success or failure. It carries the message that a particular way of going about solving the problem is or is not a good one. But a Story is an argument that claims there is *only one* right way to solve a problem. It is a much more potent form that seeks to have the audience accept the author's conclusions.

To gain an audience's acceptance, an argument (Story) must appeal to both logic and feeling. To make the logical part of this argument, all the *inappropriate*[1] ways a to resolve a problem need to be addressed and shown to fail. Each one must be given its due and shown not to work, except the one touted by the author. This is carried out by looking at the characters and the plot objectively, much like a general on a hill watching a battle down below. The big picture gives a clear view of the scope of the battle and the ramifications of the individual soldiers' actions and decisions.

To make the emotional part of the argument, however, the audience must become involved in the story at a personal level. To this end, they share a Subjective view of the story through the eyes of the Main Character. Here they get to share in the battle as if they were one of the soldiers in the trenches. It is the difference between the subjective view of the Main Character and the objective view from the Overall Story of the whole battle that produces dramatic tension from which the message of the story is created.

By comparing the two views, the argument is made to the audience that the Main Character must change to adapt the big picture, or the Main Character is on the right track and must hold his resolve if he hopes to succeed. Of course, the Main Character cannot see the big picture, so he must make a leap of faith near the end of the story, deciding if he wants to stick it out or change.

Now this relationship between the Main Character and the Overall Story makes him a special character. In fact, he holds the key to the whole battle. He is the crucial element in the dramatic web that (through action or inaction) can wrap the whole thing up or cause it to fall apart. As a result, the personal problem he faces reflects the nature of the Overall Story problem of the story at large.

To the audience there are two problems in a story. One is the Overall Story problem with which everyone is concerned; the other is the Subjective problem with which the Main Character is personally concerned. Although the problems may be greatly different in the way they are expressed, they both hinge on the crucial element in the Main Character as their common root. So, to be a complete argument a story must explore an objective AND a subjective problem, and show how they are both related to the same source.

JURASSIC PARK Analysis:

JURASSIC PARK attempts to be a story (not a tale) but does not make it because its exploration of the Subjective problem is lacking.

The Overall Story problem is clearly shown to be caused by the relationship of Order to Chaos. The message of the logical side of the argument is the more you try to control something, the more you open yourself up to the effects of chaos. As Princess Leia put it to the Gran Mof Tarkin in STAR WARS, "The more you tighten your grip, the more star systems will slip through your fingers."

If Order is the problem, then Chaos is the solution. They vaguely allude to this in JURASSIC PARK when the Tyrannosaurus comes in unexpectedly and wipes out the Raptors, unknowingly saving the humans. Although the point is not stated strongly, it is *sort of* there in the background. We will come back to this point later to show how it should have been a much more dramatically integral event than it was. The important idea at the moment is the Overall Story is fairly close to what it should be, which is true of most action-oriented stories.

It is the Subjective Story that fails to fulfill its dramatic mandate in JURASSIC PARK. To see how, we must go back to the beginning of the film, to our Main Character, Dr. Alan Grant.

As the Main Character, Dr. Grant contains the crucial element, so we would expect him to intersect the Overall Story's problem by representing Order or Chaos. Clearly the author intended him to represent Order. This means that he contains what has been set up as the Problem Element (the inappropriate attitude or approach that is the underlying source of the Story's troubles), rather than the Solution Element, and he must Change if he is to succeed.

The first scene with Grant at the dig *should have* illustrated his love of Order. All the elements were there: A disruptive boy, a randomly sensitive computer, and a helicopter that comes out of nowhere and disrupts the dig. All of these things *could have* illustrated Grant's hatred of Chaos and his quest for Order. Using the same events and incidents, the point might have been made in any number of ways, the easiest being a simple comment by Dr. Grant himself.

Unfortunately without any direct allusion to Order being his primary concern, Dr. Grant comes off simply as finding disruptions inconvenient, faulty equipment annoying, and kids as both.

Why is it so important to set up the nature of the problem so early? Well, one of the major problems with the JURASSIC PARK storyform is that we don't know what the problem is supposed to be until near the end of the first act. Certainly almost every moviegoer must have been aware that this was a picture about an island where cloned dinosaurs come to life, and then run amok wreaking havoc — that's all story*telling*. But that alone doesn't say *why* this problem occurred. The "Why" is the heart of the story*form*: The reason, if you will, for having a story to tell. If the point of conflict had been established up front, the whole thrust of the picture would have been given direction from scene one.

Just stating that Dr. Grant shares the same problem as the story is not enough. The relationship between his view of the problem and the Overall Story view of the problem is what explores the concept, makes the argument, and allows the Main Character to grow. Eventually, it is the difference between the two views of the problem that brings a Changing (versus Steadfast) Main Character to suspect the error of his ways and make a positive leap of faith. He sees the problem outside himself, and then finds it inside himself. He changes the inside, and the outside is forced to follow suit.

What does this mean for JURASSIC PARK? As it is, Doctor Grant's attitude toward John Hammond's ability to control the dinosaurs is one of skepticism, but not because of Order, because of Chaos. Grant simply agrees with Ian Malcolm, the mathematician. This makes the same point through two characters. Instead, Grant's function should not be to tout Chaos, but to favor Order. Only this point of view would be consistent with his feelings toward children.

As illustrated in the meeting scene with Hammond, Ian, and Elissa, Grant jumps from representing one approach to representing the opposite. This neutralizes his effectiveness in the story as owner of the crucial element and taking the wind out of the dramatic sails.

This problem could have been avoided easily and replaced with strong drama by having Dr. Grant continue to believe the park is unsafe, *but for a different reason*.

(Note: The following proposed scene is designed to illustrate how Grant's and Ian's positions on what is needed for the park to be safe is different. The storytelling is slight so as not to distract from the storyforming argument.)

> GRANT
> How can you be sure your
> creations won't escape?
>
> HAMMOND
> Each compound is completely
> encircled with electric
> fences.

                    GRANT
How many fences?

                    HAMMOND
Just one, but it is 10,000
volts.

                    GRANT
That's not enough....

                    HAMMOND
I assure you, even a T-Rex
respects 10,000 volts!

                    GRANT
No, I mean not enough fences.
It's been my experience that
Dr. Malcolm is right. You
can't count on things going
the way you expect them. You
need backups to your backups.
Leave a soft spot and Chaos
will find it. Put three fences
around each compound, each
with a separate power source
and then you can bring people
in here.

                    MALCOLM
That's not the point at all!
Chaos will happen no matter
how much you prepare. In fact,
the more you try to control
a situation, the greater the
potential that chaos will
bring the whole thing down.

   In the scene, Grant stresses the need for even MORE control than Hammond
used. This clearly sets up his reluctance to giving in to chaos. Ian illustrates the
difference in their points of view by stating the greater the control you exercise, the
more you tighten the spring of chaos.

What would this mean for the middle of the story? Plenty. Once Grant and the children are lost in the open with the thunder lizards, he might learn gradually that one must allow Chaos to reach equilibrium with Order. Several close encounters with the dinos might result in minor successes and failures determined by applying Order or allowing Chaos.

As it stands, Dr. Grant simply learns to care about the children. But what has really changed in him? What did he learn? Would it not have been more dramatically pleasing to have the children teach him how chaos is not just a disruptive element, but also sometimes an essential component of life? And would it not make sense for someone who has spent his whole life *imagining* the way dinosaurs lived to be surprised by the truth when he sees them in person? What a wonderful opportunity to show how the orderly interactions he had imagined for his beloved beasts are anything but orderly in the *real* world. So many opportunities to teach him the value of Chaos, yet all we get is "They DO travel in herds... I was right!" Well, that line is a nice place to start, especially if you spend the rest of the story showing how wrong he was about everything else. Truly a good place from which to start growing.

Perhaps the most disappointing aspect of the Subjective Story throughline is the meaningless manner in which they escape in the end. Grant and the kids are sealed in the control room, but the Raptors are right outside. The girl struggles to get the computer up so they can get the door locked. This of course, merely delays the Raptors until the helpless humans can escape into another Raptor attack. Then out of nowhere, T-Rex conveniently barges in, kills the Raptors and allows the humans to escape. Why? Why *then*? Was T-Rex just waiting in the wings for his cue?

Let's describe one possible ending that would've tied in Chaos, Dr. Grant's personal problem of Order in the Subjective throughline, his growth as a character and eventual change, AND have all this *force* a successful outcome in the Overall Story Throughline.

Imagine that earlier in the story, when the power went down it only affected some of the electric fences, not all. So only some of the areas were open to the roving dinos. Rather than having Elissa get the power back on for the fences, she merely powers up the computer system, but even with power to the computer restored no one can boot it up.

Dr. Grant and the kids make it back to the control room, barely escaping the T-Rex trapped by one of the functional electric fences. They climb over the fence on a tree knocked down by the Tyrannosaurus. The Raptors are at the door of the control room; the girl goes to the computer to lock the door. She locks it, and then tells Grant she can bring up the rest of the fences. There might be some kind of visual reminder in the room (such as a dino picture) that Grant (and the audience) associate with his major learning experience with the kids about the need to accept

Chaos. Grant almost allows her to bring up the power, and then yells for her to stop. He tells her not to bring it up, but to *cut* the power on *all the* fences, as he come to believe that Chaos will somehow help them.

The girl pauses for a beat, unsure if she should follow his instructions. Then, based on *her* learning experience that established her trust in Grant, she puts aside her personal assessment and brings all the fences down. By opening all the compounds, all the dinosaurs are released, allowing Chaos to rule the day while the dinosaurs rule the Earth.

Why would Grant do this? His argument for Order was based on logic. Over the course of the story, he was presented another argument that affected his feelings. So, when the crisis arrives, he must choose between what his head and his heart are telling him. His intellect makes a definitive case that bringing the fences up will reestablish Order. But his gut instincts now insist that is the last thing they should do. By letting Chaos reign, says his instinct, somehow things will work out. He doesn't have any clue HOW they will work out, just a strong feeling that bringing down the fences is what he must do if they are to survive.

Now, how do we convey all Grant's considerations to the audience so it will understand all of this? Simple! First we see briefly see the computer display showing the power going off around the various compounds, including that of our old friend, T-Rex. Just as before, the Raptors break in, the humans escape onto the dino skeletons. NOW, when T-Rex charges in to save the day, it is solely because of Dr. Grant's decision to cut the power to the fence that was holding him in. Indeed, Grant's invitation to Chaos has saved them.

Having learned his lesson about the benefits of Chaos and the folly of Order, Grant is a changed man. The author's proof of this being the correct decision is the group's salvation, courtesy of T-Rex.

Equilibrium is established on the island, Grant suddenly loves kids, he gets the girl, and they escape with their lives, and all because the crucial element of Order connected both the Overall Story and Subjective throughlines.

Dramatica has many more suggestions for Building a Better Dinosaur, but, leapin' lizards, that's enough for an introduction to the theory!

VOCABULARY

Vocabulary Grammar

Dramatica's terminology has its own grammar with structures, designations, and usages that are reflected in the vocabulary listings. The individual Vocabulary listings are constructed as follows:

Vocabulary Item • *[the type of item]* • if a Vocabulary term is a semantic item, the term's Dynamic Pair (*dyn.pr.*) will be noted • short definition • long definition • synonyms (*syn.*)

Example:

Chaos • *[Element]* • *dyn.pr.* Order<—>Chaos • random change or a lack of order • Chaos is disorder, randomness, anarchy. The Chaos characteristic is brilliant at cutting through a Gordian knot. But then it just keeps cutting every rope it sees until the chandelier falls on its head. It "stirs the pot" just to see what will bubble up to the top • *syn.* randomness, anarchy, disorder, formlessness, noncohesion

The varieties of items noted in the Vocabulary references include:

Structural Semantic Items:

[Classes]

The 4 basic areas a story can affect: Situation, Activity, Manipulation , and Fixed Attitude.

[Types]

The 16 basic categories of what can be seen from a specific point of view or Class.

[Variations]

The 64 terms which describe the thematic message and its development within a story as well as the ways of evaluating this message (semantic items).

[Elements]

The 64 descriptions which represent the highest resolutions of approaches and attitudes required to solve a story's problem (semantic items).

Story Points Items:

[Overview Story Points]

Items relating to the widest appreciation of your entire story, including the Character and Plot Dynamics which describe its dramatic mechanism and basic feel.

[Character Dynamics]

Items relating to your Main Character's essential nature, behaviors, and attitudes.

[Plot Dynamics]

Items relating to the entire story (both Objective and Subjective Story) in terms of the forces that drive the plot forward and the outcome to which they lead.

[Structural Items]

Items relating to the thematic arenas to be emphasized in a particular Storyform, focusing on goals, events, and activities.

[Archetype]

A specific type of character reflecting one of eight quintessential arrangements of 64 Characteristics required to solve a story's problem.

[Dynamic Pairs]

Implied by every term is a specific term that is its reciprocal. Together they create a paired unit where the presence or absence of one affects the presence or absence of the other. Every term that is a structural semantic item is part of a dynamic pair.

[Storyform]

The skeletal blue print of story points that are at work in any single story. It contains the story points at work in the story which are independent of how an author chooses to illustrate them.

[Throughlines]

The story points that are developed from the four distinct perspectives common to all stories (the Overall Story, Subjective Story, Main Character, and Impact Character perspectives) create a line of observations from each of those points of view which can be followed through the course of the story. These are called the throughlines—one throughline for each perspective.

[Storyforming]

Determining the story points that will be explored in a story, the perspectives from which they will be explored, and the order in which these explorations will occur within the world of a story is called Storyforming. This is independent of any Storytelling and instead deals with ordering the pieces common to all stories.

[Storytelling]

Illustrating a storyform with the cultural signs and artistry that an author feels are appropriate to his story.

[Storyweaving]

Combining the Storytelling of a story with its Storyform.

Dramatica Vocabulary

Ability • Most terms in Dramatica are unique, however, four items have two uses, serving both as Variation and Element. This is a result of the fundamental importance of the concepts represented by these four items: Thought, Knowledge, Ability, and Desire.

[Variation] • *dyn.pr.* Desire<—>Ability • being suited to handle a task; the innate capacity to do or be • Ability describes the actual capacity to accomplish something. However, even the greatest Ability may need experience to become practical. Also, Ability may be hindered by limitations placed on a character and/or limitations imposed by the character on himself. • *syn.* talent, knack, capability, capacity, faculty

[Element] • *dyn.pr.* Desire<—>Ability • being suited to handle a task; the innate capacity to do or be • An aspect of the Ability element is an innate capacity to do or to be. Although all characters will have abilities of one sort or another, only the character containing the Ability characteristic will seem to have them all. This does not mean he have developed any of his Abilities, but just that he has the capacity to do so. The positive side is that the character containing the Ability Characteristic can develop any skill he may need. The negative side is that just because something can be done does not mean it should be done. In other words, sometimes Ability is more a curse than a blessing because it can motivate a character to exercise capacities that may be negative • *syn.* innate capacity, capability, talent for, inherent proficiency

Acceptance • *[Element]* • *dyn.pr.* Non-acceptance<—>Acceptance • a decision not to oppose • When a character represents Acceptance, it simply adapts to whatever comes its way without opposition. Of course, this can eliminate many potential conflicts by refusing to stand against inequity. On the other hand, if the source of the inequity keeps churning out trouble Acceptance will allow that negative process to continue unencumbered • *syn.* acquiescence, tolerance, allowance for, consent, submission

Accurate • *[Element]* • *dyn.pr.* Non-accurate<—>Accurate • being within tolerances • Not all concepts work all the time. When an understanding has uses within limitations or is mostly or often true, it can still provide a useful way of looking at the broad issues. The more accurate an understanding, the more specifically one can apply it with certainty. The character possessing the Accurate characteristic will accept rough approximations and will make judgments and perform activities that are "within tolerance" or "good enough" for the purpose at hand. The advantage is that little energy is wasted on "the law of diminishing returns." The disadvantage is that appraising things as Accurate can lead to gross generalizations. If the character containing Accurate is not careful it may assume that an understanding applies to every instance all the time • *syn.* within tolerance, sufficient, adequate, acceptable, passable

Act • [Structural Term] • The largest sequential increments by which we can measure the progress of a story • an Act is a noticeable division in the dramatic flow of a story which is created by the convergence of the elements of Character, Theme, and Plot. This division has been noticed in studies of narrative dating back thousands of years, but never with the precision with which we see it in Dramatica. A complete storyform contains all the thematic story points that will be explored in a story, the perspectives from which they will be explored, and the order in which they will be explored from those perspectives. When a particular perspective has explored the nature of a Type by paying tribute to the Variations connected with it, that perspective has completed an act. Each perspective has its own throughline and there are four acts for every throughline, making up a complete storyform.

Action • *[Plot Dynamic]* • in terms of the objective plot, actions force decisions • All stories have both Action and Decision, however one will take precedence over the other. Typically, one defines an Action story as having more Action or more intense Action than a Decision story. This view is overly influenced by how the story is told rather than what it represents. Dramatica takes a different view of Action and Decision. Either Actions force the need for Decisions or Decisions force the need for Actions to advance the plot. Over the course of the story as a whole (independent of the nature of the Main

Character), if Actions precipitate the progression of the plot, it is an Action story. The question to ask in regards to any particular story is which comes first to move the story along?—not which is there more of. Action stories will begin with an Action, be marked at the beginning and end of every Act by an Action, and will end with a climactic Action. If it were not for unforced Actions taking place in an Action story, the story would dwindle until another Action occurred.

Activity (Physics) • *[Class]* • *dyn.pr.*
Manipulation<—>Activity • an activity • The Activity Class is one of action. Whereas the Situation Class describes a fixed situation, Activity (Physics) is a Class of dynamics. Situations evolve, develop, and change. Activities are engaged in and endeavors undertaken. • *syn.* an activity, an enterprise, an initiative, an endeavor, an operation

Actual Dilemma • *[Overview Appreciation]* • The Main Character's decision to change results in success • In an Actual Dilemma, the Main Character cannot succeed if he keeps to the path he began on. Unless he changes, he is doomed to failure. Of course, the Main Character cannot see the future and therefore can never be absolutely sure if he should change or not. That is why Main Characters must often make a "leap of faith" at the moment of climax and decide to Change or Remain Steadfast. Other times, the Main Character is slowly drawn towards his Resolve of Changing or Remaining Steadfast, however it is still clear which way he's gone by the end of the story. In stories where the Main Character Changes and, succeeds as a result, he is said to have been in an Actual Dilemma.

Actual Work • *[Overview Appreciation]* • The Main Character's decision to remain steadfast results in success • A Work story is one in which remaining steadfast is the path to success. When the Main Character's appraisal matches the reality of the situation, his assessment of the Work required is said to be Actual.

Actuality • *[Element]* • *dyn.pr.* Perception<—>Actuality • an objective reality — the way things are • Actuality refers to the true state of things. A character who represents Actuality sees right through image and pretense, preferring to get to the heart of the matter. It also will not accept foregone conclusions until they have materialized. It feels that without substance there is no meaning. The problem is that anything that does not meet its strict

definitions is ignored as irrelevant. It is often surprised when the undefined or unformed turns out to be very real • *syn.* the true state of things, objective reality, factuality, demonstrable existence, demonstrable reality

Analysis • *[Variation]* • *dyn.pr.* Strategy<—>Analysis • evaluation of the situation and/or circumstances • Analysis sits on one side of planning and strategy sits on the other. Analysis is the interpretation of available data to establish the approach most likely succeed. If the Analysis is faulty, it limits the potential of a Strategy. If a Strategy is faulty, it limits the effectiveness of Analysis • *syn.* evaluation, examination, breakdown of situation, close investigation, scrutinization

Antagonist • *[Archetype]* • An archetypal Overall Story player who is in every way opposed to the Protagonist • Antagonist and Protagonist are diametrically opposed. If one is pursuing, the other avoids. If one is avoiding, the other pursues. If one's goal is to cause something, the other's goal is to prevent the same thing and vice versa. Together, Antagonist and Protagonist form a Dynamic Pair centered around the core issue of the Overall Story Problem in stories which contain these archetypal characters. In order for one to succeed the other MUST fail.

Apparent Dilemma • *[Overview Appreciation]* • The Main Character's decision to change results in failure • Apparent Dilemma describes a story where the Main Character mistakenly believes he is on the wrong path. An Actual Dilemma story, by contrast, is one in which the Main Character's original path cannot lead to success. If the Main Character Changes when only Remaining Steadfast would have led to success, he is said to have been in an Apparent Dilemma.

Apparent Work • *[Overview Appreciation]* • The Main Character's decision to remain steadfast results in failure • Apparent Work describes a story where the Main Character mistakenly believes he is on the proper path. An Actual Work story is one in which Remaining Steadfast is the path to success. If the Main Character maintains his course when indeed he needs to Change, he is said to have been in an Apparent Work story.

Appraisal • *[Variation]* • *dyn.pr.* Reappraisal<—>Appraisal • an initial understanding • When determining which parts of evidence he should investigate and which parts he doubts and therefore chooses to ignore, a character makes an initial Appraisal of where the evidence seems to be leading. Although there is not enough evidence to really draw a conclusion, there is enough to indicate the direction evidence seems to be leading. That which is not in line is doubted, and the more out of line, the more doubt. That which is in line is investigated. Of course, since this Appraisal is based on insufficient evidence, the big picture can change dramatically over the course of investigation. Yet, like everyday people, a character is strongly influenced by first impressions and can become attached to an Appraisal and fail to see that the direction of evidence has changed • *syn.* first impression, preliminary understanding, initial approach, initial assimilation.

Appreciations • Commonly shared dramatic concepts • *see Story Points*

Approach • *[Character Dynamic]* • The Main Character's preferred method of general problem solving • By temperament, Main Characters (like each of us) have a preferential method of approaching problems. Some would rather adapt their environment to themselves, others would rather adapt themselves to their environment. There is nothing intrinsically right or wrong with either approach, yet it does affect how one will respond to problems. Choosing "Do-er" or "Be-er" does not prevent a Main Character from using either approach, but merely defines the way he is likely to first approach a problem, using the other method only if the first one fails.

Approach • *[Variation]* • *dyn.pr.* Attitude<—>Approach • one's methodology of doing or being • Approach is the manner in which a character chooses to seek the solution to a problem. This might be a specific method or just a general set of tools or guidelines that is deemed appropriate for the job. These tools can be physical or mental ones, depending on the nature of the problem and the determined solution • *syn.* method, procedure, style, manner, manner of doing, one's own way.

Archetypal Characters • Of all the ways the 64 Overall Story Character elements of Dramatica might be grouped, there is one arrangement that is akin to an alignment of the planets. When all elements from one "family" of like elements are placed in each character, eight Archetypal Characters are created. They are Archetypal because their homogeneous nature

accommodates all levels a character must have to be fully dimensional, yet line up by content so well there is little internal dissonance. Archetypal Characters are useful in stories that seek to concentrate on plot, action, or external themes. This is because they do not "get in the way" or clutter the Author's purpose. However, because they are so predictable, Archetypal Characters are not easily used to explore the human psyche and are most readily employed in stories designed more for entertainment than message.

Argument • *[Dramatica Term]* • the underlying message that is made by a story's combined structure and dynamics • The dispassionate argument is the story's contention that a particular approach is the most appropriate one to solve a problem or achieve a goal in a given context. The passionate argument is the story's contention that one world view is better than another in terms of leading to personal fulfillment. An author can use his story's argument to convey a personal message directly, or indirectly if he makes an exaggerated argument *supporting* what he is against. The argument of a story exists within the story and, if it is complete, it can be discerned whether the author realizes it's there or not. (Also see Grand Argument Story.)

Attempt • *[Variation]* • *dyn.pr.* Work<—>Attempt • applying oneself to something not known to be within one's ability • When there is a question as to the match-up of one's abilities to the demands of a task, one may still elect to attempt to complete the task. However, sometimes a character has lost sight of the purpose of the task or underestimated his progress and has actually done the work while continuing to try beyond the point originally aimed at. Why does one beat a dead horse? Why does a billionaire struggle to earn one more million? • *syn.* try, uncertain undertaking, speculative endeavor, dubious effort, endeavor, unlikely venture

Attitude • *[Variation]* • *dyn.pr.* Approach<—>Attitude • one's demeanor while doing or being • Attitude describes the manner in which a character proceeds with an approach. One character might be hard-driven, another laid back. One may be willing to sacrifice efficiency for the sake of a pleasant approach. Another might sacrifice pleasure to make the approach most efficient. Sometimes an approach can be pushed too hard or not hard enough. It requires not only the proper approach but the appropriate attitude to arrive at the solution to a problem. • *syn.* demeanor, manner of approach, countenance, behavioral outlook, perspective on doing

Attraction • *[Variation]* • *dyn.pr.* Repulsion<—>Attraction • drawing or being drawn to something • How hard should one try? How much work should one do? This is modulated by the Attraction of what one is trying to achieve. Attraction is a directional factor that indicates what lies ahead is a positive reward. When a character strives toward a goal, he passes many veils along the way. Each one is a curtain to the future that must be ripped away to see what lies beyond. Attraction describes the nature of the curtain itself. Can you judge the pleasure of a book by the art on its cover? In the parable of the carrot and the stick, Attraction is the carrot. • *syn.* allure, enticement, charm, captivate, appeal, draw, lure

Author's Proof • *[Storytelling]* • the epilogue or follow-up to a story that proves the "outcome" of the story is real or imagined, good or bad • Technically speaking, the moment of climax in a story is the intersecting point where the nature of the Main Character crosses paths with the nature of the objective story. It is here that the course of one, both or neither of them may be altered by the interaction. The only way an audience can be sure what, if anything, has changed course is to plot one more dramatic point past the climax, as part of Act 4 to illustrate the new direction of the objective story and Main Character. This might be the "?" after the words "The End" in a monster story or a formerly mean man sharing his sandwich with a stray dog on the way home. The purpose is simply to illustrate that the suspected effect of the climax has or has not truly resulted in a change in course. As such, it functions as the Author's Proof and is a key component of the denouement.

Avoid • *[Element]* • *dyn.pr.* Pursuit<—>Avoid • stepping around, preventing or escaping from a problem rather than solving it • Like its counterpart Pursue, the Avoid characteristic causes a character to be a real self-starter. The difference is that just as strongly as Pursuit tries to close in on the something, Avoid tries to escape it. Avoid can take the forms "escape" or "prevent" depending on whether the focus of the effort is an object or a process. Avoid might be seen as running away, but that has its place. And certainly, when seen as "prevent" it might be applied to stopping something very negative from happening. Of course, it could also prevent something positive or really just be running away from something that should be faced. Pursue and Avoid are not value judgments but directions. • *syn.* evade, dodge, elude, escape, steer clear of, prevent

Aware • *[Element]* • *dyn.pr.* Aware<—>Self-Aware • being conscious of things outside oneself • A character that represents Awareness misses nothing that happens around him. A drawback is he may forget to figure himself into the equation. • *syn.* outward perceptiveness, external sensitivity, consciousness of the external, responsive

Backstory • *[Storytelling]* • Although often embellished greatly in the storytelling, Backstory is nothing more than a description of how a Main Character's justification built up over time, leading him to intersect with the story's problem, or how a story problem developed over time, leading it to intersect with the Main Character. Backstory outlines the sequence of events and the combination of forces that make the Main Character the central connecting point between the subjective and objective problem. Backstory need not be presented to the audience as it is not essential to the story's argument about how to or how not to solve a problem. However, inclusion of Backstory can offer the additional benefits of showing the audience how to avoid the problem before it becomes a problem. Sometimes Backstory is presented at the beginning of storytelling, making it appear to be part of the story itself into which it can smoothly and seamlessly segue. More often, Backstory is explored episodically in Flashbacks or through other forms of revelation. Sometimes the focus of the storytelling is on the Backstory itself and the story is told episodically through flashforwards. Even more complex implementations not only present Backstory episodically but also out of order, leaving it to the audience to ultimately put the pieces together and thereby solve a riddle necessary to solving the problem of the story itself.

Bad • *[Plot Dynamic]* • The Main Character ultimately fails in resolving his personal problems • If at the end of the story the Main character is still nagged by his personal problem, then the judgment of the story can be considered bad. Even though the effort to achieve the story's goal may result in success, this is not necessarily a good thing for the Main Character. In fact success might be obtained in the objective story even though the Main Character fails to resolve his personal problems. Conversely, the effort to achieve the story goal might end in failure, yet with the Main Character ultimately overcoming his personal problems. Regardless of whether the objective story ends in Success or Failure, if the Main Character fails to resolve his personal problems, the outcome is deemed Bad.

Be-er • *[Character Dynamic]* • The Main Character prefers to adapt himself to his environment • Every Main Character will have a preference to deal with problems by either physical effort or by mental/emotional effort. When a Main Character prefers adapting himself to the environment over working directly in the external environment to resolve problems, he is a Be-er.

Becoming • *[Type]* • transforming one's nature • *see Changing One's Nature*

Being • *[Type]* • temporarily adopting a lifestyle • *see Playing A Role*

Benchmark • *[Type]* • the indicator of the depth of a throughline's difficulties • The Benchmark is a measuring stick which is used to judge progress in whichever throughline it is operating in. In the Overall Story, it is used to see how close the Overall Story Characters think they are to solving their problem. It describes where they apply their efforts, and thus is where they look to see how it is coming along.

Blind Spot • *[Character Appreciation]* • The motivations of the Subjective Characters which they are unable to see about themselves • Both the Main Character and the Impact Character (who stands in the Main Character's path) are driven by their particular motivations. In a story, each has a prime motivation that describes the one issue in each that they cannot see in themselves. It is *because* they cannot see it in themselves that it works below the level of their consciousness to motivate them. Because they cannot see it, it is called a Blind Spot. In a change character, the Blind Spot is the actual source of the problem common to both the Objective and Subjective stories. In a steadfast character, the Blind Spot represents what

drives him to become the agent of the common solution to both the Objective and Subjective stories. In either case, although other characters may see it quite clearly in the Main and Impact Characters, neither Main nor Impact can see the Blind Spot in themselves.

Both • *[Overview Appreciation]* • both women and men will tend to empathize with the main character in this story • Although there is much common ground in a story that is appreciated equally by women and men, some dramatic messages speak to one group more profoundly than the other. One particular area of difference is the relationship of female and male audience members to the Main Character. In some stories an audience member will feel Empathy with the Main Character, as if he/she were standing in the Main Character's shoes. In other stories, an audience member will feel Sympathy, a less intense emotional attachment, for the Main Character as if the Main Character is a close acquaintance. The dynamics that control this for women and men are quite different. "Both" indicates that, as a result of this storyform's dynamics, both male and female audience members will tend to empathize with the Main Character. Neither will sympathize.

Catalyst • *[Variation]* • The item whose presence always pushes the story forward toward the climax • The Catalyst is what creates breakthroughs and seems to accelerate the throughline it is affecting. In both the Objective and Subjective Stories there occur dramatic "log-jams" when things seem to be approaching a halt. This is when the Catalyst is necessary, for its introduction will either solve the puzzle that's holding things up or else make the puzzle seem suddenly unimportant so the story can continue.

Cause • *[Element]* • *dyn.pr.* Effect<—>Cause • the specific circumstances that lead to an effect • The character containing the Cause characteristic is concerned with what is behind a situation or its circumstances. This can lead it right to the source of trouble, the source of control. However, sometimes many things came together to create a particular effect. In that case, the Cause characteristic may fail by either looking for a single source or trying to address them all while ignoring the option of simply dealing with the effect. • *syn.* reason for, effector, source, agent, antecedent

Certainty • *[Element]* • *dyn.pr.* Potentiality<—>Certainty • a conclusion that something is absolutely true • The character representing the Certainty characteristic is not a risk taker. It must be completely sure before it takes action or accepts information as true. The slightest potential for error or change will stop it in its tracks. On the plus side, it never goes out on a limb far enough to break it; on the minus side, it might never get out far enough to get the fruit either. Many opportunities are lost to it because it hesitates until it is too late. • *syn.* sureness, definiteness, having no doubts, total reliability, indisputability, irrefutability, unmistakability, certitude, conviction

Change Character • *[Character Appreciation]* • the subjective character who changes his approach or attitude in a story • The Change Character is the single character who *does* change in a story in an attempt to resolve his personal problem. The Change Character must be either the Main Character or the Impact Character but cannot be both. A Change Character cannot tell until the end of the story whether or not he will change, and even then, a Change Character has no way of knowing whether or not changing will lead to success or to resolving his personal problem. However, in every story, either the Main Character or the Impact Character will Change in response to the other's Steadfastness and become that story's Change Character.

Change • *[Character Dynamic]* • The Main Character changes his essential nature while attempting to solve his problems • Every Main Character represents one special character element. This element is either the cause of the story's problem or its solution. The Main Character cannot be sure which it represents since it is too close to home. Near the climax of the story, the Main Character must demonstrate whether he is going to stick with his original approach in the belief that it is the solution or jump to the opposite trait in the belief he has been wrong. In "Leap of Faith" stories this will occur during a "moment of truth." In "Non-Leap of Faith" stories this will occur over the course of the story and be assessed for Change or Steadfastness in the end of the story. When a Main Character abandons his original story-long approach for its counterpart, he is said to Change.

Change • *[Element]* • *dyn. pr.* Inertia<—>Change • an alteration of a state or process • Change is the force that alters. A characteristic representing change is quick to adapt but also cannot leave well enough alone. It feels that if things have been one way long enough to establish a pattern, it is time to change it. • *syn.* altering, altering force, modify, reshape, adjust, adapt

Changing One's Nature (Becoming) • *[Type]* • *dyn.pr.* Playing A Role<—>Changing One's Nature • transforming one's nature • Changing One's Nature means achieving an identity with something. This is different from "being" which merely requires posing as something. To become, one must do more than just pretend to be by mimicking all the traits of what one wants to become. Rather, one must also lose all those parts of oneself that are inconsistent with what one wants to become. "Giving up" a part of oneself is always the hardest part of becoming and the reason so many characters spend a lot of time "being" without ever becoming • *syn.* embodying, manifesting, personifying, incarnating, transforming

Chaos • *[Element]* • *dyn.pr.* Order<—>Chaos • random change or a lack of order • Chaos is disorder, randomness, anarchy. The Chaos characteristic is brilliant at cutting through a Gordian knot. But then it just keeps cutting every rope it sees until the chandelier falls on its head. It "stirs the pot" just to see what will bubble up to the top. • *syn.* randomness, anarchy, disorder, formlessness, noncohesion

Character • *[Dramatica Definition]* • In Dramatica, there are two major divisions of Characters: the Subjective Characters and the Overall Story Characters. In the most frequently told kinds of stories, Subjective Characters are the smaller group, consisting of only the Main Character and the Impact Character. Both of these are concerned with providing the audience with a Subjective view of the story. There can be, and frequently are, many more Overall Story than Subjective Characters. An Overall Story Character is defined as a specific collection of dramatic *Elements or characteristics* that remains consistent for the entire story. There are sixty four elements in the Dramatica Structure which represent the building blocks of Characters. All sixty four elements must be used to fully develop the story's argument. To have meaning to an audience, the group of elements that makes up each objective character must present a consistent viewpoint (with regards to the story goal/problem) during the course of the story. In this way the relative attributes of each of these elemental approaches can be clearly explored during the course of the story. Sixty four elements may at first sound too limited to create interesting characters, but when you consider that the number of arrangements of the elements is multiplied by the way the might be grouped, the total number of characters that can be created is in the millions. In regard to story, the Overall Story Characters present the story to the audience and the Subjective Characters allow the audience to participate in the story. Because of this, Subjective Characters are unique in that they do double duty by having a special relationship with the audience and pulling their weight as Overall Story Characters as well. This is because they are concerned both with the Main Character's personal problem and also the Overall Story problem.

Charge • *[Dynamic Term]* • Since there are two of each kind of pair in a quad (Dynamic, Dependent and Companion), it is useful to have a way of identifying each one by its position in the quad. Dramatica uses the concept of a dramatic CHARGE to accomplish this. As with electrical charges, positive or negative does not mean one is good and the other bad but simply that they have opposite attributes. So in a quad the Dynamic (diagonal) pair that is negatively charged simply means that it runs from the upper right item in the quad to the lower left unit of the quad. The other Dynamic pair is referred to as positively charged. The top Companion (horizontal) pair is positive; the bottom Companion pair is negative. The left Dependent (vertical) pair is positive; the right Dependent pair is negative. By using the CHARGE method, any pair in any quad can be directly and specifically referred to.

Choice • *[Variation]* • *dyn.pr.* Delay<—>Choice • making a decision • Choice is simply a decision as to which is the best path toward resolving a problem. A character will ponder all the information and factor in all his feelings and arrive at a decision. Sometimes a character will choose before all the information is in. This can lead him to take steps that may ultimately prove to be counterproductive or even self-destructive. On the other hand, such intuitive leaps can bypass many obstacles on the way to a story's conclusion. Still, "snap judgments often lead to

regrets for those whose only exercise is jumping to conclusions." — Dramatica fortune cookie • *syn.* decision, selection, determination, pick

Circumstances • *[Variation]* • *dyn.pr.* Situation<—>Circumstances • the relationship of oneself to the environment • Circumstances describes the way a character feels about his environment. Whereas Situation is rated in terms of satisfaction, Circumstances are rated in terms of fulfillment. Emotion, therefore, is the standard of measurement a character uses to evaluate his Circumstances. Often a character must accept unfulfilling Circumstances because he needs the benefits of the Situation. Or a character may accept an unsatisfying Situation because it comes with fulfilling Circumstances. Over the course of a story, the balance between the two measurements can vary greatly. • *syn.* how things stand emotionally, emotional evaluation of the environment, value of existing conditions, relationship to others

Class • *[Structural Term]* • The broadest classification of where problems can exist • The possible places where problems can exist can be divided into four areas, and we call these areas the four Classes. The Classes are separated by distinctions between inner and outer states and processes. Situation (Universe) and Activity (Physics) represent external states and processes respectively, and Mind and Manipulation (Psychology) represent internal states and processes respectively. Though Classes have the same names as Throughlines, they represent only a structural ordering of semantic terms and are not the same as Throughlines which are more dynamic story points created by matching a Class with one of the four throughlines.

Closure • *[Variation]* • *dyn.pr.* Denial<—>Closure • bringing something to an end • Closure can be seen in two ways. One, it can be an ending. In this sense, it prevents what has happened from being changed; it protects a memory or a situation because the window of opportunity for change has ended. In the other sense, Closure can be seen as a continuance. This is because a process made into a closed loop will just go on forever, repeating the same course. In some stories Closure settles all the dramatic potentials to show that the issue of the story has been resolved. In other stories, Closure is used to show that even though the immediate problem has been resolved, the volatile relationships among the characters is never-ending. Closure is useful in letting one know when the job is done. Negatively, Closure tries to bring everything to a conclusion even if it is a continuously growing process that is completely open-ended. The attempt to stop such an evolution would be either fruitless or disastrous. But is a process closed or not? When is a career at an end? • *syn.* finishing, completion, resolution, recursive

Co-Dynamic Pair • *[Structural Term]* • When one of the two dynamic pairs in a quad is selected as the "Reference Pair," the remaining dynamic pair is referred to as its CO-DYNAMIC PAIR.

Commitment • *[Variation]* • *dyn.pr.* Responsibility<—>Commitment • a decision to stick with something regardless of the consequences • A commitment forms the essence of the steadfast character. When a character makes a commitment, it is a decision not to quit regardless of the obstacles that may come. This allows the character to accept much higher costs on the way to a goal than he would if he reevaluated every time something went wrong. A problem arises, however, when one of those obstacles turns out to be impassable. If a character reaches this point, he cannot achieve the goal. But since he is Committed, he does not reevaluate and instead continues to beat his head against a brick wall. • *syn.* dedication, devotion, steadfastness, zeal

Companion Pair • *[Structural Term]* • In any given quad, the two top items share a relationship between them in the same way the bottom two share a relationship. What separates the two pairs is what dramatic focus they create. Each pair in each quad will be focused in a slightly different place, creating a gradual shift in the model from one point of view to its opposite. In many quads, the top pair will appear to be more oriented toward the environment in comparison to the bottom pair which is more oriented toward the mind. Either the top or bottom pair can be referred to as a Companion Pair, meaning that the two items that make up the pair are companion rather than in conflict.

Complex Characters • Whenever even a single element is added or removed or swapped in an Archetypal character, that character becomes Complex. The more elements that differ from the Archetypal, the more complex the character becomes. Characters in a story need not all be Archetypal or all be complex. Making some characters more complex than others is a valuable storytelling tool that allows for more exploration of certain areas of the story while underplaying others.

Conceiving An Idea (Conceiving) • *[Type]* • *dyn. pr.* Developing A Plan [Conceptualizing]<—>Conceiving An Idea • coming up with an idea • Conceiving An Idea is the process of arriving at an idea. If there were no artificial light in the world, one might conceive the need for some form of electric torch. That would be conceiving. But the design of an actual incandescent bulb versus a fluorescent one would require conceptualizing a specific implementation of the idea one has conceived. Conceiving An Idea need not come before conceptualizing. For example, a common dramatic technique is to give a character a very clear mental image of an object or arrangement that holds the solution to the story's problem. But the character does not know the solution lies in the conceptualization. It is only when he finally conceives of the need for a particular kind of solution that he realizes he had the answer all along. Simply put, Conceiving An Idea defines the question, Conceptualizing clarifies the answer • *syn.* originating, inventing, devising, engendering, hatch ideas

Conceptualizing • *[Type]* • visualizing how an idea might be implemented • *see Developing A Plan*

Concern (Overall Story) • *[Type]* • the goal or purpose sought after by the objective characters • The Overall Story Concern is the area which all the Overall Story Characters are hoping to have a good grasp of by the end of the story. Their goals and purposes will all share some aspect of the Type item which is their story's concern. There is also a Subjective Story Concern which is the area of concern between the Main Character and the Impact Character. This is also a Type item which describes the nature of what the Main and Impact Characters are seeking from each other.

Conditioning • *[Variation]* • *dyn.pr.* Instinct<—>Conditioning • responses based on experience or training • Conditioning describes learned responses to various stimuli. Similar to Instinct in that the Consciousness in not involved until after the fact, Conditioning differs insofar as it was not inherent in the basic nature of a character but acquired though training or familiarity to impose its triggers on the mind. Since Instincts are intrinsic and Conditioning is learned, they frequently come in conflict over how to respond. This concept alone has provided the theme for many intriguing stories. • *syn.* habituation, trained response, accustomed response, adaptive adjustments

Confidence • *[Variation]* • *dyn.pr.* Worry<—>Confidence • belief in the accuracy of an expectation • Confidence points to the future. It is not a rating of the present situation but a positive evaluation of how things will turn out. Confidence, therefore, is a great motivator in unknown situations. This is because Confidence is not based on predicting a situation but on the experience of past situations. The downside is that Confidence erodes the motivation to prepare for the unexpected. If past experience has always shown that even the most threatening disasters have worked themselves out, then one will ignore potential danger that may turn out to be real. We see this in history time and time again, such as the way the people of Pompeii remained in their homes while Vesuvius bellowed smoke for the umpteenth time. • *syn.* hopeful prospects, positive expectations, faithful anticipation, optimism

Conscience • *[Element]* • *dyn.pr.* Temptation<—>Conscience • forgoing an immediate benefit because of future consequences • Conscience is the motivation that negative consequences are unavoidable if a present desire is acted on. Conscience can serve a character well in overcoming strong transient desires that would bring disasters on him. If the negative consequences are purely imaginary, however, Conscience constricts the free expression of one's heart . • *syn.* forgoing for fear of consequences, forgo, forbearance, temperance, abstinence, restraining oneself

Conscious (The Conscious) • *[Type]* • considerations • *see Contemplation*

Consequence (Overall Storyline) • *[Type]* • The area that best describes the result of failing to achieve the goal • For every goal there is a consequence. Consequence describes the results of failing to achieve the goal. This predisposes the goal to be something desirable but this is not necessarily true. Sometimes the difference between goal and consequence can be one of choosing the lesser of two evils. More optimistically put, goal and consequence might be measures of magnitude of two favorable outcomes. Sometimes the Consequence will occur if the goal is not met, other times the consequence already exists and can only be eliminated by meeting the goal. So if they are

close in their negative or positive value, it may be difficult to be sure which is the consequence and which is the goal. An easy way to be certain is to see which one the Main Character hopes to achieve.

Consider • *[Element]* • *dyn.pr.* Reconsider<—>Consider • weighing pros and cons • A Consideration is the act of deliberation. A character possessing the Consideration characteristic keeps pondering an issue, running it over in his mind. Once he has latched onto a topic, he refuses to let it go until it is resolved. This trait aids in keeping one's motivations impervious to erosion. On the other hand, the Consideration characteristic may not let sleeping dogs lie. Therefore it can lead to stirring up all kinds of negative reactions. • *syn.* deliberate, contemplate, ponder, weigh in the mind, mull

Contagonist • *[Archetype]* • An Archetype representing the motivations of temptation and hinder • A concept unique to Dramatica, the Contagonist is the character that balances the Guardian. If Protagonist and Antagonist can archetypically be thought of as "Good" versus "Evil," the Contagonist is "Temptation" to the Guardian's "Conscience." Because the Contagonist has a negative effect on the Protagonist's quest, it is often mistakenly thought to be the Antagonist. In truth, the Contagonist only serves to hinder the Protagonist in his quest, throwing obstacles in front of his as an excuse to lure him away from the road he must take to achieve success. The Antagonist is a completely different character, diametrically opposed to the Protagonist's successful achievement of the goal

Contemplation (Conscious) • *[Type]* • *dyn.pr.* Memory<—>Contemplation • considerations • When one has all the facts, knows all the impact — both positive and negative; when one is fully aware of detrimental consequences and still decides on the poor course of action, there is something wrong with the way one arrives at conclusions. This is the subject of stories focusing on Contemplation. The key here is not to redefine who a character is but to lead him to relearn how to weigh an issue so his conclusions are less destructive to himself and/or others. • *syn.* considerations, sensibilities, cognizant, ability to consider, sensible, informed contemplation, contemplation

Control • *[Element]* • *dyn.pr.* Uncontrolled<—>Control • a method based on organization and constraint • The Control characteristic causes a character to methodically direct its actions and deliberations to the specific purpose at hand. This leads to a great degree of focus. The drawback is that when one focuses, one loses peripheral vision. The purpose can become so all consuming that many peripheral yet essential parts of the equation are ignored until it is too late to save the whole project • *syn.* regulate, organized management, steer, conduct, guide, manipulate, focused organization

Cost (Overall Story) • *[Type]* • the price that must be paid while meeting the requirements of the goal • Requirements are not always met just by applying effort. Sometimes they involve trade-offs calling for accepting loss in another area to meet the requirement. The damages sustained in the process of meeting the requirement are the Cost of achieving the goal. Cost should not be confused with Consequence. Consequence is a state of things that either exists and will be vanquished by the goal or will come to exist unless the goal is achieved. In contrast, Cost builds over the course of the story all the way to the climax. Sometimes by the end of the story, the consequence of not achieving the goal is far less than the cumulative cost of achieving it. If there is a single large cost to be paid right at the moment of the climax, the Main Character may decide he has paid enough already and determine the goal is just not worth it, electing to stop trying. If there is no large cost at the end, the Main Character may decide to keep on going for an insignificant goal motivated by the thought of how much they already invested. In the words of the songwriter/singer Don McLean, "The more you pay, the more it's worth."

Critical Flaw • *[Variation]* • The Subjective Character trait that inhibits the effectiveness of that Subjective Character's Unique Ability • To balance the Main Character's extraordinary status conveyed by his Unique Ability, he must also be shown to be especially vulnerable in one area as well. This vulnerability is called his Critical Flaw. The Main Character's Critical Flaw is his Achilles heel that prevents him from being too one-sided. Just as with Unique Ability, the Critical Flaw can be quite mundane as long as it can threaten him with failure from an unprotectable direction. The specific Critical Flaw must be unique to the Main Character in the story. However, the more common the Critical Flaw is to the audience, the more it will identify with the Main Character's predicament. In Start stories, the Critical Flaw inhibits the Main Character from using his Unique Ability. In Stop stories, the Critical Flaw undoes the work done by the Unique Ability after the fact. Only when the Main Character learns to either Start or Stop as required by the story can the Critical Flaw be avoided, allowing his Unique Ability to solve the problem. The Impact Character in any story also has a Unique Ability which makes him uniquely qualified to thwart the Main Character. But in his character as well is a Critical Flaw which prevents him from just totally overwhelming the Main Character. This is again a trait which is unique to this particular character, but its effects are felt in a different area than the Main Character Critical Flaw because of the Impact Character's different purposes.

Crucial Element • *[Element]* • The single element in the story that needs to be exchanged for its dynamic pair to correct the imbalance that began the story

Current • *[Dynamic Term]* • The flow of a process • One way to measure the relationship of items in a quad is to classify them as Potential, Resistance, Current, and Outcome (or Power). In this manner, we can see how dramatic components operate on one another over the course of the story. Current simply means the flow of a process. When a dramatic current exists it does not necessarily create change. Rather, until it is directed to a specific purpose as Power, the current will have no impact at all. So in a quad, assigning one of the items as the current does not mean it will alter the course of the story. Instead, it might function to encourage purpose by providing a ready motivation. This is a useful tool for Authors since it allows for the subtle relationship of unused, inferred, threatened, or anticipated dramatic interactions that shape the fabric of a story in ways other than conflict.

Decision • *[Plot Dynamic]* • in terms of the objective plot, decisions force actions • All stories have both Action and Decision. Typically, one defines a Decision story as having more intense Deliberation than Action. This view is overly influenced by how the story is told rather than what it represents. Dramatica takes a different view of Action and Decision. Either Actions force the need for Decisions or Decisions force the need for Actions to advance the plot. Over the course of the story as a whole (independent of the nature of the Main Character) if Decisions precipitate the progression of the plot, it is a Decision story.

Deduction • *[Element]* • *dyn.pr.* Induction<—>Deduction • a process of thought that determines certainty • Deduction is the process of thought that arrives at a determination of what is by limiting out all that cannot be. It has been said, "When you have ruled out the impossible, whatever is left, no matter how improbable, must be true." The characteristic representing Deduction will arrive at conclusions by eliminating all competing theories that have holes until only one remains. This is fine for cutting away the nonsense and discovering understanding, unless the competing theories were not all the available theories and the real answer was never even considered. Also, Deduction often fails to look for situations in which alternative truths exist. A famous story had a detective narrowing down murder suspects only to discover that they all did it! • *syn.* drawing a conclusion, process of elimination, demonstrative reasoning, narrowing to a single point

Deficiency • *[Variation]* • *dyn.pr.* Permission<—>Deficiency • motivation based on lack • When a character lacks something in the sense of having Deficiency, he may not even comprehend what he lacks. But this lack drives him and fulfilling the lack would end the drive caused by the Deficiency. Deficiency is closely related to Need, but where Needs are always defined by their context and the purpose which makes them seem necessary, Deficiency does not require a purpose. When a character lacks, he is NOT content with what he has and REQUIRES something more to become content. Fulfilling a lack may appear to be the last thing a character Needs because it does not lead to his purpose, but once the lack has been taken care of, a character may find his purpose has changed and his Need has been eliminated. • *syn.* inadequacy, insufficiency, deficit, unfulfilled need

Delay • *[Variation]* • *dyn.pr.* Choice<—>Delay • putting off until later • Delay is the decision not to make a decision. Whenever the options are too closely balanced to see a clear path, whenever there is not enough information to be confident of an outcome, a character will Delay. The purpose is to wait until one gathers more information or until the situation changes to present a clear best course. But how long does one wait? And what if something distracts the character and he forgets to check and see if things have changed? Now the character has left a problem unresolved, and unless it intrudes on his thinking, it will never be thought of again. Yet deep within him, he will be influenced to avoid what created that problem or to take steps to protect against its recurrence. Until the original problem is addressed and a choice of path is made, the character will not be free of the problem's influence. • *syn.* put off, retard, postpone, defer, suspend, prolong, procrastinate

Denial • *[Variation]* • *dyn.pr.* Closure<—>Denial • the refusal to let something go • Denial is the refusal to accept that something is or has become closed. How many people continue to make a point after they have won the argument? More than just not accepting a conclusion, Denial can also be not accepting that a process will just keep repeating. A repeating process has a cycle. In a story, a character comes into such a circle at one point and follows it around back to start. At that point, a theme of Denial would have that character refusing to believe that he has been just been chasing his own tail. At the leap of faith he will just push off again and keep on circling a no-win situation in the hopes it will change this time around. Inertia does not always travel in straight lines. • *syn.* not accepting, refusal to end, unwillingness to let go, refusal to back down, stubbornness

Dependent Pair • *[Structural Term]* • A pair of items whose relationship is complementary • In any given quad, the two items directly above and below each other are referred to as a Dependent Pair. Since a quad consists of four items, it therefore contains two Dependent Pairs.

Desire • Most terms in Dramatica are unique, however four items have two uses, serving both as Variation and Element. This is a result of the fundamental importance of the concepts represented by these four items: Thought, Knowledge, Ability, and Desire.

[Variation] • *dyn.pr.* Ability<—>Desire • the motivation to change one's situation or circumstances • Desire describes an awareness that something better exists than what currently is. This doesn't mean things have to be bad now, just that one perceives something better. The key word here is "perceives." Desires are based not on what is truly better but on what one

imagines will be better. Often there is a large gap between the two. (Recall the story of the dog with the bone which jumped into the pond to get the bone from his reflection and ended up with no bone at all.) Little tension is produced if a character can try out his desires at no cost. But great tension is produced when he must give up something good forever in the belief that something else is better. ("Do you want [desire] what's in the box or what's behind door number 3?") • *syn.* want, favor, like, covet, prefer, wish, aspire

[Element] • dyn.pr. Ability<—>Desire • the motivation to change one's situation or circumstances • The Desire element is the essence of motivation. A characteristic representing Desire is mindful of a future in which situation or circumstances are improved. This does not mean that it is unhappy with what it has but rather that it can imagine something better. On the plus side, Desire primes the characteristic to seek to better its environment or itself. On the minus side, Desire is not always coupled with an ability to achieve that which is Desired. In this case, Desire may no longer be felt as a positive motivator but as a negative lack and may become a measurement of one's limitations and constraints • *syn.* drive, motivational goal, unfulfillment, source of discontent, essence of motivation •

Destiny • *[Variation]* • dyn.pr. Fate<—>Destiny • the future path an individual will take • Destiny is the path to a particular fate or through a series of fates. Fates are experiences or conditions one must encounter along the way as one's Destiny directs one's course. The nature of Destiny is such that no matter how much a character is aware of the nature and location of an undesirable fate, nothing he can do is enough to pull him off the path. Characters often try to deny Destiny by jumping to an entirely different path only to discover that all roads lead to Rome. • *syn.* inescapable path, predetermined trajectory, set direction of the future, inevitable path, unavoidable trajectory

Determination • *[Element]* • dyn.pr. Expectation<—>Determination • a conclusion about the cause behind a particular effect • Determination is an evaluation of the forces driving a process. This allows one to anticipate future effects or to take action to stop or enhance a current effect. However, it may just be that a completely different set of forces is really behind the process, causing one to put his efforts in the wrong place. When a person swims directly toward the shore, the current can carry him far down shore. As long as the character possessing Determination sticks with a particular concept of the powers that be, there is the potential it may not get what it expects. • *syn.* ascertaining causes, discovering causes, finding the reasons why, figuring out factors, discerning antecedents

Developing A Plan (Conceptualizing) • *[Type]* • dyn.pr. Conceiving An Idea<—>Developing A Plan • visualizing how an idea might be implemented • Developing A Plan means coming up with a practical implementation of an idea. It is not enough to simply have the idea. To conceptualize, one must develop an actual mental model of how such an idea might be made manifest. In other words, one might have an idea to build a spacious house. But to conceptualize the house one must imagine everything that makes up the house — the design, the layout, the colors and textures, everything that is essential to understanding what that specific house is. A character that deals with conceptualizing would be well aware of the kind of solution that will eliminate the problem but spend his time trying to devise a specific way of achieving that solution • *syn.* visualizing, imagining, envisioning, visualizing implementation

Dilemma Stories versus Work Stories • A distinction between stories where the Main Character decides to Change and where the Main Character remains Steadfast • Work describes the activities of a Main Character who remains steadfast and resolute throughout the story. This kind of character believes in the correctness of his approach to the problem and sticks by his guns come what may. Dilemma describes the situation of a Main Character who ultimately changes at the end of the story. This kind of character becomes convinced that he cannot solve the problem with his original approach and adopts a new approach. So a Work Story is concerned with a Steadfast Main Character and a Dilemma Story concerns itself with a Change Main Character. However, just because the Main Character has decided to remain Steadfast or to Change does not mean he made the right choice. Only in the end will he find out if he succeeded or failed. If in a Work Story the Steadfast Main Character really should have Changed and fails because he did not, then it was really an Apparent Work Story since work alone could not solve it. If in a Dilemma Story the Change Main Character really should have remained Steadfast and fails because he did not, then it was really an Apparent Dilemma Story since there wasn't actually a dilemma after all. Steadfast means Work, Change means Dilemma. These are modified by their pairing with Success, which means Actual, and Failure which means Apparent

Dilemma • The Main Character Changes • A Dilemma story is one in which the Main Character believes his path cannot lead to success. In the end, when the Main Character Changes, he may or may not jump to the correct path so he may or may not succeed. Either way, Dilemma describes a story where the Main Character Changes.

Direction • *[Character Dynamic]* • The way a character grows in his attempt to solve his problems, toward either "Start" or "Stop" • *see Growth*

Direction (Overall Story) • *[Element]* • the apparent remedy for the principal symptom of the story problem • *see Response*

Direction Element (aka Perspective Element) • *see Response Element*

Disbelief • *[Element]* • *dyn.pr.* Faith<—>Disbelief • the belief that something is untrue • Disbelief is not the same thing as a lack of faith. Lack of faith is the absence of absolute confidence that something is or will be true. Disbelief is absolute confidence that something is not true. Disbelief may make one a skeptic but sometimes it makes a character the only one with the confidence to tell the Emperor "You have no clothes!" • *syn.* refusal to accept, distrust, find unconvincing, find false, unpersuadability

Dividend (Overall Storyline) • *[Type]* • the benefits gathered while meeting the requirements of the goal • Although meeting the requirements of a goal can incur costs, it can also provide dividends along the way. Sometimes solving one of the prerequisites or attaining one of the preconditions of the requirement has its own reward. Though these rewards are not individually as significant as the promised reward of the goal, sometimes cumulatively they are enough to cause a Main Character to quit while he's ahead and avoid a particularly large cost that would be unavoidable if the goal

were to be achieved. Other times, a particularly large dividend may loom just ahead in the story, providing the Main Character with a boost in motivation to continue on an otherwise costly path

Do-er • *[Character Dynamic]* • As an approach, the Main Character prefers to adapt his environment to himself • Every Main Character will have a preference to deal with problems by either physical effort or by mental/emotional effort. When a Main Character prefers working in the external environment, he is a Do-er.

Doing • *[Type]* • *dyn.pr.* Obtaining<—>Doing • engaging in a physical activity • Doing is the process of being physically active. In and of itself, Doing does not require any purpose but simply describes engaging in a process, task, or endeavor, whether for pleasure or by necessity or compulsion. • *syn.* performing, executing, effecting action, acting

Domain • *[Throughline]* • An item that describes the area in which any one of the four throughlines occurs—Main Character, Impact Character, Overall Story, and Subjective Story • There are four Domains in every complete story, each representing a different perspective in the structure of that story. One is assigned to the Overall Story Throughline and contains the story points attributed to the dispassionate argument of the story while also describing the area in which the Overall Story occurs. Another is for the Subjective Story Throughline and contains the story points which concern the passionate argument of the story and describe the relationship between the Main and Impact Characters. The Main and Impact Character Throughlines are each assigned Domains as well, which contain the story points attributed to their character and describe the area in which they each operate. Each Throughline is the matching of a particular Class (either Situation (Universe), Activity (Physics), Manipulation (Psychology), or Mind) with a particular throughline (either Overall Story, Main Character, Impact Character, or Subjective Story). Each Throughline describes the general area in which the problems of its throughline will lie and from what perspective the audience will be directed to view those problems. Domains determine large, genre-like positions in the relationship of audience to story.

Domain Act Order • *[Plot Structure]* • the area in which the solution to the story's problem is sought, act by act

Doubt • *[Variation]* • *dyn.pr.* Investigation <— > Doubt • questioning validity without investigating to be sure • Here Doubt is defined as the lack of faith that evidence leads to a certain conclusion. This means that even though evidence supports a particular concept, the character is unwilling to abandon the belief that alternative explanations can be found. Certainly this approach has the advantage of keeping one's mind open. But sometimes a mind can be too open. If a character Doubts too much, he will not accept solid evidence no matter how conclusive. This can prevent the character from ever accepting the obvious truth and continuing to labor under a delusion. • *syn.* pessimism, uninformed misgivings, uncertainty, trepidation, distrust

Dream • *[Variation]* • *dyn.pr.* Hope <—> Dream • a desired future that requires unexpected developments • Dream describes a character who speculates on a future that has not been ruled out, however unlikely. Dreaming is full of "what ifs." Cinderella Dreamed of her prince because it wasn't quite unimaginable. One Dreams of winning the lottery even though one "hasn't got a hope." Hope requires the expectation that something will happen if nothing goes wrong. Dreaming has no such limitation. Nothing has to indicate that a Dream will come true, only that it's not impossible. Dreaming can offer a positive future in the midst of disaster. It can also motivate one to try for things others scoff at. Many revolutionary inventors have been labeled as Dreamers. Still and all, to Dream takes away time from doing, and unless one strikes a balance and does the groundwork, one can Dream while hopes go out the window for lack of effort. • *syn.* aspire, desiring the unlikely, pulling for the doubtful, airy hope, glimmer, far fetched desire

Driver (Story Driver) • *[Plot Dynamic]* • the kind of activity focused on in the effort to solve the story's problem • Action or Decision describes how the problem of the Story will primarily be explored. The primary concern is the kind of storytelling you want to do. If you want action to be the focus of your storytelling, choose action. If you want deliberation to be the focus of your storytelling, choose decision. It's that simple.

Dynamic Pair • *[Structural Term]* • A pair of items whose relationship is that they are extreme opposites • In any given quad, Dynamic Pairs are represented as two items that are diagonal to each other. A quad consists of four items and therefore contains two Dynamic Pairs. Their relationship can imply conflict, or it can imply synthesis. These are the negative and positive aspects of Dynamic Pairs.

Dynamics • Dramatic forces that determine the course a story will take. • The power of a story is divided between two realms. First is the structure that represents the dramatic potentials that exist in character, plot, and theme at the beginning of a story. Second are the dynamic forces that will act on the dramatic potentials to change the relationship between characters, change the course of the plot and develop the theme as the story unfolds. In Dramatica, choices between alternative forces such as "Success or Failure" and "Change or Steadfast" determine the dynamics that will act on a story.

Effect • *[Element]* • *dyn.pr.* Cause <—> Effect • the specific outcome forced by a cause • Effect is the end product of an effort or series of efforts. One might argue its pros and cons, yet ignore how the Effect came to be in the first place. On the plus side, concentrating on Effect keeps the effort focused on the problem or goal. On the minus side, it can lead to beating a dead horse. Failure may follow if one puts all one's efforts into dealing with the Effect while ignoring the cause. Should a mayor add to the police force to battle crime or improve social services? • *syn.* result, consequence, outcome, culmination, the ensuing

Element • *[Structural Term]* • There are 64 elements in each class. The same 64 elements appear in every class, arranged differently by position. Elements represent the most refined and highly detailed approaches and attitudes in the attempt to solve the story's problem. Primarily, they are the building blocks of the characters. To fully argue the thematic message, it must be addressed from all possible directions. This is accomplished by making sure that all 64 elements are divided among a story's objective characters. If an element is not used it will leave a hole in the logic or emotion of the story. If one is used more than once, it will obscure the point by showing it in two different incarnations. The reason that elements are repeated from class to class is because they represent the heart of the problem. When all else is stripped away, the problem must be evaluated by these same building blocks no matter where it was approached from. The reason the elements are arranged differently from class to class is that the way they are grouped depends on the direction from which the story approaches them. When the story is approached from a given class, it is like looking at the problem from a particular direction. All the same elements are seen, but from a different point of view.

Emotion • *[Archetype]* • An Archetype who represents the motivations of Feeling and Uncontrolled • The Emotional Archetypal Character reacts passionately to turns of events without considering the consequences or best course to achieve his purpose. Frequently portrayed as a "screamer" or "big dumb ox" this character is really not stupid. He actually represents feeling and frenzy. So his nature is to feel deeply about issues but be unable to focus that heartfelt intensity in any useful direction. Rather, he tends to go off the deep end and thrash out aimlessly, frequently to the detriment of himself and those around them. Such a character can prove to be a Trojan horse by storytelling him into the enemy's camp where he will almost certainly wreak havoc.

Empathy • Empathy describes the complete identification of the audience with the Main Character such that the audience sees the story through his eyes.

Ending • *[Element]* • *dyn.pr.* Unending<—>Ending • coming to a conclusion • The Ending characteristic causes a character to look toward the conclusion in every process or situation. He may wish to prevent it or to hasten it, but his primary concern is when it's going to be over. A very useful trait in dealing with steps or phases. Not very useful if the process or situation is really unending. Since the character representing the Ending characteristic assumes that everything must end sooner or later, he cannot accept that some things never end. Some relationships will last a lifetime, come what may. But if one partner believes it can end, he will always worry, looking for signs of its demise. If he was an Ending person, Prometheus was sorely mistaken. (Weeds grow back and Rust never sleeps!) • *syn.* conclusion, finish, completion, termination, close

Enlightenment • *[Variation]* • *dyn.pr.* Wisdom<—>Enlightenment • an understanding that transcends knowledge • Not all meaning comes from experience. The mind has the ability to synthesize abstract truth that has not been or cannot be observed. When a character is able

to come to an understanding of the whole that exceeds the sum of the observed parts, he is said to be Enlightened. A truly refined thematic conflict can be explored in the relationship between the practical Wisdom born of great experience and the aesthetic Enlightenment born of great insight • *syn.* insight, illumination, intuitive discernment, transcendent comprehension

Equity • *[Element]* • *dyn.pr.* Inequity<—>Equity • a balance, fairness, or stability • Equity is balance. The Equity characteristic makes a character want everything to work out fair and square. He will spend his time trying to maintain balance and will judge the acceptability of a situation by its apparent equilibrium. On the downside, he may not realize that without inequity there is no motivation and hence no progress. Also, there may not be enough to go around. By "robbing Peter to pay Paul" he might be moving resources back and forth in a way that stresses the whole system which might crumble from the strain • *syn.* balance, fairness, parity, equilibrium, level, even

Essence • *[Overview Appreciation]* • the primary dramatic feel of a story • A story can be appreciated as the interaction of dynamics that converge at the climax. From this point of view, the feel of the dramatic tension can be defined. Dramatic tension is created between the direction the Main Character is growing compared to the author's value judgment of that growth. A Change Main Character will either grow out of something or grow into something. In the first case, he possesses a characteristic that he will let go. In the second case, he adds a new characteristic to his make-up. But is he correct in stopping something he has been doing or starting to do something new? This is determined by the author's value judgment of Good or Bad. When a Main Character Stops doing something Bad, that is positive. When a Main Character Starts doing something Good, that also is positive. However, when a Main Character Starts doing something Bad or Stops doing something Good, these are negative. Positive and Negative affect where the audience places its focus on the story. In a Positive story, the focus is on the effort to find the solution. In a Negative story, the focus in on the effort to escape the problem.

Evaluation • *[Element]* • *dyn.pr.* Reevaluation<—>Evaluation • an appraisal of a situation and/or circumstances • Evaluation is the meaning a character finds in a situation or circumstances. Rather than just grappling with the bits and pieces, the character creates an understanding of how all the parts fit together. This gives him a better grasp of how to deal with the issue. The danger is that once he has Evaluated, the situation or circumstances change, yet he is still using the old evaluation as a unit of measure. Meanings change over time and need to be updated to maintain accuracy • *syn.* appraisal, analysis, assessment, survey, examination

Evidence • *[Variation]* • *dyn.pr.* Suspicion<—>Evidence • information supporting a belief • Evidence is information one gathers to develop an understanding about something. When looking at Evidence, a character does not necessarily have to know exactly what he is looking for, just that the information pertains to the nature of what he is trying to learn about. As a result, he tends to examine the Evidence only in terms of whether or not it is something that falls into a predetermined category. Therefore, errors can occur when the Evidence (although it pertains to the subject of interest) actually holds much more information in another area. This can lead a character to "not see the forest for the trees" because he is looking at the small picture and ignoring the big one. For example, in a mystery a detective may be looking for Evidence of who committed a murder, when in truth the victim died of natural causes which is clearly indicated if the detective had only thought to look for that • *syn.* proof, indicator, supporting information, corroborating facts, grounds for belief, substantiation

Expectation • *[Element]* • *dyn.pr.* Determination<—>Expectation • a conclusion as to the eventual effect of a particular cause • Expectation is the projection of what one expects to find at the end of a path. Expectations allow one to anticipate and make plans for both rewards and troubles. However, if the character representing Expectation does not occasionally question the basis of his projections, he may find the world has turned under his feet • *syn.* anticipated results, eventual outcome, presumed prospects, probable denouement, likely consequences

Expediency • *[Variation]* • *dyn.pr.* Need<—>Expediency • most efficient course considering repercussions • It is important not to consider Expediency as only meaning efficiency. In terms of story, Expediency describes what a character *feels* he must do or be to avoid potential consequences. These consequences can come from his environment, in the form of disapproval by others, or from within in the form of self-recrimination. If the perceived consequences are internal, Expediency feels like a "moral" pressure but is really the emotional retribution one flails against oneself for not living up to one's own self-image. If they are external, Expediency feels like peer pressure or a threat to social standing. Expediency is as important an emotional motivation as Need is a motivator of reason. Since Expediency is based on avoiding future punishments or disappointments that may or may not be real, dramatic tension can be easily created between the subjective and objective views. A way to think of Expediency is that when it pops up, characters who are being influenced by it will think of it in terms of "Should." "I should really do this, even though I may not want to." • *syn.* advisability, convenience, prudent efficiency

Experience • *[Variation]* • *dyn.pr.* Skill<—>Experience • the gaining of familiarity • Experience refers to the cumulative effect of observing or participating in mental or physical activities until they become familiar. However, just because the activities become second nature does not mean a character is necessarily good at them. To excel, a character need both Experience AND the innate Skills that can be honed by that experience. If either is lacking or deficient, the character's real ability will be less than its Experiential potential. • *syn.* familiarization, level of practice, seasoning, accumulated feelings, accumulated dealings with

Fact • *[Variation]* • *dyn.pr.* Fantasy<—>Fact • belief in something real • Fact is something that is truly real as opposed to just seeming to be real. Of course, from a character's subjective view, when something seems to be real it is impossible to tell from actual fact. No matter how strongly a belief, understanding, or knowledge of something is held, subjectively there is always the possibility some change in the situation or additional information will prove it to be unfactual. Optical illusions are a good case in point. The moment a character accepts something as fact is the moment a thematic conflict might begin to grow. Nevertheless, Fact represents beliefs that turn out to be real. • *syn.* belief in the genuine, ultimately real beliefs, truly real beliefs, authentic notion, authentic idea, correct knowledge, correct beliefs

Failure • *[Plot Dynamic]* • the original goal is not achieved • Every overall story throughline in a Grand Argument Story has at its beginning a desired outcome to be sought after. Ultimately, the characters will either achieve that outcome or Fail to do so. The reasons for Failure (and in fact the Failure itself) may not be bad. For example, while trying to arrive at an outcome, the characters may decide it was wrong to want it or learn that achieving it would hurt people. Whatever the reason, be it nobility or no ability, if the outcome desired at the story's beginning is not achieved, the story ends in Failure.

Faith • *[Element]* • *dyn.pr.* Disbelief<—>Faith • accepting something as certain without proof • Faith is a belief in something without the support of proof. Since the future is uncertain, Faith in one's ability to arrive at one's purpose is a very strong motivator. However, when one has Faith, it cannot be argued with since it does not rely on logic or proof. The danger of Faith is that it does not allow one to determine if obstacles are signs that ones motivations are misplaced, because the obstacles seem to be tests that must be overcome through steadfast belief • *syn.* acceptance without proof, steadfast belief, confidence in unproven, credence, unquestioned trust

Falsehood • *[Variation]* • *dyn.pr.* Truth<—>Falsehood • that which has been shown to be erroneous • Falsehood does not mean incorrect but in error. In other words, what is presented may be absolutely accurate and yet not reflect what is really going on. Perhaps only a portion of the truth is expressed or more information than is pertinent causes one to misconstrue. A danger is that Falsehood can get away from the control of its creator. Once an error has been passed off as truth, some will continue to accept it as truth even if it is recanted by the person that gave the False account • *syn.* erroneousness, untruth, erroneous notion, mistaken, astray, dishonest

Family • *[Structural Term]* • In the Dramatica structure, all units are divided into four major groups according to their most general natures. These groups are *Elements, Variations, Types,*

and *Classes.* Each of these groups is called a Family.

Fantasy • *[Variation]* • *dyn.pr.* Fact<—>Fantasy • belief in something unreal • Fantasy is something that although seemingly real, truly is not. Fantasies exist subjectively so they can either be misinterpretations of the meaning of actual things or internal fabrications of meanings that are not accurate. Neither one can be consciously intentional or one would be aware of the untruth of the Fantasy. Fantasies are not necessarily bad. In fact, they can be the best way for a character to clarify the nature of his goal. Maintaining the Fantasy allows one to practice responses so that Fantasy might actually turn into fact. Of course, when one lets a Fantasy grow such that it extends beyond the goal and into the means of evaluating progress toward the goal, the Fantasy can become self-sustaining and only imagined progress is ever made • *syn.* false belief, faith in the imaginary, delusion, erroneous conviction

Fate • *[Variation]* • *dyn.pr.* Destiny<—>Fantasy • a future situation that will befall an individual • The distinction between Fate and destiny is an important one. Destiny is the direction one's life must take, Fate is any given moment along that direction. So whereas one can have many Fates, one can only have one destiny. Fate describes a state of situation and circumstance that exists at a particular point in time. In other words, Fate is something of an outcome, or perhaps a step — just one of a number of Fates along the path of one's destiny. Characters often either make the mistake of assuming that they have only one Fate and are therefore stuck with it, or they mistakenly believe they can achieve their destiny without "passing through" unattractive fates that lie along the path. The nature of a Fate is that no matter how you try to avoid it, it tracks you. All options that you might exercise still lead to that Fate. That is what also defines Destiny as the limitations on free will that force you to arrive at your Fate no matter how you alter what you do or what kind of person you are. If we knew the future, there would be no free-will • *syn.* inevitable events, unpreventable incidents, eventual events, destined occurrence, destined events, unavoidable situations

Feeling • *[Element]* • *dyn.pr.* Logic<—>Feeling • an emotional sense of how things are going • Feeling is the mental process of seeking the most fulfilling course or correct explanation based on emotion. The Feeling characteristic believes "ya gotta have heart." It cares not for what is efficient or even practical as long as it is "feels" right. This makes the Feeling characteristic very empathetic to the emotional atmosphere in a situation, yet apt to ignore or pay little attention to necessities • *syn.* empathy, emotional sensibility, affective outlook, sentiment, emotional assessment

Female Mental Sex • *[Character Dynamic]* • The Main Character uses female problem solving techniques • A choice of female creates a Main Character whose psychology is based on assessing balance. A female Main Character resolves inequities by comparing surpluses to deficiencies. The manner employed in resolving the inequity will involve creating a surplus where a surplus is desired, creating a deficiency where a deficiency is desired, creating a surplus so a deficiency is felt elsewhere, creating a deficiency so a surplus will be felt elsewhere. Through the application of one's own force, hills and valleys can be created and filled either to directly address the inequity or to create a change in the flow of energies that will ultimately come together in a new hill or disperse creating a new valley. These are the four primary inequity resolving techniques of a female character. It is important to note that these techniques are applied both to others and to oneself. Either way, manipulating surplus and deficiency describes the approach. When selecting female or male, typically the choice is as simple as deciding if you want to tell a story about a man or a woman. But there is another consideration that is being employed with growing frequency in modern stories • putting the psyche of one sex into the skin of another. This does not refer only to the "sex change" comedies but also to many action stories with female Main Characters (e.g. Aliens) and many decision stories with male Main Characters (Prince of Tides). When an author writes a part for a woman, he/she would intuitively create a female psyche for that character. Yet by simply changing the name of the character from Mary to Joe and shifting the appropriate gender terms, the character would ostensibly become a man. But that man would not seem like a man. Even if all the specific feminine dialogue were changed, even if all the culturally dictated manifestations were altered, the underlying psyche of the character would have a female bias rather than a male bias. Sometimes stereotypes

are propagated by what an audience expects to see which filters the message and dilutes the truth. By placing a female psyche in a male character, preconceptions no longer prevent the message from being heard. The word of warning is that this technique can make a Main Character seem "odd" in some hard to define way to your audience. So although the message may fare better, empathy between your audience and your Main Character may not.

Female • *[Overview Appreciation]* • women will tend to empathize with the main character in this story; men will tend to sympathize • Although there is much common ground in a story that is appreciated equally by women and men, some dramatic messages speak to one group more profoundly than the other. One particular area of difference is the relationship of female and male audience members to the Main Character. In some stories an audience member will feel Empathy with the Main Character, as if he/she were standing in the Main Character's shoes. In other stories, an audience member will feel Sympathy for the Main Character, as if the Main Character is a close acquaintance. The dynamics that control this for women and men are quite different. "Female" indicates that as a result of this storyform's dynamics, female audience members will tend to empathize with the Main Character. Male audience members will tend to sympathize

Fixed Attitude (Mind) • *[Class]* • *dyn.pr.* Situation <—> Fixed Attitude • a fixed attitude, fixation, or bias • The Fixed Attitude Class describes a fixed attitude. This can be a bias, prejudice, or even a "positive" opinion about anything at all. The key is that the attitude is fixed, meaning it is accepted as a given and not reevaluated. Often the Fixed Attitude Throughline is represented by a group of people who share a common bias for or against something. • *syn.* attitude, fixation, position on an issue, fixed point of view, disposition

Flashbacks and Flashforwards • *[Storytelling]* • Storytelling techniques for developing the story and the backstory simultaneously • Often the purpose of telling a story is not just to document the effort to solve a problem but to convey understanding as to how such a problem came to be in the first place. If the author wants to develop both story and backstory simultaneously during the course of the storytelling by alternating between them, two primary techniques are available: the Flashback and the Flashforward. In the Flashback, the story proper is assumed to take place in the present. Flashbacks then reveal key episodes in the development of the problem (the Backstory), sometimes in the past, to underscore or contrast specific points in the story as appropriate and as desired. In the Flashforward, the Backstory is assumed to take place in the present and the story is revealed to the audience in episodes illustrating the future outcome of forces presently put into play. In either case, by the end of the storytelling, both Backstory and Story have been fully illustrated to the extent desired to convey the intended message

Focus • *[Element]* • the principal symptom of the story problem • *see Symptom.*

Forewarnings (Overall Storyline) • *[Type]* • the indications that the consequence is growing more imminent • Whether or not the Consequences ever befall the Main Character, there are Forewarnings that indicate their approach and help force the limit of the story and bring the Main Character to the moment where he can be assessed in terms of his Main Character Resolve. These Forewarnings could be a quick look at a growing crack in the dam which no-one sees, or it could be a mad scientist installing the final component in his doomsday device; however it is represented, its nature will be described by the Type appreciation of Forewarnings.

Future (The Future) • *[Type]* • what will happen or what will be • A story focusing on the Future concerns itself with what will be. This does not require the story to be "set" in the Future — only that the Future state of external or internal issues is the subject that is being addressed. A character centered on Future may be trying to discover what will be or may be trying a achieve a particular state of affairs down the line. In both the Story and Character sense, the end is more important than the present although it still may not justify the means • *syn.* what is to come, what will be, prospect, prospective • *dyn.pr.* Progress

Gathering Information • *[Type]* • gathering information or experience • *See Learning*

Goal (Overall Story) • *[Type]* • the central objective of a story • A Goal is that which the Protagonist of a story hopes to achieve. As such, it need not be an object. The Goal might be a state of mind or enlightenment; a feeling or attitude, a degree or kind of knowledge, desire or ability. Although it is his chief concern, the Goal which a Protagonist seeks is not necessarily a good thing for him nor is it certainly attainable. Only through the course of the story does the value and accessibility of the Goal clarify. Dramatica points out the nature of Goal that is consistent with an Author's dramatic choices, but it remains for the Author to illustrate that nature. For any given category of Goal, an unlimited number of examples might be created.

Good • *[Plot Dynamic]* • If at the end of the story the Main Character is no longer nagged by his personal problems, the judgment of the story can be said to be Good • The Main Character ultimately succeeds in resolving his personal problems • Even though the effort to achieve the story's goal may result in success, this is not necessarily a good thing for the Main Character. In fact, success might be obtained in the objective story even though the Main Character fails to resolve his personal problems. Similarly, the effort to achieve the story goal might end in failure yet the Main Character ends up overcoming his personal problems. Regardless of whether the objective story ends in Success or Failure, if the Main Character succeeds in resolving his personal problems the outcome is deemed Good.

Grand Argument Story • *[Dramatica Term]* • A story that illustrates all four throughlines (Overall Story, Subjective Story, Main Character, and Impact Character) in their every appreciation so that no holes are left in either the passionate or dispassionate arguments of that story • A Grand Argument Story covers all the bases so that it cannot be disproven because, from the perspective that it creates, it is right. There are four views in a complete story which look at all the possible ways the story could be resolved from all the possible perspectives allowed; these are represented by the perspectives created by matching the four Throughlines with the four Classes—(the Overall Story, Subjective Story, Main Character, and Impact Character Throughlines matched up with the Classes of Situation (Universe), Activity (Physics), Manipulation (Psychology), and Mind to create the four perspectives of the particular story they are operating in). Every complete storyform explores each of these perspectives entirely so that their view of the story's problem is consistent and that they arrive at the only solution that could possibly work, allowing the givens built into the story from the start. When this is done, a Grand Argument has been made and there is no disproving it on its own terms. You may disagree that the things it takes for givens really are givens, but as an argument it has no holes.

Growth • *[Character Dynamic]* • The way a character grows in his attempt to solve his problems, toward either "Start" or "Stop" • Change Characters see their problems as being inside themselves. Steadfast Characters see their problems as being outside themselves. Sometimes a problem is created by too much of something, other times by too little. Growth describes whether a problem is "too much" of something, or "too little." It appears differently depending on if the Main Character Changes or Remains Steadfast.

If a character must change, he has one of these two kinds of problems. Either he is bullheaded in sticking with an inappropriate approach or he simply doesn't use an approach that would be appropriate. In the "too much" scenario, the character comes off as aggressively obstinate. In the "too little" scenario the character comes off as stubbornly ignorant. The "too much" Change Character needs to "stop." The "too little" Change Character needs to "start."

If the Main Character remains Steadfast, though, then the kinds of problems they'll face will involve either holding out for something to Start or holding out for something to Stop. Metaphorically, the Steadfast Character is either a storm trying to weather away an island, or an island trying to hold out against a storm. Both Change and Steadfast Characters' Growth can be called "Start" or "Stop."

Guardian • *[Archetype]* • An archetype that represents the motivations of Conscience and Help • This Archetypal character acts as teacher/helper to the Protagonist. As Conscience, he provides the audience with the story's assessment of what is good and bad in the world it describes. In his Dynamic Pair relationship, the Guardian counterbalances the efforts of the Contagonist to hinder progress and tempt the Protagonist from the proper path. Since, according to Archetypal convention, the Protagonist must ultimately face the Antagonist without assistance, both the Guardian and Contagonist must be dramatically nullified

before the climax of the story so that they cannot interfere. This often occurs as a separate confrontation between them, just prior to the Protagonist meeting the Antagonist, or it may occur concurrently, but concludes before the actual climax of the story is reached.

Help • *[Element]* • *dyn.pr.* Hinder<—> Help • a direct assistance to another's effort to achieve their goal • The Help characteristic assists another's efforts. This can be a real boon to someone struggling to achieve. Sometimes, however, someone doesn't want any help. He either wants to do it on his own or what he is trying to do has been misread by the character representing the Help characteristic who is actually hindering him. Did you hear the one about the Boy Scout who helped the little old lady across the street and then she bashed him with her handbag because she had been waiting for a bus? • *syn.* aid, assist, support, bolster, abet

Hinder • *[Element]* • *dyn.pr.* Hinder<—>Help • a direct detraction from another's effort to achieve their goal • The Hinder characteristic strives to undermine another's efforts. This might be seen as a negative, as it often is. But sometimes a character functions to hinder an "evil" character, disrupting his plans. Hinder merely indicates the effect on the plans not whether that is a good or bad thing. • *syn.* retard, obstruct, impede, fetter, undermine, block, burden, encumber, thwart

Holistic or Intuitive • *[Character Dynamic]* • The Main Character uses female problem solving techniques • *see Female Mental Sex*

Hope • *[Variation]* • *dyn.pr.* Dream<—>Hope • a desired future if things go as expected • Hope is based on a projection of the way things are going. When one looks at the present situation and notes the direction of change, Hope lies somewhere along that line. As an example, if one is preparing for a picnic and the weather has been sunny, one Hopes for a sunny day. If it was raining for days, one could not Hope but only Dream. Still, Hope acknowledge that things can change in unexpected ways. That means that Hoping for something is not the same as expecting something. Hope is just the expectation that something will occur unless something interferes. How accurately a character evaluates the potential for change determines whether he is Hoping or dreaming. When a character is dreaming and thinks he is Hoping, he prepares for things where there is no indication they will come true. • *syn.* desired expectation, optimistic anticipation, confident aspiration, promise, encouraging outlook

How Things Are Going *[Progress]* • *[Type]* • *dyn.pr.* Future<—>How Things Are Going • the way things are progressing • Progress concerns itself with change • what direction and how fast? It is not so important where things were, are, or will be, but rather how the struggle between inertia and change seesaws over the course of the story. • *syn.* flowing, advancing, proceeding, moving forward, developing step-by-step, graduated, staging, successive, procession, the way things are going

Hunch • *[Element]* • *dyn.pr.* Theory<—>Hunch • a conclusion based on intuition • A Hunch is an understanding arrived at by circumstantial evidence. The phrase "where there's smoke, there's fire" describes the concept. The advantage is that when evidence mounts, even without direct connections, one may draw an analogy that has a substantial likelihood of being correct as in "I've seen that pattern before!" Of course, a Hunch is merely a suspicion. The danger is acting on it as if it were fact. • *syn.* intuition, premonition, impression, suspicion

Impact Character • *[Subjective Character]* • The Subjective Character that forces the Main Character to face his personal problem • Every Main Character has a single Impact Character that forces him to face his personal problems. From the Main Character's point of view, the Impact Character may seem to be *blocking* the road to the solution of the Main Character's personal problem, or he may seem to be trying to knock the Main Character off the road to the solution. In a more objective view, the Impact Character functions to block the Main Character from sweeping his personal problem under the carpet, forcing the Main Character to address it directly. In every act, a story problem is introduced that requires the Main Character to expose his personal problem to solve the story problem. It is the Impact Character that creates the most personal tension for the Main Character. Frequently, the Main Character is chosen by the author to be the Protagonist as well, and often the Impact Character function is combined with the Guardian or the Contagonist. In this way, they each do double duty as prime movers of both the objective and subjective concerns of the story. This arrangement is not essential, however, and in many cases it is prudent to assign the Main and Impact

Character roles to characters other than the Protagonist and Guardian/Contagonist to clearly explore the relationship between the Overall Story and Subjective problems of the story.

Impact Character's Benchmark • *[Type]* • The standard against which the Impact Character's concern is measured • The way of telling how much the Impact Character is dealing with the issues at stake for him in the story is by choosing an item in the story and using it as a measuring stick. This can be subtle or obvious, illustrated perhaps by the number of empty beer cans next to an alcoholic's bed, the severity of a facial tick, or the amount of perfume a character puts on. However it is illustrated, it needs to be there to give both the audience and the Impact Character some way of judging how deep his concern is and how far along in the story he is.

Impact Character's Concern • *[Type]* • The area of the Impact Character's cares, interests, or goals • The Impact Character will be interested in achieving some degree of growth or control over things described by this appreciation. This could be in terms of concrete or abstract things, depending partly on the Impact Character's Throughline and partly on the twist the author wants to put on that Throughline.

Impact Character's Critical Flaw • *[Variation]* • The item that undermines the Impact Character's efforts • The Impact Character's Critical Flaw undermines his effectiveness against the Main Character in general, but especially in regards to his Unique Ability. The Impact Character in any story has a Unique Ability which makes him uniquely qualified to thwart the Main Character. But in his character as well is a Critical Flaw which prevents him from just totally overwhelming the Main Character. This is again a trait which is unique to this particular character.

Impact Character's Issue • *[Variation]* • the nature of The Impact Character's efforts • An Impact Character's Issue captures the essence of what that character will represent in the story. The nature of the things he does, intends to do, and effectively means to the passionate argument of the story are all linked in this appreciation.

Impact Character's Problem • *[Element]* • The source of the Impact Character's drive • In every Impact Character there exists some inequity that is driving him. If the Impact Character Changes something in himself in response to the Main Character's Steadfastness, it is this item, his Problem, which he changes by exchanging it for his Solution. If the Impact Character is Steadfast, though, then he holds onto his problem, deepening his resolve to keep the same motivations at the end of the story as he had when he began the story.

Impact Character's Response • *[Element]* • The direction of the Impact Character's efforts • An Impact Character can never be sure if what he believes to be the source of his problem really <u>is</u> the source of his problem. Regardless, based on his way of seeing things, he will determine a potential solution or Direction in which he hopes to find the solution. The dramatic unit that describes what a Subjective Character believes is the path to a solution is his Response.

Impact Character's Solution • *[Element]* • what is needed to truly satisfy The Impact Character's motivation • The Solution Element is the "flip side" of the Problem Element. For the Impact Character, it is the element that would alleviate the Impact Character's drive which his Problem Element supplies. It is not necessarily applied during a story, but it exists in every story nevertheless.

Impact Character's Symptom • *[Element]* • Where the Impact Character's attention is most directed • The Impact Character concentrates his attention where he thinks his problem lies. Just as in the Main Character, an inequity exists in the Impact Character between himself and his environment which is driving him. The actual nature of this inequity is described by the Impact Character Problem Element. The nature of what is required to restore balance is described by the Impact Character Solution Element. From the Subjective view afforded to the Impact Character though, the inequity does not appear to be *between* himself and the Environment but wholly in one or the other. The Symptom Element describes the nature of how the problem appears to the Impact Character from his Subjective point of view. Symptom really describes the effects of the Impact Character Problem element, but because the Problem element is on the level of his own motivations, Subjective Characters can never see his actual problems without solving them.

Impact Character's Throughline • *[Throughline]* • The broadest description of the Impact Character's impact in a specific story • Everything that emanates from what the Impact Character does and represents which primarily relates to his impact alone, as opposed to specific relationships he has with other characters, can be said to be part of the Impact Character Throughline. There are four different Throughlines in the structure of any story, represented by the combination of each of the four Classes with each of the four throughlines— the Overall Story Throughline, the Subjective Story Throughline, the Main Character Throughline, and the Impact Character Throughline. The Impact Character Throughline describes, in the broadest single term, what the Impact Character represents and the area in which the Impact Character operates within the story.

Impact Character's Unique Ability • *[Variation]* • The item that makes the Impact Character uniquely able to thwart the Main Character • The reason the Impact Character is able to carry half of the Subjective Story is his unique suitability to take the opposite position to the Main Character on the Crucial Element of the story. The Impact Character Unique Ability gives the Impact Character a power which no one else in the story has to be able to affect the Main Character. The nature of this power is what is described by this appreciation.

Impulsive Responses (Preconscious) • *[Type]* • *dyn. pr.* Innermost Desires <—> Impulsive Responses • immediate responses • Built into the mind is an instinctual base of reactions and attitudes that cannot be altered but merely compensated for. When a story's problem revolves around the unsuitability of someone's essential nature to a given situation or environment, the central issue is the Impulsive Responses. The solution lies in the character conditioning himself to either hold his tendencies in check or develop methods of enhancing areas in which he is naturally weak in reason, ability, emotion, or intellect. • *syn.* unthinking responses, immediate responses, impulse, impulsive response, instinctive response, innate response, reflex

Inaction • *[Element]* • *dyn.pr.* Protection <—> Inaction • taking no action as a means of response • Inaction does not mean simply sitting still. The Inactive characteristic might choose to allow a course of action by not interfering. Or it might refuse to move out of harm's way, thereby forming a resistance to the progress that drives the harm. Both of these are efficient tools for altering the course of an interaction. However, the Inactive characteristic may also drag its feet in all areas and form a resistance to both good and bad things so that its influence simply hinders everything but changes nothing. • *syn.* passive reaction, inactive response, achieve through not doing

Induction • *[Element]* • *dyn.pr.* Deduction<—>Induction • a means of determining possibility • Induction is the process of thought that determines where an unbroken line of causal relationships leads. The purpose is to see if it is possible that something connects to something else. The character containing the Inductive characteristic has an advantage in taking seemingly unrelated facts and putting them in an order that establishes a potential causal relationship. This allows him to arrive at conclusions that "limit in" something as a possibility. The drawback is that the conclusion only illustrates one possibility out of an unknown number of possibilities. Unlike deduction, Induction does not rule out competing theories until only one remains. Rather, Induction simply determines that a particular theory is not ruled out. Problems occur when it is assumed that simply because a causal relationship might exist that it does exist. This leads to blaming and holding responsible both people and situations that were not actually the real cause. Only if all possible Inductions are compared can the likelihood of any single one be determined • *syn.* postulate, predicate, conjecture, infer, hypothesize, determine possibility

Inequity • *[Element]* • *dyn.pr.* Equity<—>Inequity • an unbalance, unfairness, or lack or stability • When a character focuses on Inequity he is evaluating in terms of what is wrong or unfair with a situation. No matter how much is working right or how much is good, it is the part that is out of balance that occupies his attention. A character with this trait will spot trouble before anyone else, but he will also never be satisfied unless absolutely everything is worked out • *syn.* imbalance, unfair, disparity, unequal, uneven, disproportionate

Inertia • *[Element]* • *dyn.pr.* Change<—>Inertia • a continuation of a state or process • Inertia is a tendency to maintain the status quo. That which is moving wants to keep moving. That which is at rest wants to stay at rest. An Inertia-oriented character concerns himself with keeping things on an even keel. He tries to

avoid or prevent anything that rocks the boat. He also does not adapt well to change. • *syn.* tendency to continue, a change resistant pattern, continuation, following an established direction

Innermost Desires (Subconscious) • *[Type]* • dyn.pr. Impulsive Responses<—>Innermost Desires • basic drives and desires • Innermost Desires describes the essential feelings that form the foundation of character. These feelings are so basic that a character is often not aware of what they truly are. When the Innermost Desires is involved, a character is moved right to the fiber of his being. • *syn.* libido, id, basic motivations, basic drives, anima

Instinct • *[Variation]* • *dyn.pr.* Conditioning<—>Instinct • intrinsic unconditioned responses • Instinct describes those built-in responses to situations and circumstances that are not learned, yet drive one to comply with their urges. How much sway they have over an individual depends both on the nature of the instinct and the intensity of conditioning against the instinct that he has experienced by accident, design, or choice. When one acts or responds according to instinct, there is no conscious consideration beforehand. Only after the fact does the consciousness become aware that an instinct has been triggered. Nonetheless, one can learn to inhibit instinctual commands until the consciousness has the opportunity to consider the propriety of conforming to it. • *syn.* involuntary drive, innate impulse, unconditioned response, automatic response, unconditioned motivation

Interdiction • *[Variation]* • *dyn.pr.* Prediction<—>Interdiction • an effort to change a predetermined course • Interdiction is the effort to change the course of one's destiny. Once a character determines that his destiny is pulling him toward an undesirable fate, he tries to Interdict and thereby avoid the fate. But has he correctly identified the course of his destiny or in actuality is what he sees as Interdiction is just another pre-destined step toward his fate? • *syn.* altering the future, interfering with the predetermined, hindering the inevitable, escaping the predestined

Interpretation • *[Variation]* • *dyn.pr.* Senses<—>Interpretation • determination of possible meaning • Once an observation is made, its meaning must be Interpreted by the mind. Even if seen exactly as it happened, the forces or intents behind what is seen are often misconstrued. Stories revolving around eye witness accounts frequently employ Interpretation (and its Dynamic Partner, Senses) to great dramatic advantage • *syn.* construe, rendition, rendering meaning, elucidate, translating meaning

Intuitive or Holistic • *[Character Dynamic]* • The Main Character uses female problem solving techniques • *see Female Mental Sex*

Inverse • *[Structural Term]* • Anytime a pair of items is being considered, each item in the pair is referred to as the INVERSE of the other

Investigation • *[Variation]* • *dyn.pr.* Doubt<—>Investigation • gathering evidence to resolve questions of validity • Investigation is a pro-active word for it describes a character who makes an effort to seek out evidence. Obviously this usually tends to bring one closer to a conclusion sooner than without the effort. But Investigation can cause trouble since the character must predetermine where to look. This leads to a meandering path through the evidence that may miss whole pockets of essential information. Sometimes a single missed piece can flip the entire conclusion 180 degrees. So Investigating to one's satisfaction depends on random success and the limits of one's tenacity, not necessarily on learning what the whole picture is. • *syn.* inquiry, research, probe, sleuthing, delving, query

Issue • *[Variation]* • The thematic meaning of the Throughline being explored • Each of the four Throughlines: Overall Story, Subjective Story, Main Character, and Impact Character, have a thematic nature which is described by its Issue. The Overall Story Issue, for example, describes the nature of the Overall Story Characters' efforts in that story. Whatever kinds of things are done by the Overall Story Characters in relation to the Story Goal can be said to be linked thematically by this particular item.

Item • *[Structural Term]* • Sometimes it becomes convenient to group a number of units of similar nature together and treat the group as if it were a single unit itself. When units are grouped together in this manner the larger entity is referred to as an item.

Judgment • *[Plot Dynamic]* • The author's assessment of whether or not the Main Character has resolved his personal problem • The notion that the good guys win and the bad guys lose is not always true. In stories, as in life, we often see very bad people doing very well for themselves (if not for others). And even more often we see very good people striking out. If we only judged things by success and failure, it wouldn't matter if the outcome was good or bad as long as it was accomplished. The choice of Good or Bad places the author's moralistic judgment on the value of the Main Character's success or failure in resolving his personal problems. It is an opportunity not only to address good guys that win and bad guys that fail, as well as good guys that fail and the bad guys that win, but to comment on the success or failure of their growth as human beings.

Justification • The complex hierarchy of experience and expectation that helps one reconcile exceptions to personally held truths while maintaining our position on those personally held truths • All understanding comes from determining connections between processes and results, causes and effects. All anticipation comes from accepting these connections as unchanging and absolute. In this manner we are able to respond to new situations based on our experience and to plan for the future based on our expectations. But our knowledge of our world and ourselves is incomplete. We are constantly learning and redefining our understanding and our anticipation. Sometimes we have built up such a complex hierarchy of experience and expectation that it becomes easier (more efficient) to formulate or accept what might seem an unlikely and complex explanation than to redefine the entire base of our knowledge. After all, the enormity of our experience carries a lot of weight compared to a single incident that does not conform to our conclusions. Unfortunately, once conflicting information is explained away by presupposing an unseen force it is not integrated into the base of our experience and nothing has been learned from it. The new and potentially valuable information has bounced off the mental process of Justification, having no impact and leaving no mark. This is how preconceptions, prejudices, and blind spots are created. It is also how we learn, for only by accepting some things as givens can we build complex understandings on those foundations. Justification also creates the motivation to change things rather than accept them, but in so doing also creates a blind spot that keeps us from seeing a solution in ourselves in situations where it would be better to accept. Because we cannot know if a point of view should be held onto or given up and reexamined, we have no way of being certain that we are approaching a problem correctly. But either way, we will not question our Justification, only the propriety of applying it to a particular instance. In the case of a Main Character who must remain steadfast, he needs to hold onto his Justifications long enough to succeed with them. But in the case of a Main Character who must change, he needs to give up his Justifications and re-examine his basic understanding. Stories explore the relationship of the inequity between the way things are and the way the Main Character sees them or would have them be. Then it can be evaluated by the audience as to whether or not the decision to remain steadfast or change was the proper one. So Justification is neither good nor bad. It simply describes a mind set that holds personal experience as absolute knowledge, which is sometimes just what is needed to solve the problem and other times is actually the cause of the problem.

Knowledge • Most terms in Dramatica are unique, however four items have two uses, serving both as Variation and Element. This is a result of the fundamental importance of the concepts represented by these four items: Thought, Knowledge, Ability, and Desire.

[Variation] • dyn.pr. Thought<—>Knowledge • that which one holds to be true • Knowledge is something a character holds to be true. That does not necessarily mean it IS true but just that the character believes it is. The gulf between what is known and what is true can create enormous misconceptions and inaccurate evaluations. • *syn.* held truth, maintained information, presumed facts, accepted ideas

[Element] • *dyn.pr.* Thought<—>Knowledge • that which one holds to be true • The Knowledge characteristic urges a character to rely on what is held to be true. The Character representing Knowledge will tap the resources of its information to find parallels and understanding that he can apply to the issue at hand. The advantage of Knowledge is that one need not learn what is already known, thereby skipping non-essential reevaluations and getting a head start with solving a problem. The difficulty is that Knowledge can be wrong. Without reevaluation dogma sets in — rigor mortis of thought, leading to inflexibility and closed minded-ness because the Character

believes no reconsideration is needed since the subject is already "known." • *syn.* learnedness, held truths, authoritative certainty, generally agreed on truths

Leap of Faith • Having run out of time or options and come to the moment of truth, the Main Character decides to either Change or remain Steadfast with no way of knowing which will best lead him to his goal or resolve his personal problem • No Main Character can be sure that he will succeed until the story has completely unfolded. Up until that moment, there is always the opportunity to change one's approach or one's attitude. For example, a Main Character may determine that what he thought was the true source of the problem really is not. Or he may reconsider his motivation to try and resolve it; whether he should give up or try harder. Again, there is no way for him to tell with certainty which path will lead to success. Nevertheless, when these scenarios close in on a single moment in the story, the moment of truth, where the Main Character has their last opportunity to remain steadfast in their approach and attitude or to change either or both, there will be a Leap of Faith. After that, all that remains is to see it to its conclusion, good or bad. That moment of truth is called the Leap of Faith because the Main Character must choose a course and then commit himself to it, stepping into the unknown with blind faith in a favorable outcome or resignation to an ostensibly poor one.

Learning • *[Type]* • *dyn.pr.* Understanding<—>Learning • gathering information or experience • Learning describes the process of acquiring knowledge. It is not the knowledge itself. When a portion of a story focuses on learning, it is the gathering of an education that is of concern, not the education that ultimately has been gathered. Learning need not be an academic endeavor. One might learn to express one's feelings or learn about love. Learning does not even require new information as sometimes one learns simply by looking through old information from a different perspective or with a new approach. It is not important if one is learning to arrive at a particular understanding or just to gather data. As long as the focus is on the process of gaining information, Learning is the operative word. • *syn.* cultivating experience, acquiring information, collecting data, gathering knowledge

Level • *[Structural Term]* • The relationship between families (Elements, Variations, Types and Throughlines) of dramatic units is similar to turning up the power on a microscope: each has a different resolution with which to examine the story's problem. Throughlines take the broadest view. Types are more detailed. Variations are even more refined and Elements provide the greatest detail available in a story. Each of the families, therefore, represents a different level of resolution or simply a different Level.

Limit • *[Plot Dynamic]* • The restricted amount of time or options that, by running out, forces the story to a climax • The Limit is what forces the story to a close. One of the functions of a story is to give the audience the value of experiences it has not had itself by living through the Main Character. As such, the Main Character in the story Changes or Remains Steadfast and hopes for the best, and we learn from his accomplishments or disappointments. Yet, even a Main Character would not jump into the void and commit to a course of action or decision unless forced into it. To force the Main Character to decide, the story provides all the necessary information to make an educated guess while progressively closing in on the Main Character until he has no alternative but to choose. This closing in can be accomplished in either of two ways: either running out of places to look for the solution or running out of time to work one out. Running out of options is accomplished by an Optionlock; a deadline is accomplished by a Timelock. Both of these means of limiting the story and forcing the Main Character to decide are felt from early on in the story and get stronger until the climax. Optionlocks need not be claustrophobic so much as they only provide limited pieces with which to solve the problem. Timelocks need not be hurried so much as limiting the interval during which something can happen. Once an established Limit is reached, however, the story must end and assessments be made: is the Outcome Success or Failure? is the Judgment Good or Bad? is the Main Character Resolve Change or Steadfast? etc.

Linear or Logical • *[Character Dynamic]* • The Main Character uses male problem solving techniques • *see Male Mental Sex*

Logic • *[Element]* • *dyn.pr.* Feeling<—>Logic • a rational sense of how things are related • Logic is the mental process of choosing the most efficient course or explanation based on

reason. The Logic characteristic exemplifies the theory behind "Occam's Razor," that the simplest explanation is the correct explanation. Therefore, the Logic characteristic is very efficient but has no understanding or tolerance that people do not live by reason alone. As a result, the character with the Logic characteristic often ignores how other's "unreasonable" feelings may cause a very real backlash to his approach. • *syn.* linear reasoning, rationality, structural sensibility, syllogistics

Main Character • A story has a central character that acts as the focus of the audience's emotional attachment to the story. This Main Character is the conduit through whom the audience experiences the story subjectively. The Main Character may be the Steadfast Character who needs to hold on to his resolve or the Change Character who alters his nature in an attempt to resolve his problems. Either way, it is mostly through his eyes that we see the passionate argument of the story, if not also the dispassionate argument.

Main Character's Benchmark • *[Type]* • the nature of the Main Character's effort to solve his personal problem; the standard by which the Main Character judges the degree of his concern • the way of telling how much the Main Character is dealing with the issues at stake for himself in the story is by choosing an item in the story and using it as a measuring stick. This can be subtle or obvious, illustrated perhaps by the number of empty beer cans next to an alcoholic's bed, the severity of a facial tick, or the amount of perfume a character puts on. However it is illustrated, it needs to be there to give both the audience and the Main Character some way of judging how deep his concern is and how far along in the story he is.

Main Character's Concern • *[Type]* • The Main Character's personal objective or purpose, the area of the Main Character's concern • The Main Character Concern describes the kinds of things the Main Character is striving to attain. This could be in terms of concrete or abstract things, depending partly on the Main Character's Throughline and partly on the twist the author wants to put on that Throughline.

Main Character's Critical Flaw • *[Variation]* • the quality that undermines The Main Character's efforts • To balance the Main Character's extraordinary status conveyed by his Unique Ability, he must also be shown to be especially vulnerable in one area as well. This vulnerability is called his Critical Flaw. The Main Character's Critical Flaw is his Achilles heel that prevents him from being too one-sided. Just as with Unique Ability, the Critical Flaw can be quite mundane as long as it can threaten him with failure from an unprotectable direction. The specific Critical Flaw must be unique to the Main Character in the story. However, the more common the Critical Flaw is to the audience, the more it will identify with the Main Character's predicament. In Start stories, the Critical Flaw inhibits the Main Character from using his Unique Ability. In Stop stories, the Critical Flaw undoes work done by the Unique Ability after the fact. Only when the Main Character learns to either Start or Stop as required by the story can the Critical Flaw be avoided, allowing his Unique Ability to solve the problem.

Main Character's Direction • *[Element]* • The efforts of the Main Character to solve his apparent problems • *see Main Character Response*.

Main Character's Focus • *[Element]* • where The Main Character believes the problem to be • *see Main Character Symptom*

Main Character's Issue • *[Variation]* • the nature of The Main Character's efforts; the Main Character's thematic focus • A Main Character's Issue captures the essence of what that character will represent in the story. The nature of the things he does, intends to do, and effectively means to the passionate argument of the story are all linked in this appreciation.

Main Character Problem • *[Element]* • source of The Main Character's motivation; the source of the Main Character's problems • In every Main Character there exists some inequity that is driving him. If the Main Character Changes something in himself at the leap of faith, it is this item, his Problem, which he changes by exchanging it for his Solution. If the Main Character is Steadfast, though, he holds onto his problem, deepening his resolve to keep the same motivations through the end of the story as he had when he began the story.

Main Character's Response • *[Element]* • The efforts of the Main Character to solve his apparent problems • A Main Character can never be sure if what he believes to be the source of his problem really <u>is</u> the source of his problem. Regardless, based on his apparent

problems he will determine a potential solution or Response which he hopes will work as a solution. The dramatic unit that describes what a Main Character holds as the path to a solution is the Main Character Response.

Main Character's Solution • *[Element]* • what is needed to truly satisfy The Main Character's motivation; the solution to the Main Character's problems • The Solution Element is the "flip side" of the Problem Element. In a story, the focus may be on the Problem Element ("The Main Character should not be this way") or the focus may be on the Solution Element ("The Main Character should be this way"). If the Main Character should not be a certain way, we say it is a "Stop" story as he must stop being a certain way. If the Main Character should be a certain way, we say it is a "Start" story as he must start being a certain way. So in a sense the Problem Element is not by itself the cause of the story's problem, but works in conjunction with the Solution Element to create an imbalance between two traits that need to be balanced. The choice to present one as a negative trait defines it as the Problem Element and its positive partner becomes the Solution Element.

Main Character's Symptom • *[Element]* • where The Main Character believes the problem to be; where the Main Character's attention is focused • When a Main Character is at odds with his surroundings, a problem exists between himself and his environment. The actual nature of this gap between Main Character and environment is described by the Problem Element. The nature of what is required to restore balance is described by the Solution Element. This is the Overall Story view of the problem. The Main Character, however, is not privy to that view and must work from the Subjective view instead. From the Subjective view, the problem does not appear to be *between* the Main Character and the Environment but wholly in one or the other. Sometimes a Main Character is a "Do-er" type and will perceive and first try to solve the problem in the environment. Other times a Main Character is a "Be-er" who will first try to solve the problem by adapting to the environment. A "Do-er" focuses the problem in the environment; a "Be-er" focuses the problem in himself. The Symptom Element describes the nature of how the problem appears to the Main Character when he places it wholly in one area or the other.

Main Character's Throughline • *[Throughline]* •
the general area in which The Main Character
operates • Everything the Main Character does
and represents that primarily relates to him
alone, as opposed to specific relationships he
has with other characters, can be said to be part
of the Main Character Throughline. There are
four different perspectives in the structure of
any story represented by the combination of
each of the four Classes with each of the four
Throughlines— the Overall Story Throughline,
the Subjective Story Throughline, the Impact
Character Throughline, and the Main Character
Throughline. The Main Character Throughline
describes in the broadest single term what the
Main Character represents and the area in which
the Main Character operates within the story.

Main Character's Unique Ability • *[Variation]* • the
quality that makes The Main Character uniquely
qualified to solve the story's problem/achieve
the goal • Just as a requirement defines the
specific nature of things needed to achieve
a particular goal, Unique Ability defines the
specific quality needed to meet the requirement.
Unique Ability is another way in which the Main
Character is identified as the intersecting point
between the Subjective and Objective stories as
it is only he who ultimately has what it takes to
meet the test of the requirement and thereby
achieve the goal. The Unique Ability need not
be anything extraordinary but must be the
one crucial quality required that is shared by
no one else. Frequently, the Unique Ability is
in keeping with the Main Character's position
or profession, however it can be much more
interesting to assign an incongruous Unique
Ability. In either approach, it is essential to
illustrate the existence of the Unique Ability in
the Main Character several times throughout
the story, even if it is not employed until the
climax. In this way, it becomes integrated into
the nature of the Main Character and does
not seem conveniently tacked on when it is
ultimately needed. Also, the Unique Ability
can be extremely mundane. The key is that the
ability does not have to be unique by nature,
but just possessed uniquely in that specific
story by the Main Character. Clever storytelling
may arrange the climax of the story so some
completely ordinary and insignificant Unique
Ability makes the difference in the outcome of a
cosmic struggle.

Male Mental Sex • *[Character Dynamic]* • The Main
Character uses male problem solving techniques
• A choice of male selects a psychology for the
Main Character based on causal relationships.
A male Main Character solves problems by
examining what cause or group of causes is
responsible for an effect or group of effects.
The effort made to solve the problem will focus
on affecting a cause, causing an effect, affecting
an effect, or causing a cause. This describes
four different approaches. Affecting a cause
is manipulating an existing force to change
its eventual impact. Causing an effect means
applying a new force that will create an impact.
Affecting an effect is altering an effect after it
has happened. Causing a cause is applying
a new force that will make some other force
come into play to ultimately create an impact.
These are the four primary problem solving
techniques of a male minded character. It is
important to note that these techniques can be
applied to either external or internal problems.
Either way, manipulating cause and effect is
the modus operandi. When selecting female
or male, typically the choice is as simple as
deciding if you want to tell a story about a man
or a woman. But there is another consideration
that is being employed with growing frequency
in modern stories: putting the psyche of one
sex into the skin of another. This does not refer
only to the "sex change" comedies but to many
action stories with female Main Characters
(e.g. ALIENS) and many decision stories with
male Main Characters (PRINCE OF TIDES).
When an author writes a part for a man, he/she
would intuitively create a male psyche for that
character. Yet by simply changing the name of
the character from Joe to Mary and shifting the
appropriate gender terms, the character would
ostensibly become a woman. But that woman
would not seem like a woman Even if all the
specific masculine dialogue were changed, even
if all the culturally dictated manifestations were
altered, the underlying psyche of the character
would have a male bias rather than a female
bias. Sometimes stereotypes are propagated by
what an audience expects to see which filters the
message and dilutes the truth. By placing a male
psyche in a female character, preconceptions no
longer prevent the message from being heard.
The word of warning is that this technique can
make a Main Character seem "odd" in some hard
to define way to your audience. So although the
message may fare better, empathy between your
audience and your Main Character may not.

Male • *[Overview Appreciation]* • men will tend to empathize with the main character in this story; women will tend to sympathize • Although there is much common ground in a story that is appreciated equally by women and men, some dramatic messages speak to one group more profoundly than the other. One particular area of difference is the relationship of female and male audience members to the Main Character. In some stories an audience member will feel Empathy with the Main Character, as if he/she were standing in the Main Character's shoes. In other stories, an audience member will feel Sympathy for the Main Character, as if the Main Character is a close acquaintance. The dynamics that control this for women and men are quite different. "Male" indicates that as a result of this storyform's dynamics, male audience members will tend to empathize with the Main Character. Female audience members will sympathize.

Manipulation (Psychology) • *[Class]* • *dyn.pr.* Activity<—>Manipulation • a manner of thinking • The Manipulation Class is where the evolution or change in an attitude is explored, unlike the Fixed Attitude Class which describes the nature of a fixed state of mind. This is a more deliberation-oriented class where the focus is not on the attitude itself, but whether it is changing for better or for worse. • *syn.* ways of thinking, thinking process, activity of the psyche, manipulation of others

Memory • *[Type]* • *dyn.pr.* Contemplation [Conscious]<—>Memory • recollections • The Past is an objective look at what has happened. In contrast, Memory is a subjective look at what has happened. Therefore, Memory of the same events varies among individuals creating many different and possibly conflicting recollections. Often one's current feelings come from memories, both pleasant and unpleasant. Many a taut story revolves around a character's effort to resolve open issues from his memories. • *syn.* linear reasoning, rationality, structural sensibility, syllogistics

Mental Sex • *[Character Dynamic]* • a determination of the Main Character's mental operating system • Much of what we are as individuals is learned behavior. Yet the basic operating system of the mind is cast biologically before birth. Talents, intellectual capacity, instincts — all of these are not learned but inherited. Among these traits are those specific to females and others specific to males. To be sure, we can go a long

way toward balancing out those traits yet that does not eliminate them nor diminish their impact. In dealing with the psychology of a Main Character, it is essential to understand on which foundation his experience rests.

Methodology • the elements a character will implement to achieve his Purposes • When a character is motivated toward a particular purpose, there remains the decision of what means should be used to reach it. Not every possible Methodology is as appropriate as every other under unique circumstances. For example, if one wants to pound in a nail, a wrench would not work as well as a hammer. In fact, sometimes the whole problem in a story is created because someone is using the wrong tool for the right job. In creating Overall Story Characters for a given story, 16 of the 64 elements will be selected as the Methodology elements of the character set.

Mind • *[Class]* • a fixed attitude • *see Fixed Attitude*

Morality • *[Variation]* • *dyn.pr.* Self Interest<—>Morality • doing or being based on what is best for others • Not to be taken as a spiritual or religious sense of right and wrong, Morality here is intended to describe the quality of character that puts others before self. This is not, however, always a good thing. If a character is besieged by Self-Interested parties that grasp and take whatever they can, Morality (in this limited sense) is most inappropriate. Also, Morality does not always require sacrifice. It simply means that a Moral character will consider the needs of others before his own. If the needs are compatible, it can create a win/win scenario where no one need suffer. • *syn.* selflessness, altruism, benevolence, generosity

Motivation • The elements that represent the drives behind a character's Purposes • Motivation is the force that drives a character in a particular direction. For the problem in a story to be fully explored, all motivations pertaining to that topic must be expressed. This is accomplished by assigning characteristic elements that represent these motivations to the various objective characters. In this way, different characters represent different motivations and the story problem is fully explored. In creating Overall Story Characters for a given story, 16 of the 64 elements will be selected as the Motivation elements of that character set.

Nature • *[Overview Appreciation]* • the primary
dramatic mechanism of a story • The nature of
a story will be one of four possibilities: Actual
Work Story, Actual Dilemma Story, Apparent
Work Story, or Apparent Dilemma Story. A story
can be appreciated as a structure in which the
beginning, middle, and end can all be seen
at the same time. From this point of view, the
Objective and Subjective throughlines can
be compared. The Overall Story Throughline
determines if the solution to the problem can
be found in the environment or if the problem
is actually caused by a character flaw of the Main
Character himself. The Subjective throughline
determines if the Main Character will remain
steadfast in the belief the problem can be solved
in the environment or will change in the belief
that he himself is the cause of the problem.
When the Main Character remains steadfast, he
spends the entire story doing work to try and
solve the problem. This is called a Work Story.
If the Main Character is correct in believing the
solution to the problem lies in the environment
it is an Actual Work story. If the steadfast Main
Character is wrong and is the true cause of the
problem, it is an Apparent Work story since he
believes Work is all that is necessary and that is
not the case. When the Main Character changes,
he has come to believe that he is the real
cause of the problem. This is called a Dilemma
Story because the Main Character spends the
story wrestling with an internal dilemma. If
the Main Character is correct in believing that
he is the source of the problem, then it is an
Actual Dilemma Story. If he is incorrect and
changes, even though the problem was truly
in the environment, it is an Apparent Dilemma
Story. Each of these four combinations creates
a different mechanism to arrive at the climax
with the appropriate match up between the
true location of the problem and the Main
Character's assessment of where to find the
solution.

Need • *[Variation]* • *dyn.pr.* Expediency<—>Need
• that which is required • Needs are always
based on a purpose. It is often assumed that
Need describes something absolutely required
in an objective sense. But Need is really a
subjective judgment of what is lacking to fulfill
a requirement. To illustrate this, we might
consider the statement, "We all need food and
water." This statement seems to make sense,
but is not actually correct. In truth, we only
need food and water if we want to live. For a

paralyzed patient who wishes to be allowed to
die, the last thing he *Needs* is food and water.
Clearly, need depends on what one subjectively
desires. That which is required to fulfill that
desire is the subjective Need. • *syn.* subjective
necessity, urge, demand, imperative

Negative Feel • *[Overview Appreciation]* •
the problem is closing in on the objective
characters • Overall, stories feel like "uppers" or
"downers." This is not a description of whether
or not things turn out okay in the end, but a
sense of direction created by the kind of tension
that permeates the story up to the moment
of climax. When the focus is on characters
doggedly pursuing a Solution, the story feels
positive. When the focus is on characters being
dogged by a relentless Problem, the story
feels negative. Another way to appreciate the
difference is to look at the Main Character. An
audience can sense whether the author feels a
Main Character should or should not change.
If the character is growing toward the proper
choice, the story feels positive. If he is growing
toward the improper choice, the story feels
negative. Both these views are created by the
friction between the Overall Story view that
indicates what is truly needed to solve the
problem and the Subjective view of the Main
Character as to what *seems* to be the solution to
the problem.

Neither • *[Overview Appreciation]* • both men and
women will tend to sympathize with the main
character in this story • Although there is much
common ground in a story that is appreciated
equally by women and men, some dramatic
messages speak to one group more profoundly
than the other. One particular area of difference
is the relationship of female and male audience
members to the Main Character. In some stories
an audience member will feel Empathy with
the Main Character, as if he/she were standing
in the Main Character's shoes. In other stories,
an audience member will feel Sympathy for the
Main Character, as if the Main Character is a
close acquaintance. The dynamics that control
this for women and men are quite different.
"Neither" indicates that as a result of this
storyform's dynamics, neither male and female
audience members will tend to empathize with
the Main Character, both will sympathize.

Non-Acceptance • *[Element]* • *dyn.pr.*
Acceptance<—>Non-Acceptance • a decision
to oppose • The character containing the Non-

Acceptance characteristic will not compromise. He stands his ground regardless of how unimportant the issue may be. Certainly, this characteristic nips attrition in the bud but also loses the benefits of give and take relationships. • *syn.* run counter to, reject, decline, repudiate, resist, refusal to compromise

Non-Accurate • *[Element]* • dyn.pr. Accurate<—>Non-Accurate • not within tolerances • Non-Accurate describes a concept that is not functional for the purpose at hand. There may be some value in the concept in other areas, but for the intended use it is not at all correct. The Non-Accurate characteristic will find the exceptions to the rule that ruin an argument. This makes it nearly immune to generalizations. Unfortunately this can also make it unable to accept any explanation or concept that has an exception, even if the exception has no real effect on how the concept is being applied. Anything that is not right all the time for every use is rejected as Non-Accurate • *syn.* not within tolerance, insufficiency, inadequacy, deviancy, deficient to the purpose

Overall Story Benchmark • *[Type]* • The standard by which progress is measured in the Overall Story • The Overall Story Benchmark is the gauge that tells people how far along the story has progressed. It can't say how much longer the story may go, but in regards to seeing how far away the goal is, both the Overall Story Characters and the audience will look to the stipulation to make any kind of judgment. This Type item describes the nature of the measuring stick which will be used in the story.

Overall Story Catalyst • *[Variation]* • The item whose presence always pushes the Overall Story forward • The Overall Story Catalyst is what creates breakthroughs and seems to accelerate the development of the Overall Story. In both the Objective and Subjective Stories there occur dramatic "log-jams" when things seem to be approaching a halt. This is when the Catalyst is necessary, for its introduction will either solve the puzzle that's holding things up or else make the puzzle seem suddenly unimportant so the story can continue.

Overall Story Concern • *[Type]* • The area of concern in the objective story • *see Concern.*

Overall Story Consequence • [Type] • The area that best describes the result of failing to achieve the goal • *see Consequence.*

Overall Story Costs • [Type] • The area that best describes the costs incurred while trying to achieve the goal • *see Costs.*

Overall Story Dividends • [Type] • The area that best describes the dividends accrued while trying to achieve the goal • *see Dividends.*

Overall Story Focus • *[Element]* • Where attention is focused in the objective story • *see Symptom.*

Overall Story Forewarnings • [Type] • The area that best describes the imminent approach of the story consequences • *see Forewarnings.*

Overall Story Goal • [Type] • The common goal of the objective characters • *see Goal.*

Overall Story Inhibitor • *[Variation]* • The item that impedes the objective story's progress • The Overall Story Inhibitor is what prevents a story from just rushing full speed to the solution. It is like a brake mechanism which can be applied as the author pleases. The introduction of this item will always slow the progress of the story and it works as the antidote to the Overall Story Catalyst.

Overall Story Issue • *[Variation]* • The objective story's thematic focus • *see Issue*

Overall Story Line • the plot as it concerns the story goal • The Overall Story Line is a distinct act by act sequence of events that involves all of the Overall Story story points and none of the Subjective Story story points. It represents the dispassionate argument of the story, emphasizing events and relationships in a purely cause and effect way. This is not to say that it has nothing to do with the meaning of a story, only that it is not the WHOLE story. Meaning in stories comes from comparing the Overall Story view of a story with the Subjective view that comes from within the story.

Overall Story Preconditions • [Type] • The area that best describes the conditions imposed on meeting the story's requirements • *see Preconditions.*

Overall Story Prerequisites • [Type] • The area that best describes what is needed to meet the story requirements • *see Prerequisites.*

Overall Story Problem • *[Element]* • The source of the objective story's problems • *see Problem*

Overall Story Range • *[Variation]* • The objective story's thematic focus • *see Issue*

Overall Story Requirements • [Type] • The area that best describes the requirements that must be met prior to achieving the goal • *see Requirements.*

Overall Story Response • *[Element]* • The direction of efforts in the objective story • *see Response.*

Overall Story Solution • *[Element]* • The solution to the objective story's problems • *see Issue*

Overall Story Symptom • *[Element]* • Where attention is focused in the objective story • *see Symptom.*

Overall Story Stipulation • *[Type]* • The standard by which progress is measured in the Overall Story • *see Overall Story Benchmark*

Overall Story Throughline • *[Class]* • The domain in which the objective story takes place • *see Throughline.*

Overall Story Type Order • *[Plot Structure]* • the kind of activity employed to arrive at a solution to the story's objective problem, act by act • As the Overall Story progresses act by act, it covers the Overall Story Perspective (the Perspective created by matching the Overall Story Throughline with one of the four Classes) Type by Type around the quad of Types which it contains. These four explorations make up the four acts and describe the kinds of things that will have to happen to arrive face to face with the Overall Story Problem.

Overall Story versus Subjective Perspectives • In Dramatica, we can examine a story from the outside as a dispassionate observer, noting the relationship of Character to Plot to theme. We can also examine a story from the inside, by stepping into the shoes of the Main Character to discover how things look to himself. In the first case, we see the story like a general watching a battle from atop a hill. We are concerned with the outcome, but not actually involved. This is the Overall Story perspective. In the second case, we see the story from the point of view of a Main Character. This is more like the view of a soldier in the trenches. We are watching the same battle, but this time we are personally involved. This is the Subjective perspective. An audience is provided access to both Overall Story and Subjective views by the author. When the audience is only shown information that the Main Character also receives, it is in the Subjective perspective. When the audience receives additional information that the Main Character does not receive, it is in the Overall

Story perspective. The dramatic potentials of a story are largely created by the differential between the Overall Story and Subjective perspectives. At appropriate times, Dramatica aids the author in focusing his attention on the perspective that will most effectively support his dramatic intentions.

Obligation • *[Variation]* • *dyn.pr.* Rationalization<—>Obligation • accepting a task or situation in exchange for someone's potential favors • Obligation is a mental trick we play when we accept a poor situation now in the hopes it will lead to a better one later. If we do not feel Obligated, we know we are really in control of the situation since we can leave at any time. However, we would then lose any chance of a reward at the end and even risk consequences that might befall us as a result of leaving. But by focusing on the hope of a reward and protection from consequences, our current suffering can be tolerated and we feel we have no choice but to stick it out. The problem is that as long as we continue to feel we have no choice, the suffering can increase way beyond any realistic hope of recouping and yet we "must" stay. • *syn.* agreement, pledge, contract, accepted compulsion, emotional contract

Obstacle Character • *[Subjective Character]* • The Subjective Character that forces the Main Character to face his personal problem • *see Impact Character*

Obtaining • *[Type]* • *dyn.pr.* Doing<—>Obtaining • achieving or possessing something • Obtaining includes not only that which is possessed but also that which is achieved. For example, one might obtain a law degree or the love of a parent. One can also obtain a condition, such as obtaining a smoothly operating political system. Whether it refers to a mental or physical state or process, obtaining describes the concept of attaining • *syn.* controlling for oneself, possessing, having, keeping.

Openness • *[Variation]* • *dyn.pr.* Preconception<—>Openness • willingness to reevaluate • Openness simply means entertaining alternatives. When a character's preconceptions come into conflict with new information, if he is open, he will not be biased or blind to it. He puts openness above holding on to a point of view. Of course, this can easily be carried to extremes, when someone seems to have no opinion at all and just goes with whatever anyone else says. Some degree of preconception is necessary to benefit from the value of one's own experience. • *syn.* broad mindedness, tolerancy, willingness to reevaluate, receptiveness

Oppose • *[Element]* • *dyn.pr.* Support<—>Oppose • an indirect detraction from another's effort • The Oppose characteristic causes a character to speak out against any effort, although he does not actively engage in preventing it. As in "the Loyal Opposition," an opposing view can be useful in seeing the negative side of an endeavor. However it can also wear thin really fast with the constant nag, nag, nag. • *syn.* object to, speak out against, argue against, protest, dispute, show disapproval of, detract from

Optionlock • *[Plot Dynamic]* • the story climax occurs because all other options have been exhausted • If not for the story being forced to a climax, it might continue forever. When a story is brought to a conclusion because the characters run out of options, it is said to contain a Optionlock. As an analogy, one might think of a story as the process of examining rooms in a mansion to find a solution to the story's problem. Each room in the mansion will contain a clue to the actual location of the solution. In an optionlock, the Overall Story Characters might be told they can examine any five rooms they want, but only five. They must pick the five rooms ahead of time. They can take as long as they like to search each one and go thoroughly examine four of the rooms. After getting through their fourth pick they are given a choice: based on the clues they have found so far, do they wish to stick with their original fifth room or pick another room instead out of all that remain? Either choice may lead to success or failure, but because running out of options forced the choice it is an Optionlock story. This choice represents the Optionlock which brings the story to a close and forces such story points as Main Character Resolve (Change or Steadfast), Outcome (Success or Failure), and Judgment (Good or Bad).

Order • *[Element]* • *dyn.pr.* Chaos<—>Order • an arrangement in which patterns are seen • The character containing the Order characteristic is concerned with keeping things organized. Change is not a problem as long as it is orderly. However, sometimes you can't get there from here and the whole system has to be blown apart to rebuild from the ground up. Sometimes

a little chaos needs to reign so that a log jam can be broken or a process speeded up. The character representing Order is an organization fiend. • *syn.* structure, patterned arrangement, organization, patterned formation, formation, configuration, patterned sequence

Outcome • *[Plot Dynamic]* • an assessment of how things ended up • When one is creating a story, one must consider how it all comes out. This will not just be a description of the situation but also of what potentials remain and how they have changed over the course of the story. Often, an author may wish to show the Outcome of a dramatic movement at the beginning or middle rather than the end. In this way the audience will focus more on how that eventuality came to be rather than trying to figure out what is going to happen.

Overview Story Points • Story points items relating to the widest appreciation of your entire story, including the Character and Plot Dynamics which describe its dramatic mechanism and basic feel are called Overview Story Points. For example, Essence, Nature, Reach, Apparent or Actual Dilemma stories, etc.

Past • *[Type]* • *dyn.pr.* Present<—>Past • what has already happened • The past is not unchanging. Often we learn new things which change our understanding of what past events truly meant and create new story points of how things really fit together. A Story that focuses on the Past may be much more than a documentation of what happened. Frequently it is a reevaluation of the meaning of what has occurred that can lead to changing one's understanding of what is happening in the present or will eventually happen in the future. • *syn.* history, what has happened, former times, retrospective

Perception • *[Element]* • *dyn.pr.* Actuality<—>Perception • the way things seem to be • Perception is a point of view on reality. In truth, we cannot truly get beyond perception in our understanding of our world. A character that represents Perception is more concerned with the way things seem than what it is. Therefore he can be caught off-guard by anything that is not what it seems. • *syn.* appearance, how things seem to be, discernment, a particular reading of things, a point of view on reality, a way of seeing

Permission • *[Variation]* • *dyn.pr.* Deficiency<—>Permission • one's ability based on what is allowed • Permission means Ability limited by restrictions. These constraints may be self imposed or imposed by others. When a Character considers what he can or cannot do, he is not assessing his ability but the limitations to his ability. When one worries about the consequences born of disapproval or self-loathing, one halts for the lack of Permission. The frustration of a character suffering a vice-grip on his ability may eventually erupt in an explosive reaction if the noose gets too tight. • *syn.* constrained ability, limited capability, restricted capacity, hindered performance, allowed limitations, restrained utility

Perspective • *[Throughline] [Class]* • The combination of one of the four throughlines with one of the four Classes • To complete the creation of one of the four perspectives (or Throughlines) for any particular story, a throughline must be matched to a Class so that the place which the perspective is looking from is defined and the nature of the perspective is defined. The four throughlines include the Overall Story, the Subjective Story, the Main Character, and the Subjective Character and they are the four places where a perspective or Throughline can be assigned. Situation (Universe), Activity (Physics), Manipulation (Psychology), and Mind are the four classes which represent the four broadest classifications which describe the nature of a perspective. In every story, each throughline is assigned one Class. Then the pair relationships of the Classes and the terms which fall under them suddenly apply to the Perspectives which have been created by this merging of throughlines and Classes. Only by fully exploring all four perspectives can a Grand Argument Story be completed.

Physics • *[Class]* • an activity • *see Activity*

Playing A Role (Being) • *[Type]* • *dyn.pr.* Changing One's Nature <—> Playing A Role • temporarily adopting a lifestyle • "Being" is an elusive word, subject to inconsistent common usage. For purposes of story, Playing A Role is meant to describe the condition of existing in a certain manner. This does not mean that whomever or whatever is being a particular way is truly of that nature to the core. In fact, it may be put on, as an act or to deceive. However, as long as there is nothing more or less to the functioning of person or thing, it can be said to "be" what it appears to be. Stories often focus on someone who wants to "be" something without actually

"becoming" it. The important difference is that to "be" requires that all the elements of what one wants to be are present in oneself. To "become" requires that there are no elements in oneself that are not in what one wants to become • *syn.* pretending, appearing, acting like, seeming as, fulfilling a role

Positive Feel • *[Overview Appreciation]* • the objective characters in the story are closing in on the problem • An author can pass judgment on the appropriateness of a Main Character's approach to the problem. When a Main Character's approach is deemed proper, the audience hopes for him to remain steadfast in that approach and to succeed. Regardless of whether he actually succeeds or fails, if he remains steadfast he wins a moral victory and the audience feels the story is positive. When the approach is deemed improper, the audience hopes for him to change. Whether or not the Main Character succeeds, if he changes from an improper approach to a proper one he also win a moral victory and the story feels Positive.

Positive versus Negative • Positive and Negative are not evaluations of the ultimate outcome of a story, but evaluations of how the story feels during its course toward the outcome. Does the story feel like it is drawing closer to a satisfying and fulfilling conclusion or farther away from an unsatisfying, unfulfilling conclusion? Then it is positive. Does the story feel like it is drawing closer to an unsatisfying and unfulfilling conclusion or farther away from a satisfying, fulfilling conclusion? Then it is negative. Any given story will have either a positive or negative feel to it. This is caused by a combination of two kinds of dynamics, one of which describes the Main Character, the other describes the Author. Every Main Character's personal problem is either caused because he is doing something he needs to stop or because he is not doing something he ought to be. In other words, his problem exists because he needs to remove or add a trait. In a sense, the Main Character must either move toward something new or move away from something old. That alone does not give a positive or negative feel to a story, as what he is moving toward or away from could be good or bad. Every Author has feelings about which traits are good ones to have and which are bad. Just because a Main Character successfully solves his problem by removing or adding a trait does not mean he has become a better person for it. The Author's message may be that failure in problem-solving is preferable to diminishing one's overall character. So the Author's identity is exposed to the audience by passing a value judgment on whether removing or adding a trait (Start or Stop) was good or bad. Taken together, Start and Stop, and a value judgment on what the Main Character is growing in relation to of *good* or *bad* create four combinations. Two of these are positive and two of them are negative. Start and *good* means the Main Character is moving toward something good and that feels positive. Stop and *bad* means the Main Character is moving away from something bad and that also feels positive. Start and *bad* means the Main Character is moving toward something bad and that feels negative. And Stop and *good* means the Main Character is moving away from something good and that feels negative as well.

Possibility • *[Element]* • *dyn.pr.* Probability<—>Possibility • a determination that something might be true • The Possibility element endows a character with an open-minded assessment of his environment and relationships. However, it gives less weight to the single most likely explanation, looking instead at the whole range of known alternatives. Since the most likely scenario does not always happen, the Possibility element aids in having "Plan B" ready. On the downside, this characteristic may "over think" things and lose track of what is most probable. • *syn.* plausibility, viability, conceivable eventualities, open assessment

Potential • *[Dynamic Term]* • One way to measure the relationship of items in a quad is to classify them as Potential, Resistance, Current, and Outcome (or Power). In this manner, we can see how dramatic components operate on each other over the course of the story. Potential simply means a latent tendency toward some attitude or action. Though a dramatic Potential may exist, it is not necessarily applied. Rather, until a Resistance interacts with a Potential, the Potential has nothing to act against and will remain latent. So in a quad, assigning one of the items as the Potential does not mean it will become active in the story. Instead, it might function to deter the Resistance item from a certain course rather than risk conflict with Potential. This is a useful tool for Authors since it allows for the subtle relationship of unused, inferred, threatened, or anticipated dramatic interactions that shape the fabric of a story in ways other than conflict.

Potentiality • *[Element]* • *dyn.pr.* Certainty<—>Potentiality • a determination that something has the capacity to become true • The element of Potentiality drives a character to take risks on long odds. Always looking at what is not specifically ruled out, he is even beyond the realm of possibility and spends his time focusing on the greatest possible potential. As long as there is no reason why something should not be a certain way, the character representing Potentiality acts as if it is. Of course this leads him to see benefits and dangers others might miss, but it also leads him to starve on "pie in the sky." This characteristic always looks at what might be, never stopping to take stock of what is. • *syn.* chance, precariousness, focusing on the uncertain, going with the improbable

Power (Outcome) • *[Dynamic Term]* • One way to measure the relationship of items in a quad is to classify him as Potential, Resistance, Current, and Power (or Outcome). In this manner, we can see how dramatic components operate on each other over the course of the story. Power simply means the effect of a process. When a dramatic Power exists it does not necessarily create change. Rather, until it is applied for the necessary period of time by Current, the Power will have not have the impact sufficient to affect change. So in a quad, assigning one of the items as the Power does not mean it will alter the course of the story. Instead, it might function to direct effort by providing a specific target. This is a useful tool for Authors since it allows for the subtle relationship of unused, inferred, threatened, or anticipated dramatic interactions that shape the fabric of a story in ways other than conflict.

Preconception • *[Variation]* • *dyn.pr.* Preconception<—>Openness • unwillingness to reevaluate • Preconception is a preconception that prevents one from entertaining information contrary to a held conclusion. When one shuts his mind to additional data, there is no way to realize the conclusion might be in error. Contradictory observation no longer becomes part of experience so experience ceases to grow. Obviously, this can lead to all kinds of actions and attitudes that work to the detriment of oneself and others. On the other hand, Preconception can steel one against temporary exceptions that tempt one to veer from the true path. Question • Is it bad to have

Preconceptions against evil? • *syn.* prejudice, closed mindedness, narrow mindedness, intolerancy, stubbornness, unwillingness to reevaluate

Preconditions (Overall Story) • *[Type]* • unessential restrictions imposed on the effort to reach the goal • When meeting the requirement is made contingent on some non-essential restriction, the extra baggage is referred to as Preconditions. Depending on the nature of the Preconditions and the nature of a character, it may turn out that although the prerequisites will achieve the goal, the goal itself is improper and only the Preconditions can actually solve the problem. Misplaced emphasis is a common thematic exploration.

Preconditions • *[Variation]* • *dyn.pr.* Prerequisites<—>Preconditions • limitations tacked on to an effort • When access to resources necessary to meeting prerequisites is made contingent on some non-essential accomplishment or limitation, the extra baggage is referred to as Preconditions. Depending on the nature of the Preconditions and the nature of a character, it may turn out that although the prerequisites will achieve the goal, the goal itself is improper and only the Preconditions can actually solve the problem. Misplaced emphasis is a common thematic exploration. • *syn.* provision, prescribed specification, imposed stipulation, limiting parameters, imposed limitations

Preconscious • *[Type]* • immediate responses • *see Impuslive Responses*

Prediction • *[Variation]* • *dyn.pr.* Interdiction<—>Prediction • a determination of a future state of affairs • Prediction explores the effort to learn the course of one's destiny. Destiny is the path to a particular fate or through a series of fates. Fates are experiences or conditions one must encounter along the way as one's destiny directs one's course. The nature of destiny is such that no matter how much a character is aware of the nature and location of an undesirable fate, nothing he can do is enough to pull him off the path. However, if one could know the future course, one could prepare for each eventuality to minimize or maximize its effect. • *syn.* foresight, foreseeing, anticipation, envisioning one's future, prophecy, forecast, foretell, prognosticate

Prerequisites (Overall Story) • *[Type]* • the essential parameters that must be met to complete the requirement • Prerequisites are the essential or necessary steps or accomplishments that must be achieved in order for something to occur. If a goal has a single requirement, there may be many prerequisites to achieving that requirement.

Prerequisites • *[Variation]* • *dyn.pr.* Preconditions<—>Prerequisites • preliminary steps that must be met • Prerequisites are the essential or necessary steps or accomplishments that must be achieved in order for something to occur. If a goal has a single requirement, there may be many prerequisites to meeting that requirement. • *syn.* essential steps, necessary requisites, compulsory stipulation

Present (The Present) • *[Type]* • *dyn.pr.* Past<—>Present • the current situation and circumstances • "Present" does not refer to the way things are going, but to the way things are. It is a here and now judgment of the arrangement of a situation and the circumstances surrounding it. A story that focuses on the Present is not concerned with how events led to the current situation nor where the current situation will lead, but defines the scenario that exists at the moment . • *syn.* how things stand, the here and now, current situation, as of this moment

Proaction • *[Element]* • *dyn.pr.* Reaction<—>Proaction • taking initiative action to achieve one's goals • The Proactive characteristic will urge a character to begin problem solving on his own. This character will be a self-starter who is up and at it the moment he realizes a potential problem exists. Sometimes, however, a potential problem may not actually materialize and would have disappeared in short order by itself. Proaction may actually cause the problem to occur by irritating the situation. Worse yet, the character representing Proaction may act before the true nature of the problem is seen, leading him to cause damage to innocent or non-responsible parties, sometimes actually aiding the real source of the problem. • *syn.* to initiate action, execute, undertake, commit, implement

Probability • *[Element]* • *dyn.pr.* Possibility<—>Probability • a determination of likelihood • The character having the Probability characteristic puts its beliefs and efforts behind what is most likely. It is not as bound to safety as a character containing the Certainty characteristic, yet will still only take "calculated" risks. It is always playing the odds and changes direction in midstride if the odds change. This allows it to steer clear of many dangers but also tends to make it fickle. • *syn.* likelihood, prospective, predictable, promising

Problem (Overall Story) • *[Element]* • the underlying cause of the story's difficulties • Of all the Elements, there is a single one that describes the essence of the story's problem. The inclusion of this element in an Overall Story Character identifies him as the Main or Impact Character. This is because it makes that character the only one who can solve both the Overall Story and Subjective problems in a single stroke by addressing the problem (changing).

Problem-Solving Style (Mental Sex) • *[Character Dynamic]* • a determination of the Main Character's mental operating system • *see Mental Sex*

Process • *[Element]* • *dyn.pr.* Result<—>Process • the mechanism through which a cause leads to an effect • A Process is a series of interactions that create results. The character representing Process will concentrate on keeping the engine running smoothly. Unfortunately, he often forgets to look where the car is actually going. Sometimes the experiences along the way are the important part, other times it is arriving at the destination. • *syn.* chain of interactions, manner of procedure, cause/effect relation, progression, ongoing pull or tendency

Production • *[Element]* • *dyn.pr.* Reduction<—>Production • a process of thought that determines potential • Production is a process of thought that determines potential. Almost like deduction in reverse, rather than arriving at a present truth by limiting out what cannot be, Production arrives at a future truth by limiting out what can not happen. Anything that remains has potential. The problem for the character representing the Production characteristic is that Potentiality is often mistaken for Certainty if he fails to realize that any overlooked or unknown information can completely alter the course of the future. • *syn.* determining potential, noticing possibilities, ruling out future impossibilities, discovering of potential

Progress *[How Things Are Going]* • *[Type]* • *dyn.pr.* Future<—>Progress • the way things are going • See *How Things Are Going*

Projection • *[Element]* • *dyn.pr.* Speculation<—>Projection • an extension of probability into the future • Projection is a means of anticipating events and situations by extending the line of how things have been happening into the future. A character that represents Projection has a good grasp of what he might look for in things to come. However, this character will give great weight to past experience so abrupt changes in direction might be ignored until it is too late. • *syn.* anticipation, how things will be, most likely, probable

Protagonist • *[Archetype]* • An archetype who represents the motivations of Pursuit and Consider • An Overall Story Character charged with the responsibility of pursuing a solution to the story's objective problem. An objective problem does not mean it can't be personal. Rather, it means that all the dramatically functioning characters in the story are concerned about the outcome. The true Archetypal Protagonist pursues the solution against the Antagonist. In other stories a close cousin of the Protagonist shares all the same elements except he tries to avoid the Antagonist's plan. For the Pursuing Protagonist the goal is to cause something. For the Avoiding "Protagonist" the goal is to prevent something.

Protection • *[Element]* • *dyn.pr.* Inaction<—>Protection • an effort to prevent one's concerns from being vulnerable to interference • Protection is the act of building one's defenses against actual and potential threats. Certainly, preparing for problems brings a character advantages should the problems occur. However, the very act of building defenses can be interpreted as a threat to others who rely on Proaction and thereby precipitate the very aggression the character had tried to protect against. Also, a character representing Protection may stifle another's need for risk-taking or become so wrapped up in preparations that there are no resources left to use for advancement. • *syn.* defense, safeguard, preservation, precaution

Proven • *[Element]* • *dyn.pr.* Unproven<—>Proven • a rating of knowledge based on corroboration • Proven refers to an understanding that has been shown to be correct enough times to enough people to hold it as fact. The character representing Proven will judge truth only by what has been sufficiently verified. This makes it wary of unsubstantiated rumors, evidence, or conclusions. In the negative column, determining something is Proven requires drawing an arbitrary line that says, "Enough it enough, it's true!" The moment one assumes that the understanding is Proven, one ceases to look for exceptions. When a connection is made between two events or people based on a series of "Proven" facts, all it takes is one exception to ruin the argument. • *syn.* verified, confirmed, corroborated, established, demonstrated, shown

Psychology • *[Class]* • a manner of thinking • *see Manipulation*

Purpose • The intentions which any character has in a story • Purpose and Motivation are often confused. Whereas Motivation is the *reason* or *emotion* the character must fulfill or satisfy, Purpose is the specific way he intends to do so. Sometimes a character will attempt to satiate his Motivation by achieving several Purposes, each of which does part of the job. Other times, a single Purpose can assuage multiple Motivations. Many interesting stories are told about characters who struggle to achieve a Purpose that really will not meet their Motivation or about characters who achieve a Purpose for the wrong Motivation. But other, less common arrangements sometimes present more Deliberation oriented stories where the character achieves a Purpose near the beginning and then must search to find a Motivation that gives it value, or a character who has a strong Motivation but must search for the Purpose that truly accommodates it.

Pursuit • *[Element]* • dyn.pr. Avoidance<—>Pursuit • a directed effort to resolve a problem • The character representing Pursuit is a real self-starter. The Pursuit characteristic leads a character to determine what he needs to achieve and then make a bee-line for it. This may seem admirable and it can be. Unless of course he is trying to pursue something bad for himself and/or for others. In fact, it may be that the object of the Pursuit doesn't want to be pursued. "If you love something let it go... If it loves you, it will come back. If it doesn't come back, hunt it down and kill it." • *syn.* seek, go after, attempt to achieve, look for, directed effort

Quad • *[Structural Term]* • For every dramatic unit, three others can be found that possess a similar quality.

APPROACH	SELF INTEREST
MORALITY	ATTITUDE

A relationship exists in this group of four units that allows them to act as potentiometer controlling dramatic direction and flow. These groups can be represented as a square divided into four quadrants — hence the name QUAD. In each quad of four dramatic units, special relationships and functions exist between diagonal, horizontal, and vertical pairs.

Range • *[Variation]* • The thematic meaning of the Throughline being explored • *see Issue*

Rationalization • *[Variation]* • dyn.pr. Obligation<—>Rationalization • a logical alternative used to mask the real reason • Rationalization is the attempt to have your cake and eat it too. When a character expects that catering to his desires will bring about some cost or punishment, he tries to do what he'd like in a way he thinks will avoid retribution. One way is to come up with an excuse. Rationalization involves fabricating an artificial reason for one's attitude or actions that will excuse them. The reason must make sense as being a possible actual cause of the character's activities. In fact, it might very well have been the reason, except that it wasn't, which is what makes it a Rationalization. • *syn.* fabricated excuse, ulterior explanation, false justification, artificial reason

Reach • *[Overview Appreciation]* • the manner in which the audience identifies with the Main Character • The Reach of a story describes the relationship between the audience and the Main Character. An audience might Empathize with a Main Character in which case the audience identifies with the Main Character and sees the story through his eyes. Alternatively, an audience might Sympathize with the Main Character in which case it stands next to the Main Character as if it were a close acquaintance. The story dynamics that determine Empathy or Sympathy are different for men than for women. Women tend to identify and Empathize with a Main Character of either sex who is limited by a Optionlock. Men tend to only Empathize with male Main Characters. Women tend to Sympathize with a Main Character of either sex who is limited by a timelock. Men tend only to Sympathize with female Main Characters.

As a result of these dynamics, sometimes both women and men will Empathize, sometimes women only, sometimes men only, sometimes neither (both will Sympathize). It should be noted that these are tendencies only. Training, experience, and personal choice in any individual audience member can slip the balance wholly to the other side. Nevertheless, at the subconscious level these tendencies will hold true.

Reaction • *[Element]* • *dyn.pr.* Proaction<—>Reaction • actions made in response • The Reaction characteristic leads a character to strike back at the source of a problem. Reaction is less precipitous than Proaction requiring the problem to materialize before it acts. It does not take preemptive first strikes nor does it turn the other cheek. As a result, it often waits too long to tackle a problem that could easily have been prevented, then gets in a brawl that actually becomes a problem. Many authors try to pit one Proactive character against another. This actually diminishes the drama of the conflict as both characters are taking the same approach. By making one character Proactive and another Reactive, a much more real and powerful interaction is created. • *syn.* response, reply, acting from stimulus, goaded to action

Reappraisal • *[Variation]* • *dyn.pr.* Appraisal<—>Reappraisal • a reconsideration of a conclusion • When one has made an initial appraisal as to where preliminary evidence seems to be leading, there comes a time when one must make a Reappraisal of the evidence to see if its direction has changed. This tends to keep one on the right track. But characters, like everyday people, are influenced by what has occurred most recently — "What have you done for me lately?" As a result, during Reappraisal a character might discount the body of evidence in favor of that which is most fresh in his mind. • *syn.* reassess, rechecking, checking up, reexamining a conclusion, reevaluating a conclusion

Reason • *[Archetype]* • An Archetype who represents the motivations of Logic and Control • The Reason Archetypal Character evaluates and acts solely on the basis of calm logic, never becoming enraged, passionate or emotionally involved in a decision. Although common in simple stories, the Reason character is hard to empathize with. As a result, it is one of the characters most often altered slightly from its archetypal arrangement

to provide more potential for empathy from the audience. A frequent choice is to swap the trait of calm with the Emotional character's trait of frenzy. The result is that both characters become more interesting, the Reason character being both logical and frenetic, the Emotional character being highly passionate yet in control

Reconsider • *[Element]* • *dyn.pr.* Consider<—>Reconsider • questioning a conclusion based on additional information • The Reconsideration characteristic represents the drive to reexamine one's conclusions to see if they are still valid. This leads to a pragmatic approach to one's own beliefs but also undermines resolve with every new obstacle that crosses one's path. • *syn.* re-examining conclusions, rethinking, to mull over again, further deliberation, additional scrutiny

Reduction • *[Element]* • *dyn.pr.* Production<—>Reduction • a process of thought that determines probability • Reduction is a process of thought that compares the likelihood of several incomplete lines of deduction. Sometimes there is not enough information to fully deduce the ultimate truth in a matter. However, there is enough information to narrow the field of possibilities. When all the possibilities are considered, each can be rated on its individual merits as to how much each has. The potentialities are compared, arriving at the most likely conclusion. This allows the Reduction characteristic to act with a greater degree of confidence than if no "favorite" theory or explanation had emerged. Of course, dealing with incomplete data is a horse race where even the most unlikely explanation may surge ahead when the last piece is in place and prove to be the actual fact of the matter. It is when the Reduction characteristic gives probability the weight of certainty or fails to reevaluate that problems can arise. • *syn.* determining probability, comparisons of potentiality, measurement of likelihood, judging probabilities

Reevaluation • *[Element]* • *dyn.pr.* Evaluation<—>Reevaluation • a reappraisal of a situation or circumstances • Reevaluation is the act of reconsidering one's first impressions. This may be in regard to a person, situation, goal, or even oneself. Reevaluation is a helpful characteristic in dispelling incorrect initial assessments of the meaning behind things, but is a real drawback when a person or situation conspires to lure one's understanding away from an accurate

Evaluation. Perhaps a series of coincidences or a concerted effort can present information that conflicts with an earlier Evaluation that was actually quite on the mark. A character containing the Reevaluation characteristic can be swayed by new misleading information and form new, mistaken understandings. • *syn.* reappraisal, further assessment, subsequent analysis, scrutiny of first impressions

Repulsion • *[Variation]* • *dyn.pr.* Attraction<—>Repulsion • pushing or being pushed away from • A character's path to his goal is blocked by many curtains. The future beyond each cannot be seen until he has passed through to the other side. Sometimes the curtain itself is attractive, encouraging one to continue. Other times it is negative, indicating danger or loss, or that something unsavory lies behind. This is the nature of Repulsion. The warning is, "I'd go back if I were you" or "Don't spit into the wind." But does the curtain truly represent something distasteful that waits beyond or is it simply a false front, a mask to scare off the less tenacious? • *syn.* unattractive, repellent, foreboding, unsavory, pushing away, forcing back

Requirements (Overall Story) • *[Type]* • the necessary precursor to achieving the goal • Achieving a goal is not a one-step activity. Rather, all the cogs and wheels of a situation must be adjusted and realigned first to enable the goal. That can entail taking a certain number of steps in sequence and/or involve "tuning" the orchestra of the dramatics until they support the harmony of the goal. Both the sequential and holistic approach to these prerequisites and preconditions are described by the nature of the overall requirement to achieving the goal. In other words, the requirement describes the condition requisite to the goal and is made up of prerequisites and preconditions.

Resistance • *[Dynamic Term]* • One way to measure the relationship of items in a quad is to classify them as Potential, Resistance, Current, and Outcome (or Power). In this manner, we can see how dramatic components operate on each other over the course of the story. Resistance simply means a tendency toward inertia. When a dramatic Resistance exists it does not necessarily come into play. Rather, until a Potential interacts with a Resistance, the Resistance will have no impact at all. So in a quad, assigning one of the items as the Resistance does not mean it will alter the course of the story. Instead, it

might function to deter the Potential item from a certain course rather than risk conflict with Resistance. This is a useful tool for Authors since it allows for the subtle relationship of unused, inferred, threatened, or anticipated dramatic interactions that shape the fabric of a story in ways other than conflict.

Resolve • *[Character Dynamic]* • the degree to which the Main Character feels compelled to remain on the quest • There are two major ways in which an author can illustrate the best way to solve the problem explored in a story. One is to show the proper way of going about solving the problem, the other is to show the wrong way to solve the problem. To illustrate the proper way, your Main Character should hold on to his resolve and remain steadfast because he truly is on the right path. To illustrate the improper way of dealing with a problem, your Main Character must change for he is going about it the wrong way.

Response (Overall Story) • *[Element]* • the apparent remedy for the principal symptom of the story problem • Characters do the best they can to deal with the Overall Story Problem, but because the Overall Story Characters of a story are all looking at the problem from their subjective point of view, they can't get enough distance to actually see the problem right away. Instead they focus on the effects of the problem, which is called the Overall Story Symptom, and choose to follow what they feel will be a remedy, which is called the Overall Story Response.

Response Element (aka Perspective Element) • A Subjective Character can never be sure if what he believes to be the source of the problem really is the source of the problem. Regardless, based on his belief he will determine a potential solution or Response in which he hopes to find the solution. The dramatic unit that describes what a Subjective Character holds as the path to a solution is his Response Element.

Responsibility • *[Variation]* • *dyn.pr.* Commitment<—>Responsibility • the belief that one is best suited to accomplish a task • The instinct for survival is paramount under normal circumstances. Still, even animals throw themselves into danger to help a human friend. The drive that overcomes self-interest is Responsibility. Responsibility exists when one cares more for others than for oneself. The problem occurs when a character believes he knows what is best for someone and that someone doesn't agree. "It's for your own good," and "This is going to hurt me more than you" are two expressions that exemplify this attitude. Sometimes the character is right in believing he knows best, other times not. But either way, Responsibility can cause problems when it is imposed on another rather than offered to them. Responsibility can both be given or taken. • *syn.* assumed propriety, believed appropriateness, self designated aptness, accepted suitability

Result • *[Element]* • *dyn.pr.* Process<—>Result • the ramifications of a specific effect • Result is a holistic view of all the end products of a process. When a cause generates an effect, how does the effect upset the overall balance of a situation? In a balance of power, one must consider the results of arming an ally not just the immediate effect of strengthening its military. The character possessing the Result characteristic considers the ripples that might occur because of a given effect. The negative aspect is that it often over-thinks the situation until its considerations are ranging far beyond the scope of any real concerns. This can inhibit useful actions for insignificant reasons. Stop a new factory that will create jobs to protect a previously unknown species of gnat? It depends on the scope of the concern. • *syn.* ramifications of an effect, consequence, repercussion, impact, end product

Security • *[Variation]* • *dyn.pr.* Threat<—>Security • an evaluation of one's protections • Before one can expand to greater achievements, it is important to protect what one has already achieved. When a character is concerned with Security, he builds defenses against threats both known and anticipated. However, actual dangers may or may not fall within the ability of the protections to keep one secure. Subjectively, a character must determine when he feels secure, based on his experience. For example, a famous comedian once related that he always bought so many groceries he had to throw many away when they spoiled. This, he said, was because he had gone hungry so often as a child. When a character's experiences motivate him to over or under prepare for dangers, Security may actually become a danger itself. • *syn.* evaluation of safety, measure of safeguards, appraisal of one's protections, gauge of defenses

Self-Aware • *[Element]* • *dyn.pr.* Aware<—>Self-Aware • being conscious of one's own existence • When a character possesses Self-Awareness

he fully appreciates all his feelings, thoughts, abilities, and knowledge. Everything he experiences or observes is couched in terms of his own point of view. As the downside, he may not be able to understand that some things that happen don't pertain to him at all and in fact happen best without him. • *syn.* self-conscious, conscious of one's existence, self-perceiving, self-appreciating, self-cognizant

Self-Interest • *[Variation]* • *dyn.pr.* Morality<—>Self-Interest • doing or being based on what is best for oneself • In its pure form, Self-Interest is defined as the quality of ALWAYS choosing what is best for oneself with NO consideration as to the effect on others. This does not require ill intent toward others. A character who is Self-Interested simply focuses on the personal ramifications of decisions. In fact, in stories that show the evil nature of an oppressive society or regime, Self-Interest can be a very positive thing. • *syn.* self-serving, self-centered, narcissistic, selfishness, self-absorbed, egocentric

Sense Of Self • *[Variation]* • *dyn.pr.* State of Being<—>Sense of Self • one's perception of oneself • Simply put, Sense of Self is our own Self-Image. A character may not truly know who he is but he always knows who he thinks he is. This inward-looking view may be right on the mark or not even close. The difficulty a character has is that from inside himself it is impossible to be sure who he is. All he can do is take clues from the reaction of those around him. Interesting storytelling sometimes places a character among those who provide a warped feedback that creates a false Sense of Self in the character. This erroneous image may be far better, far worse, or simply different than his actual state of being. Other stories force a character to come to grips with the fact that he is wrong about himself, and the opinions of others are accurate. In a Main Character, the differential between Sense of Self and State of Being is part of what separates the Subjective from the Objective story lines. • *syn.* perception of self, self-image, self-identity, self-attribution

Senses • *[Variation]* • *dyn.pr.* Interpretation<—>Senses • sensory observations • Senses refers to the raw data supplied to the mind to interpret. Sometimes the data is accurate, other times it is faulty even before the mind gets hold of it. Senses describes the overall accuracy of an observation (such as seeing a crime or checking the results of a test). When taken with its Dynamic Pair of Interpretation, all manner of error or accuracy can be created. This provides the author with a powerful storytelling tool to create comedies and tragedies based in error and misunderstanding. • *syn.* perceptual data, raw sensations, sensory impressions, immediate impressions, perceptions

Set • *[Structural Term]* • A set is a grouping of 16 units. Although the set contains four separate quads and the units are all in specific positions according to their natures, the quads are not considered in the set. This is because the concept of the set is to define a group of 16 that all have similar natures. In other words, a set is an umbrella that equally covers each of 16 individual units in a group.

Sidekick • *[Archetype]* • An Archetype who represents the motivations of Faith and Support • The Sidekick is the absolutely faithful and supportive member of the Archetypal character set, the cheerleader for the Overall Story. Although frequently attached to the Protagonist, the Sidekick is identified by what his qualities are, not by who he is working for. In fact, the Sidekick might be attached to the Antagonist or not attached at all. His function is to represent the qualities of faith and support, not specifically to be in service of any other character. However, if the Sidekick is bound to the Protagonist, he can be effectively used to mirror the Author's feelings about the conduct of the Protagonist. Moving scenes can be created by a misguided Protagonist actually alienating the faithful, supportive Sidekick. Although the Sidekick would never turn against the Protagonist, he can turn away from him, leaving rather that being a party to something he finds immoral or disappointing.

Situation (Universe) • *[Class]* • a situation • The Situation Class is where any fixed state of affairs is explored, such as an institution, system, or situation that remains stable and unchanging. The point may be to show the system is good, bad, or neutral, but the focus must be on the system not on how the system is changing. • *syn.* a situation, a set of circumstances, state of affairs, predicament, environment, milieu

Situation • *[Variation]* • *dyn.pr.* Circumstances<—>Situation • the arrangement of one's environment • Situation describes the ins, outs, and practical considerations of the environment in which a character finds himself. Throughout

a story, the situation may evolve or may remain constant, depending on the essence of the message and the nature of the plot. Since it is limited to the practical, Situation can only be measured and/or interpreted though Reason. • *syn.* how things stand rationally, a reasoned evaluation of environment, arranged context, environmental state, surroundings, predicament

Skeptic — *[Archetype]* — An Archetypal Character possessing the qualities of disbelief and oppose — If a Sidekick is a cheer leader, a Skeptic is a heckler. The Skeptic still wants to see its team win, but doesn't think it can and is sure this is because the team members are going about it all wrong. Therefore, the Skeptic exhibits disbelief and opposes all efforts. Of course, when the team really is misguided, the Skeptic is in fact right on track. As with all Overall Story Archetypes, the Skeptic applies its outlook to hero and villain alike. In other words, the qualities of disbelief and oppose describe the nature of the Skeptic - not just its opinion about a particular issue. So, the Skeptic also doubts the bad guys are as powerful (or bad) as they are said to be, and opposes them as well. One purpose of stories is to illustrate how well different personality types fare in the effort to solve a particular kind of problem. Archetypal Characters represent the most broad categories into which personality types might be categorized. The Skeptic provides the opportunity to explore how well a doubter and naysayer does in resolving the story's troubles

Skill • *[Variation]* • *dyn.pr.* Experience<—>Skill • practiced ability • Skill is the innate potential to accomplish either that which is physical or mental. It does not require the practical experience necessary to tap that potential, just that the latent capacity exists. Skill might be seen as raw physical ability, talent, or intellectual or emotional aptitude which may or may not ever be developed. • *syn.* proficiency, aptitude, competence, adeptness, degree of expertise, practiced ability, honed ability

Solution • *[Element]* • the specific element needed to resolve the story's problem • The Solution Element is the "flip side" of the Problem Element. In a Change story, for instance, the focus may be on the Problem Element ("The Main Character should not be this way") or the focus may be on the Solution Element ("The Main Character should be this way"). So in a sense the Problem Element is not by itself the cause of the story's problem, but works with the Solution Element to create an imbalance between two traits that need to be balanced. The choice to present one as a negative trait defines it as the Problem Element and its positive partner becomes the Solution Element. In Steadfast stories, the Solution Element represents the nature of the things that would resolve the Overall Story Problem. Again it is the "flip side" of the problem, but it has exclusively to do with the Overall Story since the Main Character does not, in these cases, share the same problem as the Overall Story.

Speculation • *[Element]* • *dyn.pr.* Projection<—>Speculation • an extension of possibility into the future • Speculation is the effort to determine what could conceivably happen in the future even though it is not the most likely scenario. Speculation leads a character to expect the unlikely if it actually occurs. Difficulties arise when Speculation runs rampant and a character puts effort into preparing for things that are so unlikely to be unreasonably improbable. • *syn.* prognostication, surmising possibilities, conjecturing

Start • *[Character Dynamic]* • The audience wants something in the story, which is directly connected to the Main Character, to begin • Start means something different in a story where the Main Character has a Resolve of Change than in a story where the Main Character has a Resolve of Steadfast. If the Main Character must Change because he lacks an essential trait, then he must Start doing or being something they currently are not. If the Main Character is holding out Steadfastly until something begins in his environment, then he is waiting for something to Start. The term simply describes an aspect of the growth which happens in the Main Character.

State of Being • *[Variation]* • *dyn.pr.* Sense of Self<—>State-of-Being • one's true self • State of Being describes the actual nature of a character. The character himself is often not aware of the true nature of his being. In fact, there may be no one at all who fully understands all that he is. However, in the communication between Author and Audience, the essence of a character must be fully explained or the story's message will be obscured. • *syn.* essence, one's true self, true self, essential nature, core being

Steadfast Character {*Character Appreciation*}
• the Subjective Character who ultimately retains his original approach or attitude from the beginning of the story to the story • Every Subjective Character (both the Main and Impact Character) represents one special character element. This element is either the cause of the story's problem or its solution. The Subjective Character cannot be sure which he represents since it is too close to home. Near the climax of the story, each Subjective Character must demonstrate whether he has stuck with his approach in the belief that it is the solution or jumped to the opposite trait in the belief that he is the cause of the problem. There will only be one Steadfast Character in every story, however when a Subjective Character decides to stick with his story-long approach, he is said to Remain Steadfast.

Steadfast • *[Character Dynamic]* • The Main Character sticks with his essential nature while attempting to solve the problem • Every Main Character represents one special character element. This element is either the cause of the story's problem or its solution. The Main Character cannot be sure which he represents since it is too close to home. Near the climax of the story, the Main Character must demonstrate whether he has stuck with his original approach in the belief that it is the solution or jumped to the opposite trait in the belief he has been wrong. When a Main Character decides to stick with his story-long approach, he is said to remain Steadfast.

Stipulation • *[Type]* • the indicator of the depth of a throughline's difficulties • *see Benchmark*

Stop • *[Character Dynamic]* • The audience wants something in the story, which is directly connected to the Main Character, to desist • Stop means something different in a story where the Main Character has a Resolve of Change than in a story where the Main Character has a Resolve of Steadfast. If the Main Character Changes because he possesses a detrimental trait, then he Stops doing or being something he has been. If the Main Character is Steadfast in holding out for something outside himself to be brought to a halt, he is hoping that it will Stop. The term simply describes an aspect of the growth which happens in the Main Character.

Story Mind • The central concept from which Dramatica was derived is the notion of the Story Mind. Rather than seeing stories simply as some characters interacting, Dramatica sees the entire story as an analogy to a single human mind dealing with a particular problem. This mind, the Story Mind, contains all the characters, themes, and plot progressions of the story as incarnations of the psychological processes of problem solving. In this way, each story *explores* the inner workings of the mind so we (as audience) may take a more objective view of our decisions and indecisions and learn from the experience.

Story Driver • *[Plot Dynamic]* • the kind of activity focused on in the effort to solve the story's problem • Action or Decision describes how the problem of the Story will primarily be explored. The primary concern is the kind of storytelling you want to do. If you want action to be the focus of your storytelling, choose action. If you want deliberation to be the focus of your storytelling, choose decision. It's that simple.

Story Points • Commonly shared dramatic concepts • Story Points are items of dramatic meaning that are common to all stories. When a person attempts to deal with troubles, certain considerations and perspectives are commonly adopted; "goals," for example, "requirements," and "consequences." Stories, which represent analogies to this problem solving process, also incorporate these aspects. In Dramatica, these shared considerations are referred to as "story points."

Story versus Tale • A tale describes a problem and the attempt to solve it, ultimately leading to success or failure in the attempt. In contrast, a story makes the argument that out of all the approaches that might be tried, the Main Character's approach *uniquely* leads to success or failure. In a success scenario, the story acts as a message promoting the approach *exclusively*; in the failure scenario, the story acts as a message *exclusively* against that specific approach. Tales are useful in showing that a particular approach is or is not a good one. Stories are useful in promoting that a particular approach is *the only* good one or *the only* bad one. As a result of these differences, tales are frequently not as complex as stories and tend to be more straightforward with fewer subplots and thematic expansions. Both tales and stories are valid and useful structures, depending on the intent of the author to either illustrate how a problem was solved with a tale or to argue how to solve a specific *kind* of problem with a story.

Storyform • *[Dramatica Term]* • The structural and dynamic skeleton of a story • When a story is stripped of all its details and Storytelling, what is left are the story points and thematic explorations that make up a Storyform. When a story fully illustrates the Storyform it is working from it will make a complete argument without any "plot holes" because the argument of a story is its Storyform.

Storyforming versus Story telling • There are two parts to every communication between author and audience: the storyforming and the storytelling. Storyforming is the actual dramatic structure or blueprint that contains the essence of the entire argument to be made. Storytelling is the specific way the author chooses to illustrate that structure to the audience. For example, a story might call for a scene describing the struggle between morality and self-interest. One author might choose to show a man taking candy from a baby. Another might show a member of a lost patrol in the dessert hoarding the last water for himself. Both what is to be illustrated and how it is illustrated fulfill the story's mandate. Another way of appreciating the difference is to imagine five different artists each painting a picture of the same rose. One may look like a Picasso, one a Rembrandt, another like Van Gogh, yet each describes the same rose. Similarly, different authors will choose to tell the same Storyform in dramatically different ways.

Storyforming • the process of creating the dramatics of a unique story by arranging structure and dynamics • When an author thinks of the way he wants his story to unfold in terms of the point he wants it to make and how his characters will solve their problems, what that author is doing is Storyforming. Before Dramatica, the tendency was to actually blend the two processes of Storyforming and Storytelling together so that authors thought of what they wanted to say and how they wanted to say it more or less simultaneously. But these are really two distinct acts which can be done separately, especially with the help of Dramatica.

Strategy • *[Variation]* • *dyn.pr.* Analysis<—>Strategy • a plan to achieve one's purpose or a plan of response • The specific plan or series of interconnected plans that are intended to produce a desired result is called a Strategy. The sophistication of a strategy can range from complex to non-existent (if a character prefers to wing it). Sometimes a strategy is on the mark, other times it is completely inappropriate to its intended purpose. Either way, for the audience to appreciate its apt or inept construction, the plan must be spelled out in full. In storytelling, Strategy can define limits and draw out parameters for a story. This is a useful variation to use for connecting theme to plot. • *syn.* scheme, tactic, plan, ploy, decided approach

Subconscious • *[Type]* • basic drives and desires • *see Innermost Desires*

Subjective Story • the story as it relates to the conflict between the Main and Impact Characters • The passionate argument of a story is carried by the relationship between the story's Subjective Characters— namely, the Main and Impact Characters. The examination of their internal states and the articulation of the story's passionate argument makes up the Subjective Story Line. This is not the view from within the shoes of either the Main or Impact Characters, but is rather like an objective view of their subjective relationship. It is a view of their story together which always sees both of them.

Subjective Story Benchmark • *[Type]* • The standard by which growth is measured in the Subjective Story • The Subjective Story Benchmark is the gauge that tells people how far along the Subjective story has progressed. It can't say how much longer the story may go, but in regards to seeing how far away the concerns are, both the Main and Impact Characters, as well as the audience, will look to the stipulation to make any kind of judgment. This Type item describes the nature of the measuring stick which will be used in the Subjective story.

Subjective Story Concern • *[Type]* • The area of concern between the Main Character and the Impact Character • The nature of the things which the Main and Impact Characters want from their relationship; the Subjective Story Concern describes how the audience sees the concern of the Main and Impact character's relationship with each other being.

Subjective Story Catalyst • *[Variation]* • The item that acts as the catalyst to move the subjective story forward • The Subjective Story Catalyst is what creates breakthroughs and seems to accelerate the Subjective Story. In both the Objective and Subjective Stories there occur dramatic "log-jams" when things seem to be approaching a halt. This is when the Catalyst is

necessary, for its introduction will either solve the puzzle that's holding things up or else make the puzzle seem suddenly unimportant so the story can continue.

Subjective Story Inhibitor • *[Variation]* • The item that impedes the subjective story's progress • The Subjective Story Inhibitor is what prevents the Subjective Story from just rushing full speed to the solution. It is like a brake mechanism which can be applied as the author pleases. The introduction of this item will always slow the progress of the Subjective Story. It works as the antidote to the Subjective Story Catalyst.

Subjective Story Issue • *[Variation]* • the thematic focus between the Main Character and the Impact Character • The nature of the activities which make up the relationship between the Main and Impact Characters which is the Subjective Story is described by this item. The Subjective Story Issue describes the way the relationship between the Main and Impact Characters will work thematically in the Grand Argument of the story, so at the same time it generally describes the kinds of things that will pop up to illustrate this theme.

Subjective Story Problem • *[Element]* • the underlying cause of the difficulties between the Main Character and the Impact Character • This is the actual source of the inequity between the Subjective Characters which lies at the level of their motivations. Only by applying the Subjective Story Solution can the effects of this inequity finally be dealt with.

Subjective Story Response • *[Element]* • The direction of efforts in the subjective story; the *apparent* remedy for the symptom of the difficulties between the Main Character and The Impact Character • Subjective Characters do the best they can to deal with the Subjective Story Problem, but because the Main and Impact Characters are all looking at the problem from their subjective points of view, they can't get enough distance to actually see the problem right away. Instead they focus on the effects of the problem, which is called the Subjective Story Symptom, and choose to follow what they feel will be a remedy, which is called the Subjective Story Response.

Subjective Story Solution • *[Element]* • the specific element needed to resolve the difficulties between the Main Character and The Impact Character • This is the item

which will, if introduced, restore balance in
the Subjective Story and neutralize the effects
of the Problem by replacing it. It may not be
actually implemented, but if it were adopted in
the relationship between the Main and Impact
Characters, it would end the source of their
conflict and change their relationship.

Subjective Story Symptom • *[Element]* • the
principal symptom of the difficulties between
the Main Character and the Impact Character,
where attention is focused in the subjective story
• When there is a problem in the relationship
between the Main and Impact character, they
look at it from their subjective point of view and
cannot see its actual nature because it lies on
the level of their motivations. Instead they focus
their attention on what they believe to be the
source of their problems which is really an effect
of the problem. This area is called the Subjective
Story Focus.

Subjective Story Throughline • *[Throughline]* • the
general area in which the subjective story takes
place • *see Throughline.*

Subjective Story Type Order • *[Plot Structure]* • the
kind of activity employed to arrive at a solution
to the story's subjective problem, act by act •
As the Subjective Story progresses act by act,
it covers the Subjective Story Perspective (the
Perspective created by matching the Subjective
Story Throughline with one of the four Classes)
Type by Type around the quad of Types which it
contains. These four explorations make up the
four acts and describe the kinds of things that
will have to happen to arrive face-to-face with
the Subjective Story Problem.

Subplot • *[Storytelling]* • An amplification of a
branch or aspect of a storyform • Subplots
are often misunderstood to be secondary
subordinate stories running in parallel to the
main story. Such secondary stories are a valid
storytelling technique but they are not Subplots.
A Subplot in not a separate independent story
but an amplification of a branch or aspect of the
main story. Each Subplot is, indeed, a story in its
own right but it is connected to the main story
through one of the objective characters. This
objective character does double duty as the Main
Character (a subjective character) in the subplot.
As a result, it is inappropriate to hinge a subplot
around either the Main or Impact Characters
of the main story as the two story lines would
become blurred and create confusion as to
the message intended. To keep Subplots from

appearing to be the main story, it is important to
draw them with less detail. This does not mean
they should be incomplete or sketchy, rather
that the Subplot should be explored in less
depth. There can be as many Subplots as there
are objective characters. Many subplots will
become unwieldy, however, and can needlessly
complicate telling a story, blurring or diverting
the audience's understanding of the main story.
Similar to the Main Character of the main story,
the Main Characters of the subplots should be
limited to one story each. Not all "multiple plot"
stories consist of subplots attached to a main
plot. Frequently in serial programs such as soap
operas, certain forms of episodic television, and
some written serials such as comic strips, several
complete stories run in parallel, connected
only by their common setting or by using the
same ensemble of characters. In this form of
storytelling, characters do double duty, playing
multiple roles in a number of separate plots
which really do not directly affect each other.
The point of note is that an author should be
aware of the difference between subplot and
multiple plot constructions so the proper
dramatic connections can be made to create the
greatest impact.

Success • *[Plot Dynamic]* • the original goal is
achieved • Every overall story throughline in
a Grand Argument Story has at its beginning a
desired outcome to be sought after. Ultimately,
the characters will either Succeed in achieving
that outcome or fail to do so. However, Success
is not always a good thing. For example, it
may be that a character succeeds at something
hurtful or evil. Even a well intentioned character
might achieve something that he is unaware
will cause harm. Whatever its quality, worth
or ramifications, if the outcome desired at the
story's beginning is achieved, the story ends in
Success.

Support • *[Element]* • *dyn.pr.* Oppose <—> Support
• an indirect assistance given to another's
efforts • Support is not direct help. Direct help
is actively joining someone in an effort. Support
is aiding the effort without actually participating
in it. For example, a character possessing the
Help characteristic would join someone in
digging a ditch. The character representing
Support would provide a shovel and cheer them
on. Support is a fine thing to keep one's spirits
up, but is awfully frustrating when you just need
someone to lend you a hand. • *syn.* commend,
extol, endorse, back, compliment, laud

Suspicion • *[Variation]* • *dyn.pr.* Evidence<—
>Suspicion • questioning a belief based
on evidence • Suspicion is a preliminary
conclusion arrived at with insufficient evidence.
It is valuable in helping one know what kinds
of things to look for in gathering additional
evidence. But it can also be a detriment because
once a character suspects something, he is
less likely to examine all the evidence for a
completely alternative explanation. • *syn.* wary
approach, partially justified apprehensiveness,
informed doubt, doubt based on evidence,
sensible caution

Sympathy • *[Overview Appreciation]* • The
audience will care about the Main Character,
but it will not identify with him • Sympathy
describes the relationship of the audience to a
Main Character whom it cares about yet does
not identify with. To identify with the Main
Character, empathy is needed, but some story
forms do not allow for empathy from either
male or female audiences, and some exclude
both at once. But sympathy can still be a strong
emotion, and creating a storyform which will
elicit sympathy can be a way to emphasize the
intricacies in a story's storytelling and Overall
Story elements rather than its emotional side.

Symptom • *[Element]* • the principal symptom of
the story problem • When a Main Character
is at odds with his surroundings, a problem
exists between himself and his environment.
The actual nature of this gap between Main
Character and environment is described by
the Problem Element. The nature of what is
required to restore balance is described by
the Solution Element. This is the Overall Story
view of the problem. The Main Character,
however, is not privy to that view but must
work from the Subjective view instead. From
the Subjective view, the problem does not
appear to be *between* the Main Character and
the Environment, but wholly in one or the
other. Sometimes a Main Character is a "Do-
er" type and will perceive and first try to solve
the problem in the environment. Other times
a Main Character is a "Be-er" who will first
try to solve the problem by adapting to the
environment. A "Do-er" focuses the problem in
the environment; a "Be-er" focuses the problem
in himself. The Symptom Element describes the
nature of how the problem appears to the Main
Character when he places it wholly in one area
or the other.

Temptation • *[Element]* • *dyn.pr.* Conscience<—
>Temptation • the urge to embrace immediate
benefits despite possible consequences •
Temptation is the draw to belief that the negative
consequences of an action are imaginary or can
be avoided. Often this is just a pipe dream, and
when one gives into Temptation one must pay
a price. However, just as often one can avoid
negative consequence and indulge one's desires.
It is our Faith and Disbelief in consequences
that defines the struggle between Conscience
and Temptation. ("Psssst... We've got this new
Dramatica program that will solve all your
story problems but it's going to cost you some
bucks...") • *syn.* indulge, embracing immediate
benefits, intemperance, immoderation

Tendency • *[Overview Appreciation]* • the degree
to which the Main Character feels compelled to
accept the quest • Not all Main Characters are
well suited to solve the problem in their story.
They may possess the crucial element essential
to the solution yet not possess experience in
using the tools needed to bring it into play. Like
most of us, Main Characters have a preference
for how to go about solving problems. Some
prefer to immediately take action. We call these
characters Do-ers. Others prefer to deliberate
first to determine if the problem might go away
by itself or perhaps they can adapt to it. We call
these characters Be-ers. When a Do-er finds
himself in a story driven by Action he is quite at
home. Similarly, when a Be-er finds himself in a
Decision driven story, he is quite content. Both
of these combination lead to Main Characters
who are more than Willing to accept the quest
for a solution to the story's problem. They are
comfortable with the tools they will be required
to use. But if a Do-er is placed in a Decision
story or a Be-er is drawn into an Action story,
the Main Character will be very Unwilling to
participate in the quest at all for the tools he
must use are not in his area of experience.
Willing Main Characters force the plot forward.
Unwilling Main Characters are dragged along by
circumstances beyond their control.

Test • *[Element]* • *dyn.pr.* Trust<—>Test • a trial
to determine something's validity • To test is
to try out a supposition to determine if it is
correct. "Run it up the flagpole and see if people
salute it" is the concept here. Any explanation
that makes sense has the potential to be correct
or incorrect once it is actually tried in "the real
world." The Test characteristic will always want

to try things out before using it. This can weed out faulty items before they break down when one relies on them. However, it can also waste time when it is of the essence or waste one of the three wishes just to see if it works. • *syn.* trial of validity, examination, audit, inspection, scrutinization

Theme • [Dramatica term] • The author's statement about the relative worth of different value standards as they are compared in all contexts essential to the story. • Theme is developed by creating varying perspectives within a story on an issue which is central to the story. Presenting these perspectives in such a way that the most appropriate one, according to the author, moves to the forefront conveys theme to an audience. Theme occurs in both progressive and static elements of a story's structure and is a consideration in all four stages of communication (Storyforming, Storyencoding, Storyweaving, and Reception).

Theory • *[Element]* • *dyn.pr.* Hunch<—>Theory • an unbroken chain of relationships leading from a premise to a conclusion • A Theory is an unbroken web of relationships that describes a mechanism. To be a theory, the actual mechanism of each relationship in the Theory must be known as well. Unless it is understood how point A gets to point B, it might just be coincidental. For example, if two completely different and separate mechanisms are working in the same area, it may appear that one is causing a certain effect when it is really the other. Developing Theories gives the character representing Theory the ability to understand and predict how things work and fit together. The drawback is that he will not accept an obvious relationship unless all its steps can be discovered. As a result, many "common sense" approaches and understandings are not used, despite their proven value. • *syn.* structured explanation, concrete hypothesis, systematized descriptive knowledge, description of linear connections

Thought • *[Element]* • *dyn.pr.* Knowledge<—>Thought • the process of consideration • When a character represents Thought, he illustrates the process of consideration. Unlike the logic element that is only concerned with arriving at a conclusion via reason, Thought deliberates both logical and emotional aspects of a problem, not particularly to decide an issue so much as to examine it from all perspectives.

This has the advantage of illuminating every side of an issue, but has the potential disadvantage of Thought becoming an endless loop where consideration runs round in circles, chasing its mental tail and never coming to rest in a decision. • *syn.* the process of consideration, thinking, contemplation, mental attention, running over in your mind

Thought • *[Variation]* • *dyn.pr.* Knowledge<—>Thought • the process of consideration • Thought is not always directed. Often it wanders, experiential and without conscious purpose. Thought might be about a topic or simple random musings or creative daydreaming or inspiration. At its most essential level, Thought is simply the mental force of change that rearranges the inertia of knowledge. • *syn.* consideration, contemplation, ponderence, musing, reflection

Threat • *[Variation]* • *dyn.pr.* Security<—>Threat • an evaluation of one's vulnerabilities • Threats are indicators or warnings that danger lurks. Avoiding real danger can be enhanced by acting at the first sign of a Threat. However, reading the indicators is a subjective endeavor. One's biases and experiences may lead to inaccurate assessments of Threats. They may be real or imagined. When a character avoids actions or behaviors because he perceives a Threat that is truly imaginary, he might stunt his own progress toward his purpose based on an unreal fear. • *syn.* perceived danger, indication of peril, perceived vulnerability, warning, detected hazard

Throughline • *[Dramatica Term]* • The sequence of story points over a story that describe one of the four Perspectives in a story • The Throughlines are really the four structural perspectives which each move toward facing its own problem as the story reaches a climax. The Overall Story, Subjective Story, Main Character, and Impact Character Throughlines all have their own distinct story points which have to be illustrated to create a Grand Argument Story, but Storytelling choices can be made to accentuate a particular throughline and emphasize it more than the others and create stories that have an unusual feel to them.

Timelock versus Optionlock • The two kinds of limits that can force a story to its climax • Stories would go on forever unless they were limited in some way, forcing an end to action and/or decision. One way to bring a story to a conclusion is with a timelock which limits how long the characters have to solve the problem. The limit might be a bomb set to go off, the timing mechanism on a safe, or the poison that takes effect in 24 hours- anything that has a specific deadline and needs to be prevented or achieved. The other way to force a story to end is with a optionlock which limits how many things the characters can try to solve the problem — trapped aboard a spaceship with a vicious creature with no one coming to the rescue, trying to escape from Alcatraz, struggling to save a relationship — anything that has a specific scope and needs to be resolved. So in short, in a timelock the characters run out of time, in a optionlock the run out of options. As a side note, timelocks and optionlocks can coexist but only one can be the real limit that forces the climax.

Timelock • *[Plot Dynamic]* • the story climax is forced by a time limit • If not for the story being forced to a climax, it might continue forever. When a story is brought to a conclusion because the characters run out of time, it is said to contain a Timelock. As an analogy, a story might be thought of as the effort to find the solution to the story's problem which is hidden in one of the rooms of a mansion. Each room contains a clue to the actual location of the solution. The Main Character is told he may search as many rooms as he likes in five minutes. At the end of five minutes he is given a choice. Based on the clues he has already found, he must decide if the solution is in one of the rooms he already searched or in one of the rooms he has not yet searched. Either choice may lead to success or failure, but because running out of time forced the choice it is a Timelock story. The choice represents the Timelock which brings the story to a close and forces such story points as Main Character Resolve (Change or Steadfast), Outcome (Success or Failure), and Judgment (Good or Bad).

Trust • *[Element]* • *dyn.pr.* Test<—>Trust • an acceptance of knowledge as proven without first testing its validity • To Trust is to accept without trial. Whether a concept, relationship, person, or mechanism, it will be accepted by the character possessing the Trust characteristic without supportive evidence. This helps him to get on with the job at hand in the most efficient manner, but opens him up to disastrous surprises when an assumption is proven

incorrect at a critical moment. • *syn.* untried acceptance, untested belief in, accept implicitly, assumed dependability, unquestioned reliance on

Truth • *[Variation]* • *dyn.pr.* Falsehood<—>Truth • that which has been proven correct • Truth is more than facts and accuracy. Truth is meaning. Whenever someone is quoted out of context, what is reported may be factual and may be accurate but it is not Truthful. Meaning depends on intent and purpose. That is the beauty of the legal system — that even if someone is caught red-handed, the jury can acquit because it feels there were mitigating circumstances. The problem with Truth is that it is an interpretation and therefore open to debate. One person's Truth is another's Falsehood. • *syn.* honesty, correct information, correct notion, verity

Type • *[Structural Term]* • The 16 terms which are grouped directly beneath the Classes which are the next most general areas in which problem elements can lie • There are 16 Types in the Dramatica structure, four to each Class. The Classes each represent a different point of view and the Types in that Class represent a more refined exploration of that point of view. In a sense, Types describe the basic categories of what can be seen from a given point of view. Just as Throughline level story points create genre-like brush strokes in the story structure, Type level story points determine the nature of the plot.

Unending • *[Element]* • *dyn.pr.* Ending<—>Unending • a continuance without cessation • The Unending characteristic sees nothing as ever coming to completion. What others may see as an end, this characteristic sees as a change of direction. For example, obtaining a diploma is seen not as an end of college but as another step in one's career (which is Unending). This has an advantage of "never saying 'die'," which helps the motivation stay alive to keep trying. On the other hand, seeing a bad thing as unending can rob one of motivation. Also, when something is really over, the character representing Unending can't see it. This might be a former relationship or a current job that he takes for granted. • *syn.* continual, ongoing, perpetual, ceaseless, interminable, incessant, perennial

Uncontrolled • *[Element]* • *dyn.pr.* Control<—>Uncontrolled • a disorganized response • The character representing Uncontrolled spreads himself very thin by expending his energy and motivation in all directions at once. As a result, he is fully involved in his environment, which covers all the bases. Yet, because his attention is randomly distributed, there is not single direction to his thrust. Therefore, the Uncontrolled character frequently spends a lot of energy getting nowhere. • *syn.* unregulated, disorganized, unfocused, rampant, unguided, open, frenzy

Understanding • *[Type]* • *dyn.pr.* Learning<—>Understanding • appreciating the meaning of something • Understanding is different from knowledge. From knowledge one gets awareness, from Understanding one gets meaning. To obtain meaning requires not only knowing the substance of its nature but the context of its essence. In other words, one must not only define what something is but how it fits into the larger picture as well. To this end, Reason describes the function and Emotion defines the purpose. So Understanding is not just an intellectual pursuit but requires an empathy with the meaning as well. It is useful to note that many Eastern and ancient philosophies define Understanding as "becoming one with" that which is being considered. Until one joins his subject in unity, he cannot understand it. • *syn.* comprehending, grasping, appreciating, obtaining meaning, acquiring meaning

Unique Ability • *[Variation]* • The item that makes the Main Character uniquely able to resolve the Overall Story Problem; the item that makes the Impact Character uniquely able to thwart the Main Character's efforts • Just as a requirement defines the specific nature of things needed to achieve a particular goal, Unique Ability defines the specific quality needed to meet the requirement. Unique Ability is another way in which the Main Character is identified as the intersecting point between the Subjective and Objective stories as it is only he who ultimately has what it takes to meet the test of the requirement and thereby achieve the goal. The Unique Ability need not be anything extraordinary but must be the one crucial quality required that is shared by no one else. Frequently, the Unique Ability is in keeping with the Main Character's position or profession, however it can be much more interesting to assign an incongruous Unique Ability. In either approach, it is essential to illustrate the existence of the Unique Ability in the Main Character several times throughout the story,

even if it is not employed until the climax. In this way, it becomes integrated into the nature of the Main Character and does not seem conveniently tacked on when it is ultimately needed. Also, the Unique Ability can be extremely mundane. The key is that the ability does not have to be unique by nature, but just possessed uniquely in that specific story by the Main Character. Clever storytelling may arrange the climax of the story so that some completely ordinary and insignificant Unique ability makes the difference in the outcome of a cosmic struggle.

Unit • *[Structural Term]* • Dramatica breaks down the components of story into the smallest possible building blocks that have meaning for an author. These essential building blocks are called Units.

Universe • *[Class]* • a situation • *see Situation*

Unproven • *[Element]* • *dyn.pr.* Proven<—>Unproven • a rating of knowledge that has not been tested • Unproven describes an understanding suspected to be true but not substantiated enough to call it fact. The character representing Unproven will not accept anything as fact just because the theory has worked so far. No matter how many times or how many ways evidence builds to support the contention, Unproven will not be satisfied until the conclusion is absolutely drawn in hard data not just road tests. This keeps the character representing Unproven from jumping to conclusions, but makes him less able to accept the obvious conclusion unless it is directly observed in a way that is not open to alternative interpretation. • *syn.* unverified, unconfirmed, unestablished, undemonstrated, untried

Unwilling • *[Overview Appreciation]* • The Main Character unwillingly participates in the effort to find a solution to the story problem • Unwilling describes a Main Character who would prefer not to become involved in neither the problem nor the search for a solution. As a result, some sort of leverage must be applied to "force" him to join the quest. Once the Main Character is enticed or coerced into beginning the journey toward a solution, he requires outside encouragement or compulsion to keep up the effort.

Value • *[Variation]* • *dyn.pr.* Worth<—>Value • the objective usefulness or desirability of something in general • Value is a good indicator by which to predict its import to others. However, no one really thinks completely objectively so there is always a degree of personal preference included in a determination of Value. Difficulties arise when a character neglects the personal worth someone else may or may not find in something of specific value. For example, a Boss may find it of no direct Value, but placing a candy bar on each employees desk for them to find in the morning can have a lot of worth to the employee. Indirectly, then, Value is returned to the Boss in the form of a better day's work. But seeing the indirect Value is difficult from the subjective view. Learning to see items and actions not just for their intrinsic Value, but for their conditional Value is a strong thematic message. • *syn.* utility, objective appraisal, general usefulness

Variation • *[Structural Term]* • The 64 items that represent the thematics under which problem elements can occur • The variations describe the thematic message and the development of that message in the story. Variations are measuring sticks by which the author wishes his message to be evaluated. It is the discrepancy between opposing ways of evaluating the meaning of the story that creates the thematic statement as to which is the best way or that one-way is no better or worse than another. There are 64 Variations in the Dramatica structure, 16 to each Class.

Willing • *[Overview Appreciation]* • The Main Character willingly participates in the effort to find a solution to the story problem • Willing describes a Main Character who is self-motivated to find a solution to the story's problem. Even if the going is tough, he requires no outside encouragement or compulsion to keep up the effort.

Wisdom • *[Variation]* • *dyn.pr.* Enlightenment<—>Wisdom • understanding how to apply Knowledge • Wisdom is the meaning of what is known. A Character may be aware of facts but unless he sees the pattern that organizes those facts, the knowledge alone may be useless. Wisdom, therefore, does not describe just being aware of something but understanding how many bits of knowledge fit together .• *syn.* mental mastery, integrated understanding, seasoned understanding, comprehension, astute cogency

Work • *[Plot Dynamic]* • the kind of activity focused on in the effort to solve the story's problem • *see Driver*

Work • *[Variation]* • *dyn.pr.* Attempt<—>Work • applying oneself to something known to be within one's ability • When a task lies within one's known abilities, effort applied to the task is Work. There are no surprises; no shortcomings. But has one accurately judged both one's abilities and the demands of the task? If not, perhaps the task is not achievable or of a size that one must increase one's abilities before undertaking it. • *syn.* appropriate undertaking, suitable task, manageable labor, a performable activity

Worry • *[Variation]* • *dyn.pr.* Confidence<—>Worry • concern for the future • Like confidence, Worry looks toward the future but is based on a projection of negative experience. When in the past seemingly innocuous situations have developed into disasters, one learns to Worry at the slightest evidence of instability. Worry has the positive quality of motivating one to prepare for the worst. If the worst happens, the character representing Worry is truly prepared. But how often does the worst actually happen? The downside is that resources one might use to make advances are wasted just trying to protect the status quo. And those who worry tend to avoid unknown situations that might hold substantial rewards. • *syn.* anxiety, concern, apprehension, misgivings

Worth • *[Variation]* • *dyn.pr.* Value<—>Worth • a rating of usefulness or desirability to oneself • Worth describes the subjective value of an item or action to an individual. Of course, this varies greatly from individual to individual. This is the nature of garage sales • one woman's trash is another woman's treasure. Making choices on the basis of Worth is an efficient way to get the most with one's resources. But there may be all kinds of potential locked in something a character considers worthless because objectively it has great Value. For example, Native Americans used gold simply as a decoration. To them it had little other Worth. Of course to Europeans it had significant Value. A character who ignores potential value because of low Worth can live to regret the deals he makes in a story, both physically and emotionally. • *syn.* subjective value, individual appraisal, personal importance

Z Pattern • *[Dynamic Term]* • There is a relationship between the function of dramatic items and the order in which they interact. Changing the order can drastically affect how an audience interprets

the meaning of events and information. For
example, if a person makes a rude comment
and is slapped, an audience will react differently
than if a person is slapped then makes a rude
comment. One of the ways in which drama is
built is to control the order in which events
happen. To do this, there must be some standard
or measure that defines the "at rest" or "initial"
order of events. In Dramatica, the patterns of
a "Z" (either forward or backward, from top
to bottom or bottom to top) drawn through
the four items of a quad describes one of the
sequences in which dramatic units might be
brought into play.

Dramatica Synonyms

Ability • *[Element]* • innate capacity, capability, talent for, inherent proficiency

Ability • *[Variation]* • talent, knack, capability, capacity, faculty

Acceptance • *[Element]* • acquiescence, tolerance, allowance for, consent, submission

Accurate • *[Element]* • within tolerance, sufficient, adequate, acceptable, passable

Activity [Physics] • *[Class]* • an activity, an enterprise, an initiative, an endeavor, an operation

> **Actuality** • *[Element]* • the true state of things, objective reality, factuality, demonstrable existence, demonstrable reality

Analysis • *[Variation]* • evaluation, examination, breakdown of situation, close investigation, scrutinization

Appraisal • *[Variation]* • first impression, preliminary understanding, initial approach, initial assimilation

Approach • *[Variation]* • method, procedure, style, manner, manner of doing, one's own way

Attempt • *[Variation]* • try, uncertain undertaking, speculative endeavor, dubious effort, endeavor, unlikely venture

Attitude • *[Variation]* • demeanor, manner of approach, countenance, behavioral outlook, perspective on doing

Attraction • *[Variation]* • allure, enticement, charm, captivate, appeal, draw, lure

Avoid • *[Element]* • evade, dodge, elude, escape, steer clear of, prevent

Aware • *[Element]* • outward perceptiveness, external sensitivity, consciousness of the external, responsive

Becoming (Changing One's Nature) • *[Type]* • embodying, manifesting, personifying, incarnating, transforming

Being (Playing A Role) • *[Type]* • pretending, appearing, acting like, seeming as, fulfilling a role

Cause • *[Element]* • engender, induce, elicit, determinant, reason for, factor, effector, source, agent, antecedent

Certainty • *[Element]* • sureness, definiteness, having no doubts, total reliability, indisputability, irrefutability, unmistakability, certitude, conviction

Change • *[Element]* • altering, altering force, modify, reshape, adjust, adapt

Changing One's Nature (Becoming) • *[Type]* • embodying, manifesting, personifying, incarnating, transforming

Chaos • *[Element]* • randomness, anarchy, disorder, formlessness, noncohesion

Choice • *[Variation]* • decision, selection, determination, pick

Circumstances • *[Variation]* • how things stand emotionally, emotional evaluation of the environment, value of existing conditions, relationship to others

Closure • *[Variation]* • finishing, completion, resolution, recursive

Commitment • *[Variation]* • dedication, devotion, steadfastness, zeal

Conceiving An Idea • *[Type]* • originating, inventing, devising, engendering, hatching ideas

Conceptualizing (Developing A Plan) • *[Type]* • visualizing, imagining, envisioning, visualizing implementation

Conditioning • *[Variation]* • habituation, trained response, accustomed response, adaptive adjustments

Confidence • *[Variation]* • hopeful prospects, positive expectations, faithful anticipation, optimism

Conscience • *[Element]* • forgoing for fear of consequences, forgo, forbearance, temperance, abstinence, restraining oneself

Conscious (Contemplation) • *[Type]* • considerations, sensibilities, cognizant, ability to consider, sensible, informed contemplation, contemplation

Contemplation (Conscious) • *[Type]* • considerations, sensibilities, cognizant, ability to consider, sensible, informed contemplation, contemplation

Consider • *[Element]* • deliberate, contemplate, ponder, weigh in the mind, mull

Control • *[Element]* • regulate, organized management, steer, conduct, guide, manipulate, focused organization

Deduction • *[Element]* • drawing a conclusion, process of elimination, demonstrative reasoning, narrowing to a single point

Deficiency • *[Variation]* • inadequacy, insufficiency, deficit, unfulfilled need

Delay • *[Variation]* • put off, retard, postpone, defer, suspend, prolong, procrastinate

Denial • *[Variation]* • not accepting, refusal to end, unwillingness to let go, refusal to back down, stubbornness, uncompliant

Desire • *[Element]* • drive, motivational goal, unfulfillment, source of discontent, essence of motivation

Desire • *[Variation]* • want, favor, like, covet, prefer, wish, aspire

Destiny • *[Variation]* • inescapable path, predetermined trajectory, set direction of the future, inevitable path, unavoidable trajectory

Determination • *[Element]* • ascertaining causes, discovering causes, finding the reasons why, figuring out factors, discerning antecedents

Developing A Plan (Conceptualizing) • *[Type]* • visualizing, imagining, envisioning, visualizing implementation

Disbelief • *[Element]* • refusal to accept, distrust, find unconvincing, find false, unpersuadability

Doing • *[Type]* • performing, executing, effecting action, acting

Doubt • *[Variation]* • pessimism, uninformed misgivings, uncertainty, trepidation, distrust

Dream • *[Variation]* • aspire, desiring the unlikely, pulling for the doubtful, airy hope, glimmer, far fetched desire

Effect • *[Element]* • result, consequence, outcome, culmination, the ensuing

Ending • *[Element]* • conclusion, finish, completion, termination, close

Enlightenment • *[Variation]* • insight, illumination, intuitive discernment, transcendent comprehension

Equity • *[Element]* • balance, fairness, parity, equilibrium, level, even

Evaluation • *[Element]* • appraisal, analysis, assessment, survey, examination

Evidence • *[Variation]* • proof, indicator, supporting information, corroborating facts, grounds for belief, substantiation

Expectation • *[Element]* • anticipated results, eventual outcome, presumed prospects, probable denouement, likely consequences

Expediency • *[Variation]* • advisability, convenience, prudent efficiency

Experience • *[Variation]* • familiarization, level of practice, seasoning, accumulated feelings, accumulated dealings with

Fact • *[Variation]* • belief in the genuine, ultimately real beliefs, truly real beliefs, authentic notion, authentic idea, correct knowledge, correct beliefs

Faith • *[Element]* • acceptance without proof, steadfast belief, confidence in unproven, credence, unquestioned trust

Falsehood • *[Variation]* • erroneousness, untruth, erroneous notion, mistaken, astray, dishonest

Fantasy • *[Variation]* • false belief, faith in the imaginary, delusion, erroneous conviction

Fate • *[Variation]* • inevitable events, unpreventable incidents, eventual events, destined occurrence, destined events, unavoidable situations

Feeling • *[Element]* • empathy, emotional sensibility, affective outlook, sentiment, emotional assessment

Fixed Attitude (Mind) • *[Class]* • attitude, fixation, position on an issue, fixed point of view, disposition

Future • *[Type]* • what is to come, what will be, prospect, prospective

Help • *[Element]* • aid, assist, support, bolster, abet

Hinder • *[Element]* • retard, obstruct, impede, fetter, undermine, block, burden, encumber, thwart

Hope • *[Variation]* • desired expectation, optimistic anticipation, confident aspiration, promise, encouraging outlook

How Things Are Going • *[Type]* • flowing, advancing, proceeding, moving forward, developing step by step, graduated, staging, successive, procession, the way things are going

Hunch • *[Element]* • intuition, premonition, impression, suspicion

Impulsive Responses (Preconscious) • *[Type]* • unthinking responses, immediate responses, impulse, impulsive response, instinctive response, innate response, reflex

Inaction • *[Element]* • passive reaction, inactive response, achieve through not doing

Induction • *[Element]* • postulate, predicate, conjecture, infer, hypothesize, determine possibility

Inequity • *[Element]* • imbalance, unfair, disparity, unequal, uneven, disproportionate

Inertia • *[Element]* • tendency to continue, a change resistant pattern, continuation, following an established direction

Innermost Desires (Subconscious) • *[Type]* • libido, id, basic motivations, basic drives, anima

Instinct • *[Variation]* • involuntary drive, innate impulse, unconditioned response, automatic response, unconditioned motivation

Interdiction • *[Variation]* • altering the future, interfering with the predetermined, hindering the inevitable, escaping the predestined

Interpretation • *[Variation]* • construe, rendition, rendering meaning, elucidate, translating meaning

Investigation • *[Variation]* • inquiry, research, probe, sleuthing, delving, query

Knowledge • *[Element]* • learnedness, held truths, authoritative certainty, generally agreed on truths

Knowledge • *[Variation]* • held truth, maintained information, presumed facts, accepted ideas

Learning • *[Type]* • cultivating experience, acquiring information, collecting data, gathering knowledge

Logic • *[Element]* • linear reasoning, rationality, structural sensibility, syllogistics

Manipulation (Psychology) • *[Class]* • ways of thinking, thinking process, activity of the psyche, manipulation of others

Memory • *[Type]* • remembering, recollections, reminiscence, recalling, retention

Mind (Fixed Attitude) • *[Class]* • attitude, fixation, position on an issue, fixed point of view, disposition

Morality • *[Variation]* • selflessness, altruism, benevolence, generosity

Need • *[Variation]* • subjective necessity, urge, demand, imperative

Non-Acceptance • *[Element]* • run counter to, reject, decline, repudiate, resist, refusal to compromise

Non-Accurate • *[Element]* • not within tolerance, insufficiency, inadequacy, deviancy, deficient to the purpose

Obligation • *[Variation]* • agreement, pledge, contract, accepted compulsion, emotional contract

Obtaining • *[Type]* • controlling for oneself, possessing, having, keeping

Openness • *[Variation]* • broad mindedness, tolerance, willingness to reevaluate, receptiveness

Oppose • *[Element]* • object to, speak out against, argue against, protest, dispute, show disapproval of, detract from

Order • *[Element]* • structure, patterned arrangement, organization, patterned formation, formation, configuration, patterned sequence

Past • *[Type]* • history, what has happened, former times, retrospective

Perception • *[Element]* • appearance, how things seem to be, discernment, a particular reading of things, a point of view on reality, a way of seeing

Permission • *[Variation]* • constrained ability, limited capability, restricted capacity, hindered performance, allowed limitations, restrained utility

Playing A Role (Being) • *[Type]* • pretending, appearing, acting like, seeming as, fulfilling a role

Physics (Activity) • *[Class]* • an activity, an enterprise, an initiative, an endeavor, an operation

Possibility • *[Element]* • plausibility, viability, conceivable eventualities, open assessment

Potentiality • *[Element]* • chance, precariousness, focusing on the uncertain, going with the improbable

Preconception • *[Variation]* • prejudice, closed mindedness, narrow mindedness, intolerance, stubbornness, unwillingness to reevaluate

Preconditions • *[Variation]* • provision, prescribed specification, imposed stipulation, limiting parameters, imposed limitations

Preconscious (Impulsive Responses) • *[Type]* • unthinking responses, immediate responses, impulse, impulsive response, instinctive response, innate response, reflex

Prediction • *[Variation]* • foresight, foreseeing, anticipation, envisioning one's future, prophecy, forecast, foretell, prognosticate

Prerequisites • *[Variation]* • essential steps, necessary requisites, compulsory stipulation

Present • *[Type]* • how things stand, the here and now, current situation, as of this moment

Proaction • *[Element]* • to initiate action, execute, undertake, commit, implement

Probability • *[Element]* • likelihood, prospective, predictable, promising

Process • *[Element]* • chain of interactions, manner of procedure, cause/effect relation, progression, ongoing pull or tendency

Production • *[Element]* • determining potential, noticing possibilities, ruling out future impossibilities, discovering of potential

Progress • *[Type]* • flowing, advancing, proceeding, moving forward, developing step by step, graduated, staging, successive, procession, the way things are going

Projection • *[Element]* • anticipation, how things will be, most likely, probable

Protection • *[Element]* • defense, safeguard, preservation, precaution

Proven • *[Element]* • verified, confirmed, corroborated, established, demonstrated, shown

Psychology (Manipulation) • *[Class]* • ways of thinking, thinking process, activity of the psyche, manipulation of others

Pursuit • *[Element]* • seek, go after, attempt to achieve, look for, directed effort

Rationalization • *[Variation]* • fabricated excuse, ulterior explanation, false justification, artificial reason

Reaction • *[Element]* • response, reply, acting from stimulus, goaded to action

Reappraisal • *[Variation]* • reassess, rechecking, checking up, reexamining a conclusion, reevaluating a conclusion

Reconsider • *[Element]* • reexamining conclusions, rethinking, to mull over again, further deliberation, additional scrutiny

Reduction • *[Element]* • determining probability, comparisons of potentiality, measurement of likelihood, judging probabilities

Reevaluation • *[Element]* • reappraisal, further assessment, subsequent analysis, scrutiny of first impressions

Repulsion • *[Variation]* • unattractive, repellent, foreboding, unsavory, pushing away, forcing back

Responsibility • *[Variation]* • assumed propriety, believed appropriateness, self designated aptness, accepted suitability

Result • *[Element]* • ramifications of an effect, consequence, repercussion, impact, end product

Security • *[Variation]* • evaluation of safety, measure of safeguards, appraisal of one's protections, gauge of defenses

Self-Aware • *[Element]* • self-conscious, conscious of one's existence, self-perceiving, self-appreciating, self-cognizant

Self-Interest • *[Variation]* • self-serving, self-centered, narcissistic, selfishness, self-absorbed, egocentric

Sense of Self • *[Variation]* • perception of self, self image, self identity, self attribution

Senses • *[Variation]* • perceptual data, raw sensations, sensory impressions, immediate impressions, perceptions

Situation (Universe) • *[Class]* • a situation, a set of circumstances, state of affairs, predicament, environment, milieu

Situation • *[Variation]* • how things stand rationally, a reasoned evaluation of environment, arranged context, environmental state, surroundings, predicament

Skill • *[Variation]* • proficiency, aptitude, competence, adeptness, degree of expertise, practiced ability, honed ability

Speculation • *[Element]* • prognostication, surmising possibilities, conjecturing

State of Being • *[Variation]* • essence, one's true self, true self, essential nature, core being

Strategy • *[Variation]* • scheme, tactic, plan, ploy, decided approach

Subconscious (Innermost Desires) • *[Type]* • libido, id, basic motivations, basic drives, anima

Support • *[Element]* • commend, extol, endorse, back, compliment, laud

Suspicion • *[Variation]* • wary approach, partially justified apprehension, informed doubt, doubt based on evidence, sensible caution

Temptation • *[Element]* • indulge, embracing immediate benefits, intemperance, immoderation

Test • *[Element]* • trial of validity, examination, audit, inspection, scrutinization

Theory • *[Element]* • structured explanation, concrete hypothesis, systematized descriptive knowledge, description of linear connections

Thought • *[Element]* • the process of consideration, thinking, contemplation, mental attention, running over in your mind

Thought • *[Variation]* • consideration, contemplation, ponderence, musing, reflection

Threat • *[Variation]* • perceived danger, indication of peril, perceived vulnerability, warning, detected hazard

Trust • *[Element]* • untried acceptance, untested belief in, accept implicitly, assumed dependability, unquestioned reliance on

Truth • *[Variation]* • honesty, correct information, correct notion, verity

Unending • *[Element]* • continual, ongoing, perpetual, ceaseless, interminable, incessant, perennial

Uncontrolled • *[Element]* • unregulated, disorganized, unfocused, rampant, unguided, open, frenzy

Understanding • *[Type]* • comprehending, grasping, appreciating, obtaining meaning, acquiring meaning

Universe (Situation) • *[Class]* • a situation, a set of circumstances, state of affairs, predicament, environment, milieu

Unproven • *[Element]* • unverified, unconfirmed, unestablished, undemonstrated, untried

Value • *[Variation]* • utility, objective appraisal, general usefulness

Wisdom • *[Variation]* • mental mastery, integrated understanding, seasoned understanding, comprehension, astute cogency

Work • *[Variation]* • appropriate undertaking, suitable task, manageable labor, a performable activity

Worry • *[Variation]* • anxiety, concern, apprehension, misgivings

Worth • *[Variation]* • subjective value, individual appraisal, personal importance

Reference
PART 2

SEMANTIC ITEMS

Dramatica's Structural Semantic Items

The following is an alphabetical list of the semantic items that appear in the structural part of the Dramatic model. The items have been subdivided into four parts based on their structural nature: Classes, Types, Variations, and Elements.

Classes (Throughlines)

1. Activity (*Physics*)
2. Fixed Attitude (*Mind*)
3. Manipulation (*Psychology*)
4. Situation (*Universe*)

Types (Concerns)

1. Changing One's Nature (*Becoming*)
2. Playing A Role (*Being*)
3. Conceiving An Idea
4. Developing A Plan (*Conceptualizing*)
5. Contemplation (*Conscious*)
6. Doing
7. The Future
8. Learning
9. Memory
10. Obtaining
11. The Past
12. Impulsive Responses (*Preconscious*)
13. The Present
14. How Things Are Going (*Progress*)
15. The Innermost Desires (*Subconscious*)
16. Understanding

Variations (Issues)

1. Ability	33. Investigation
2. Analysis	34. Knowledge
3. Appraisal	35. Morality
4. Approach	36. Need
5. Attempt	37. Obligation
6. Attitude	38. Permission
7. Attract	39. Preconception
8. Choice	40. Preconditions
9. Circumstances	41. Prediction
10. Closure	42. Prerequisites
11. Commitment	43. Rationalization
12. Conditioning	44. Reappraisal
13. Confidence	45. Repel
14. Deficiency	46. Resolution
15. Delay	47. Responsibility
16. Denial	48. Security
17. Desire	49. Self-Interest
18. Destiny	50. Sense of Self
19. Doubt	51. Senses
20. Dream	52. Situation
21. Enlightenment	53. Skill
22. Evidence	54. State of Being
23. Expediency	55. Strategy
24. Experience	56. Suspicion
25. Fact	57. Thought
26. Falsehood	58. Threat
27. Fantasy	59. Truth
28. Fate	60. Value
29. Hope	61. Wisdom
30. Instinct	62. Work
31. Interdiction	63. Worry
32. Interpretation	64. Worth

Elements (Problems)

1. Ability	33. Logic
2. Acceptance	34. Non-acceptance
3. Accurate	35. Non-accurate
4. Actuality	36. Oppose
5. Avoid	37. Order
6. Aware	38. Perception
7. Cause	39. Possibility
8. Certainty	40. Potentiality
9. Change	41. Proaction
10. Chaos	42. Probability
11. Conscience	43. Process
12. Consideration	44. Production
13. Control	45. Projection
14. Deduction	46. Protection
15. Desire	47. Proven
16. Determination	48. Pursuit
17. Disbelief	49. Reevaluation
18. Effect	50. Reaction
19. Ending	51. Reconsideration
20. Equity	52. Reduction
21. Evaluation	53. Result
22. Expectation	54. Self-Aware
23. Faith	55. Speculation
24. Feeling	56. Support
25. Help	57. Temptation
26. Hinder	58. Test
27. Hunch	59. Theory
28. Inaction	60. Thought
29. Induction	61. Trust
30. Inequity	62. Unending
31. Inertia	63. Uncontrolled
32. Knowledge	64. Unproven

Reference
PART 3

STRUCTURAL MODELS

The Dramatica Structural Model

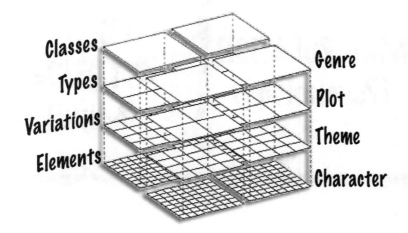

The Dramatica Structural Matrix is a framework for holding dramatic topics. These topics are pertinent to Genre, Plot, Theme, and Character and describe their effect on one another. During the process of storyforming, these topics (called "*themantics*") are re-arranged much as a Rubik's cube might be scrambled, all in response to the author's choices regarding the impact they wish to have on their audience. As a story unfolds, the matrix unwinds, scene by scene and act by act until all dramatic potentials, both large and small have been completely explored and have fully interacted.

4 Classes

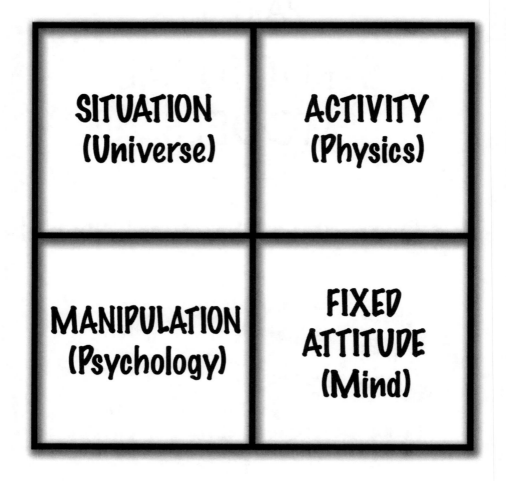

| SITUATION (Universe) | ACTIVITY (Physics) |
| MANIPULATION (Psychology) | FIXED ATTITUDE (Mind) |

16 Types

Situation Types   **Activity Types**

Past	How Things Are Going (Progress)	Under-standing	Doing
Future	Present	Obtaining	Gathering Information (Learning)

Developing A Plan	Playing A Role	Memory	Impulsive Responses (Preconscious)
Changing One's Nature	Conceiving An Idea	Innermost Desires (Subconscious)	Contempla-tions (Conscious)

Situation Types   **Activity Types**

64 Variations

Situation Variations

Fate	Prediction	Fact	Security
Interdiction	Destiny	Threat	Fantasy

Openness	Delay	Work	Attract
Choice	Destiny	Repel	Attempt

State of Being	Situation	Knowledge	Ability
Circumstances	Sense of Self	Desire	Thought

Rationalization	Commitment	Permission	Need
Responsibility	Obligation	Expediency	Deficiency

Activity Variations

Instinct	Senses	Wisdom	Skill
Interpretation	Conditioning	Experience	Enlightenment

Approach	Self Interest	Pre-requisites	Strategy
Morality	Attitude	Analysis	Pre-conditions

Truth	Evidence	Value	Confidence
Suspicion	Falsehood	Worry	Worth

Closure	Hope	Investigation	Appraisal
Dream	Denial	Re-appraisal	Doubt

Manipulation Variations   **Fixed Attitude Variations**

64 Elements

Situation Elements   ## Activity Elements

Knowledge	Ability		Actuality	Aware		Proven	Theory		Effect	Trust
Desire	Thought		Self-Awre	Perception		Hunch	Unproven		Test	Cause

Order	Equity		Inertia	Projection		Accurate	Expectation		Result	Ending
Inequity	Chaos		Speculation	Change		Determina-tion	Non-accurate		Unending	Process

Consider	Logic		Pursuit	Control		Certainty	Probability		Proaction	Inaction
Feeling	Reconsider		Un-controlled	Avoid / Prevent		Possibility	Potentiality		Protection	Reaction

Faith	Conscience		Support	Help		Deduction	Reduction		Acceptance	Evaluation
Temptation	Disbelief		Hinder	Oppose		Production	Induction		Re-evaluation	Non-acceptance

Manipulation Elements   ## Fixed Attitude Elements

Situation Class
(Universe)

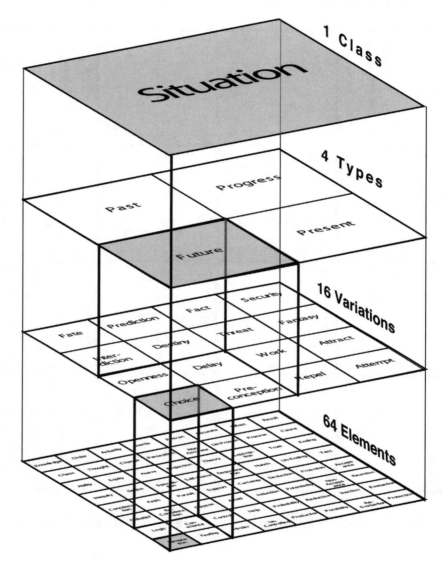

Situation Types
(Universe)

Situation Variations
(Universe)

Past Variations

Progress Variations

Fate	Prediction
Interdiction	Destiny

Fact	Security
Threat	Fantasy

Openness	Delay
Choice	Destiny

Work	Attract
Repel	Attempt

Future Variations

Present Variations

Situation Elements
(Universe)

Past Elements

Progress Elements

Knowledge	Order	Actuality	Inertia
Chaos	Thought	Change	Perception

Proven	Accurate	Effect	Result
Non-accurate	Unproven	Process	Cause

Ability	Equity	Aware	Projection
Inequity	Desire	Speculation	Self-Aware

Theory	Expectation	Trust	Ending
Determination	Hunch	Unending	Test

Consider	Faith	Pursuit	Support
Disbelief	Reconsider	Oppose	Avoid / Prevent

Certainty	Deduction	Proaction	Acceptance
Induction	Potentiality	Non-acceptance	Reaction

Logic	Conscience	Control	Help
Temptation	Feeling	Hinder	Un-controlled

Probability	Reduction	Inaction	Evaluation
Production	Possibility	Re-evaluation	Protection

Future Elements

Present Elements

Activity Class
(Physics)

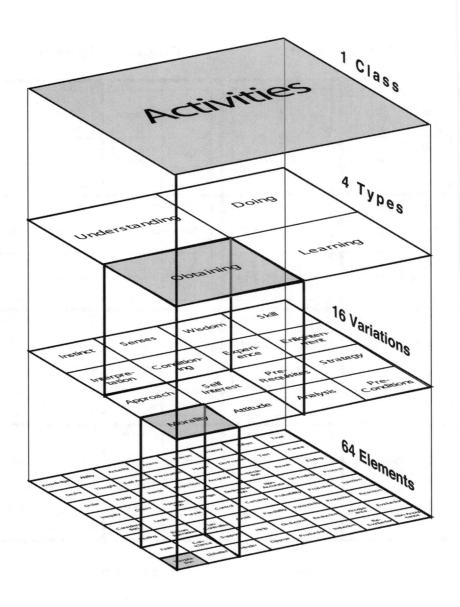

Activity Types
(Physics)

Activity Variations
(Physics)

Understanding Variations   **Doing Variations**

Instinct	Senses
Interpreta-tion	Condition ing

Wisdom	Skill
Experience	Enlighten-ment

Approach	Self Interest
Morality	Attitude

Pre-requisites	Strategy
Analysis	Pre-conditions

Obtaining Variations   **Learning Variations**

Activity Elements
(Physics)

Understanding Elements   **Doing Elements**

Knowledge	Ability
Desire	Thought

Actuality	Aware
Self-Aware	Perception

Proven	Theory
Hunch	Unproven

Effect	Trust
Test	Cause

Order	Equity
Inequity	Chaos

Inertia	Projection
Speculation	Change

Accurate	Expectation
Determination	Non-accurate

Result	Ending
Unending	Process

Consider	Logic
Feeling	Reconsider

Pursuit	Control
Un-controlled	Avoid / Prevent

Certainty	Probability
Possibility	Potentiality

Proaction	Inaction
Protection	Reaction

Faith	Conscience
Temptation	Disbelief

Support	Help
Hinder	Oppose

Deduction	Reduction
Production	Induction

Acceptance	Evaluation
Re-evaluation	Non-acceptance

Obtaining Elements   **Learning Elements**
(Gathering Information)

Manipulation Class
(Psychology)

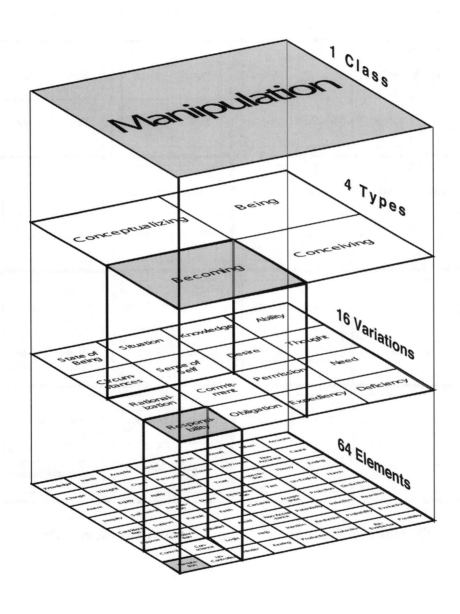

Manipulation Types
(Psychology)

Developing A Plan	Playing A Role
Changing One's Nature	Conceiving An Idea

Manipulation Variations
(Psychology)

**Developing A Plan
Variations**
[Conceptualizing]

**Playing A Role
Variations**
[Being]

State of Being	Situation
Circum-stances	Sense of Self

Knowledge	Ability
Desire	Thought

Rationali-zation	Commit-ment
Responsi-bility	Obligation

Permission	Need
Expediency	Deficiency

**Changing One's Nature
Variations**
[Becoming]

**Conceiving An Idea
Variations**
[Conceiving]

Manipulation Elements
(Psychology)

Developing A Plan Elements
(Conceptualizing)

Playing A Role Elements
(Being)

Knowledge	Inertia	Actuality	Order
Change	Thought	Chaos	Perception

Proven	Result	Effect	Accurate
Process	Unproven	Non-accurate	Cause

Aware	Equity	Ability	Projection
Inequity	Self-Aware	Speculation	Desire

Trust	Expectation	Theory	Ending
Determin-ation	Test	Unending	Hunch

Consider	Support	Pursuit	Faith
Oppose	Reconsider	Disbelief	Avoid / Prevent

Certainty	Acceptance	Proaction	Deduction
Non-acceptance	Potentiality	Induction	Reaction

Control	Conscience	Logic	Help
Temptation	Un-controlled	Hinder	Feeling

Inaction	Reduction	Probability	Evaluation
Production	Protection	Re-evaluation	Possibility

Changing One's Nature Elements
(Becoming)

Conceiving An Idea Elements
(Conceiving)

Fixed Attitude Class
(Mind)

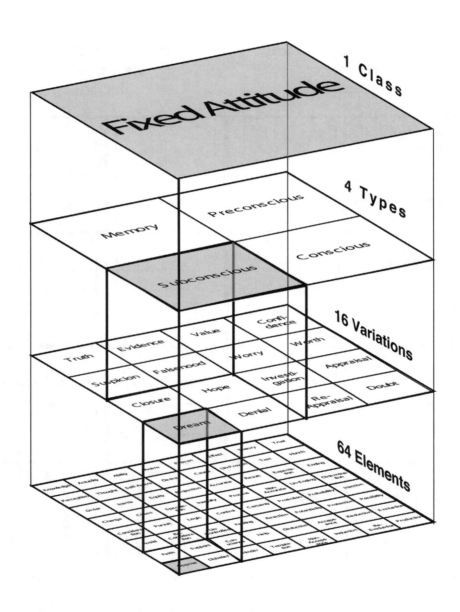

Fixed Attitude Types
(Mind)

Memory	Impulsive Responses (Preconscious)
Innermost Desires (Subconscious)	Contempla-tions (Conscious)

Fixed Attitude Variations
(Mind)

**Memories
Variations**
(Memory)

**Impulsive Responses
Variations**
(Preconscious)

Truth	Evidence
Suspicion	Falsehood

Value	Confidence
Worry	Worth

Closure	Hope
Dream	Denial

Investiga-tion	Appraisal
Re-appraisal	Doubt

**Innermost Desires
Variations**
(Subconscious)

**Contemplation
Variations**
(Conscious)

Fixed Attitude Elements
(Mind)

**Memories
Elements**
(Memory)

**Impulsive Responses
Elements**
(Preconscious)

Knowledge	Ability	Actuality	Aware	Proven	Theory	Effect	Trust
Desire	Thought	Self-Aware	Perception	Hunch	Unproven	Test	Cause

Order	Equity	Inertia	Projection	Accurate	Expectation	Result	Ending
Inequity	Chaos	Speculation	Change	Determin-ation	Non-accurate	Unending	Process

Consider	Logic	Pursuit	Control	Certainty	Probability	Proaction	Inaction
Feeling	Reconsider	Un-controlled	Avoid / Prevent	Possibility	Potentiality	Protection	Reaction

Faith	Conscience	Support	Help	Deduction	Reduction	Acceptance	Evaluation
Temptation	Disbelief	Hinder	Oppose	Production	Induction	Re-evaluation	Non-acceptance

**Innermost Desires
Elements**
(Subconscious)

**Contemplation
Elements**
(Conscious)

64 Characteristics of Overall Story Characters

Purpose Elements

Knowledge	Ability		Actuality	Aware
Desire	Thought		Self-Awre	Perception

Order	Equity		Inertia	Projection
Inequity	Chaos		Speculation	Change

Evaluation Elements

Proven	Theory		Effect	Trust
Hunch	Unproven		Test	Cause

Accurate	Expectation		Result	Ending
Determina-tion	Non-accurate		Unending	Process

Consider	Logic		Pursuit	Control
Feeling	Reconsider		Un-controlled	Avoid / Prevent

Faith	Conscience		Support	Help
Temptation	Disbelief		Hinder	Oppose

Certainty	Probability		Proaction	Inaction
Possibility	Potentiality		Protection	Reaction

Deduction	Reduction		Acceptance	Evaluation
Production	Induction		Re-evaluation	Non-acceptance

Motivation Elements

Methodology Elements

Characteristics of Archetypal Characters

	Motivations	Methodologies	Means of Evaluation	Purposes
Protagonist	Consider Pursuit	Certainty Proaction	Proven Effect	Knowledge Actuality
Antagonist	Reconsider Avoid	Potentiality Reaction	Unproven Cause	Thought Perception
Emotion	Feeling Uncontrolled	Possibility Protection	Hunch Test	Desire Self-Aware
Reason	Logic Control	Probability Inaction	Theory Trust	Ability Aware
Skeptic	Disbelief Oppose	Induction Non-Acceptance	Non-Accurate Process	Chaos Change
Sidekick	Faith Support	Deduction Acceptance	Accurate Result	Order Inertia
Guardian	Conscience Help	Reduction Evaluation	Expectation Ending	Equity Projection
Contagonist	Temptation Hinder	Production Reevaluation	Determination Unending	Inequity Speculation

Index

C

COMING IN SPRING 2005

Dramatica for Screenwriters

By Armando Saldaña Mora

Unlike *Dramatica: A New Theory of Story* which focuses on the nature of the Dramatica story theory, *Dramatica for Screenwriters* is a "how-to" book for screenwriters using Dramatica.

Here's how Armando describes the book:

> *It covers the practical use of* Dramatica *and the art of screenwriting. Content-wise, this is book contains creative approaches, comprehensive exercises and illustrative explanations to writing screenplays. Style-wise it uses a personal experience approach—more 'this is what works for me' instead of the 'This Is The Word Of God' style favored by authors like* [fill-in-your-favorite-Hollywood-story-guru-here].

ABOUT THE AUTHOR

Armando Saldaña Mora (born in Mexico City, 1964) has been a professional writer since 1985. "The key to succeed in this profession," he says, "is being able to create with top quality for any genre, any format, any medium." Accordingly, his career has taken him from authoring and producing stage plays, to crafting and editing novels, to originating and redrafting screenplays, to scriptwriting and conducting writer's workshops for TV networks.

Write Brothers Press

Dramatica® Pro
The Ultimate Creative Writing Partner

Rating: Excellent *"The most versatile and dynamic program of its kind, Dramatica is a sophisticated, intuitive tool that can benefit both the novice and professional."*

Writer's Digest

Wes Craven
Writer/Director
Scream, Music of the Heart Nightmare on Elm Street

"At the beginning of the project, Dramatica Pro is great....It puts you so far ahead. It saves you time because you're not writing stuff you'll eventually have to throw away because you hadn't thoroughly thought it through."

Got an idea for a story? Dramatica Pro is the place to start! Dramatica Pro will ensure that all your characters serve their dramatic purpose, your themes stay true to your characters, and plots stay on track. You'll cast and build your characters, plot out your story, layer in themes with universal meaning, and put it all together to create an unforgettable story.

Structure Your Plot...

Answer Dramatica's thought-provoking questions about your characters and plot. This narrows down the possible ways of telling your story to the one that best expresses your personal vision— and prompts Dramatica to supply some answers of its own. Amazingly, it can show you which parts of your story are strong, and which need punching up!

Illustrate Your Story...

Write specific examples of how each of your story decisions about character arc, theme, conflict, tension, story goal, plot points, etc., will play out in your story's scenes. At the click of a button, see how the great writers illustrated the same story points in their classic stories by looking at in-depth breakdowns of over 60 films, novels, plays, and short stories .

Create Scenes...

Now weave together all the parts of the story you've developed so far.

Determine how elements of character, plot, and theme will be revealed to your audience over time, and place your written examples directly into specific Acts, Scenes, or Chapters. Your step outline or plot synopsis is complete, ready to be honed into a killer first draft!

Develop Your Characters...

Interesting. Deep. Real. Memorable. Dramatica helps you craft characters that leap off the page and into the hearts and minds of your audience. Visualize your characters by casting them from your choice of over 500 icons. Name them from a database of over 5,000 unique names.

Structure Templates...

Open one of the structure template files to use a pre-built dramatic structure for your novel, screenplay, or short story—complete with instructions on what to write about in each scene or chapter. You'll never be alone when you work alongside the "Ultimate Creative Writing Partner." Together you'll solve the plot and character problems that prevent many good stories from becoming great enough to sell. Dramatica's StoryGuide will handhold you from initial idea all the way through to completed narrative treatment, inspiring you and supporting you along the way. It's like having a successful author sitting by your side and mentoring you.

"I had my pitch meeting with a producer... Everything he wanted to know I'd been forced to game out with my ol' friend Dramatica... the program will make your job as a writer not only easier, but more fun. By the way, I got the deal."

David Obst, Wired Magazine

Rating: 5 Stars *"This program is an amazing tool for helping both professional and wanna-be writers create, deepen, and refine their stories."*

PC Magazine

Words of Praise for Dramatica Pro, the award-winning writing software based on the Dramatica Theory of Story:

"Dramatica instructs gently with the possibility of grand results. Used accordingly, the program can help a writer to create a flawless story blueprint. It actually has the ability to assist almost anyone to form a compelling tale that only that individual is capable of producing."

Writers' Journal

Rating: 5 Stars "This program is an amazing tool for helping both professional and wanna-be writers create, deepen, and refine their stories."

PC Magazine

Rating: Excellent "The most versatile and dynamic program of its kind, Dramatica is a sophisticated, intuitive tool that can benefit both the novice and professional."

Writer's Digest

"[Dramatica Pro] doesn't supply canned prose or purport to do any actual writing. Instead, it helps you define your characters and organize your plot."

Walter S. Mossberg
The Wall Street Journal

"A program to help the Steven Spielbergs of tomorrow work their way through writer's block."

CNN Future Watch

"Dramatica Pro may teach you more about the intricacies of the writing craft than any other product on the market."

Back Stage West

"Dramatica Pro is a totally revolutionary creative writing tool and partner that delivers what it promises... This new theory is a proven approach that systematically eliminates the pitfalls of writing to formula. Users of the system will find Dramatica Pro indispensable for developing, or enhancing, the story they really want to tell."

Eden Maxwell
LAMG Digest

"Dramatica Pro represents a major leap for novelists, playwrights, screenwriters, and fiction writers. Dramatica Pro's user interface unquestionably stands head and shoulders above its other top three competitors, StoryLine Pro, Collaborator, and Plots Unlimited. Simply put, you can create a tightly structured story within Dramatica Pro's unique environment..."

Randy Sydnor, KLA Radio

"By helping to clarify your intentions before you begin writing, Dramatica has the potential to shave weeks (possibly months!) off of the frequently frustrating, hit-or-miss rewriting process."

NYScreenwriter

"The best program for either a novice or a blocked writer. While you still, of course, offer the raw material, it truly does help you arrange it."

Fiction Writer

"Run any story through Dramatica Pro and it'll come out stronger, richer, and more dynamic. In short, just plain better... Recently, I've been using the Dramatica Pro approach to storytelling to teach my students and guide our screenwriting faculty."

Prof. Charlie Purpura
Head of Screenwriting, *New York University Tisch School of the Arts Dept. of Dramatic Writing*

"In my recent memoir Silent Fire (New York: Crown Books, 2002), I used Dramatica to bring to life the people as I remembered them, so that they could live not only in my memory, but in the story as well."

James A. Connor
Writer, *Silent Fire*

"The story for "Copy Shop" was in my head for 10 years. Dramatica is with me for 5 years - long enough to burn the 12 essential questions into my subconscious. The 12 minute film won 25 international awards and an Oscar-nomination."

Virgil Widrich
2001 Oscar® Nominee Best Short Film: "Copy Shop"

"Dramatica Pro is a true brainstorming partner! No other story software offers this level of involvement and efficiency in the story creation process; what a liberating experience. You guys have built a valuable tool that will continue to inspire for years to come."

Shayne Wilson
Associate Producer, *Dead Like Me*

"Dramatica Pro is a story development tool I am pleased to recommend to other writers. It can either develop a story with minimal feedback from the writer or significantly enhance an existing idea by fanning writer passion to an unexpected level. This has allowed my story development process to shift in several truly systemic ways."

David O'Neal
Novelist, *Fool Me Twice, What Goes Around The Pact With Bruno, Choosing to Kill*

"Having writer's block or even paradoxically too many ideas can prevent you from getting that great concept or pitch off the ground. That's where Dramatica comes into play. It's not only the ultimate objective brainstorming partner but it guides you through the in-depth- process of character, plot and theme development without which there can be no good screenplay. There is a lot of painstaking 'homework' in the development process but Dramatica actually draws you into it almost effortlessly. It makes the next step-the screenwriting process-virtually devoid of the dreaded writer's block. In one case Dramatica has provided an angle and idea for the storyline that no one thought about. It made the story better; it was actually brilliant and it was free! Now that's a novel concept in this town !"

Jean - Philippe Girod
Producer, *Windhorse Entertainment*

"Dramatica Pro is a great way to start out and organize a story."

Robin Cowie
Producer, *The Blair Witch Project*